Since 1947

Since 1947

Partition Narratives among Punjabi Migrants of Delhi

Ravinder Kaur

OXFORD
UNIVERSITY PRESS

OXFORD
UNIVERSITY PRESS

Oxford University Press is a department of the University of Oxford.
It furthers the University's objective of excellence in research, scholarship,
and education by publishing worldwide. Oxford is a registered trademark of
Oxford University Press in the UK and in certain other countries.

Published in India by
Oxford University Press
2/11 Ground Floor, Ansari Road, Daryaganj, New Delhi 110 002, India

First Edition published in 2007
Oxford India Paperbacks 2018

ISBN 13: 978-0-19-948357-0
ISBN 10: 0-19-948357-4

Typeset in AGaramond 10.5/12
by Star Compugraphics Pvt Ltd, Delhi

CONTENTS

TABLES

Acknowledgements

Financial support for this study was offered by Danish Social Sciences Research Council (FSE), while Institute for Society and Globalisation (ISG) at Roskilde University and Danish Institute for International Studies (DIIS) served as its academic home. My colleagues at these two institutions have contributed tremendously in shaping this work in multiple ways. Thomas Blom Hansen as my supervisor and Ninna Nyberg Sørensen as co-supervisor have helped nurture it from the very beginning till the time of its final publication. Both Ninna and Thomas helped me look at Delhi and the Punjabi resettlement colonies anew by digging deeper into what I thought was thoroughly familiar to me. It allowed me to see much that was unfamiliar beneath the layers of familiarity. And though my writing period coincided with Thomas's transnational academic journeys and long stretches of fieldwork, I was always assured of lengthy critique of my writing, useful advice, and unbounded encouragement from him at frequent pace. I could hardly have wished for a better mentor, advisor, and friend.

This work has also benefited much from detailed critical comments offered by Paul Brass, Gyanendra Pandey, Steen Bergendorff and, at an earlier stage by, Jan Breman and Fiona Wilson. Similarly, I am thankful everyone who facilitated the fieldwork, of whom the survivors of Partition contributed the most by letting me in their homes and personal histories. I gained much from advice given by Khushwant Singh, Sardar Tarlok Singh, Surinder Saini, I.K. Gujral, Kuldip Nayyar, Dipankar Gupta, V.N. Dutta, S.D. Muni, and Balraj Bahri Malhotra. I also wish to thank colleagues from the 'Partition panel' at British Association for South Asian Studies (BASAS) and European Conference on Modern South Asian Studies (ECMSAS), especially Ian Talbot, Yasmin Khan, Pippa Virdee, Shinder Thandi, Pritam Singh, Ishtiaq Ahmed, and Iftikhar Malik. Likewise, Finn Stepputat, Helene Maria Kyed, Steffen Jensen, Marianne Larsen, Christian Lund, Lars Buur, Nicholas Van Hear, and Simon Turner generously took time out to read and comment on various drafts. Inge Jensen at the Graduate School ironed out all practical hurdles confronting this work.

Finally, I must thank my husband Anders, my son Anton, and my family in Delhi for supporting me throughout. The usual disclaimers of author's sole responsibility etc., apply to this work as well.

Copenhagen   Ravinder Kaur
1 December 2006

Curating the Wound
Introduction to the Paperback Edition

In the heart of Delhi, a sprawling neighbourhood called Rehgar Pura hums with sounds and sights of busy urban life. The streets are lined with narrow buildings, residences stacked above bustling commercial establishments, wholesale and retail shops, godowns and small production units, all packed in this compact urban terrain. The neighbourhood is well known as a primary trading hub for leather goods and a variety of commodities in Delhi. Yet for all its commercial renown and central location, Rehgar Pura barely marks its presence in the social landscape of the city. It is a kind of place that remains invisible in plain sight. The upwardly mobile residents of Delhi usually do not visit it unless they have to, and when they do, they mostly do not acknowledge it. Indeed the city is dotted with many such neighbourhoods that garner little outside interest or excitement. These invisible spaces almost never make it to the tourist guides or the list of 'happening places' in the colourful city newspapers. What makes this neighbourhood different is its complicated entanglement with the history of postcolonial India and Pakistan—the history of Partition.

It was not until I began my fieldwork in 2001 that I first discovered the connections between this locality and the events of Partition. In the now defunct archives of the old Ministry of Relief and Rehabilitation, Rehgar Pura was listed as a site of resettlement for 'Harijan' community displaced during the violent upheavals of territorial Partition. I was no stranger to this neighbourhood. I was born about 2 kilometers from this location, and had been a frequent visitor to the bazaar through my childhood. What had been unfamiliar to me was how Rehgar Pura was deeply woven, and yet concealed, in the story of Partition migration and resettlement. In 1947–48, the refugees classified as 'Harijan', 'Scheduled Caste', 'Scheduled Tribe', or 'untouchables' as such were resettled in this colony by the newly liberated postcolonial Indian state. Already at the turn of the twentieth century, this location was a marked site for the Harijan residents of Delhi often in the employment of the city municipality as sweepers. It also became a site of resettlement for the newly arrived refugees deemed 'untouchable' from West Punjab and the North West Frontier Province (NWFP), separated and set apart from the 'regular' resettlement locations. This spatial separation somehow also meant separation from the history of Partition, and an absence in the popular narratives of collective trauma and loss experienced by millions of people across the subcontinent. Or more precisely, its near absence in the history of Partition migration. The history of Partition remains, with some notable exceptions, more or less still oblivious to the question of caste. Perhaps this is the paradox of contemporary Partition historiography—even as the project of oral history and memorialization of Partition gains greater currency in the public sphere, the history itself remains confined within the old parameters of upper caste and middle class. If the stories of Dalit refugees of Partition occupied a tentative space a decade ago, they still remain on the edges of Partition history. The questions, at once old and new, are these: Which experiences of human suffering are found worthy of being memorialized? What kind of wounds precisely can be preserved, exhibited, and remembered in the public domain? And what form might the public memory itself take when an array of absences continues to underpin the project of memorialization?

The project of memorializing the human suffering at the heart of Partition history of violence and displacement has by now become vastly popular—both within and beyond the academy. The urgency to record and document testimonies, the lived experiences of now ageing survivors has especially fueled several popular initiatives of oral history archives. Like the new category of 'citizen journalists' shaped in the accelerated age of social media, the digitally empowered 'citizen historians' now seek testimonies of Partition survivors in public interest. These testimonies are not stored in a state archive but are openly accessible on the Internet. And for the first time, the history of Partition is the subject of a museum that collects and exhibits memories and objects that we are left with. These are laudable projects, and the involvement of young citizen historians commendable. The past is mediated to a new generation so that the collective wound continues to be remembered. To underline non-partisanship, these efforts are even publicized as 'apolitical' that solely focus on what is popularly called the 'human dimension' of Partition. Yet there is something deeply unsettling in this increasingly depoliticized notion of human suffering in the project of memorialization. It fails to recognize that what we choose to remember or forget, to publicly speak or remain silent about are, and always have been deeply political gestures.

The domain of public memory that Partition history now inhabits—very visible and plentiful—increasingly irons out the complexities of Partition politics to narrate highly affective albeit simple accounts of human suffering. The *human* subject in this project is often a free-floating agent disconnected from the realm of politics—a word almost invoked with disapproval—where politics is largely understood as state or national level negotiations by big leaders. That personal and collective negotiations, transgressions, and compromises underpinning disorderly social relations in everyday life also constitute politics is barely acknowledged. The subject of memorialization increasingly is a passive victim of circumstances and almost never a willing participant in the events that unfolded. In other words, the space for complexities and contradictions is steadily erased once the affective project of memorialization overshadows the project of critical history. The point here is that the work of public memorialization refashions particular kinds of histories reiterated within the limits of upper caste and middle-class worlds. The kind of remembrance of human suffering that is formed within this depoliticized space secedes from the messiness of everyday life, a kind of messiness that also includes Dalit refugees edged out of history, the wealthy migrants who were able to exchange property, the victims who happened to be aggressors too, or the bureaucratic machinery that created a hierarchy of victimhood that ironically favored the already resourceful elite. The project of memorialization is too often taken to be a project of sacralization of suffering, recognition of the wound inflicted on the victim, and therefore beyond debate. Yet in a moment when the historical wound of Partition is being curated for display, even dressed up afresh for public consumption, we need to be ever more attentive to the messiness of the wound that is left outside the public gaze. The near-absence of Rehgar Pura from the spatial map of Partition history is precisely a sign of discomfort, a discomfort with the politics of caste, and possibly fears of politicizing a human tragedy. We might ask, then, what is this tragedy, and who is the *human* in it. Perhaps the tragedy is the continuous absence of the Dalit subject in this imaginary of the human figure.

June 2017
Delhi/Copenhagen

1. Narrating Everyday Forms of Past
An Introduction

'Since 1947'. This is a phrase often encountered in Delhi, sometimes engraved as an inscription on shop fronts and business letterheads, or more frequently as an opening to personal and collective narratives of turmoil and exodus resulting from Partition. It also signifies a series of events that collate and condense the British departure from India, the inauguration of the post-colonial Indian nation-state, and an unprecedented flow of forced migration across the newly carved borders between India and Pakistan. Most important, it summarizes a nearly six-decade-long period of post-Partition personal and governmental efforts at restoration of loss experienced through loss of homes, livelihoods, and national territory in 1947. The phrase has by now emerged as a powerful metaphor, an encrypted code, that is often employed emotively to define 'before' and 'after' periods of Partition that seek to cut through personal narrations and modern Indian history, and convert them into distinct and comparative episodes.

In this book, this phrase is used to pave the way for an incursion into the embedded themes of disruption in one's everyday life: forced migration, and then reparation; rearrangement; and renewed embodiment of the migrant's personal and social bearings. The entire journey begins and culminates in Delhi. It aims to reproduce and comprehend the move from the North West Frontier Province (NWFP) and West Punjab to Delhi. The move is layered by multiple levels of class, caste, and gender experience, and shows how *past encounters* are routinely remodelled as present and how *present circumstances* reshape the remembrance of past. Such narratives challenge our absolute notions of past and present and constitute the very underpinnings of this study. The personal and collective narratives emerge as *living monuments* to the tragic upheavals of Partition and continue to be passed from one generation to another, though not necessarily in their original form.

EVERYDAY FORMS OF PAST

We can best take a synoptic glance at this study by examining a conflict which took place between the residents of a south Delhi colony and the Municipal Corporation of Delhi (MCD) in February 2002, when the municipality finally implemented its long-standing threat of demolishing unauthorized building extensions in Lajpat Nagar area.[1] The MCD in a day-long operation demolished burgeoning illegal modifications—extra rooms covering street space, small shops, and extended balconies—to the flat buildings in the area called Old Double Storey. As the name suggests, each building in the area was originally constructed as a two-storeyed house, which had by now given way to four flats at four elevated levels. The original flats were no more than 100 square yards (86 sq m), each with one living room, verandah, and a kitchen. In one corner of the building there was a common bathroom and toilet for every four flats. Over the years, the verandah (the small open area) had been converted into a room, toilets/bathrooms carved out, and extension areas built out on to the street. The two-storeyed flats were built in the 1950s for Partition refugee families, as part of the permanent resettlement scheme. The children in refugee families had grown into adults and now had children of their own. Some families who had achieved a better economic status moved to better localities; others sold the flats to realize a profit from the fast-rising real estate value of the area, while the remaining families partitioned the same living space to accommodate two or more families.

As the heavy bulldozers came to a halt, the residents began retrieving their belongings from the razed properties. The streets in the Old Double Storey quarter were littered with fresh piles of concrete, broken bricks, mangled wires, the remnants of numerous boundary walls, and extra rooms and balconies added on to these small apartments over the years. The main wall of a kitchen in an affected building had been razed in the operation, since it was constructed on the street space. The gas stove, drinking water bottles, assorted pots and pans now lay in the open, guarded by a woman and her daughter. Neena Khanna, as I found out, was a 42-year-old primary school teacher and had lived in the area all her life.[2] She was born in one of the flats in the locality and had later got married two streets away from her family home. She had a teenage daughter and a son, and it was the daughter who was now helping her with cleaning up. Her husband and son were away with the other men, probably meeting the area MLA to find a solution. Elections were imminent, so they were sure that some way would be found to stop the demolitions. She assured me that she was not staying at home merely because of traditional beliefs that kept women out of public; rather it was a practical necessity that someone watch over the house at that time. As it turned out later, women were fully engaged in strategy-making and implementation to counter the MCD's actions.

My curiosity and presence in the area did not need much explanation. The place was full of onlookers, local journalists, representatives of the MCD, local-level politicians, and brokers of various kinds. In any case, there was too much activity going on in the locality for residents to focus on visitors. The presence of unfamiliar faces was taken as granted in this chaotic situation. The residents—both men and women—stood huddled in groups, recounting their loss of living and commercial space, the callous attitude of the municipality, and the general disruption the demolitions had caused in their daily lives. Many parents were worried about the impact it would have on their children, especially with the annual school exams due to start in less than four weeks. There were concerns about loss of income from extra rooms that had been rented out, and most important, whether they would be allowed to rebuild their destroyed properties. There were agitated voices from the older generation of residents, who repeatedly said, 'We came here after we had lost everything. Now we are going to lose everything again.'

Several among them had tears in their eyes as they recalled their individual stories of how they had been forced to leave their homes during the 1947 Partition of India and Pakistan, and how they came to live in Lajpat Nagar in Delhi. The area was described as a jungle where no one was prepared to live four to five decades ago. The local Delhi residents were afraid to venture here for the fear of professional Gujjar criminal gangs located in the nearby villages. Madan Kapoor, an 85-year-old resident recounted his journey from Lyallpur to Delhi. Of the 16 members in his family, only four had survived the communal violence and the hazards of the journey in 1947. The government constructed these apartments for them in a completely uninhabited area where no one wanted to live. The government had to offer easy instalments schemes for refugees to be able to take possession of the flats. As a conclusive claim over Lajpat Nagar and its public and private space, he remarked,

It is we who have brought glory and life to this area that no one wanted initially. Now the property prices have escalated, which is why the government wants to interfere. They never came here when Lajpat Nagar was a concrete jungle with rows upon rows of empty houses.[3]

The inherent gloom over this immediate calamity was however, balanced by a pragmatic stance, since disruptions were not seen as an entirely unusual occurrence by the residents. The older generation reminded their children and grandchildren of the long arduous journey they had undertaken 55 years ago, to reach Delhi from towns and villages that are now a part of Pakistan. They had been forced to leave their well-established homes, farms, and businesses in a hurry, in order to escape almost certain death during the internecine Hindu–Muslim communal violence. They were rendered homeless and empty-handed, but through persistence and skill, they successfully built their homes, shops, businesses, friendships, and new relationships all over again. Old Double Storey area was a living testimony to that personal and collective struggle the residents had waged to successfully reconstruct ordinary lives. In less than half-a-century, they had transformed themselves from homeless refugees to homeowners and loyal citizens of modern India. The disruption had been overcome within their lifetimes.

Such positive determination to overcome fresh disruptions was evident when the residents—old and young—decided to confront the municipality fiercely and strategically. The local politicians were approached to intervene in the matter, while the Supreme Court of India was simultaneously petitioned to legally bring the demolitions to a halt.[4] The main roads in the area became a battleground, where the residents camped each day during peak traffic hours.

The staged nature of the protests notwithstanding, the southern part of the city came to a halt, drawing sufficient attention to the demolitions in the area. The demolitions in this area were completely a local affair of Delhi and hardly attracted any attention outside the city pages of local newspapers. The residents' perspective on the demolition and its subsequent news coverage had an extra-local edge, however, which took the issue far beyond its present context. Each time demolitions in the area were mentioned, reports would unfailingly mention that the colony was a resettlement colony built by the government to house Partition refugees of 1947. The demolitions were presented as yet another breach in the residents' lives. The narration of a local event—demolitions by the municipality—was immediately connected to the five-decade-old history of Partition violence, bringing in its wake the creation of Pakistan, and the forced mass migration that had caused ruptures in their everyday lives. The children of original migrants, who now had children and grandchildren of their own, had not experienced that journey themselves, but somehow—probably through repeated narration—it had become an integral part of their lives.

The residents' response to the *present* crisis was clearly getting shaped by both acquired and inherited experiences of *past* disruption. They were determined to persevere and battle with the municipality, the government, and the courts, just as their parents and grandparents had done in the years following the 1947 uprooting. At once, such a response reduced the dividing line between the past and present to a fuzzy blur. To the residents, the present confrontation had simply become an extension of their experienced or inherited past, which may to historians seem too far removed in time, context, and magnitude for any kind of reasonable comparison. Clearly, the past in this case is not confined to history but continues to live an everyday life, appearing in unusual places and contexts, shaping people's strategies and responses to their present in ordinary and extraordinary circumstances.

This study, then, is about *everyday forms of past*, used to contextualize and make sense of *present* situations through a repository of *past* experiences that have been lived or inherited.[5] Everyday past, in this sense, does not represent a unitary, fixed, and unchanging representation of history; but rather refers to popularly remembered versions of past events that tend to attain a mythical character of their own.[6] This anoints one's present as well as past with a state of suspense—that is, the unfolding of events can hardly be predicted in advance. In other words, just as the events taking place currently do not reveal a road map before the developments have actually taken place, the past also tends to be remembered and revised in current contexts. In everyday life, the scholarly distinctions between past and present hardly make sense, as people remember and narrate their situations and personal stories in a historically linear context, in which their individual present lives get connected with distant ancestors, journeys, and events in faraway places, time periods, and traditions that have roots in an ancient historical past. Thus, past is frequently invoked in one's everyday life. Past connects distant places and events with people who, through their singular experiences, bear the burden of collective memory. It is often articulated dramatically and visibly through memorials and commemorations, but it does not cease to exist even in its publicly unarticulated form. It is not an entire chronology of personal or national histories that we are concerned with in this study, but rather those cataclysmic events that cause disruptions in the lives of ordinary people and force them to renew their personal histories and rearrange their social relationships. In the lives of Delhi Punjabis, the 1947 Partition remains such a cataclysmic event, which rearranged their ordinary lives through physical dislocation.

The field, substance, and source of this study are formed around the everyday life of Punjabi migrants in Delhi. The study is woven with memories of personal and inherited experiences, and national histories of Partition. The broad aim of this study is to explore how past is employed to repair ruptures in people's ordinary lives. The partition of Punjab province in 1947 and the forced migration of more than five million Hindus and Sikhs into India, open up an unexplored area within modern Indian history. The resettlement process after the migration, the relationships the migrants have formed with their former homeland Pakistan, and their post-Partition homeland in India, points to a hitherto restricted field of enquiry. The specific aim of this study is to (1) delve into the forms of past (Partition experience) used by Punjabi Hindu refugees to evolve coping strategies when forced to leave their homes in 1947, and (2) examine the emerging identification process which remains shadowed by an uneasy relationship that the migrants have developed, both with their former homelands as well as the Indian state.

BOMBS, CRICKET, AND MUNICIPAL THREATS

In the context of other events that took place in 1998 and 2004, disenchantment with the municipal incarnation of the Indian state establishes the inherent complications in a study of displacement and resettlement; in other words, the ambivalent, unsettled nature of relationships (with the former homeland as well as the place of settlement) makes any study of migrant resettlement extremely challenging. When do migrants get fully resettled? Or, rather, when do they begin to feel at home? Where primarily do they locate *home* in their imagination? The suggested complications become apparent with the following description of a seemingly unrelated event when India conducted six nuclear tests in May 1998.

One of the first strategic decisions made by the newly elected Bharatiya Janata Party (BJP)-led coalition government was to test a series of nuclear bombs in Pokhran, a desert location in Rajasthan. India had previously conducted nuclear tests in 1974 at the same location under the Congress regime. While the earlier tests had been meant for 'peaceful' use of nuclear technology, with the 1998 tests, there were no such pretences. This time the purpose was to enhance India's security vis-à-vis Pakistan.[7] The bomb was quickly nicknamed the 'Hindu bomb' since it challenged India's arch-rival, Muslim Pakistan, with which it shares a tragic history of territorial division in 1947; three full-fledged wars fought over border disputes in 1947, 1965, and 1971; low-intensity conflicts in Punjab, and continued hostilities in Kashmir; and an incessant rivalry to achieve a superior balance of power. The test explosions were greeted by nation-wide celebrations and euphoria. The celebration over India's nuclear acquisition became a visible expression of one's loyalty and patriotism towards the nation. The failure to do so was popularly considered disloyal and treacherous to India. The notion of enemy and friend was also qualified on the nuclear measure: there were inimical countries that had publicly condemned the tests, withdrawn their diplomatic representatives and frozen trade ties and development aid; and there were friendly countries that had, if not celebrated along with India, at least not joined the international protests.

Against this background, the scene in Delhi can be considered exceptional. The streets of Delhi were sites of full-scale public celebration, complete with drum-beating and flashy victory-signs. The newspapers were replete with photos of Hindus and Sikhs, often BJP supporters, dancing with greater gusto than their countrymen elsewhere in the country. It was not just the scale of celebration that set them apart from others but rather the fact that they were celebrating the possible demise of Pakistan in a nuclear attack. A vast majority of Punjabis living in Delhi are Partition refugees or their descendants, who made Delhi their home after they were forced to leave their homes in West Punjab and NWFP in Pakistan. Thus, the celebrations took place in the knowledge that their former homeland was being threatened by the Indian state. The public celebration was, in a way, finally de-linking them from their former homeland. The nostalgia and emotional tie that binds migrants to the place they were forced to leave was starkly unacknowledged here. The emotional severance from their land of origin was inexplicable. So was their uneasy relationship with their new home in Delhi and with the Indian state.

The Indo–Pak camaraderie witnessed during the 2004 India–Pakistan cricket series further complicates this picture. The Indian cricket team agreed to visit Pakistan on a goodwill tour, for which the Pakistani government allocated 8250 'cricket visas' to Indian spectators.[8] This was an unprecedented gesture that was widely applauded both in India and Pakistan. A number of Indians, many non-Punjabis among them, visited Pakistan for the first time and were reportedly overwhelmed by the response from ordinary people.[9] For the Punjabi migrants in Delhi, this was a unique opportunity to visit the land their parents or grandparents came from.[10] The gesture was reciprocated in 2005 by the Indian side, which offered a similar number of 'cricket visas' to Pakistani visitors for an India–Pakistan series hosted by India. The half-century-long Indo–Pak hostility and mutual mistrust was put on hold, revealing the friendliness and goodwill underneath. What made this historic turnaround possible at people-to-people level? While the idea of people-to-people diplomacy between India and Pakistan dates back to the early 1990s, it failed to take a popular form till 2004.[11] This time the initiative was backed by the state authorities from both sides, which made a significant difference. The notion of being anti-national, unpatriotic, and disloyal through association with Pakistan—with its cricket team and its people—was not an issue, since the Indian government itself was facilitating such association (see Chapter 7). State involvement in determining the relationship migrants have with their former homelands, thus, presents an obvious theme that needs to be followed up.

Clearly, the migrants' relationship with the Indian state does not exist in a dialectic mode but rather in a triangular formation: India, Pakistan, and the displaced population. Such a conflation gives rise to expressions of enmity, belonging, home, loyalty, revenge, etc., wherein the nation-state of Pakistan remains as relevant a consideration as the Indian nation-state. The history of Partition is far from being consigned to the archives and the historians. It remains a living theme that frequently emerges at the most unexpected moments. The everyday life of Punjabi migrants and their descendants in Delhi is where one finds living testimony to the events considered long-forgotten by the Indian state and the Indians who were not directly involved in the Partition migration.

The gaps between Partition in 1947, the 1998 nuclear tests, and the 2002 demolitions in Delhi have emerged on many planes, not only time and space. A number of crucial developments took place in between that helped move the Punjabi migrants from 'refugees' to local residents of

Delhi. The Indian state had conceived a massive orchestrated resettlement plan that helped the migrants to get permanent housing, easy loans, free education, and state jobs among other benefits. The entire residential and commercial area in Lajpat Nagar was an example of state supported urban development aimed at resettling refugees. This aspect of state involvement in their personal lives is rarely mentioned by the Punjabi migrants. This represents a breach in the collective memory that begins from the *past* of Partition violence and migration and moves straight to the *present*, where the migrants and their descendants appear as well-settled people who are at home in Delhi. The decades of the 1950s and 1960s, which were crucial to making Delhi their home, either get compressed or are completely lost in most narrations. This opens another area of exploration significant to this study, as it once again highlights the uneasy relationship between the state and the former refugees.

After half-a-century, the narratives of Partition are no longer a dominant part of the everyday life of the survivors and their descendants, but neither have they ceased to exist in collective and personal memory. The past is remembered in the most unlikely and routine situations, and not necessarily in specific grand situational settings. It is not unusual to find old men and women standing in long queues for milk, talking about their days in Lahore or Rawalpindi where it was still possible to get unadulterated milk, cheap and plentiful food, and the latest trend-setting fashions in their local bazaars. People were in good health and good humour back there. Crime was almost non-existent under the British and women had much more freedom to move publicly than they have now. Everyday life in Delhi was hard, the cost of living was crushing, and the food was adulterated most of the time.

Despite occasional disillusionments with their circumstances, Punjabis are considered, by themselves and others, a 'success story' of Partition re-settlement. They have integrated in Delhi in an ideal way without causing any visible local–refugee conflict as in Karachi in Pakistan. Often their ethnic attributes are cited as reasons for them doing better than other Partition migrants, for example, those from East Bengal. An approximate image is that of successful, well-integrated citizens of modern India who have taken to Indian nationalism in a far deeper manner than Indian citizens in other parts of India who are still bound by provincial or regional, rather than national, considerations. Their journey from being refugees/migrants to modern citizens stands as a unique example that needs to be explored thoroughly. The following questions help to chart a course in this exploration:

(1) When and how do refugees transform into 'locals'? The entire process—from refugee to local—is contextualized in the tragic event of Partition and the

accompanying communal violence where half a million people died and roughly 5 million Hindus and Sikhs were forced to move from West Pakistan to India. The process of becoming a local in instances of forced migration (often preceded by ethnic violence) is deeply connected with personal-emotive issues that are frequently ignored. The expression 'local' does not here entail any legal-technical issues of citizenship, but rather the subtle and complex social interactions that make newcomers claim a locality as their own. This requires creating a space alongside the previously settled residents, besides negotiating with and inducing the state authority to facilitate their settlement. The critical circumstances of violence and forced movement at once simplify and complicate these twin tasks.

(2) How are the singular events of forced migration experienced by divergent categories based on caste, class, and gender? Partition divided Punjab society along religious lines, that is, the identities 'Hindu', 'Muslim' and 'Sikh' became paramount. In a way, the resulting social divide was vertical, not horizontal, which meant that hierarchical divisions along caste, class, and gender were retained undisturbed even in a religiously polarized society. These differing experiences have so far remained absent in the popular narratives of Partition. The history of Partition migration is marked by such noticeable absences and blanks: untouchables, women, and the very poor seldom make an appearance.

(3) How are social conflicts interpreted and then reflected in the state policies of refugee resettlement? During instances of displacement and resettlement, social conflicts—based on caste, class, and gender—confront not only the refugees but also the state authorities, since the latter make administrative policies to reorder and govern the displaced population. Displacement also offers a moment where changes, social or political, can be introduced. Thus, such historical moments present an opportunity to explore whether and how pre-migration social conflicts are reproduced, ignored, or re-interpreted in the course of resettlement.

A short note must be added here on the use of terms like 'refugee' and 'migrant' in this book. Both these terms are used throughout the following chapters but they do not have interchangeable meanings and implications. The term 'migrant' implies a broad allusion to all those who moved from one place to another during and after Partition. The term 'refugee' alludes to a specific section within this broad group that sought state protection in refugee camps, and later in the government-constructed housing colonies. The conceptual understanding of 'refugee' stems from a legal position and must therefore be used sparingly.[12]

The underlying assumption for employing two terms is that the event of Partition did not produce a single category of migration. Migration in significant numbers started taking place soon after the 5 March riots in Rawalpindi when British India was still undivided and no international border had yet been created. The term 'refugee' technically pertains to those who seek shelter outside their own national borders, which in the case of Partition migrants did not happen till 15 August 1947. The large-scale migration after this date was, however, across the international borders between India and Pakistan, which in the process created refugees in international legal terminology. Thus, it will be safe to deduce that a category of refugees existed within the overall category of Partition migrants of whom not all can be classified as refugees for the above mentioned reasons. While mass migration was largely induced under threat and coercion, individuals and families used different strategies of exit, of which not all were undertaken in chaotic circumstances. Many people had begun migrating long before Partition took place, while others had evacuated and secured their belongings without state sponsorship. The important difference lies in the relationship the migrants had with the state, since statelessness is a prime factor in the legal and conceptual understanding of refugees.

NARRATIVES AS REPOSITORIES OF EVERYDAY PAST

A unique characteristic of Partition violence and forced migration has been the *absence* of any commemorative memorial or monumental embodiment that serves as a sacred pilgrimage for Partition survivors in India. This stands much in contrast to the Holocaust, a comparable event in many ways, which has many well-known memorials, museums, and even a commemorative day that is observed around the world every year.[13] A Partition memorial remained conspicuously absent until the Indian government established a nondescript five-metre-tall structure at the India–Pakistan border at Attari in Punjab in 1997 to mark fifty years of Independence. The structure is paved with shiny black granite stone, a kind often used in modernized kitchens of middle class Indian homes, with an inscription in bold letters: 'Dedicated to 10 Lakh Punjabis who died unsung in 1947'. The monument does not attract much attention among the thousands of Indian and foreign tourists who visit the border every evening to witness the dramatic flag exchanging ceremony between the Indian and Pakistani border police. The lack of attention is clear from the absence of any sacred or ceremonial marks like red thread, incense, and vermilion, which usually appear around a site, object or person considered holy or worthy of pilgrimage in India. Often ordinary things turn sacred when invested with such public displays of reverence. In short, a state-supported memorial, chiefly constructed to commemorate half-a-century of independence, has hardly been acknowledged by the survivors.

The absence of publicly revered memorials does not, however, mean that remembrance of the past ceases to exist altogether. Among the Partition survivors, such remembrance continues to live in everyday forms expressed chiefly through *narratives*. Thus, narratives of Partition migration and resettlement are the primary sources where everyday forms of past among Punjabi migrants can be located. At a casual level, narrative very simply suggests a story or an account of an event that is currently taking place or has already taken place in the past.[14] Narratives mainly comprise verbal or written communications, in which an event or a series of events are transmitted between narrator and the audience. The narrator often collates different scattered events or happenings into a single, inextricably connected body. Narrators may position themselves as eyewitnesses to the events being described, as participants, or simply as neutral bearers of an oral tradition that hands down narratives of the past from one generation to another.

The significance and utility of popular narratives of past is similar to that of myths: to explain larger happenings that are deemed to be out of one's personal control. It is a way to read meanings into events, persons, and places that seem distant and inaccessible when one encounters them. Lévi-Strauss, in his structural study of myths identifies *langue* and *parole* as two time referents of past events and a myth comes into existence only when it is activated through a third referent that makes it timeless, that is, capable of explaining present, past, and the future (Strauss 1955). Such a mythical quality can be isolated in narratives as well, since they tend to explain not only the past but also one's present circumstances. Narratives as a form of communication are used both in fictional story-telling as well as in non-fictional works. The difference does not lie in the method of communication, but rather in the process of production of a given narrative. Clearly, in this study, narrative in its non-fictional form is a matter of interest to us. The expanse of non-fictional narrative thus goes beyond the literary 'story' as a source, since non-fictional narratives are routinely produced in news reports, history books, personal memoirs, private letters, judicial testimonies, and even in gossip, where day-to-day events are narrated in informal settings.[15]

Three broad narrative themes, together with several supplementary narratives, commonly seek to compress and present the entire life histories of Punjabi migrants:

(1) *Everyday life before Partition*: The description of houses they lived in, occupational intricacies, anecdotes about daily life, neighbours, relatives, Muslim acquaintances and British officials, and myths, plots and intrigues within the extended joint family that appear as an indelible part of the family history;

(2) *The last journey*: Everyday life began to crumble when faced with communal violence, the intensity of violence, the role of Muslim neighbours and friends in escaping, disappointments and betrayals by the political class, discrepancy and sometimes even close family members, personal and material losses, hardships, routes of travel, mode of transport, and arrival in refugee camps; and, finally,

(3) *Life after Partition*: The fresh beginnings, restoration of loss, building new homes, recreating community networks through marriages within the migrant communities, livelihood strategies, commercial success through persistence and hard labour, and a thriving new everyday life.

Thus, the *narratives of events* that forced people to move from one place to another form the basic construct of this study. This is because most people like to narrate their life experiences as simple, uncomplicated tales that help plot their own role in the larger drama unfolding around them.

The uncomplicated, uninterrupted narration does not mean that the experiences being narrated are uncomplicated and entirely comprehensible in themselves. It is their construction as fluent, effortless narratives that make them interesting; but such fluency is achieved only at a later stage. Several disconnected episodes are joined together so that spatial and historical gaps are significantly reduced. For instance, I was told by Mohan Kapoor, a Punjabi Hindu refugee, of his experience during Partition violence and how he found himself in Delhi as a result:

I lived in Rawalpindi with my family. I had recently got married and my wife was expecting our first child. I had a clerical job at the military depot in the cantonment and basically kept to myself. The killings had already started in our area, even before August. My father said that I should take my wife to a safe place, so we joined a group of people who had got a military truck to transport them out of the city. We arrived in Delhi and had no place to stay. The camps were already overflowing with refugees. My brother-in-law made a plan and we would go to the Muslim houses in the city and threaten them with physical violence to vacate their places. We said that we have been thrown out of our homes and we will not let Muslims live in Delhi now. Muslims would leave because they were frightened of us. For centuries Muslims had ruled India and oppressed the Hindus and this is what they were doing again during Partition. They were killing and raping Hindu women. We had to stop that (personal interview).

This narrative has multifarious themes embedded in it: his personal situation, recent marriage, wife's pregnancy, safe and permanent job; communal violence, its history in the area (it had started before August), the significance of the month of August 1947 in Partition history; personal vulnerability due to the larger situation, potential risks to the pregnant wife and the unborn child; the journey from Rawalpindi to Delhi, overflowing camps in Delhi, lack of residential space; corrective measures planned and executed by the narrator and his brother-in-law to drive Muslims out; and, finally, the centuries-long history of Muslim oppression in India that had to be recti-fied now. The narrative is actually crowded with different themes, each of which require full elaboration separately and would make lengthy accounts in themselves. But here they appear in a compact, conjoined and fluent version that includes the 10th-century account of Muslim invasion as an integral explanation of the narrator's life story. It has historical and spatial gaps, moving from the 10th century to the 20th century and from Rawalpindi to Delhi in a single leap. Thus, narratives allow one to figure out what is being told, as well as what is being left out in one's account of personal history. The verbalized spaces and the gaps in between are equally important to understand the way people identify themselves in relation to their old and new surroundings.

The most significant inter-relation of the main and supplementary themes varies along class/caste distinctions, that is, the volume of sub-themes invoked is directly proportional to the class/caste identity of the narrator. The upper caste/middle class migrants narrate their life histories and experiences in nuanced detail, with rich anecdotes and descriptive background of their prestigious jobs, the amount of lost wealth, and the comparative privilege with which they migrated. Here the ritual of narrating their past lives becomes a mode of displaying their earlier possessions, jobs, social ranks, and prestige. On the other hand, the lower class/lower caste/Dalit migrants avoid such detailed and lengthy narratives, probably for two reasons: one, that there is nothing much in terms of material or social prestige worth recounting; and, two, they are generally not used to having patient listeners of their personal stories. Thus, narratives in the second category are usually bereft of detailed supplementary themes.

To a large extent, our knowledge about Partition migration has so far been obtained from the narratives of upper caste/middle class migrants, because not only are these narratives repeated orally in their detailed forms, they are also made available frequently in print as memoirs, biographies, autobiographies, newspaper reports, public speeches, etc. The lower class/ untouchable migrants are not entirely lost in knowledge thus produced; rather, they form the inevitable large canvas—the background—against which the upper caste/middle class stories are told. Partition was a mass event and its narration cannot be authenticated without the appearance of the masses. Thus, upper caste/middle class narrators not only tell their 'own' stories, but also define the experiences of 'others'. The body of lower class/untouchable experience is appropriated and produced as a supplementary narrative to the mainstream oft-narrated story of the middle classes in Punjabi migrant society.

It must be emphasized that the notion of class in this study must not be understood strictly in Marxist terms, that is, as social classification according to an individual's relationship to means of production. A complex web of socio-economic-political relationships, as witnessed in pre- and post-Partition Punjabi society, calls for a more nuanced understanding. Bourdieu's conception of class distinctions—as ownership of various capitals, social, cultural and economic, that are generated through affiliations with educational and other elite institutions, through the expansion of social networks, etc., and that can only be accumulated through generations— offers a deeper comprehension of the class divisions in Punjab. However, class alone does not explain the hierarchies and distinctions in Punjab and most of South Asia; it must be studied together with the institutions of the caste system.

The act of frequent repetition, an authoritative authorship of the narrative and its popular acknowledgement by others produces a master version from a conglomerate of narratives. A master narrative has shaped up over the years from among the Partition narratives as well. The interesting aspect of such a master version is that the author of the narrative is also the main character in the narrative: distinguished men among the migrants have themselves authored such narratives. Their authority to narrate and define the history of migration is derived from their pre-migration standing within their community. Broadly these prominent men can be classified into three categories based on their occupation and accruing social prestige.

At the very top are the *Rais* (pronounced *ra-ees*) born into wealthy families who traditionally took up social causes and political engagement as a community service. Such men were often at the helm of affairs, for example, Diwan Chaman Lall, a rich barrister from West Punjab who was a prominent Punjabi leader before Partition. He migrated to Delhi in 1947 and became a member of the Upper House of Parliament. He was thoroughly engaged in the resettlement problems faced by Punjabi migrants in Delhi before he was appointed India's Ambassador to Turkey. He regularly wrote newspaper articles and delivered public speeches on resettlement problems.

The second is a new social category with clear origins within the colonial administrative system: the *sarkari afsar* (government officers). These men were educated in the English educational system, had decent salaries, official accommodation, and prestige that came with their rank. While some came from wealthy families who could afford a proper English education in England, there were others at lower ranks in the hierarchy, for whom government jobs were a route to upward social mobility. In a well-established tradition of British Indian bureaucracy, most officers would mark their retirement with memoirs. A good example is Justice G.D. Khosla, whose memoirs offer an insight into narrative-making.

While these two categories account for the bulk of authoritative writing, there are others like the middle-level prosperous traders, businessmen, teachers, and local community leaders who produce oral accounts of Partition, deriving their authority from the community resettlement efforts they had been deeply engaged with.

The acknowledgement of the authority of authors of oral or written narratives also suggests that authors have the influence to exclude characters, sequences, locations, etc. Popular exclusion thus becomes another basis for narrative classification. Within the same narrative, exclusion works at a split level, as two levels (we shall name them A and B) of narratives are commonly recounted together. Level A draws a larger picture of the events taking place, and Level B is where the author, who is both the narrator and the main character, enters the scene. These two levels often overlap, but do not necessarily coincide or resonate with each other, since personal experiences often vary from the mass-scale happenings. The urban poor, big and small peasants, untouchables, and women fill in Level A of narrative, along with the urban and rural middle classes, traders, government officers, and other prominent people who become a part of similar circumstances. The characters at this level remain mute and do not yet have personal stories of their own. The exclusion becomes clearly visible at Level B, where the narrative begins taking up its master version, that is, characters begin narrating their own experiences. Here women, untouchables, and the urban poor disappear, not because they do not have a story to tell but because they do not get to tell that story. The characters who speak at this level contribute to the production and maintenance of a common minimum narrative or the master version that various authorities agree to.

One could add a third level, C, where the vocal characters begin digging deeper into their personal experiences to rise above the common minimum character of the narratives. Here the narrative may depart from the master version, even challenge it, since personal experiences of a single event often differ to produce contrasting accounts. In this study narratives are analysed at three levels with two main objectives: (1) to restore the absences, blanks, or breaches (untouchables, single women, the urban poor) in the history of Partition migration, and (2), to challenge the master version from a deeper level where the narrator's own experiences depart from it and therefore challenge it. This third level of unfolding narratives helps restore absences and blanks in the history as well.

MEMORIES IN A PICKLE JAR AND THE NARRATIVES THEREIN

The entire discussion on collective memory can be roughly formed around the experiential moments of formative events; their private expressions; public performances of narration; and the production of master narratives. The overriding aim is to understand how and when historical events get memorized into catch-all *common minimum narratives* that claim to tell of widely experienced moments. As a shortcut, one can descend a metaphorical stepladder—of preservatives and pickle jars—into such a question so as to make the discussion accessible.

The most eye-catching, ordinary and universal items in all Punjabi households are jars of mango pickles lined up on kitchen shelves. Though recipes and spices are part of common knowledge, yet the pickles appear different in their texture, taste, and smell in different households. These are subtle differences, almost invisible to the uninitiated, but they give precious clues to the ingredients that have gone into the jars and, more important, the ones that were kept away from the preservative process. The choice of ingredients and recipes is neither incidental nor random; it is influenced by the social origins—class and caste—of the family that owns a given pickle jar. The mangoes are pickled, preserved, and stored away in plain glass or colourful ceramic jars during the summer months. The jars travel daily between the storage shelves and the eating space to become an unexceptional, mundane part of a family's everyday life. It is this *everyday preservative and consumptive* feature of the pickle jars that makes it so apt a metaphor for our discussions of collective memory.

The memories of Partition violence, migration, and resettlement are similarly as common a feature in Punjabi families in Delhi as the ubiquitous pickle jars on their kitchen shelves. The versions that one gets to hear depend largely on the social space in terms of class and caste occupied by the families before and after Partition, not unlike the pickle jars that contain a universal Punjabi recipe with clear marks of familial preferences and traditions of adding or omitting certain ingredients. Our task is not only to engage with the overwhelming body of collective memory of Partition migration but also to liberate the individual and familial narratives that may deviate from the dominant version.

In order to do so, we need to isolate the basic ingredients from the additive spices and the preservative mediums that create different smells, flavours, and tastes. If the main *ingredient* is one's 'self', then class, caste, and gender become the *additives* that lead to different variations. This tempered mix is then *preserved* with the minor sequences of everyday life: the aftermath of tumultuous events and the memory of accumulated experiences. When one is able to see through the mixed product as a confluence of different ingredients and processes, it becomes easier to comprehend the single human category of forced migrants as a highly stratified and complicated one. This enables us to understand the differing social spaces that the forced migrants of a single historical event come to occupy.

As a methodology, when one engages with a given problematic on the plane of memory, the space thus created occupies previously unmarked areas between the past and present. This becomes more acute when memory is extracted not from documentary sources but from survivors who become the active link between past events and their public recital. In a way, such a study follows a sort of *ethnographic journey into historical spaces*, giving rise to disciplinary breaches. While anthropological studies are understood as studies of 'here and now' (Auge 1977), history is seen as 'an unending dialogue between the present and the past' (Carr 1987: 30). However, this distinction seems superficial when confronted with studies of contemporary historical processes that leave behind not only traditional historical sources consisting of written, printed, and dated archives, but also *living sources* in the form of people who were actually a part of that historical process. This living testimony to past events not only belongs to those at the forefront—the political leadership—but also to ordinary people, bystanders who become part of the indistinguishable mass that constitutes the crowd inhabiting the larger backdrop.

Memory-making is clearly the first step in the production of narratives. The personal experiences of cataclysmic events like violence and forced migration form the raw material that later takes the shape of narratives. Following our earlier arguments, it is clear that various pieces in one's memory are joined to produce a fluent account. This means that the available constructs contain both remembered and forgotten bits of information. It also suggests that individual narrative is produced out of collective accounts. At a theoretical level, this requires defining what is 'collective' and what is 'individual' in the formation and continuation of collective memory[16]— in other words, *how* historical events are experienced and remembered by individuals, in *what forms* they are articulated outside the intimate sphere and, more important, *who* gets to narrate them or remember them publicly. Often memory is discussed in terms of computerized processes that involve feeding, storing, and retrieving memory bits.[17] At the end of such a process the memory *product* gets delinked from the memory *process*. Thus, memory-making becomes a universal, natural and therefore inevitable, and unalterable process.

It may be safely deduced, however, that all memory is shared and 'contains an element of recollection' (Connerton 1989: 6). The normative character of memory—that is, the fact that all events are experienced and recollected in terms of current norms—is emphasized. This leaves the challenge of being able to appreciate individual experiences in larger collective happenings. It is important to ensure that individual experiences do not stand dissolved in a collective body of memory. Recent scholarship, following the psycho-social constructivist approach to memory, suggests that even overwhelmingly political events are mostly remembered and articulated in autobiographical terms, that is, as 'memory for the events of one's own life' (Conway 1997: 22). *Autobiographical memory* (AM) is used not only to retrieve personal experiences but also employed to recollect large events of social and political significance. For example, the episodes of Partition history are not told in terms of the grand narrative traditionally found in the textbooks, which starts from 15 August 1947 when the British government transferred power to the independent states of Pakistan.

I was six years old in 1947 when I heard about Pakistan. We lived in a big house in Dabbi Bazaar in Lahore city. We actually owned an entire lane that connected our locality with rest of the bazaar. We had a gate at the entrance and kept it locked so that none other than our family could use it. This way the women in our family had greater scope to move freely within the house without being watched by the strangers. My father and uncles said that Muslims had started killing Hindus. So we started collecting stones in the balcony to throw at Muslims in case we were attacked.[18]

It is clear from this example that the memory of Partition was basically a memory of, first, the personal position of the narrator at that moment as a six-year-old boy; and, second, the description of the house he lived in, a big house with a private lane. None of these remembrances are about flags, political leaders or motivating political speeches that one would otherwise associate with the achievement of independence. It is remembrances about one's self and one's immediate surroundings that are situated at the forefront. Conway describes this as three-layered autobiographical knowledge, that is, knowledge that refers to: (1) lifetime periods measured in length of time, years and themes of self and goals during that period, (2) general events (records of extended and repeated events that occur over weeks and months), and, finally, (3) event-specific knowledge that consists of images, sensations, smells, and other sensory perceptual features associated with an event (Conway 1997; Conway and Rubin 1993). These layers of autobiographical knowledge form knowledge structures or pools of knowledge in long-term memory, and can be accessed by specific cues stored in general events and lifetime periods.

This helps us understand the formation of collective memory better wherein an individual self does not get dissolved in the larger narrations. The individual self informs the source from where the memory springs, that is, whether it has been experienced by the narrator, or the narrator is reproducing someone else's experience. There is often a thin line between what one *experiences* and what one *imagines* one has experienced. This imagined experience can be borrowed and reproduced from what one has seen, read, or heard. The narrative form where one places oneself inside or outside the event then becomes a crucial pointer that aids in discerning this thin line. The direct personal narrations that one gets from Partition survivors are often narrated the first time in the third person plural, and that narration is normally an attempt to conjoin one's personal experience with the 'authentic' experience one is expected to have had during Partition migration. Upon repeated narrations, the pronoun changes to the first person, and then it is not unusual to find that the narrator's personal experience was vastly different from the one narrated the first time.

Another useful tool to sift through memories is the 'framing device' or interpretative practices as patterned by the ways we define the situation at hand, which avoids freezing a particular 'reading' of a given memory (Irwin-Zarecka 1994: 4–5)—in other words, how we frame the story we tell or how we position it: for example, narrate it as a joke, or as something one read in a newspaper editorial, or in a history book. Each frame—joke, editorial, book—prepares the reader or audience to receive the story in a particular way. On the one hand, framing devices help the audience to know in advance what to expect, and, on the other hand, help the narrator gain distance from, and then, if need be, dismiss the story. In understanding collective memory, framing is particularly helpful as it leads one to the context and the sensitive, empirical explorations in a given theme. Collective memory is understood as 'a set of ideas, images, feelings about the past (that are) best located not in the minds of the individuals, but in the resources they share' (Irwin-Zarecka 1994: 4). Framing leads one to layers of intermediaries that could open up multiple meanings and reinterpretations, because collective memory is 'filled with reused and reusable material' (ibid.: 7). In the Partition narratives, a commonly used framing device is the narration of stories as heroic victories. One way to deal with these would be to dismiss them as plain bragging; but if we understand them as plain prefaces or frames, then it points to the socio-cultural make-up of Punjabi women and men.

The final tool to interpret memories is borrowed from gender studies. In this, one looks at the performances of narrations: that is, how the experiences are narrated (publicly or privately) and who narrates them (male or female members of the household). Linda Degh (1995) points out that in many societies there are male performers who are assigned the task of public narration. Even though many consider story-telling a female pastime, it is not publicly performed by women. Women's narrations are restricted to the household and mainly told while performing their regular vocations within the family. Though the gendered differences in the narrations are not surprising, it is important to remember who within a family is telling the story. Many times women refuse to talk about political events like Partition which they presume not to be their business. They often call their husbands or sons to tell the family story, while themselves keeping a safe distance from the entire proceedings. The husband may ask his wife to fill in some details, which she does, even correcting him at times, but the entire narration is considered his responsibility. The possibility that the versions are gendered and therefore different makes it imperative for the researcher to find alternative means to listen to the women survivors.

OPENING THE MASTER NARRATIVE OF PARTITION RESETTLEMENT

Those days were chaotic. Everyone was trying to save their lives, their children and property. People were escaping in whatever circumstances they could. The trains, even the rooftops of the trains, were full of people.. There were caravans of refugees hundreds of miles long moving from one place to another. Muslims were killings everyone. Those who did not get killed in the violence died due to hunger, thirst and disease. I was 17 years old then. I arrived in Delhi from Lahore in September 1947 with my family and we found a place to live in Kingsway camp. The Government had allotted a tent for the family and gave some rations including rice and lentils. Only children and sick people got milk. Nobody gave any cash doles to the refugees. I did a number of petty jobs and even hawked candy for children on the streets of Delhi. After a while, I became an assistant in a shop in Connaught Place. I did not have a cycle or money for a *tonga* [horse-drawn carriage] ride. I would start walking early in the morning to cover the 10-km stretch and work the whole day with dedication. The shopowner was very impressed with my hard work. He suggested that I open a shop for myself. At that time shops were being allotted in Khan Market. With some help and my own savings, I got this shop. Later I bought two neighbouring shops and made a large combined shop. Today I have a house, two cars and everything else. God has been kind to me.[19]

Locating one's point of entry into the present study through this simple abridged narrative has clear benefits. The narrative, at one and the same time, establishes the standard widespread story of movement and resettlement from Pakistan to India, produces the quintessential refugee figure that often hovers between multiplicity of myth and reality, and finally, points to the cryptic and condensed modes in which the entire resettlement process is commonly understood. Though the story 'belongs' to one individual, who when forced to leave Lahore came to Delhi and with persistence and hard work found a niche in the city, it is shared popularly among the Punjabi refugees in Delhi, to the extent that it has turned into the master narrative of movement and resettlement. However, the master narrative obscures very vital long-term processes centred around individuals on the move who, first, transformed from ordinary people into refugees, and then from refugees into citizens of the modern post-colonial Indian state.

Though it is quite 'normal' to hear and read of the unique character of Punjabi refugees in the private accounts of Partition (mostly told or written by the Punjabi refugees themselves), it is quite unusual to find the state endorsing and then authenticating such beliefs through official proclamations. The allegations of bias against Bengali refugees, therefore, do not come as a complete surprise.[20]

For many years past it has been the fashion to speak of the refugee from East Pakistan as a creature apart. Often he is held up as an object of derision and contempt, where his counterpart in the West is sung of in paeans of praise. Yes, the comparison does not flatter him. He is dubbed a bundle of apathy, impervious to the rehabilitation effort bestowed upon him. And, the severer critics proclaim, he is rebellious and obstructive, too. Yet, how thoughtless and cruel all such comment is (Rao 1967: 141).

The master narrative, therefore, does not stand alone but exists in a comparative frame, especially since the comparison between Punjabi and Bengali refugees has come to assume the status of an inevitable preface that foregrounds any discussion on Partition resettlement. Similar comparisons with Indian Muslims who migrated to Pakistan are not uncommon either, especially in the context of ethnic conflict in Karachi. Incidentally, a large number of Muslims from Delhi city resettled in Karachi, which was considered a cosmopolitan urban centre with thriving commercial activity. Within a short time, Muhajirs, as the Indian Muslims had been dubbed, got embroiled in the local–refugee conflict with the local Sindhi population. This assumed violent overtones through an organized separatist movement called the Muhajir Quami Movement (MQM). Most Punjabis do not fail to point out that while Delhi Muslims in Karachi were regarded as intruders, they were welcomed with open arms, both by the government and the locals in Delhi.

It indeed remains an intriguing question why Punjabi refugees were confronted with no local–refugee conflicts like in Karachi or why resettlement was considered more successful in the case of Punjab but not in Bengal. A compelling explanation, perhaps, lies in the character of Delhi city itself, where the notion of 'natives' has never been as watertight as in Karachi, whose Sindhi identity prevailed antagonistically vis-à-vis the Indian Muslim immigrants despite the city's apparent cosmopolitanism. This comparative situational advantage is, however, seldom mentioned by the Punjabi refugees. During most of my fieldwork in Delhi, I encountered highly charged explanations from the 'original' refugees, their descendants, and also the state employees who had spent large part of their lives working for the resettlement process. The 'human factor' in such refugee discourses was mentioned as a crucial factor that made a significant difference to the successful (or otherwise) implementation of the state policies. A number of terms and phrases in English, Hindi, Punjabi, and even Urdu were used to describe this human factor. The qualities that differentiated Punjabis from everybody else were variously described as *himmat* (courage), *gairat* (pride), *purusharth* (masculine capabilities), *mehnat* (ability to work hard) and an 'indomitable spirit' that does not accept defeat. This description was supplemented with stories, not necessarily personal, that are routinely told to establish the 'facts' about Punjabis. I cite two stories that I came across rather frequently in completely different settings. The first is about Punjabi refugees and their spirit of enterprise. The second story builds on the elements of pride and self-respect that are considered so much a part of the Punjabi ethnic make-up. The names of people and places always change depending upon who is telling the story, that is, Sikhs would appropriate the protagonist as their own and so would the Hindus.

Story 1: A young refugee from West Punjab came to Delhi after Partition. He had no money and no place to live but he did not go to any Government refugee camp for free grants. He had decided to make his own living. One day he went to a sugar merchant in Khari Baoli (a wholesale market in Old Delhi) and asked him for two sacks of sugar with the promise to pay by evening. Each sack cost Rs 15. The merchant took pity on this helpless refugee and gave him two sacks. This young refugee took the sacks and started selling sugar in small portions on the pavement outside the merchant's shop. He sold the sugar at the same price as the wholesale prices that the merchant charged in the shop. By evening he had sold both the sacks and paid back the merchant Rs 30. Soon this became a regular practise for the refugee and the merchant. After many days the merchant asked the refugee that how he made his living when he continuously sold sugar at cost price without leaving a profit margin for himself. The young man replied that after selling the sugar, he was left with the empty bags, which he then sold for Rs 2. This was more than enough for his upkeep. In this way he could look after himself and save a little as well. Needless to say that, merchant was impressed with the spirit of enterprise that this young man displayed (popular story).

Story 2: There is the poignant story of a young Punjabi lad hawking newspapers in New Delhi's fashionable shopping centre. On a generous impulse a kindly soul offered him a rupee-note in exchange for a paper and waived the proffered change. There were tears of chagrin in the youngster's eyes as he angrily protested that he was not a beggar. Here was a gallantry that mocked at adversity and would never admit defeat (Rao 1967: 37).

The two stories together seek to convey the 'ethnic essence' that differentiates Punjabis from all 'other' Partition refugees and also from the local Delhi population. The merchant in the story symbolizes the long-established and prosperous local Hindu mercantile community that owned most of the resources in the city. Many times, the first story is rounded off with a reminder that most of the refugees who started on the pavements have now bought out the local Hindu shopkeepers and established enviable businesses. The credit, as in the story, goes to the ingenious skills, sheer determination, and hard work that the Punjabi refugees displayed. The second story goes a step further in establishing the characteristic pride that influenced the choices made by refugees. The refusal to accept private or state charity is a theme often proudly recounted in everyday conversations.

It is not a coincidence that the main characters in both the stories are male, and attempt to restore masculine attributes lost during the Partition violence and migration when they were unable to adequately protect 'their' women, livelihoods, and homes or prevent violent territorial division of the new nation. In most such popular discourses, the state never gets to share in the glory of successful resettlement. Yet, the role of state—mainly the army and the bureaucracy—cannot be denied, as massive evidence exists, not only in archival form but also in the written memoirs/biographies of the civil–military officers involved in the resettlement process. The absence of the state in refugee discourses, however, becomes an intriguing issue that calls for further investigation.

These stories, particularly the second one, have been further authenticated through repeated references in scholarly and official works on Punjabi refugees in Delhi. For example, V.N. Dutta (1986), a renowned historian and himself a refugee, reproduced the entire story as evidence of the Punjabi spirit in his essay, 'Punjabi Refugees and the Urban Development of Greater Delhi'. In the footnotes to the story, he cites, as proof of authenticity, the official state publication, *The Story of Rehabilitation*, as the source. The same story is recounted in official and unofficial accounts innumerable times to repeat the by-now well-known point. Even a socio-economic study commissioned by the Planning Commission to measure the scale and impact of a sudden demographic change in Delhi after Partition could not escape the stereotypes. The study was conducted by the well-known economist from the University of Delhi, V.K.R.V. Rao, who paid 'high tributes to the spirit of enterprise and the hard work of the refugee population' (Rao and Desai 1965: xx). Almost as an afterthought, the author adds, 'besides, of course, [the successful resettlement] being attributable to their higher academic qualifications and skills' and 'in part, due to the help they received from the Government in respect of their residential and business accommodation, and to a smaller extent, to the special educational and financial facilities they received from the Government' (ibid.). Similarly, a government official in charge of resettlement remarks:

I would therefore like to place on record my admiration and appreciation of the high quality of the human factor in the Punjabi refugee that has enabled him to remake his life in Delhi and give to the refugee households here a position of importance that is likely to grow into one of dominance over the coming years (ibid.: xx).

The other obvious field of enquiry, then, is how the 'success' of resettlement is determined and by whom. The phrase often used by the refugees and the officials alike to describe successful resettlement was, 'We/They are well settled.' The phrase 'well settled' is as subjective and vague as the rest of the terms used to describe the distinguishing spirit of Punjabis. Any attempt to open up the meanings of such a term would require knowledge of what 'doing well' is being compared with—the local Delhi population or the pre-Partition socio-economic status of the refugees. This would also entail moving away from the monolithic, all-encompassing discursive category that Punjabi refugees have come to assume. If Partition is indeed considered a 'critical event' (Das 1995: 6), then we need to look separately at the social groups that have emerged out of such a momentous episode. The critical events are described as events after which 'new modes of action came into being which redefined traditional categories such as codes of purity and honour, the meaning of martyrdom, and the construction of a heroic life. Equally, new forms were acquired by a variety of political actors, such as caste groups, religious communities, women's groups and the nation as a whole'. It needs to be emphasized here that the pre-history of critical events is as significant as the events themselves, for that is when the ground is laid for such events and categories of actors produced.

APPROACHING PARTITION

A defining feature of British India's Partition has been the nationalization of populations (Pandey 2001: 1) and the eventual process of mass migration to the ascribed nation-states. The sheer magnitude and multiplicity of simultaneous partition processes—division of territory and assets; creation of post-colonial nation-states; unprecedented communal violence; human suffering and trauma entailed in dislocation—often hinders comprehension of the entire phenomenon. Some aspects of Partition historiography, collectively referred to as the events of 'high politics' at national level (Chandra et al. 1989; Gilmartin 1988; Inder Singh 1987; Jalal 1985; Talbot 1988) have dominated earlier writings, while recent works focus on the sufferings of individuals and micro-processes (Pandey 2001; Butalia 1998; Menon and Bhasin 1998; Major 1998; Das 1995) and the popular portrayal of Partition in literature, drama, films, paintings, and everyday life (Malik 2002; Chatterjee 2002; Chakravarty 2002; Talbot 1996; Bhalla 1994). Thus, making sense of Partition history is the first step in understanding the processes of Partition migration and identification among the Punjabi refugees. The following three broad categories will be employed here to understand Partition:

(1) as a by-product of the religious nationalism that surfaced during the Indian national struggle for independence and its culmination,
(2) as a logical beginning of post-colonial nation building exercise, and finally
(3) as a central cathartic event that has shaped the collective national psyche in India and Pakistan.

The purpose in using these categories as our frame to understand Partition is primarily in order to do away with the limiting disciplinary boundaries that have so far made it a preserve of historians. The point is not merely to circumvent the disciplinary straitjacket but also to introduce differences of approach—that is, whether we approach Partition as a *dead issue* that happened half a century ago and is routinely subjected to academic post-mortems, or as a *living theme* that did not end with the lapse of communal violence and the closure of high-level political negotiations between India and Pakistan. The choice of such approaches would decide the further course, in terms of which aspects of Partition are brought into prominence and which are dropped, or which sources are used and which are discarded.

In this study, Partition clearly stands as a *living theme* that surfaces as a regular *point of reference* among millions of survivors of communal violence and migration in 1947. The Partition survivors represent a seldom-used collective source that enables one to understand the long-term impact of traumatic events. Such insights cannot merely be captured in a few selected oral histories that immediately get converted into permanent memories once they are recorded, printed, and publicly circulated. Often one does not take into account the fact that what is narrated today may be retracted tomorrow. The reasons behind such choices—to offer a memory or to retract it—are what make the entire exercise of memory and its presentation a *living theme*.

The choices are dictated by one's present requirements, which ensure that the event never belongs to the past but keeps reappearing in everyday life. This would mean looking at the everyday lives of the survivors—individually and collectively—to see how everyday life is shaped by memories and how the memories are in turn shaped by the compulsions of everyday life. Such an approach to Partition shifts the scope away from debates that are otherwise dichotomously paired around fissures between Hindus–Muslims; Congress party–Muslim League; India–Pakistan, etc., and calls for a larger social-political field than the one offered within the discipline of history.

The decade preceding Partition, from 1937 onwards, is considered crucial by *traditionalist* historians since it marked a turning point in pre-independence Indian power politics.[21] Under the provisions of the 1935 Government of India Act, which extended franchise and self-government to the provincial level, the first open electoral exercise took place in 1937. It offered the nationalist Indian leadership an opportunity to publicly test its long-standing agendas for the first time. The election results placed the Indian National Congress as the most important political party at the all-India level, while in Punjab province the clear winner was the regional Unionist Party. The Muslim League failed to draw popular support from among the Muslims and saw its claims of being the sole Muslim political party thwarted. It also failed to reach a power-sharing arrangement with the Congress to establish a coalition government in the United Provinces. The humiliating electoral losses suffered by the Muslim League spurred its leadership to hurried campaigns and efforts to break through to the Muslim masses. Revisionist historians depart from the prevailing view that Jinnah sought solace in sectarian politics at this point, having lost the provincial political power struggle to Congress.[22] They see Jinnah's heightened emphasis on religious separatism as a tactical shift (rather than as a caving-in to religious fanaticism) that was engineered as a response to real political demands. The demand for Pakistan is further seen as a 'bargaining counter' from where to negotiate sufficient power share for the Indian Muslims (Jalal 1985).

Whether the demand for a separate state was merely tactical or genuinely sectarian, Jinnah definitely claimed to speak for the entire Indian Muslim population. Even though such a claim was rejected in the popular elections, it was pushed forward by the Muslim elites who turned to separatist policies to safeguard their interests (Hasan 1996: 4). The Muslim landowners and government officials who felt threatened by the changing power equations and fear of Hindu domination were instrumental in founding the Muslim League to spearhead a separate Muslim identity (Robinson 1974). The religious separatism, as the core of Partition politics, is traced further back to the late 19th-century religious–social reform movements like the Arya Samaj among the Hindus, and the Deobandi movement and the Aligarh movement among the Muslim masses.[23] By the early 20th century, the social movements had taken a far more political turn in the shape of disciplined 'cultural' organizations like the Rashtriya Swayamsevak Sangh (RSS)[24] and disticly communal political parties like the Hindu Mahasabha and the Muslim League. The loss of political power by the Muslims in the 19th century and the long-standing communal divide because of exclusive Hindu social practices (like taboos about food, marriage etc.) are cited as the original causes of the separatist demands (Khalique 2002: 112). In a recent three-volume study on Partition, Muslim nationalism and the cohesive communal features of Islam are brought forth (Prasad 2002). Although the study recognizes the parallel growth of Hindu communalism, it suggests:

Neither the League's adoption of the demand of Partition (1940) nor its success in securing its fulfilment within a short span of seven years can be explained without reference to the deep historical as well as socio-political foundations of Muslim nationalism, based on a belief that Muslims, although living together with Hindus and others on Indian soil, constituted a nation separate from the rest and had their own special interests to protect and promote (Prasad 2002: 11).

The emphasis on the social exclusiveness of the two communities somehow makes Partition appear an inevitable event that could not have been averted. In a way such a view disengages itself from a direct confrontation with the political negotiations among the outgoing British officials, the Muslim League and the Congress that preceded the Partition. The onus of Partition is now laid not on the political manoeuvring but on the mutually repelling social practices, beliefs, and institutions that would one way or the other have led to the breakdown.

One more approach that we will use to frame Partition is where the preceding decade is seen as a preparatory pause before independent statehood, and the final hour of independence as a long-awaited opportunity to actually practise statecraft. Partha Chatterjee (1986) terms the time when the young nation finally came into being under the leadership of Nehru as the 'moment of arrival'. The scientific, rational approach of Nehru, tempered with socialist beliefs, ensured that 'central planning' and the 'committee of experts' became the core of state policies in all spheres (Chatterjee 1994: 201). Here the entire reading of Partition is conducted away from the spheres of communal violence, conflicts, and breakdowns in political negotiations. The focus on the making of the nation-state—its independence and not partition—and its change in status, from colonial to post-colonial are dealt with in a neat and clean manner. The question why the young free nation began its life with amputated territories is never asked, because *whys* are not considered important; *hows* take precedence instead.

It is not being suggested that the period around August 1947 in Indian history cannot be studied without making references to Partition, but that its absence in studies of post-colonial state formation in India do give a very partial and incomplete picture. This is because the Indian state was not really functioning as a giant monolith, steered by the 'experts' and run according to well-prepared 'central plans'. The state was immediately besieged by the overwhelming task of refugee resettlement and restoration of law and order in disturbed regions of Punjab, Delhi, and Bengal. Further, the state needs to be studied in terms of its parts—that is, those organs that were directly created for or were connected with Partition-related administrative tasks and those that were far removed from it. The nation-building exercise was not taking place in secluded environs but was actually, in many ways, being undertaken through the resettlement work.

The third prevalent trend is to perceive Partition as the central cathartic event in the young nation's life, which left its traumatic marks on the collective national psyche. These types of studies are often conducted across the national borders dividing India and Pakistan. The trauma of Partition is traced in both ordinary and extraordinary events when 'India and Pakistan play a cricket match, or when their political leaders talk of "unfinished business"' (Kaul 2001: 4). The bilateral conflicts between India and Pakistan—over Kashmir, for example—are directly rooted in Partition politics. The inimical relationship between the two countries extends both outwards into the international politics (for example, their positioning during the Cold War was diametrically opposite each other), and also inwards among the ordinary people and their everyday lives. For example, it is not entirely uncommon in popular discourse to accuse Indian Muslims of being Pakistani agents and traitors. Similarly, during Hindu–Muslim communal clashes, Muslims are often blamed for being provocative; they must then be taught a lesson as how to stay in a Hindu-majority nation.[25] Partition violence has entered the popular vocabulary in north India, especially in Punjab (the site of the most gruesome atrocities) as a benchmark against which to measure the gravity of violence. The 1984 anti-Sikh riots in Delhi and the 2002 anti-Muslim Gujarat violence were popularly compared by media and survivors to the Partition violence. However, neither of these events compare with Partition in terms of the scale and magnitude of violence.

Religious violence in Punjab was not an entirely unknown phenomenon during the colonial period, as there were occasional inter-communal clashes between Sikh/Hindu–Muslim and Sikh–Arya.[26] The construction of deepened religious identities through 19th-century social reform movements, and the colonial practice of authenticating and fixing those modern religious identities through the census enumeration and preferences for certain ethnic material in government jobs (for example, Khalsa Sikhs in the British army) meant that new religious groups were contesting and negotiating their socio-economic control in colonial Punjab. This communal contest often took a violent shape. However, a distinction needs to be made between the communal violence that marred colonial Punjab and the Partition violence that took genocidal proportions. The differences emerge on four counts: (1) immediate cause of violence, (2) extent of killings, (3) spatial location of violence, and (4) involvement of women. The pre-Partition period was marked by violent eruptions over religious provocations like the appearance of a dead cow in a Hindu temple or a pig carcass in a mosque, controversial routes of religious processions in a locality, and provocative noise levels of religious chanting or morning calls of the muezzin to his followers. The number of deaths was very low, while the number of bodily injuries was higher; the violence was mainly seen as an urban phenomenon that took place in public spaces, that is, it rarely entered the private space; and, last, the violence took place between men of opposing communities and women hardly appeared either as victims or as perpetrators. This changed dramatically during the Partition violence, as the causes behind eruption of violence became more political than religious: the number of deaths was extraordinary, estimated at half a million, while extent of injuries was insignificant in comparison; the violence took place in rural as well as urban centres of Punjab, and also entered people's homes, as private houses were burnt, which had rarely happened before; and, finally, women appeared as chief victims of the general as well as a well-orchestrated sexual violence irrespective of all communities.

These distinctions primarily help us to understand the *intent* behind violence that changes its character from what is called 'traditional' violence to genocidal violence.[27] Often the ritualistic character of communal violence in India is pointed out to show that men in opposing communities engage in violent contest to mark boundaries and guard them fiercely.[28] Total annihilation of the 'other' is never the object, as the 'self' is defined by the mirror existence of the 'other'. However, this understanding of communal violence becomes obsolete when one looks at the intent of destruction and annihilation of the dehumanized 'other' visible in the burning of homes (to render people homeless); the sexual nature of violence, with amputation of reproductive organs in both men and women, mass rapes; and organized killings, with the presence of private communal armies of World War II demobilized soldiers—all these point out to an intent of annihilating the other. The ritual in this case is less to mark out boundaries and more to do with cleansing one's sacred national territory of ethnic pollutants. Thus, the magnitude and the mechanisms employed in cleansing territories is what makes Partition violence unparalleled in contemporary South Asian history. The violence claimed half a million lives, resulted in massive destruction of property and left around 25 million people displaced all over South Asia.[29]

FRAGMENTING MOMENTS OF PARTITION

Partition represents a momentous cataclysmic event in modern India. It is the very basis of this study, and needs to looked at thoroughly in order to be able to understand the context of immigration to Delhi. To begin with, each single act of migration from West Punjab to Delhi must be broken down further into series of moments: of turmoil, exodus, and arrival. These moments together encapsulate the transformation of people into refugees and chart the uneasy turf where state and refugees frequently meet and part. Once separated, the collective moment breaks down into a disjointed sequence, where the state occasionally shirks, hides, and then exercises its authority. In their estranged form, the three momentary strings reveal how the withdrawal of the state from the everyday lives of people during critical political processes creates turmoil, causes an exodus, and produces refugees. The active engagement of the state at a later stage gears the official apparatus towards producing lawful citizens and restoring the previously lost order in public and private lives.

The moments of turmoil occurred around the time of actual partition and represent the public chaos and incessant violence among the Hindus, Muslims, and Sikhs. They also signified personal moments of agony when individuals and families decided to leave their homes. At this juncture, the state—in its colonial and post-colonial incarnation—was characterized by a partial paralysis that made high-level negotiations on Partition of territory, assets etc., between India and Pakistan possible, but disabled its capacity to restore law and order among virulent communal groups. The unprecedented violence in Punjab spurred mass migration not only from the areas that were directly affected by violence but also from those that were considered peaceful. It was not so much the violence and chaos itself but its fearful anticipation that forced people to leave. The state was not able to assert its authority and instil confidence among people that their lives, properties, and honour were safe from violent mob. But the involuntary withdrawal of the state from the public sphere of law and order cannot in itself be taken as evidence of state collapse.[30] It needs to be localized and restricted to tumultuous events that led to population movement and not to the entire process of migration and resettlement.

The moments of exodus represent both chaos and order, depending upon the individual circumstances and time period when the last journey was undertaken. While abrupt, instantaneous, individually organized journeys to safety were common at the time of Partition, the bulk of the movement took place later through the state-organized mass exchange of population (see Chapter 3). The organization of refugee convoys, transit camps, special trains, and other transport was a gigantic exercise that involved multiple state agencies. These acts evince the reclamation of a state authority that was otherwise undermined by the unchecked violence and unceasing fear among the population. The entry of the state in the field of population movement from October 1947 onwards eased the incessant chaos that is popularly considered characteristic of the Partition migration.

It is in the moments of arrival that state seeks active engagement with the displaced population—while the state clearly failed in stemming violence and discouraging forced population movement, the arrival of refugees presented an opportunity to fully redeem and establish its authority. The 'arrival' not only signifies the physical emergence of refugees on Indian territory but also the coming of the Indian state into its own. The task of distributing emergency relief and then resettling refugees permanently provided the state with a unique opportunity to gain legitimacy and publicly display its administrative skills. This study is located in these moments of arrival, when state and refugees constantly negotiate their roles and opportunities in the new circumstances.

To begin with, the tide of forced migration had not started in August 1947 (as is popularly believed) but in March 1947 after the Rawalpindi riots. The fall of the Khizar Tiwana government in Punjab following the Muslim League agitation led to widespread riots in Rawalpindi, which soon engulfed Lahore, Amritsar, Jhelum, Attock, and Multan (Hansen 2002: 109–13). A particular feature of the March violence (apart from an unprecedented number of deaths) was the number of people who sought refuge in the camps. An official estimate from the districts of Attock, Jhelum, and Rawalpindi alone put the number of refugees at 60,000. They were in the camps either because they feared for their safety or their houses had been burnt (Hansen 2002: 113). The growing uncertainty about the future course of events, like the demarcation of the boundary line and the possible extent of communal violence, proved cataclysmic in terms of making people move away to perceived safer areas where their community was in majority. The trickle of refugees in spring had transformed into never-ending columns of refugees by the summer of 1947.

The exact number of dead, injured, and those forced to migrate in either direction has remained a source of contention among historians. The conservative estimates emanating from British sources about the number of casualties put the figure at 200,000 (Moon 1961), while the Indian estimates peg the number at around 400,000 to 500,000 (Khosla 1950). The estimates in some of the recent studies, which rely extensively on oral testimony, put the figure at 800,000 (Butalia 1998). The number of migrants is, thus, equally contested. As an approximate measure, it would be safe to assume that the population that risked being forced to migrate could not be more than the actual non-Muslim population.

Table 1.1 shows the total non-Muslim population to be less than 4 million in West Punjab. The NWFP would add another 2.8 million non-

Table 1.1 : Population in West Punjab districts in 1941

District	Total	Muslim	%	SC	%	Christians	%	Sikhs	%	Hindus	%
Lahore	1695375	1027772	60.6	32735	1.9	67686	0.4	310648	18.3	252004	14.9
Sialkot	1190497	739218	62.1	65354	5.5	73846	6.2	139409	11.7	165965	13.9
Gujranwalla	912235	642706	70.5	7485	0.8	60380	6.6	99139	10.9	100630	11.0
Sheikhupura	852508	542344	63.6	22438	2.6	59985	0.7	160706	18.9	66744	7.8
Gujarat	1104952	945609	85.6	4621	0.4	4391	0.4	70233	6.3	80022	7.2
Shahpur	998921	835918	83.7	9693	1.0	12690	1.3	48046	4.8	92479	9.2
Jhelum	629658	563033	89.4	771	0.1	730	0.1	24680	3.9	40117	6.4
Rawalpindi	785231	628193	80.0	4233	0.5	4212	0.5	64127	8.2	78245	10.0
Attock	675875	611128	90.4	1015	0.1	504	0.9	20102	3.0	42194	6.2
Mianwali	506321	436260	86.2	1008	0.2	324	0.6	6865	1.3	61806	12.2
Montgomery	1329103	918564	69.1	43456	3.2	24101	1.9	175064	13.2	167510	12.6
Lyallpore	1396305	877518	62.8	68222	4.9	51694	3.7	262737	18.8	135637	9.7
Jhang	821631	678736	82.6	1943	0.2	744	0.1	12238	1.5	127946	15.2
Multan	1484333	1157911	78.0	24530	1.7	13270	0.9	61628	4.1	225342	15.2
Muzzafargarh	712849	616074	86.4	2691	0.4	218	0.3	5882	0.8	87952	12.3
DG Khan	581350	512678	88.1	1059	0.2	46	0.1	1072	0.2	66348	11.4
Transfrontier Tract	40246	40084	99.6	0	0.0	0	0.0	2	0.0	160	0.4
Total	15717390	11773746	78.7	291254	1.4	374821	1.5	1462578	7.4	1791101	10.3

Source: Author's collation based on the 1941 Population Census of the Punjab province.

Muslims who could migrate. These figures do not include those who got killed, who were forcibly or voluntarily converted to Islam, or who simply refused to move away. To find out how many people moved to Delhi, the population censuses of 1941 and 1951 conducted in Delhi are used to compare the decadal demographic shifts to find the approximate extent of movement. The total population of Delhi in 1941 was counted at 917,939 which increased to 1,744,072 in 1951, at an unprecedented decennial growth rate of 106 per cent.[31] In absolute numbers, the increase amounts to 1.1 million people, making it the highest ever increase in the city's census history; even more so when the increase does not take into account the outward migration of approximately 300,000 Delhi Muslims to Pakistan.

Even if we assume that the increase was not entirely due to the influx of Punjabi refugees—given the factors of the usual rural–urban in-migration and natural growth at the natural growth rate of 4 per cent—the massive increase can largely be attributed to Partition-related events. The incoming Punjabi refugees became a part of the city from then on, first as inhabitants of tents in refugee camps, temporary roadside shacks, and abandoned military barracks, and later as residents of the mass-constructed refugee colonies. Throughout this journey, the Indian state remained a co-traveller (though not always in the frame), arranging and organizing the mass of refugees.

DEFINING THE CONTOURS OF DELHI

As noted earlier, the unprecedented decadal growth rate of 106 per cent in the city's population in the period 1941–51 brought into the city over one million people who required permanent housing.[32] The exceptionally high figure is on account of the incoming partition refugees, usual rural–urban migration and an overall growth in the city's population at the annual rate of around 4 per cent.[33] But converting people into figures is tricky business: one can deduce from the changing contours of the city the obvious pitfalls that lie therein.

Table 1.2: Area and population of greater Delhi, 1901–56 (urban)[34]

Census	Area (km²)	Population
1901	43.25	209000
1911	43.25	233000
1921	168.09	304000
1931	169.64	447000
1941	170.16	676000
1951	195.80	1415000
1956 (March)	280.49	1746000

Source: Economic Survey of Delhi 2002.

When the first census of the city was undertaken in 1881, it was as a part of the Delhi district of Punjab province. The district included the *tehsils* (divisions) of Sonepat and Ballabhgarh apart from Delhi itself, for a total area of 3304 sq km. In 1911, the imperial capital was shifted from Calcutta to Delhi following George V's announcement at the Delhi Durbar (court). Soon after, a separate Delhi province was formed comprising Delhi division and portions of Ballabhgarh division. An area of 119 sq km was transferred in 1915 from Ghaziabad division of United Provinces to Delhi, which led to delimiting the basic unit of Delhi, as we know it today, with a total area of 1483 sq km.

Table 1.3: Area and population of the different towns of greater Delhi, 1956[35]

| | Area | | Population | | Gross Density |
	Sq Km	%	Per 1000	%	Persons per kilometre
Old Delhi	26.5	9.27	1087	62	106.197
Red Fort	2.09	0.73	11	0.63	13.618
New Delhi	81	28.3	296	16.89	9.472
Civil Lines	20.9	7.3	75	4.28	9.248
South Delhi	52.7	18.44	67	3.82	3.287
West Delhi	30.7	10.76	91	5.19	7.698
Shahdara	23.7	8.32	69	3.94	7.564
Cantonment	43.3	15.15	32	1.83	1.909
Mehrauli	0.49	0.17	8	0.45	40.970
Najafgarh	0.36	0.13	6	0.34	41.209
Narela	3.88	1.36	11	0.63	7.133
Total	285.90	100	1753	100	16.041

Source: Rao and Desai (1965: 31).

Several changes were taking place within Delhi city at the same time. Till 1911, the areas constituting urban Delhi were Red Fort and the limits of Delhi Municipality over the walled city of Shahjehanabad, a portion of present Civil Lines in the north, and the settlements of Sabji Mandi, Sadar Bazar, and Paharganj in the west.[36] The urban portions of Delhi were no more than 27 square kilometres with a resident population of 233,000 when Delhi was announced to be the new imperial capital. The newly constituted province of Delhi was under the direct jurisdiction of the Government of India, wherein three new urban administrative units were created in addition to the existing urban expanse. These were: (1) Civil Lines Notified Area, the temporary seat of the central Government, (2) Raisina Municipality, the site of later New Delhi area, and (3) New Cantonment on the west of Raisina municipality. By 1921, urban Delhi comprised four units,[37] that is, Red Fort, Delhi municipality, Civil Lines, and New Delhi spread over an area of 104.44 sq km and with a population of 304,000. During the 1931 census, the town of Shahadra was added to the municipal units of Delhi, stretching Delhi across the Yamuna River on the eastern side. The last two units of south and west Delhi were created in 1953 to cover the new settlements established for the Partition refugees from Punjab and the NWFP.

In a survey from September 1955 till February 1957 commissioned by the Planning Commission, the questions of population growth, housing and living standards of the city dwellers were looked at in detail (Rao and Desai 1965: 6–7). The survey sample constituted 3,44,147 households with a total membership of 17,08,019 persons spread over ten municipal divisions of Delhi, namely, Old Delhi, New Delhi, Civil Lines, West Delhi, South Delhi, Shahdara, Narela, Mehrauli, Najafgarh, and Cantonment Board. The results of this survey combined with that of decennial population surveys show that the sharp demographic increase in the period 1941–51 cannot be attributed to Partition migration alone. The decadal increase in 1951 amounted to almost a million people that are inevitably linked to the momentous events of 1947 and the population movement that followed it. The survey and the census figures show that the forced migration during Partition had somehow catalysed simultaneous voluntary migration in the Punjab–Rajasthan–Delhi belt. One can get a fairer idea of the people's movements if they are followed from their place of birth to their new land.

The figures in Table 1.3 classify the Delhi population according to their place of birth. In 1921, people born within Delhi district, at over 60 per cent, formed the largest group, while the in-migration from neighbouring areas constituted the remaining 37.4 per cent. This approximate proportion of 60:40 is maintained over the next three decades till 1951, when not only is there a new category of people from 'countries of Asia' (a euphemism for Pakistan), but the district-born population is actually reduced to around 40 per cent instead of the previous figure of 60 per cent. Though the internal migration from within India to Delhi, in terms of percentage increase in Delhi's population, reduced from 40 per cent to 30 per cent, but in absolute numbers it represents a significant increase in this category of population. This distribution pattern was reflected in the 1956 survey as well, when a little less than 60 per cent of the population was found to be migrant, refugee, or otherwise.[38] Around 40 per cent of the sample population was found to be of refugee background in Delhi, of which 72.5 per cent were original refugees, 24.6 per cent were labelled as residents (that is, children born of refugee parents after their immigration to Delhi), and 2.9 per cent were classified as in-migrants, 'mostly those born during the period between the emigration of their parents from Pakistan and their final immigration into Delhi' (Rao and Desai 1965: 107).

Table 1.4: Percentage distribution of population according to place of birth (1921–51)[39] in Delhi province/union territory of Delhi

	1921	1931	1941	1951
Total population	4.884.52	6.362.46	9.179.39	17.440.72
District Born	61.9%	58.6%	59.3%	41.1%
Territories in India	37.4%	40.8%	40.0%	31.1%
Countries of Asia	0.1%	0.1%	0.3%	27.7%
Rest of the World	0.6%	0.5%	0.4%	0.1%

Source: Census of India 1951.

That these figures are not definitive was betrayed by the surveyors themselves. The difference between the refugee and non-refugee categories was rather fluid as it was based on one's place of birth. It did give clues to association with a certain place, but failed to capture the journeys and movements that individuals experienced in their lifetimes before Partition. During the survey, the refugees were found to be living within both non-refugee and resident households. The constituents of these two categories that were associated with the refugees came from the same ethnic groupings. The reason for this all-inclusive distribution of refugees was that a 'good part of the households [were] headed by "residents" who immigrated to Delhi earlier than the commencement of the reference period from presumably the same parts of Pakistan from which these kin of theirs came during the Partition to be accommodated within these households on account of old kinship ties' (ibid.). This points to the migration that was prevalent from the areas that later formed Pakistan to urban centres of Delhi, where a number of Punjabi traders lived long before the Partition. As early as mid-19th century, there are references to Punjabi localities like 'Mohalla Punjabian', 'Katra Punjabi', etc. (Gupta 1999: 54), where Punjabi Muslims lived. There was even an association of Punjabi lawyers called 'Vakil-e-Quam-Punjabian', which, in 1904, bought a separate cemetery for the Punjabi Muslims in Shidipura (Gupta 1999: 187, 191). Similarly, Punjabi Hindu traders are known to have migrated to Delhi before Partition, either in families or at least settling one male member of the family in the city.

The pre-1947 presence of Punjabis in Delhi partly explains why so many Punjabi refugees sought shelter in the city. However, the mass arrival of Punjabi refugees dramatically changed the spatial, social, economic, and political profile of Delhi. The physical alterations in the city begin with the mass housing projects that were developed by the government to provide permanent housing to the refugees. The southern, eastern, and western parts of Delhi were sites of new housing projects, while north and central Delhi was where most of the temporary refugee accommodations were located. Karol Bagh, which was once a quiet residential suburb on the western side, became part of the bustle of commercial central Delhi. The new localities which sprang up around the Old city and the British-built New Delhi are visibly identifiable by their indistinguishable design and construction. The names also mark them out separately, as they bear the names of freedom fighters and national leaders: Patel Nagar, Tilak Nagar, Lajpat Nagar, to name a few.

The continuous and rapid expansion of the urban limits of Delhi has meant that these areas are no longer on the outskirts of the city. The unabated rise in Delhi population, approximately 14 million in 2002, has added many more localities around the original refugee colonies. In a way, there are four layers of urban expansion around the core of the old city: (1) urban development projects at the turn of the 20th century, like Civil Lines, Karol Bagh, etc., (2) New Delhi capital city project following the 1911 Delhi Durbar, (3) Partition-related constructions between 1947 and the 1960s, and (4) post-1975 Emergency constructions to the present. In this study, we are mainly concerned with the areas falling in the third layer where a vast majority of the original Punjabi refugees still reside. The increase in family size often means that children and grandchildren have to move out of the old localities. Many descendants of Partition refugees therefore live in the newly developed areas situated in the fourth layer. The identifiable field site of this study is located in the expanded city contours of the third and occasionally the fourth layer.

ABOUT THIS BOOK

This book is organized in eight main chapters (apart from this introductory chapter) around the twin courses travelled by the Punjabi migrants—from ordinary people to refugees and from refugees to locals in Delhi city—over a period of half-a-century. The main focus is on the period between 1947 and 1965, that is, from Partition itself—covering the themes of displacement, loss, resettlement, and restoration—till the official closure of resettlement work in 1965, when the Indian government closed and merged the Ministry of Relief and Rehabilitation into the Ministry of Home Affairs as a department. It was a significant moment when the 'refugees' ceased to be the subject of a separate ministry within the Indian government, and became a part of the 'home affairs' instead.

The thematic organization of this book means that it does not necessarily give a decade-by-decade account of the resettlement process over the last six decades. It discusses the last journey undertaken by millions of Hindus and Sikhs from West Punjab, and challenges the popular narrative that represents migration essentially as chaotic, disorderly, and hurried. This study makes use of personal and governmental narratives to show that the population movement—multi-layered and distinguished by class- and caste-based experiences—was far more complicated than we popularly imagine.

The book also describes the government policies and practices of resettlement, wherein 'compensation' against property lost in Pakistan was the key criterion. A reference to past ownership meant that pre-Partition distinctions of class and caste were reproduced in Delhi as well. Refugee resettlement presented an opportunity to the nascent state to establish its authority by making available rehabilitation schemes and distributing resources among the displaced. The entire resettlement exercise was meant to restore the national and personal losses incurred during Partition. Somehow, the national loss and the personal loss of migrants had the same need of restoration, albeit at different levels. The restoration of social order was imbued by gendered meanings and distinctions according to the prevalent norms of morality.

The final part of the book (Chapter 8) also explores the historicity of the identification processes among the Punjabi migrants in Delhi. What defines them most of all is the ethnic amnesia that they display towards their Punjabi ethnicity. A visible delinking from their Punjabi ties has resulted in a closer identification with the Indian nation. In fact, following the inimical Hindu–Sikh relationship that shaped up after Partition, the very definition of Indian identity stands reworked in a Hindu context.

NOTES

1. A similar exercise to demolish illegal constructions was carried out in December 2005 by the MCD, targeting 18,000 buildings in various parts of Delhi. The even spread of this 'demolition drive' all over the city meant that the public discourse had clearly shifted to corruption (rather than that of recurring historic injustices) within the municipality, since the targeted localities were a mix of non-refugee and refugee resettlement colonies, like Patel Nagar.
2. Personal interview with Neena Khanna, 6 February 2002.
3. Personal interview with Madan Kapoor, 6 February 2002.
4. 'Remove Encroachments, SC tells MCD', *The Times of India*, 9 March 2002.
5. The concerns about the use of past in present have earlier been expressed by Maurice Bloch (1977) and Arjun Appadurai (1981). While the concerns are shared, the context in which this question is posed in the two referred works is quite different from the present study. The emphasis is on distinctions of past as ritualized and non-ritualized. That is not the focus of this study.
6. The term 'everyday' is used here to indicate the complex totality—constituting frequently recurring routine practices, and simultaneous singular, specialized, and individuals acts therein—that defines the rhythm of human life. Henri Lefebvre (1991: 97) defines everyday life as '"what is left over" after all distinct, superior, specialized, structured activities have been singled out by analysis'. This tends to empty the 'everyday' of its richness and complexities and somehow places it outside the field of knowledge. What Lefebvre isolates from 'everyday', namely the identifiable practices, is used by Michel de Certeau (1984) to understand the modes of behaviour in societies. Everyday life, thus, emerges as a matrix of

practices that are both singular and practical. It must be pointed out that 'everyday' is often used in diametrically opposite senses: to denote readily accessible and dominant forms of specific cultures on the one hand, and to invoke those practices and lives 'from below' that are traditionally left out of historical accounts on the other. In this study, 'everyday' is used to invoke the very fullness and inherent contradictions present in people's lives.

7. This aspect has been a source of controversy. The then defence minister George Fernandes maintained that the bomb was not meant as a threat to Pakistan; rather, it was directed against China. While the strategic experts continued debating who the real threat was, the mass of Indian population popularly believed it to be a lethal weapon against Pakistan.

8. The one-day international (ODI) cricket series was held between 13–23 March 2004 and included matches played at Karachi, Rawalpindi, Peshawar, and Lahore, the cities where a majority of the Punjabi refugees in Delhi hail from. The Pakistani Cricket Board facilitated 8250 visas for Indian spectators (*The Hindu*, 27 February 2004).

9. The newspapers were filled with reports about Indian visitors being warmly received by Pakistani families who offered them a place to stay. It was reported that the hotels, restaurants or taxi drivers would often waive the charges for their Indian guests. The Indian side extended a similarly warm welcome in 2005, when Pakistani spectators arrived in India to attend another India–Pakistan series (see, for example, the news report, 'It is love for real', *Frontline*, vol. 22, issue 8, 9–25 April 2005).

10. A number of respondents from my earlier interviews in 2002 wanted to avail this opportunity, depending on individual financial affordability, especially when the stigma attached with Pakistan was gradually diminishing. When contacted again, only those from the upper middle/middle class were found to have managed the visit.

11. The Pakistan India People's Forum for Peace and Democracy (PIPFPD), for instance, started in the early 1990s and found support among the intellectuals from both sides of the border. The activists would routinely hold candle-light vigils on the border and organize visits of students, media personnel, and academics to inculcate a better understanding of the 'other' country and its people. Yet the movement did not gain popular acceptance till the mid-2000s.

12. The UN Convention Relating to the Status of Refugees, 1951, applies to any person who

> …owing to well founded fear of being persecuted for reasons of race, religion, nationality, membership of a particular social group or political opinion is outside the country of his nationality and is unable or, owing to such fear, is unwilling to avail himself of the protection of that country; or who, not having nationality and being outside the country of his former habitual residence as a result of such events, is unable or, owing to such a fear, is unwilling to return to it (p. 16).

The characteristic feature of this definition is the condition of 'statelessness' or lack of state protection that seeks to describe those fleeing from a country, i.e., across international borders. In the case of Partition migrants, the 'statelessness' or lack of citizenship was never in doubt. The migrants from Pakistan automatically became citizens of India following Article 6 of the Indian Constitution, according to which:

> A person who has migrated to the territory of India from the territory now included in Pakistan shall be deemed to be a citizen of India at the commencement

of this Constitution if (1) he or either of his parents or any of his grand-parents was born in India as defined in the Government of India Act, 1935 (as originally enacted); and (2) (i) in the case where such person has so migrated before the nineteenth day of July, 1948, he has been ordinarily resident in the territory of India since the date of his migration, or (ii) in the case where such person has so migrated on or after the nineteenth day of July, 1948, he has been registered as a citizen of India by an officer appointed in that behalf by the Government of the Dominion of India.

13. For example, 29 January every year is commemorated as Auschwitz Day, to remember the mass extermination of Jews in the camps.

14. While introducing 'narrative' as a methodological tool in this study, it must be simultaneously placed within and distinguished from the 'narrative history' discussions. The narrative mode of representation is traditionally employed in historiography to produce historical accounts, but is often accused of being unscientific, e.g., by the French Annales group. The debate is inextricably linked with the question of what 'history' is and how historical events should be represented. Historians like Hayden White (1984: 32) perceive narrative as an integral part of historiography, where narrative is defined as 'at once a mode of discourse, a manner of speaking, and the product produced by the adoption of this mode of discourse'. Paul Ricoeur (1980: 27) uses chronology as a tool to understand narrative: 'Every narrative combines two dimensions in various proportions, one chronological and the other nonchronological. The first may be called the episodic dimension which characterizes the story made out of events. The second is the configurational dimension, according to which the plot construes significant wholes out of scattered events.' It is this 'plot' that tells the larger story within which minor events fit in. In this study, however, narrative is used largely as a method to understand how past is remembered by individuals, state authorities, cultural groups, political organizations, etc. The same events may be remembered differently, thus producing competing narratives.

15. Such an expanse also means that any ensuing confusion between narrative and discourse must be clarified. An oft-used understanding of narratives is derived from the seminal work of Vladimir Propp (1968), who first attempted a systematic study of folktales where he identified a typology of tales according to the functions of the characters therein. Following Propp, the characteristics specific to narratives are: presence of dramatis personae in the account who have definite functions or character in the account, and a sequential order, often chronological, in which the turn of events is narrated. Discourses, on the other hand, refer to historically constituted systems of meanings through which all objects and subjects are identified (Foucault 1972). In other words, all objects are objects of discourse since the meanings attached to them are derived from prevalent social constructions and systems (Laclau and Mouffe 1985). Discourses thus entail a larger area of social meanings and understandings, whereas narratives are more specific and limited. One may add here that a narrative possesses a visible structure with an opening, a closure, and a clear authorship, which may be absent in a discourse. This does not mean that narratives and discourses do not overlap, since narratives structurally embody discourses while discourses are often received publicly in narrative forms.

16. A vast body of literature on memory exists that needs to be mentioned here. Clearly, Freud (1932) remains a major influence through his psycho-experimental studies where he explained memory process in terms of ego and unconscious. He suggested that all memories are interminably stored in the unconscious, though

repressed as a preventive measure against painful or traumatic experiences. The past lives on in both repressed and expressed forms, and one needs to look at the patterns of what one chooses to celebrate, mourn or remain silent about. Another leading figure Halbwachs (1950 [1980]) perceives memory in a collective mode, where it is always constructed in the specific context of given social settings. The past is, thus, not delinked from the present, and offers material for future strategies. For example, as social communities emerge and take shape, they rely on commemorative techniques to stabilize and unite the group. This in turn helps the dominant group to establish its localized versions of the community's history. It is in such contextual settings that individual memories take a coherent shape ready for fluid uninterrupted narration. However, the incessant focus on 'groups', 'communities', and 'collective struggles' as the basis for constructing social memory forecloses the options of investigating the complex interweaving of personal or familial experiences of given events. The 'group', as the harbinger of social memory in a society, collapses the crucial categories of gender, caste, and class that offer the often overlooked analytical spaces that will allow us to look at the finer aspects of memory making. Similarly, Frederick Bartlett ([1932] 1995)argued that memorizing the past is a socially determined activity, but he substituted the word memory with remembering. The choice of the present continuous tense against the noun form was favoured since it brought forth the active ongoing nature of the memory. He suggested that all our remembering is shaped by 'schemas' or 'organized settings' that consist of layered networks of past associations, experiences that keep on arranging themselves into new settings when confronted with new experiences (Bartlett [1932] 1995: 201). This would mean that the present is encountered and evaluated against our past experiences. Each new episode rearranges past events as well and possibly presents them outwardly in a new light. This would also mean that there is really no uniqueness attached to specific incidents since they may be re-experienced and remembered in an altogether new mode. Such a reading of Bartlett's work is immensely useful in understanding contexts where references to the not-so-distant past, like Partition, appear when least expected.

17. See for example Robert S. Wyer, Jr and Thomas K. Srull (1989) *Memory and Cognition in its Social Context*, where memory construction, like an ordinary computer, is explained in terms of processing units, general systems operation and bins (semantic and referent). Such impersonal, ahistorical, and decontextualized explanations suggest, first of all, that the memory-making processes take place in an individual's head activated by external stimulation, and second, that memory is recorded photographically in the brain, like a frozen snapshot. Once it is recorded it retains its original appearance and is stored permanently in an individual's mental archive.

18. Personal interview with Purushottam Das Tandon, February 2002.

19. S.L. Mehta, personal interview, New Delhi December 2000.

20. See, for example, Joya Chatterji's (2001) article on rehabilitation in Bengal, where she draws on the fundamental differences in the nature of migration in Punjab and Bengal and the different attitude that the government adopted towards these two provinces.

21. For a detailed account of the traditional view, see Anita Inder Singh (1987).

22. See Ayesha Jalal (1985) and Asim Roy (1990).

23. For Hindu and Muslim revivalist movements, see Kenneth W. Jones (1976); J.T.F. Jordens (1978); Christophe Jaffrelot (1999); J.N. Farquhar ([1915] 1999); Bashir Ahmad Dar (1971); Barbara Metcalf (1982).

24. For the history and activities of the RSS, see Tapan Basu et al. (1993) *Khaki Shorts and Saffron Flags.*
25. The recent carnage in Gujarat in 2002 begun with stories of Muslim provocation, of Muslims trying to create mini-Pakistans in India, of being funded by Pakistani intelligence agency Inter Services Intelligence (ISI), and of taking advantage of Hindu tolerance. The result was the long-drawn pogrom which took 2000 lives and rendered thousands of Muslim families homeless.
26. For the communal violence in Punjab in the decade preceding Partition, see Hansen (2002: 109–13). The Arya–Khalsa conflict is noted in Kenneth Jones (1973).
27. For this distinction, see Hansen (2002).
28. See 'Introduction', in Das (1996). Also see Sudhir Kakar (1996).
29. The figures include displaced populations in Punjab, Sind, NWFP, Bengal, and Assam.
30. The collapse of law and order during Partition is often taken as collapse of the state. See, for example, Kamtekar (1989).
31. Census of India, 1941 and 1951.
32. Census of India, 1951, and also the Economic Survey of Delhi, 2001–2002, ch. 3, p. 22.
33. Economic Survey of Delhi 2002, Department of Planning, Government of Delhi.
34. Economic Survey of Delhi 2002. Ibid, p. 22. In 1941, the annual growth rate in the city's population was 4.4 per cent and it shot up to 7.3 per cent in 1951.
35. Table is taken from V.K.R.V. Rao (1965: 31).
36. For detailed accounts of the developments in urban Delhi in the late 19th and early 20th centuries, see Narayani Gupta (1999) and Ajay K. Mehra (1991).
37. These administrative units are invariably referred to as 'towns' in most studies on urban Delhi until the early 1960s.
38. V.K.R.V. Rao (1965: 75, 107). The refugees formed 36 per cent of the sample households, while non-refugee migrants constituted 21.3 per cent.
39. See Census of India, 1951.

2. State and Community in the Narratives of Displacement

A particularly noticeable feature of the master narrative of Partition migration is not what it intends to *reveal*, but rather what it intends to *hide*. While personal courage and human attributes are given primacy when describing the success story of Partition resettlement in Delhi, the role of governmental agencies and community organizations in facilitating such large-scale resettlement is mostly dispensed with. Such noticeable absences in the migrant narratives make it imperative for us to explore not only what is publicly narrated but also what is not. The role of state agencies, though open to critique, is well documented, among other sources, in the archival sources and memoirs of officers connected with the resettlement projects. The provision of permanent housing facilities, establishment of new commercial districts, allocation of jobs in governmental departments and educational institutions, and business loans at low rates are some of the facilities that were made available by the state that the Partition migrants could make use of. Similarly, community or *biradari* is another notional character that emerges as a strong catalyst in the resettlement process, but seldom appears in personal accounts. The question that guides our query is: do community networks and boundaries disappear in cataclysmic events of forced migration? As the subsequent chapters in this book reveal, communities take shape in the new locations as well, albeit in new forms. However, it is the theme of omission of such extra-personal contributions towards resettlement in personal narratives that calls for a fuller enquiry.

Two strands of exploration need to be followed in the succeeding chapters: one, to prop up the state as the principal organizer in the Partition resettlement process and, two, to follow the absence of the state in personal narratives publicly and privately told by the survivors. To pursue these strands, the modern Indian state needs to be understood in the historicity of its colonial past and post-colonial developments. This also requires that the official narrative—or the story told by the state—of Partition resettlement be brought within the analytical arena (see Chapters 3 and 4). The following pages will outline the key concepts used in this book—state and community—for a critical appraisal.

LOCATING THE STATE IN DISPLACEMENT

What organizing principles, on the basis of which to reorder people, does a state rely on when confronted with a human mass produced through forced migration? At such a critical time, the state requires a variety of governmental techniques to facilitate the arrangement of people into governable units, ranging from temporary refugee camps to permanent housing colonies. This becomes especially challenging when the state itself is in its formative stage, trying to deal with its own change of status from colonial to post-colonial. To understand how the state encounters forced population movements, we need to know how people are officially categorized, as a consequence of which social categories and organizations get transformed or are reproduced. This leads us to question the very character of the state, in order for us to find and measure the extent of its 'social' aspects. How is the element of the 'social' reflected in state policies to govern people who acquire the collective identities of 'migrants' and 'refugees', subsuming all other identities?

In the process of state formation, where withdrawal of the colonial state is accompanied by abrupt partition of territory, unprecedented violence and loss of life/property, and an interminable flow of refugees, the experience of *loss* is not just limited to the fleeing masses—it must extend to the post-colonial state through *loss* of territory, inability to protect its subjects and consequently its claim to sovereignty. Since *loss* dominates the violent upheavals of partition and migration, the policies and efforts of resettlement can perhaps be seen as attempts at *restoration of loss*. Such a project of *restoration* requires multiple levels of objectives and motivation for individuals, communities and state, each of which is further imbued with social conflicts of gender, class, and caste. Finally, masculine notions of family, honour and morality, which are inherently and structurally present in social organization, need to be juxtaposed with individual and collective efforts of resettlement. The debates that inevitably need to be entered to answer these questions pertain to state formation, state/society dialectics, and those that question the gender neutrality of the state.

The overwhelming body of state literature is often categorized in terms of spatially constituted vantage points that enable us to look at the state 'from above'—grand overarching state theories—and 'from below'—through specific studies of popular resistance and forms of public authority therein. The state is presented as an 'institution' (Engels 1942), a 'human community' (Weber 1958), or as an idea/system of political practices (Abrams 1988). In this study of displacement, however, the immateriality of the state is not the most essential notion that needs to be either established or contested. Rather, it is the underexplored area of *embodiment of the idea of state*— visualized through people (functionaries of state), institutions (of bureaucracy and army, for instance), and policies of government (legislations and programmes)—in its various familiar and publicly recognizable facets that needs to be brought into focus. We can frame this as a question for further perusal, that is, 'how' the idea of state authority is transmitted into organic practices and 'who' bears the state into the public domain. Though the problem of the embodiment of state is central here, it cannot be grasped without defining 'what' goes into that body, that is, the conceptual idea of the state.

The idea of state has, in recent years, been explored beyond the previous preserve of economic-political studies. One project has been to examine the state in view of the 'cultural turn' that has 'disrupted entrenched ways of thinking about familiar objects of social research by emphasizing the casual and socially constitutive role of cultural processes and systems of signification' (Steinmetz 1999: 2). The boundaries between state and society, which are often seen as being problematic, blurred, or plain unnecessary in discussions of the state, are considered significant in this cultural analysis of the state. These boundaries are seen here as the 'recurrently produced essence of modern politics' where the state is situated as an 'effect of mundane processes ... that create the world fundamentally divided into state and society ...' (Mitchell 1999: 95). The state is thus freed of the straitjacketed categorization as being a distinct object of ahistorical enquiries whose essence can be extracted only in isolation. The internally produced and maintained state/society dynamics are essential if the state has to establish distance and predominance over the rest of 'society'.

Similarly, Bourdieu's formulation of state plays on this dynamic through which the state assumes a hegemonic position at the centre of society. The state derives from a 'culmination of a process of concentration of different species of capital' (Bourdieu 1999: 57). The four types of 'capital' that collectively make up the state are: capital of physical force (army, police), economic capital (fiscal systems), informational capital (codifying population and territory), and symbolic capital (juridical systems, recognition by social actors, and value addition to other capitals) (Bourdieu 1999: 58–64). Their concentration constitutes the state as a bearer of 'meta-capital' that surpasses all other authorities derived from singular forms of capital. The meta-authority thus created, is established in society through constantly (re)produced elaborate rituals, governmental practices, and discernible symbols of the state. However, the processes that activate and necessitate accumulation of meta-capital in the first place remain unexplored. Bourdieu (1999: 57) admits that such an explanation 'of historical logic of processes' is most difficult to obtain as it requires 'boundless data of accumulated historical research' and coherent theoretical constructs.

A less ambitious project, then, would be to imbue the state with 'a historical perspective' to examine the techniques of modern political order as 'the consequence of certain novel practices of the technical age' (Mitchell 1999: 77). This can be attempted through ethnography of the state, described as 'discourses of state from the "field" in the sense of localised ethnographic sites' (Hansen and Stepputtat 2001: 5). This approach creates a distinct possibility for states (post-colonial states in particular) to be examined as historically specific confluences of a range of practical, symbolic, and performative 'languages of stateness' (Hansen and Stepputtat 2001: 7). This language is communicated through practical and symbolic modes that articulate the basic characteristics of a state, namely, its techniques of governance and institutions of public authority. For this project, it is the practical languages of governance—assertion of territorial sovereignty through monopoly of violence; mapping and archiving knowledge of population/ territory; development and management of 'national economy—that offer helpful tools of analysis' (Hansen and Stepputtat 2001: 7–8). The control and management of populations is a pre-requisite for a state to convey its effective presence, which in turn forms the basis for acceptance of its authority by the governed masses. The idea of entering the discourses of the state from the field makes it possible for us to look for languages and discursive practices of a state (instead of visible entities) in order to locate the state. This is especially useful when the paraphernalia of the state is in transition, formation, or temporary withdrawal.

To further locate the state in displacement, we need to depart from another prevalent trend in studies of the state, namely, that of looking at 'everyday forms of state' (Joseph and Nugent 1994; Fuller and Benei 2000) articulated in people's ordinary daily lives. This is because it leads us to the 'routine' and mundane aspects of one's daily life, whereas for this project, it is the cataclysmic events that form the setting. In this 'everyday view' the focus is on 'dominant culture and an examination of power, and particularly those organizations of power that provide the context for "everyday struggle"' within a nation state (Joseph and Nugent 1994: 18). The very basic pre-requisites for a nation-state—a well-defined territory and population—are presumptively there for these micro-level daily struggles and negotiations of power to take place. But in instances of territorial conflicts, civil wars, and large-scale forced migration, these basic characteristics of the state get blurred or at least challenged. While the 'everyday' analysis leads us to the 'routine' and mundane aspects of one's daily life, the cataclysmic events that form the setting for this project get separated from daily lives as exceptional and therefore not befitting such an examination. It is often forgotten that it is always difficult to ascertain what is routine and what is extraordinary since for many people civil conflicts become part of their everyday lives where the exceptional becomes the everyday norm.

If we were to describe these possibilities as collective moments—of rupture, upheaval, and reorganization—then we need different modes of deconstruction to witness the authority of the state in displacement. Refugee camps and temporary settlements are actual identifiable locations that become discernible symbols of schismatic upheavals and disorders in the scheme of nation-states. Since the state is not a naturally inherent feature of either settled or displaced populations, forms of authority need to be re-established through a variety of practices and ideologies, especially in these sites of displacement. This nascent process of establishing structures of authority must more clearly reveal the rationalities that lie beneath the state apparatuses than can be visualized in the everyday practices of state. The processes of policy-making to govern and manage the displaced populations can be seen as diminutive forms of larger structures of authority where known systems of governance are replicated and new ones are invented in response to previously unanticipated probabilities.

THE STATE AS A SOCIAL BEING

The task of reordering a displaced people involves a large degree of social manoeuvring on the part of the authorities in order to suitably arrange caste, class, and gender equations and balances. The prevention of social conflict on these grounds can only be attained if accepted social norms are not disturbed. Population displacement preceded by violence, however, is a moment when such carefully maintained balances get derailed. Mass movement means that various social classes and castes seek safety and refuge simultaneously. Gender boundaries get challenged when men and women are forced to travel together in packed trains. Do single women, untouchables, and poor migrants achieve social equilibrium with the privileged sections of society during displacement? What role does the state play in such circumstances: does it protect social barriers or facilitate new social systems? Such an explanation seeks an understanding of the social aspects of the state.

Therefore, the state/society split is another central characteristic of the state that needs to be introduced in this analytical frame. Most state-centred literature begins with the assumption that the 'state is a distinct entity, opposed to and set apart from a larger entity called society' (Mitchell 1999: 82). Though the elusive line between the two is yet to be visibly ascertained, state/society distinctions continue to be part of the theoretical debates on the state. While it has come to be accepted that the boundaries are rather blurred, the analysis of the levels of interaction between the two is limited to that of institutional exchange (for example, see Mitchell's [1999: 82–3] case in point, that of government–business cooperation). The social practices and ideologies of family, hierarchy, and community, shaped by regulatory norms of morality, sexuality, and honour, do not occupy a large space in studies of state formation. If there is such a level of transplantation of norms and ideologies, then how does this transplantation travel from state to society or society to state?

A common constitutive split employed in this regard is that of private/ public where 'private' gets associated with society since state is categorized as a form of 'public' authority. It is not very difficult to conclude that the state as public authority (detached from subjectivity) enters the private realm (where subjects are located) to establish subjectivity through repeated reminders of 'subjected identities via rituals and media of moral regulation, and not only through their manifest, concrete oppression' (Joseph and Nugent 1994: 21). In due course, 'governance becomes unified with the "private" realm...and sexualised subjectivities enter "politics"' (Corrigan in ibid.: xviii). If 'public' can seep into the 'private' realm, then it must be possible for the private to be reflected in public politics and policies. I would argue that just as ideas of government can percolate to the private sphere of families, *the private notions of sexuality and morality could be 'nationalized' and practised as public policies and guidelines.* This understanding could be helpful in deciphering the rationalities of policy processes and population management programmes that states enter into.

An obvious deduction that can be made from this discussion is that states or forms of public authority are not gender-neutral. Though the gendered facet of state is frequently seen in specific and localized state-related studies (Bacchetta 1996; Menon and Bhasin 1997; Butalia 1998), the state continues being discussed as an *asexual* entity. In Connell's idea of 'configuration of gender practice', institutions do have a definitive place in gendered analysis (Connell 1996). The notions of femininity and masculinity are configured at three levels: individuals, ideologies, and finally institutions (Connell 1996: 72). The practice of gender configuration follows a three-fold model of structure of gender: power relations (for example, patriarchal structures), production relations (gendered division of labour and related accumulation of wealth), and cathexis (emotional attachments and sexual desires). The differing male and female roles enacted in these relational capacities, either uniquely or collectively, point to gendered positions in social structures. In terms of power relations and production relations, the state is clearly categorized as a masculine institution as the 'state organisational practices are structured in relation to the reproductive arena' (Connell 1996: 73). It is not unusual to find men in the majority at the top levels of institutional structures, which can be explained by gender configuring of recruitment and promotion; of the internal division of labour and systems of control; of policy-making, practical routines, and ways of mobilizing pleasure and consent (Connell 1996). It needs to be pointed out that gender practices have social and cultural linkages that do not necessarily derive from biological functionalism. Nevertheless, biological symbolisms, processes of reproduction, and sexual imagery are routinely invoked to justify gender practices.

In a state structure, it is the institutions of civil–military bureaucracy that betray the obvious and subtle levels of gender distinctions imbibed as part of the professional curricula. The ideas of homo-erotic heterosexuality; display of authority and hierarchical subordination; and unquestioned loyalty are unstated attributes that bureaucrats are required to possess to be able to efficiently run the business of state. This is noted as a practice of the colonial state that trained its bureaucrats in the mould of 'imperial masculinity' that transformed 'real true boys' into 'real true men' (Kantikar 1994: 185, 195). Masculine notions are, therefore, inherent in the administrative frames in practice as well as at the level of ideology. The gendered role-plays within patriarchal households—the husband who controls the funds and family policies and the wife who organizes everyday routine functions in the house like cooking, cleaning, listening to problems, and helping children with homework—are played out at the state level as well. For instance, the resettlement work for the Partition refugees was divided into two distinct levels: one at the ministerial level where male government officials would make policy decisions, allocate the funds, make legal-administrative interpretations of specific cases, and the other where female social workers would organize camp functions through distribution of food, administering medical care, educating children in the camps, teaching them hygiene and etiquette, etc. Such a division of labour is considered normal and therefore inculcated as part of the state apparatus.

STATE/SOCIETY IN INDIA

Studies on the state in India often attempt to grapple with the perceived inconsistencies produced by cohabitation of Indian traditional social structures—caste hierarchies and religious diversity—with the modern state structure. Nicholas Dirks has pointed to Marx, Weber, and Dumont's reading of political institutions in India as being informed by 'orientalistic knowledge', where village communities and not the institutions of state; and caste hierarchy, not organized bureaucratic order; exist at the centre of authority and governance (Dirks 1993: 4–5). The modern state is considered a temporary repository of power, while traditional sources of authority derived from caste and village-level organization retain a sense of permanence—that is, 'while states came and went, village communities endured.'[1] This creates a theoretical wedge between society and the modern state that needs immediate attention. However, a quick look at the functioning of the Indian state shows that the state—both in its colonial and post-colonial incarnations—has intervened at various levels of society, often indulging in un/intended social engineering. For analytical purposes in this chapter, it is not only state intervention in the social space that is an important area of exploration but also its converse corollary, that is, the infiltration of social norms in state functions.

Therefore, a systematic perusal of the outlined problems above requires that the state in India be explored as a social being rather than as a political actor, that is, as an entity entwined with and not detached from society. The social aspect of the state becomes important also because of specific social goals, arising from the national movement which the state is expected to fulfil. Ashis Nandy articulates this long-standing wish of the colonial people 'brought up on western educational system [who] have waited for the day when a powerful Indian state would belong to them, be an exemplar and a social arbiter, ... and play the central role in transforming the society' (Nandy 1989: 2). That the state/society combination in India is an inevitable area of exploration can be gauged from the view that transfer of power to a state presiding over social incongruities is seen as a possible reason for territorial partition of India.

> ... an error of insight perceived by a few and resented by none...was the supposition that the unitary system of democracy in force in Britain could be transferred in toto to India. They failed to perceive that Hindus and Muslims, if not specifically two nations, were two distinct cultures. They failed to see the logical consequence that there were large areas of life in which neither community would accept dictation from the other. ...When therefore the Muslims began to demur at the prospect of being permanently under a Hindu majority, the essence of their position was not understood. ...The Hindus, however, found the idea of a sovereign Parliament attractive and their insistence on its virtues increased Muslim uneasiness (Spear 1958: 575).

State intervention in society is a well-known colonial legacy, wherein the state sets about making social reforms through the use of judiciary and state legislative. The prime examples were the ban on *sati* (the Hindu custom of widow-burning) and child marriage, and the encouragement of widow remarriage.[2] The colonial practice of mapping territories and counting populations through censuses produced a new outlook on the social order and hierarchy in India and had marked political consequences.[3] The introduction of western intellectual ideas through the English educational system was another point of intervention through which a whole intermediary class amiable to western ideas was produced.[4] Thus, the state's role as a social transformer is not without precedent and this role was inherited by the post-colonial state as well. Pranab Bardhan offers the implementation of land reform legislation as an instance of post-colonial state intervention that eroded the traditional functions of local landlords and institutions of maintenance of irrigation works and loans, and replaced it by 'an alien, large and often corrupt bureaucracy'(Bardhan 1998: 190). An important outcome of the attempts to reform was that the state became visible and known even in the remote corners of the countryside (Bardhan 1998: 190).

The character of the post-colonial state took its basic shape during the Nehruvian years (1947–64), when the Congress government was firmly established for a considerable period. The two main objectives of the Nehruvian state—industrialization and social equity—became the vehicles of social reform. The strategy was to introduce a process of institutional change that created bodies of village-level governance based on universal franchise, and cooperative societies through state-fed financial support (Frankel 1978). However, the expectations of alleviation of poverty and inequalities in social structure were not fully realized because the state could not confront the propertied classes in society (Kaviraj 1997: 237). The state failure in this context needs further explanations on two counts: (1) the state had become the sole agency in India that controlled large scale resources, and (2) it had showed its willingness to transform the traditional structures in the princely states through abolition of kingship and acquisition of territory. In other words, it had both the resources and the will to transform that were never fully employed to restructure the larger socio-economic inequities. This observation is useful for this study since the Indian state had come to control resources left behind by the Muslim refugees, and therefore had the means to perform its objectives of removing social inequalities.

The state's ineptness at playing the role of the inducer of social change is also explained through tensions that prevail between the 'imported concept of statecraft' (Nandy 1989: 4) and the prevailing multifarious social constructs. The tension is heightened because the 'increasing democratisation…and the increasing involvement in politics of the popular classes located in different linguistic and geographical regions in India, sharpened their sense of identity as constituents of distinctive linguistic and cultural communities' (Kumar 1997: 405–6). The strain is also felt in matters of representation, where a pluralist version opens space for different social groups but also challenges state sovereignty (Rudolph and Rudolph 1978: 385).

The state in India is seen as being far from the European concept of nation-state[5] where it does not preside over a nation but rather gets engaged in power politics—that is, 'the Indian state…does not merely respond to crises produced by the uneven economic development and social change, but is itself the leading force providing differential advantages to regions, ethnic groups and classes' (Brass 1997: 32). This means that the foremost project of the state is to create a society that is suited to the modern state system which in the Indian context would translate as the creation of 'a more coherent form of Indianness emerge and the diversity of the country would diminish, to make India more governable' (Nandy 1989: 4). The creation of a modern citizenship that is fit to be governed through modern statecraft is therefore, the underlying objective of state interventions. This project can be witnessed more closely during the resettlement of migrants (as we shall see later) through a variety of smaller 'social work' projects aimed at inculcating hygiene, literacy, progressive social traditions, usage of national language, and observance of newly invented national rituals.

It is suggested that the need to create a cohesive state and society was recognized as early as a decade before the transfer of power, when national reconstruction and social planning was seriously pursued as a strategy (Chatterjee 1994). A National Planning Committee was established in 1938 with Jawaharlal Nehru (who had already started experimenting with state-making) at its helm. The significant aspects of national planning were, first, that they appeared as a state policy providing the 'overall framework of a *coordinated* and *consistent* set of policies of a national state that was already envisioned as concrete idea' and, second, that it strongly emphasized committees of experts who technically evaluated policies on a 'scientific' basis (Chatterjee 1994: 201, emphasis added). It seems as if several scientific experiments in building state institutions were being smoothly organized by expert committees in the years following Partition. This interpretation of the Congress party's preparatory exercise for practising statecraft needs to be read with caution since it is completely detached from the political realities under which planning was to be implemented later. Planning as a core strategy gives us an idea of which way the policy thrust was intended to function in laboratory-like conditions. But the occasion to practise these policies upon colonial withdrawal was accompanied with unprecedented large-scale violence. The Congress leadership had no inkling, political strategy, or administrative preparation to counter Partition violence and population movement. The resettlement of Partition migrants can be analysed to see to what extent the Congress party and Nehru were able to implement their visions.

COMMUNITY OF NARRATIVES

The dispersal of communities during mass migration leads to one of the main questions in this study: namely, if and in what forms communities restate themselves. The very concept of community thus needs to be explored, especially in the Punjabi context, where the idea of biradari, comes quite close to community and yet displays deviations that require a fresh conceptual understanding. Community is popularly understood as a small organic constituent of society but is, unlike a family unit, not necessarily based on blood ties. The classical idea of community credited to the Chicago sociologists hinges upon the rural-urban dichotomy, wherein 'the folk society'[6]—characterized by small, self-contained social groups where everyone knows everyone—is seen as antithetical to urban life where direct, face to face primary relationships in the associations of individuals in the community break down, and may give way to isolation and even crime (Park 1925). These ideas have been subject to severe criticism, since they perceive mobility as a state of impermanence and a cause for the breakdown of traditional order.

Community has since been described, based on its utility as a relational idea, as a unit where 'members of a group of people (1) have something in common with each other, which (2) distinguishes them in a significant way from the members of other putative groups' (Cohen 1992: 12). The community becomes a symbolic constitution of boundaries that are constituted by the people involved, and a belief in community becomes more a matter of consciousness (Cohen 1992: 13). It is the symbolism— expressed as an emblem, sign, or an idea—with elusive meanings that binds people as a community, where the meanings of the symbolism keep on renewing themselves based on the actual users' interpretation. The symbolic aspect of the community grants a greater leverage in expanding the conceptual base and provides scope for varied interpretations.

Elizabeth Fraser (1999: 71) points to the problems in Cohen's description of community that is ideally hinged on consciousness and not on locality, but paradoxically most of the empirical examples presented by him rest precisely on studies in shared locality or of marked ethnic groups. She also questions, but does not dwell upon, why social groups (like shopping crowds and theatre audiences) that share something in common, distinguishing them from other social groups, are not recognized as communities. The impermanence and constant movement among shoppers and theatre audiences may underlie such an omission that is not readily acknowledged by community theorists. This suggests that even though community is accepted as a concept and not an entity, theorists still look for familiar faces, recognizable places or institutions that can be identified with specific communities. Fraser then tries to present community as a 'value, or an ideal, and it appears as such in ethics, in moral or normative discourse in other contexts...[and secondly] as a descriptive category or set of variables...that can only be realised and lived in episodic and fleeting moments' (Fraser 1999: 76, 84). It is the 'structurelessness' (Turner 1995) and the episodic character of the community that makes it useful for this study.

It must be emphasized here that community as a concept cannot be transplanted *in toto* as a tool to understand the Indian social context. The problem here is far from that of the rural/urban dichotomy and the contested meanings of symbolism. It lies in the widely divergent social system and practices that employ social origin—like caste—as a boundary marker. The Hindi words *samaj* and biradari roughly translate into society and community respectively, but they are often used loosely and interchangeably. There are many common features that they possess with the term 'community' in that they point to smaller social groups and share symbols and practices that mark one group from another. But unlike community in the classical sense, the village 'folk' do not share biradaris since they are formed around caste affiliations that one is born into. The same village could be home to more than one biradari where each group would occupy a separate space. The biradari cannot be joined simply by sharing a locality—to be a member one needs to be born into it. The members of the biradari may live in towns or villages, but they still form part of the same social group that intermarries and exchanges token gifts. Geographical distance is never a hindrance to the survival of such groups which share common festivals, rituals, kinship networks, etc. These biradaris are more structured than the community theorists would like them to be, since there are commonly accepted and practised codes about sharing food, marriages, etc., that tend to keep the group exclusive. Nor are they entirely structured—like formal associations would be—as the caste taboos, practices and myths keep getting reinvented, making caste boundaries rather fluid (Gupta 2001).

The caste-based biradaris are often subjected to the same sort of commentaries as communities, about 'losing the sense of community' when the scenario shifts from rural to urban. The caste boundaries are said to dilute, if not completely disappear, in urban settings where often not everyone knows everyone and it is difficult to ascertain people's caste in order to establish renewed biradaris. This is where Fraser's idea of community as a shared value realized in fleeting moments presents itself as a useful tool.

In this sense, the Partition migrants in Delhi city present a complex case as most of them migrated from West Punjab's large cities like Lahore, Gujranwala, Multan, and Lyallpur. The migrant population did not move out of their hometowns after a long history of settlement but were actually on the move after just less than five decades.[7] The last three cities mentioned above were newly settled urban townships built to ease the population pressure in East Punjab. The discourse—fictional and biographical—from these towns suggests that they were already considered modern locations where traditional social systems were being replaced by new secular ideas. The traditional biradari system was not convincingly enough in place for it to be reproduced after migration to Delhi.

This brings us to another aspect of community that stems from the *need* to belong to a human group, or what Charles Taylor (1993: 25–6) calls the 'need for recognition…a vital human need'. Zygmunt Bauman (2001: 1–2) calls it wishful thinking that everyone entertains because it conveys a safe, warm place where one can relax and be heard by people who understand one's concerns. Our changed approach to community, from *use* to *need,* underlines that community is not something that is available and can be made *use* of, rather, it is a created category that people feel they *need* to fulfil their wish to belong. The commonality, here among the Partition migrants, does not lie just in the shared history of movement and resettlement but also in the way the history is narrated publicly. If we take *narrative* as an indicator of community, then our analysis is at once freed from the geographic and symbolic restraints that despite their symbolic nature, need to be visible to others to be effective. Narratives on the other hand are far less discernible and extend their scope to a hugely varied group that may not otherwise come across as a single community. The acceptance and public recital of a common master narrative helps us identify communities that are otherwise lost to social research.

SOURCES: COLLECTING NARRATIVES

The choice of methods to follow any given research theme depends on the existence and availability of sources of knowledge. A prime source in the studies of the 'aftermath' of mass violence, subjection or population movement is to be found in the *survivors* of the event. The Partition survivors may or may not have experienced violence and other dramatic moments directly, but they remain a part of the larger scenario. The act of movement was a matter of choice, however limited, to save their lives and protect their families. The Partition survivors retain an element of guilt, of being castigated as cowards who chose to escape and not confront the Muslim onslaught. Thus, their very existence becomes a questionable option that needs to be justified both to themselves and others. Giorgio Agamben (1999), drawing on the Holocaust survivors, suggests that the survivors act as eyewitnesses who carry the narration of the sequence of events to those who were absent from the scene. How do Partition survivors justify their own existence?

While the events of Partition may be far removed from those of the Holocaust, the primal reasons for the wish to survive are not entirely dissimilar. The difference lies in the sentiment of *triumph* that survivors of Partition cherish for having braved the incessant violent attacks. While Holocaust survivors were primarily the victims of the Nazi onslaught, Partition survivors were both victims as well as perpetrators of the communal violence. Thus, Partition violence represents a kind of civil war where the opponents were more or less equally matched. Survival from such an evenly matched contest endowed *heroism* on the survivors who battled to live and tell their story. This does not mean that each act of survival was imbued with heroism in reality, since most survivors were essentially attempting to escape violence to save their lives, their dependents, and their moveable property. But being a survivor meant that one had borne witness to the event, having lived through the experience personally. This allowed the survivors to *edit* the memory strategically and tactically when narrating their episode of survival. Here, hero, witness and narrator become a single person who can create his/her own character, role and act in the Partition drama. In this way, a moral economy of survival is produced and sustained through frequent acts of narration of the past.

Another outcome of such narration is that one's individual self gets connected to a larger cause of community and nation. One is not surviving for one's self alone but for the nation. The survivors therefore become the flag-bearers of nationhood or whatever other issues may have led to their confinement. Further, the testimonies produced by the survivors become part of a systematic record, the archive that preserves the memory of events to gain crucial inputs for the national history and to gain immortality.

How does one really define the survivors? In instances of communal violence, both victims of violence as well as the perpetrators gain knowledge of unfolding events through direct participation—as a part of the crowd, leaders of the crowd or as objects of the crowd's violent wrath, and alternatively as onlookers to others actions as well as their own. The participants tend to be the book-keepers of their own role during the event that they later narrate as personal memories. Though the struggle to survive may be explained as a natural wish to prolong one's life, the very motivation that makes survivors of traumatic events choose life over death is highly intriguing. Agamben (1999: 1) draws on Primo Levi's narratives of his personal experiences in the Nazi concentration camp in Auschwitz to suggest that for many victims the only reason to live is to bear witness to what happened during that extraordinary event. In the case of Partition survivors, another, perhaps stronger argument of nation-building can be added. A lot of survivors introduce their arrival in Delhi as an inevitable act since they had to fight the Muslims and help create a Hindu India. The survivors may be described as those who struggle to live (and not bring their own lives to an end) because they bear crucial *agency* which they alone can bear and reproduce for others. Their decision to live or die, despite personal pain and loss, is no longer their own, since as survivors they become both *dramatis personae* and their own narrators.

Levi's own studies on the Holocaust largely draw on his personal experience in the camp where the everyday killings blurred the fine dividing line between the killers and the victims. He suggests that in this 'gray zone', where the chain of links between the victims and the killers becomes disjointed, the routine killings affect the victims and their killers in not dissimilar ways, and the wish to survive the ordeal is therefore for similar reasons (Levi 1988). The wish to preserve and publicly relay one's testimony becomes a prime motive to survive.

The unclear distinctions between the victims and the perpetrators become apparent in situations where killings and bloodshed become a part of the routine. Communal riots, as a frequent occurrence in South Asia, represent a routine violence that normalizes mass killings. The term 'survivor' then, transcends the normative distinction between victims and perpetrators. It extends to all those who survive through a traumatic event in one role or another. The testimony of a survivor however, may not contain the element of neutrality otherwise associated with a third party account.

Archives represent another prominent source where written, printed, and dated evidence can be located to construct the resettlement process among the Punjabi Hindus.[8] The survivors' testimonies, oral or written, constitute a rich archive of information that has been used in this study. In common parlance, archives also mean a vast repository of knowledge, a referral bin that can be called upon when required. The oral history project on the Indian independence movement supported by the Indian state is a good example of this exercise.[9] The project has been in progress between 2000–5 and the main aim has been to collect and record testimonies of the main actors—politicians, journalists, freedom fighters, community leaders, women activists—in the freedom struggle. The transcriptions of the oral interviews have been made available for research purposes and are maintained in the same way as the documentary evidence. Thus the oral testimonies have gained the same status and function as that of the documentary evidence which archives are traditionally associated with.

This also opens a critique of the oral histories where personal testimonies are converted into permanent evidence of given historical sequences. The documentary sources are often criticized for taking little note of how ordinary people imagine or perceive political events, that is, for keeping certain voices out. The oral histories are, as a result, a chosen method that aims at including what was previously kept out of common narration. The oral testimonies are gained chiefly through personal interviews and they are expected to present an unrepresented view that is not necessarily part of the dominant discourse. But once the personal testimony is recorded, transcribed, printed, and publicly circulated, it attains the same features as that of ordinary records. This also means that only one momentary shade or impression of that event is captured, since people talk in given frames of mind and most tend not to repeat statements exactly from one day to another. The sequence of events may alter or the expression of emotion attached with it may disappear or be accentuated. This is not to suggest that one source be valued over another, but to emphasize the constant need to critically evaluate one's sources. One single interview or testimony may not allow a full picture; rather it calls for frequent interaction with the narrator.

Survivors have clearly gained primacy in the newer studies being conducted on Partition violence and movement. The collection of oral histories through personal interviews with the survivors is a chosen method used in these studies. Urvashi Butalia's (1998) *The Other Side of Silence* is a trendsetting study that largely draws on the life stories of the women survivors of Partition violence. The point of departure for Butalia is her personal stake—as a survivor's daughter—in the history of Partition violence and population movement. Like Levi's writings on Auschwitz, personal testimonies, though collected and translated by a second person, form the basis for a documentary study that seeks to tell 'others', who were in no way involved in the Partition events, how it was to live that experience. Documentation and public presentation of the collected testimonies becomes a prime motive and explanation of one's own survival through traumatic events. It allows one to share with others what one has experienced alone in private, a simultaneous public mourning of death and celebration of life, wherein the protagonists can relive and distribute the risks they faced to survive.

In Partition history, well-known sources of survivor testimonies have been autobiographies, memoirs, and biographies of (and by) distinguished people. The accounts, needless to say, have a clear elite bias since the people who write and publish memoirs are often erudite, influential or wealthy individuals. The class distinctions do have a role in the way mass events are experienced by different segments of society. This does not mean that these accounts should be kept out of one's purview, but rather that class origins of any given account should play a prominent role in the analysis. The published memoirs offer excellent material to compare and contrast with the accounts of the lower-middle classes or poor classes that are rarely published (they have to be searched for, listened to, and often translated before they achieve a public status). The very first challenge in extracting personal testimonies of ordinary lower and middle class people in a large city like Delhi is to identify the prospective respondents. The very large number of refugees—more than half-a-million in 1951—makes it difficult to choose a cross-section of respondents from among them.

The fieldwork in this study primarily takes place in two types of locations: former *refugee colonies* where the survivors and their descendants live, and a variety of *government premises* where the documents, records, and memoirs of resettlement are maintained. The distance between these two locations is not merely physical but functional as well, that is, they provide different kinds of raw material for this study. The collection of narratives in the government premises requires systematic perusal of a wide array of written documents, whereas the task in the refugee colonies is to *generate* oral narratives through full-length personal interviews. Both written and oral narratives then get textualized in the larger context of Partition displacement. The government premises here mainly refer to the Department of Rehabilitation, Ministry of Home Affairs, New Delhi, which is the new incarnation of the former Ministry of Relief and Rehabilitation.[10]

The second type of fieldwork was conducted in the former refugee colonies, namely, Old Double Storey quarters and Amar Colony in Lajpat Nagar in south Delhi, Kingsway camp in north Delhi and Rehgar Pura in central Delhi. Since most of the third-layer post-Partition expansion in Delhi is a possible location for such a study, these specific locations were chosen on account of a number of considerations. The idea was to approach as many divergent groups and individuals as possible in terms of class and caste, in order to see if such factors yielded different responses. A location in south Delhi and another in north Delhi was meant to cast the net as wide as one could, since south Delhi is generally regarded as wealthier than its northern counterpart. Also, since poverty is associated with low castes, it would probably be easier to find them in the poorer areas.

The plan had to be revised midway through the fieldwork as I realized that I had (1) misjudged the level of poverty, and (2) not understood a basic implication of caste distinctions, namely, that upper caste people do not normally reside along with lower castes. Such considerations had not collapsed even during as extraordinary an event as Partition; therefore I searched for and found new locations (like Rehgar Pura) as part of my revised plan. Similarly I found a widows' colony that actually was not marked on the city map. Its existence was hardly known outside the immediate locality. The widows from Partition had lived here in isolation since 1947 and the place had not changed one bit over the last half century.

A quantitative sample survey was initiated at the very beginning, in order to generate broad knowledge about the refugees, their life before Partition, their moment of departure, their arrival and later life in Delhi, and their relationship with their former homeland. The survey respondents were chosen according to their ages, aiming at survivors of Partition who were at least 15 years old in 1947, that is, old enough to make sense of the events taking place around them. Thus, the minimum age that made one eligible for the survey was 69 years in 2001.

The method to identify people of that age was to use the electoral rolls produced by the Election Survey of India that list the names, house numbers, ages, and father's names of every eligible voter in a given constituency. The work was mainly situated in two Delhi Assembly constituencies: Kasturba Nagar in south Delhi that includes Lajpat Nagar in its jurisdiction, and Timarpur in north Delhi, of which Kingsway is a part. These lists helped identify the residents who could participate in the survey. They also helped in gaining information about people who had moved away from the locality.

The lists showed that these colonies have primarily remained a stronghold of Punjabis, with very few people of non-Punjabi ethnicity having moved in here. In Kingsway, some Hindu Marwari families from the old city had moved in, while in Lajpat Nagar some Sikh refugees from Afghanistan had rented accommodation. Kingsway Camp is now the site for huge residential colonies named Guru Tegh Bahadur Nagar and Mookherjee Nagar. Kingsway was the location of the 1911 Durbar that had been assembled for King George V. Four main military barracks named after British commanding officers were located here: Edwards Line, Outram Line, Reeds Line, and Hudson Line. In 1947 Kingsway became a prime (and the biggest) location for refugee camps in Delhi. It had 30,000 inmates at the height of migration in the summer and autumn of 1947. Large tents surviving from World War II were used here to house the refugees. The barracks for the soldiers were also allotted to the refugees. The tents here had become permanent, and in the1980s the government undertook a new planned construction here. The original inhabitants of the camp still live there in their newly constructed houses.

The survey results helped generate a general profile of the migrants and challenged some of the prevalent views on Partition migration. First, Punjabi migrants emerged as urbane, well-educated people who had been reasonably well-off in Pakistan. They migrated mainly from cities like Lahore, Rawalpindi, Dera Ghazi Khan, Multan, Sargodha, Sialkot, Peshawar, and Dera Ismail Khan. Barring Lahore, most other cities were located in the canal colony settlement areas that came to be populated in a planned manner in the late 19th century. They were not all traders and shopkeepers, as is popularly believed, though a large proportion of them (48.9 per cent) were engaged in trading, but a comparatively large proportion (33.3 per cent) was employed by the British government. A large number had also owned agricultural land in West Punjab, though they were not cultivating farmers. More than 70 per cent of the migrants had been at least to primary school while a fifth of that number had received college or university education. Though income level was a sensitive subject, most insisted that their salary levels had been good enough to maintain their living standards, since inflation was lower in colonial times as compared to the present.

Though the caste profile of the migrants reflected the widespread belief that the majority of migrants were upper caste Khatris (35 per cent) and

Aroras (31 per cent), it was startling to find that the survey showed no untouchable low caste individuals in the survey areas. More than 70 per cent believed in the institution of caste, especially when it came to arranging marriages. As much as 84 per cent of the respondents had married a partner not only from the same caste but also from the same sub-caste. An overwhelming majority had married off their children and grandchildren within the Partition migrant community.

Over 60 per cent reported having at least formal though cordial relations with the Muslims in their old hometowns, and the same number had heard of violence taking place around their localities. They did not necessarily have direct experience of violence at any stage. Around 45 per cent had left Pakistan even before the Partition day, while another 36 per cent had moved between the months of September and October 1947. At least 25 per cent knew of some Hindus who had chosen to remain behind. This is new evidence, though not thoroughly verified, to suggest that there were a sizeable number of Hindus and Sikhs who had chosen not to move. Among those who chose to move, 78 per cent said that they had not been helped by their Muslim neighbours/friends in moving out of Pakistan.

The survey also suggested that not everyone had come to Delhi empty-handed, even though this was a question that a lot of people chose to remain silent about. A compelling reason for this silence was the ensuing familial quarrels that would take place if the children heard about some asset their parents had not told them about. It was not always possible to talk to the concerned individuals in complete isolation. Teenage grandchildren would often sit with the grandparents while the forms were being filled out. Despite these problems, 40 per cent reported that they had brought along some movable assets, mainly cash and jewellery. The questionnaire included the options of photos, among other things, but this option was not ticked by anyone.

The mode of transport was another area where a well-known belief was authenticated: namely, that 66 per cent had travelled by train for some part of the journey. A small number had travelled with the foot convoys as well, and only 20 per cent reported their convoys being attacked. It was not surprising that there were not many who had travelled with convoys to Delhi, as this was a popular mode for rural migration while trains were the preferred mode in urban movement. For most, Delhi had not been the obvious destination for resettlement, as 70 per cent had travelled to one or more other places before arriving in Delhi. While 30 per cent took only 10 days to travel to Delhi from their point of departure, 25 per cent took over a year before they arrived in Delhi, indicating a longer span within which migrations continued. The reasons for coming to Delhi varied from simply following their fellow refugee travellers (37 per cent), prior family relations in the city (23 per cent), to seeking better opportunities through government rehabilitation schemes (13 per cent).

The new arrivals lived in refugee camps (54 per cent) and also in privately rented accommodation (17 per cent). This conflicted with the subsequent question about whether they had personal resources to support themselves. Thirty-eight per cent reported that they did, but still chose to live in the government-aided refugee camps. To an earlier question, 40 per cent had admitted to having brought assets along with them. Clearly these assets were not used for daily purposes but saved as much-needed capital to start business ventures or to marry off daughters. Half the respondents claimed to have received no assistance from the government in their resettlement, while 36 per cent said that their living standards at present were much worse when compared to their lifestyle in Pakistan (they said that they had left substantial capital behind). However, only 42 per cent acknowledged government help in establishing their homes. This is remarkable, considering that the survey was taking place in colonies that were established by the state to resettle the refugees. By that definition, each respondent had been a beneficiary of state largesse.

Plotting One's Self

The final task in this chapter is to plot *my self* in the narratives which I intend to open up in the following pages. Henrietta Moore suggests that authors are per se present in texts, whether they acknowledge this or not, more so in ethnographic studies where the entire text results from the author's personal experiences in the field. Thus the author becomes the narrator and therefore an inevitable part of the plot. However she suggests that the author *of* the text is not the same as the author *in* the text (Moore 1994). It is this subtle yet significant relationship—between the authorship of the text that I produce and my presence in the text as an author—I need to lay bare.

The narratives that I have collected and reproduced are not distant from my own personal life history. I have heard similar stories in my childhood home, as my parents had migrated in 1947 from Sargodha and Lahore in Pakistan. I grew up in one of the neighbourhoods where Punjabi migrants had made their homes after moving from Pakistan. In that sense I am technically a *native* writing my own history. Since the native/foreigner categories are too simplistic—it is difficult to define these days who is an authentic native or foreigner when travel and not rootedness has come to define a large part of humanity—they should ideally be left out of discussions.[11] However, this categorization is considered important to underscore the objectivity (or otherwise) with which researchers approach their research field and object. In other words, the distinction between 'self' and the 'other' is a distinctive ethnographic mark that prevents objectivity from becoming blurred. Thus, fear of getting too close to their subjects or 'going native' is pointed out as the ultimate threat to be avoided 'if one wants to safeguard one's professional credentials and if one wants to safeguard one's sense of self' (Moore 1994: 115). One's nativity within the field of research therefore complicates this self/other distinction, so much considered a hallmark of objectivity.

As a co-bearer (through my personal history) of the narratives of Partition migration, I did not approach the respondents or subjects of my interviews as a complete stranger. I was familiar with the stories I would hear. I was also familiar with the emotive tearful sessions that occasionally take place in migrant families when grandparents or parents begin recounting their childhoods, favourite anecdotes from their former hometowns, stories of dear ones lost in the violence and migration, and the material losses their families had to suffer in that process. Yet I was not personally acquainted with all the stories that I was to hear. The family intricacies, quarrels, and individual journeys had their own rhythm that I could not anticipate. Thus, they became *intimate strangers* to me, that is, strangers who were intimately known to me through a shared common history. I did however take care to choose a field site that was as far away from my childhood home as possible, in order to avoid interviewing my neighbours and my parent's friends.

The interaction I shared with the respondents also brought out an aspect of information gathering that is often overlooked. It is not uncommon that ethnographers report their subjects being as interested in their personal situations and life histories as the researchers are in their subjects. This is often presented as having come as a surprise, as if the role of who should ask questions and who should answer them is fixed and pre-determined. The interviewees are as interested in asking questions as the interviewer, for the simple reason that in ordinary life people *exchange* and not *extract* stories and information from others. My position as a descendant of Partition migrants allowed me a baggage of stories and personal anecdotes from my parents that I could offer to the people whom I interviewed in *exchange* for their narratives. Each interview thus became a familiar session that would often occur in my own family at times. This way, I could use my own personal history in a positive way instead of allowing the fear of native unobjectivity to hinder my work.

However, I have tried to differentiate between author *of* the text—a descendant of Partition migrants, researcher and organizer of the text—and the author *in* the text. This means that the text is not organized along the lines of my journey into this study, that is, I do not always appear as the narrator. The use of the formal third person pronoun is deliberate and consistent to emphasize this distance that I want to maintain. A compelling reason is that the entire exercise of unfolding my own history also meant discovering dark sides of my own ethnic community that I was otherwise oblivious to. The popular image of Punjabi refugees—hardworking, enterprising, brave, and honest—that I was familiar with was getting challenged. The stories of corruption, nepotism, and irregularities in the compensation schemes were also becoming visible. There were inconsistencies, gaps, and unanswered questions that needed to be filled to get a complete picture. As I discovered, the story that I had known was only a partial story. I chose to convert the collected narratives into text not in my position as a descendant of Partition migrants but rather as a detached narrator. Therefore, the occasional shift between first and third personal narration reflects the dilemmas inherent in my involvement in this study.

NOTES

1. Dirks makes a critique of Marx's view that the innocuous looking village communities are actually repositories of oriental despotism that enslave human minds through superstition and traditional rules.
2. For further details, see Kumkum Sangari and Sudesh Vaid (eds) (1989) *Recasting Women: Essays on Colonial History* and Sarkar (2001). Also see Chatterjee (1994), especially the chapter entitled 'The Nation and its Women'.
3. This argument is introduced and discussed at length in Bernard Cohn (1996).
4. For an overview of the socio-political developments in colonial and post-colonial India see Metcalf and Metcalf (2002).
5. Most Indian writings on state formation in India allude to the differences between Indian and European states. At times, while stressing upon the uneven complexities of social and political culture in India, European nation-states are presented as ideal versions of state authority. For example, Ashis Nandy (1989: 4) in his critique of the Indian state compares it to Germany where 'Bismarck had created a proper nation-state'. Such sweeping comparisons completely ignore the long, violent and complicated histories of state formation in various parts of Europe, and therefore serve little to help understand the state-making processes in India.
6. See Robert Redfield's (1947: 1955) description of rural communities in 'The Folk Society' and Robert Redfield (1955) *The Little Community*.
7. In the late 19th century, the colonial government undertook the establishment of new irrigation canal systems in West Punjab (now in Pakistan) and moved population from East Punjab (now in India) into the newly opened land. Most Hindus and Sikhs in West Punjab were originally from parts that are now Indian Punjab. The Partition happened within five decades of that first population movement. The migrants, in that sense, were returning to their orginal homelands.
8. Broadly speaking, archives suggest a collection of records that is preserved, catalogued, and ready to be retrieved for reference in future. Administrative bodies—both governmental and non-governmental—tend to maintain records of their transactions, policy decisions, and other regular business since more than one individual is involved in such processes. Thus a systematized filing system is

organized to facilitate the accession of records by more than one individual. Archives therefore pertain to organized sources of information on a particular theme that can be stored and retrieved.

9. The project is housed at the Nehru Memorial Museum and Library in New Delhi.

10. The other 'governmental' sites include the National Archives of India (NAI) in New Delhi, which has a selection of recently released files (including personal case files) concerning various aspects of resettlement. The files include official correspondence and layouts of specific refugee colonies which were being planned in the late 1940s. Another site is the Nehru Memorial Museum and Library (NMML), which possesses a rich vein of information collected from the private archives of political leaders, bureaucrats, and social workers who had been engaged in resettlement work. Finally, there are the recently released All-India Congress Committee (AICC) files from 1940 to the 1950s. A large part of the AICC archive is yet to be sorted out and catalogued for public use. I was allowed to go through the material on my own initiative, which meant that I had to pore through many files without the aid of a catalogue. The fortunate result was that I stumbled upon evidence that has never been brought out in public forums earlier. This material enables us to look upon Partition displacement and resettlement in a new way.

11. See Arjun Appadurai's (1988) discussion on the anthropological construct of natives.

3. The Last Journey
Exploring Social Class in Partition Migration

In the depth of night the last hope is shattered. The Hindu and Sikhs have no roots [any longer] here at all. They must wrench themselves together, assemble their pitiful possessions, and before sun-up are on the long unending trek to India. Here a cart dragged wearily by a lean hungry bullock, there a wheelbarrow or a push-cart, many carrying bundles on their heads. Multiply this a hundredfold. The streams mingle and flow ever eastwards. They cling together out of sheer terror, for on long way out danger lurks—bands of marauders prey on their very helplessness. The attack is launched unawares. Men, women and children perish or are badly mauled. Those who escape lick their wounds and resume their wearisome journey (Rao 1967: 8–9).

The above narrative is extracted from the official account of Partition migration compiled by the Government of India two decades after the events. The image that it conjures up is that of refugee caravans with men, women, and children on bullock carts and miles-long refugee columns on their way to India. The other powerful images, gained through government photo archives and personal accounts is that of choked railway compartments with people clambering dangerously on train tops.[1] These narratives and images help evoke a powerful symbol of the pain and trauma that ordinary people went through. Clearly, the narrative behind these images is the national narrative, the chaotic birth of the Indian nation and the excruciating pain attached to it.

However, what is often overlooked is that such popular narration is built around the experiences of the urban poor and rural folk, who, with their farming essentials and meagre belongings, set out to find a new home. The 'truth' of Partition migration, thus, *masks* the complexity and the multiple levels within the population movement. For instance, the experiences of upper class and upper caste migrants—who flew down to safety and whose household belongings and bank accounts were transferred through official means—seldom frame the popular imagination of 'what happened during Partition'. In the popular accounts, the Partition migrants thus appear united in their misfortunes, irrespective of their social class, caste and gendered experiences. The tension between the 'differing' experiences and the *master narrative* of the last journey, which seeks to condense, simplify and standardize the account of Partition migration, has seldom been explored.

This chapter takes the *means of transport* used during Partition migration as a point of entry into differing modes of how individuals or communities experienced, and now remember, Partition. While the foot journeys took weeks of travel and were fraught with dangers of violent attacks, looting and abduction on the way, air transport took no more than a couple of hours and posed no risk of attack to the travellers. In between these two options lay train and truck transport that was not always easy to obtain, and, once it became freely available, became a target of specialized attacks. The means of transport provided the vantage point from which to 'witness', and later on 'narrate', Partition.

To open up such an analysis, one can borrow Paul Virilio's (1977) concept of 'speed' as the determinant of one's world view and subject it to a class analysis. The interwoven complexities of such class-based *measured movement* inform us how movement was experienced in the first place. The differing experiences then help explain how different narratives emerged and how some of them became more popular than others. Virilio begins by emphasizing the significance of speed or mobility in modern societies. The different modes of transport that command greater speed, point to how the world is experienced when organized on fast-changing time–space–speed vectors. Space is conquered with acceleration and technology, and distances are measured on the basis of speed, and not in spatial terms. In other words, the distance between two given points is measured by how fast one can reach a point rather than by the actual spatial distance. The speed at which we cover the distance—on foot or by motor vehicle, train or airplane—determines how we experience and remember the landscape en route, witness ordinary events, and interact with the people inhabiting those landscapes. While Virilio uses 'speed' to explain the steps and gaps in the conflict-ridden, technologically advanced world, it has significant relevance to the forced movement that inevitably accompanies inter/intra-national conflicts.

MOVEMENT AND DISPLACEMENT

In Partition migration history, 3 June 1947 is as important a day as the Partition itself. It was on that day Lord Mountbatten announced the Partition plan according to which the British would hand over power as early as August 1947 instead of June 1948 as planned earlier. The advanced date meant that the entire procedure of transfer of power had to be hurried up. This included handing over authority, division of assets, and the territorial division of Punjab and Bengal provinces. Communal riots had already erupted in Rawalpindi district in the month of March, wherein 2090 people died and 1142 were seriously injured.[2] The fall of the Khizar Tiwana government in Punjab following the Muslim League agitation led to widespread riots in Rawalpindi that soon engulfed Lahore, Amritsar, Jhelum, Attock, and Multan. A particular feature of the March violence, besides an unprecedented number of deaths, was the number of people who sought refuge in the camps. An official estimate from the districts of Attock, Jhelum, and Rawalpindi alone put the number of refugees at 60,000; they were in the camps either because they feared for their safety or because their houses had been deliberately burnt (Hansen 2002: 113). The growing uncertainty about the future course of events, such as the drawing of boundary lines and the possible extent of communal violence, proved cataclysmic in terms of making people move away to perceived safer areas where their commu-nity was in the majority. A private letter (see Box 3.1) addressed to the All-India Congress Committee (AICC) points to this turmoil.

Box 3.1[3]

From: Charanji Lal Kapur
Machine Mohalla No. 2
Hitkari Buildings
Jhelum City
Dated the second of April 1947

Worthy Leader,
The recent communal disturbances and its serious consequences are very well known to you. These incidents have caused a very great panic in this area. The panic has further been enhanced by the Congress resolution demanding division of Punjab. It makes sure that whether the resolution materialises or not this side must become PAKISTAN (*sic*) within which there can be no protection of minorities, as is evident from the recent laws passed by the Sind Legislative Assembly. As a result of the above 100% capitalists of this side have either shifted to towns outside Punjab or are ready to shift very soon. This step of the capitalists, or so called leaders, has more to the panic.
Middle classes or the poor masses are unable to decide their future line which has further been darkened by the attitude of local leaders. They have got only two courses to adopt i.e., either they should remain there where they are and enrisk (*sic*) their lives in the hands of Pitiless Majority or they should arrange for their shifting which is very difficult on account of their financial circumstances. Will you therefore, the author/supporter of the division resolution very kindly guide them in this hour of distress and oblige. Thanking you in anticipation and awaiting your early reply.

To
Acharya J B Kriplani
President AICC,
New Delhi.

Source: AICC instalment II.

This letter is written by an upper caste Punjabi Khatri male who is well aware of the political developments in the country. He writes mockingly to the Congress president, the author of the division resolution, to 'kindly guide them in this hour of distress and oblige'. He refers to the landowners and the rich and influential people as 'capitalists' who had already started moving to safer places. In contrast, the middle classes and poor people were left behind as they could not afford to move immediately.

The class differences in the movement can already be traced long before the full-scale movement was to begin. The official announcement in June was a step further in the formation of a Muslim-majority Pakistan, heightening concerns for the safety of minorities. The Hindus and Sikhs in the areas that were to be part of Pakistan now feared a repetition of the Rawalpindi massacres. The cleavages in everyday life between Muslims on the one hand and Hindus/Sikhs on the other became more pronounced. While the Muslims in West Punjab were euphoric over having attained their political goal, the Hindus and Sikhs feared for their lives. But still no decision to go or stay was made by a large number of people. It was primarily among the upper-middle and middle classes, who kept abreast of political events through radio and newspapers, that this debate raged. The fear of violence was widely prevalent, as a letter addressed to Mahatma Gandhi (see Box 3.2) in the month of July shows.

Box 3.2[4]

Mandi Jagat Rai, Mianwali Dated 10.6.1947
My most beloved Mahatamaji, Since the matter of boundary has been settled by the British without any regard for our cherished goal of united India for which you have given your life long devotion, it is now time to think of saving us from the perpetual slavery in the Pakistan. Unless our beloved Hindustan helps us we are here always doomed. It is very essential we may be migrated into Hindustan zone as quickly as possible. Property, home, hearth has no value before liberty and freedom. We helpless Hindus look to you to save us from horrible destruction. Jai Hind Your most obedient servant Nand Lal Ahuja [As a final postscript he writes:] If Lord Mountbatten is sympathetic towards 'Innocent victims', he must arrange for cheap transport.

Source: AICC Instalment II.

This letter too is written by an upper caste middle class Punjabi from Mianwali in Punjab province. He writes of 'our cherished goal of united India', suggesting his sympathies for the Congress party. He appeals to Gandhi, the moral-political authority of the freedom struggle, to bail them out of a potentially violent situation. The helplessness gets accentuated with the use of passive constructions like 'we may be migrated', which indicate resignation. He signs off with a Congress-style salute to the nation: Jai Hind. The final sarcasm is aimed at Lord Mountbatten, urging him to prove his sympathy by arranging cheap transport for ordinary people. Despite these pleas, the movement was chaotic and dangerous for those who could not afford secure means of transport. A report by the Congress party President, Acharya Kriplani, after a tour of riot-torn areas drew this scenario:

Thousands of Hindus who are leaving ... at the present moment belong to the learned professions or commerce or are small landholders. They belong mostly to the middle classes. They have their own homes and lands. They have, as Indian conditions go, a high standard of living. They know that they will have to begin their life anew in India. They are leaving in the aggregate, crores worth of properties here. Few of them will get the physical comforts that they are used to. Most of them will be paupers. They know that the cities and towns in the other Indian provinces where they will go are already over-crowded and short of food. If, in spite of these facts which are well-known and well-realised, they choose to leave their native land and their ancestral homes they must have very real reasons for doing this. It cannot be mere panic. It is for the Government and the majority community to investigate these causes and afford relief.[5]

The upper-middle class migration began quite early and was a precursor to the mass migration in the months to follow.[6] As a precautionary measure, many people with substantial properties and businesses left the trouble-prone areas long before Partition took place. They would either take up temporary residences in Hindu-dominated cities or proceed to the hill stations of Simla or Mussoorie for early summer vacations while waiting to see if the situation would normalize. They even began to sell their properties or exchange them with those Muslims on the other side of the border who were contemplating migration to Pakistan.[7] This trend of early migration is also echoed in the official account.

The Hindu or Sikh landlord, merchant or money lender blessed with wealth is the first to take flight. Naturally, [because] he is the object of envy and avarice. There is nothing now to protect him from the attentions of the Muslim goonda [ruffian]. Overnight he has packed up, rushed to the nearest railhead, thence to flee eastward to safety in India. Soon after Partition there is just a fleeting moment of sanity, and the Hindu villager, peasant, artisan or petty trader fondly imagines the worst is over and lulls himself into the belief that if he accepts the fact of Pakistan he will be spared molestation and allowed to say on as a useful element of the society. But passions once aroused are hard to quench. The madness has far from subsided, it has gained in intensity (Rao 1967: 8).

The class differences between Hindus, Sikhs, and Muslims are indicated in this account as the possible grounds for conflict, fearing which the Hindu and Sikh landlords made arrangements to flee long before actual Partition. The class conflict inherent in Partition violence needs to be stripped of its religious veil. Evidently, it was not only the class differences between Hindus/Sikhs and Muslims that defined the Partition exodus—the internal class hierarchy among Hindus and Sikhs also shaped how and when migration took place.

Violence took place throughout the summer of 1947, especially in cities like Lahore and Gurdaspur that were located in the disputed border areas. In this part of Punjab, people did not know where the lines would be drawn. Each community was making pleas to include certain areas on their side. The Boundary Commission headed by Sir Cyril Radcliffe, a British bureaucrat who never visited India either before or after Partition, was flooded by petitions in favour of various areas. But Lahore went to Pakistan and Gurdaspur remained with India, leading to widespread riots. To make matters worse, the Boundary Commission award was not made public until after Independence Day on 15 August 1947. Most people in the border areas did not know which country they now belonged to and whether to stay or move. While political leaders quibbled about the boundary award, a large population had become 'minorities' and their own backyard had now turned into 'hostile territory'.

The largest ever mass migration in human history then started. Everybody was looking for a safe refuge for themselves, their families and belongings. Migration became the only alternative to certain death at the hands of organized mobs. Hindus and Sikhs 'had' to leave for 'their' nation (India) and Muslims were driven out to their 'own' Pakistan. A perverse logic that guided these forced migrations was that room had to be made for the incoming refugees from the other side. So more refugees were created on both sides to make way for more refugees.

If one imagines this migration to be an unfounded panic reaction, then the statistics of people killed and injured during the months between August and October proves otherwise. The plains of Punjab witnessed unending inter-community conflicts that created fear and uncertainty in the region. While some people were forced to move because of fear of death, others sought to escape shame and humiliation brought about by the abduction of women, rapes, and forcible conversions.

The migration continued despite the appeals of political leaders to stay put. It seems that the political leadership had not imagined that division of territory would result in population movement. This naiveté is all the more astonishing when one considers that migration was already being reported from Punjab since the Rawalpindi violence in the month of March. There were emotive appeals to rescue the minorities in West Punjab from where 'a steady stream of refugees was arriving [with] appalling stories of the experiences through which they had to pass before they could escape that doomed city [Lahore], and of the worse plight of those who are still left behind.'[8]

But Nehru made his displeasure about migration clear when he announced that he was not 'in favour of wholesale migration of population. It was not in the interest of the majority of people to be uprooted from the soil. The lives and interests had to be protected by both the governments who were responsible for the minority well being'.[9] Notwithstanding Nehru's views about migration, Sir Francis Mudie, the Governor of West Punjab, saw the refugee problem more as a nuisance, wherein only the removal of refugees could restore peace. He wrote to Jinnah:

I expect trouble in all the western districts. The refugee problem is assuming gigantic proportions. The only limit that I can see to it is that set by the [population] census reports. According to reports, the movement across the border runs into a lakh [hundred thousand] or so a day. At 'Chuharkhana' in the Sheikhupura district I saw between 1–1½ lakh of Sikhs collected in the town and round it, in the houses, on the roofs and everywhere. It was exactly like the Magh Mela in Allahabad. It will take 45 trains to move them, even at 4000 people per train; or if they are to stay here, they will have to be given 50 tons of atta (flour) a day. At Govindgarh in the same district there was a collection of 30,000 to 40,000 Mazhabi Sikhs with arms...I am telling everyone that I don't care how the Sikhs get across the border; the great thing is to get rid of them as soon as possible (K. Singh 1991: 511–13).

It was clear that organized violence had triggered off mass migration that could not now be stopped. People had left their homes to take shelter in camps, for their strength lay in numbers, and safety in togetherness. By now the newspapers had started taking note of the refugee crisis in the making. The pictures of newly installed Indian cabinet members were now accompanied by pictures of refugees.

It was not until mid-October that a Joint Evacuation Movement (JEM) Plan was formulated by the MEOs (Military Evacuation Organisation) of India and Pakistan. The target date for accomplishing the evacuation of approximately 10 million refugees in Punjab was set as December 1947. The sheer enormity of the population to be exchanged posed its own problems. In British East Punjab 4.4 million Muslims, that is, 32 per cent of the population, needed to be evacuated. The princely states and the Punjab hill states were home to another 2.3 million Muslims who were now huddled in a number of transit camps. Hence the total number of Muslims in East Punjab expected to be evacuated was 6.7 million.[10] Similarly, West Punjab had a non-Muslim population of 3.9 million that was awaiting evacuation. The non-Muslim population of Sind and NWFP would take the total number to 5.4 million. The non-Muslims included 3 million Hindus, 1.5 million Sikhs, and half-a-million Dalit Hindus among others.

The JEM plan was finalized between Brigadier H.M. Mohite of MEO (India) and Brigadier F.H. Stevens representing MEO (Pakistan) on 20 October 1947. It was estimated that since 1 August, '2.1 million Muslim refugees had already moved into West Punjab and 2 million non-Muslims into East Punjab.' Therefore, 'the object [was] to move the balance of the evacuees from East Punjab states into Pakistan and those from NWFP and West Punjab into India, as soon as possible' (K. Singh 1991: 549). The plan outlined the methods of evacuation, means of transport and even identified the routes to be used for the 'foot convoys'.

In a section entitled 'Method', the modus operandi is explained:

The rural population will be moved by foot convoys, especially those who were in possession of bullock carts and cattle. Motor transport convoys will be used by Pakistan MEO to deliver food to the foot convoys and other famished camps. Both MEOs intend to use motor transport to clear small pockets and to help the progress of the foot convoys by lifting the women, children, sick and the aged. The extra lift obtained by this method is therefore small, but it is none the less important and will save many lives. Railway trains will be used to move urban populations, rural people who have no bullock carts or cattle or who are unfit to walk. Each train will carry at least 2500 people and the total lift is considerable. Aircraft may be used, if available, but only a small lift is to be expected by this method (ibid.).

The targets for phased movement are given in Table 3.1:

Table 3.1: Joint evacuation movement targets

	Muslims	Non-Muslims
At Present	3.2 million	1.8 million
On Completion of non-Muslim foot convoy (Approximately 1st November)	2.4 million	1.2 million
On Completion of Muslim foot convoy (Estimate on 30th November)	0.5 million	0.6 million
On 15th December	0.25 million	0.3 million
On 31st December	NIL	NIL

Source: K. Singh (1991: 551).

The authorities were seemingly busy planning the final exodus down to the last detail:

Halting points for the night, food, water, medical aid and protection had to be provided for in advance. Schedules had to be drawn up to avoid clashes between caravans moving in opposite directions. All along the route of the convoys, jeeps and armoured cars kept constant patrol. Night curfew had to be clamped down on areas through which the convoys marched. Mobile dispensaries were always in attendance to care for the sick. Besides all this, when rains towards the end of September washed roads away in many regions and brought movement to a halt, the MEO had to undertake repair and construction of lines of communications (Rao 1967: 16).

The whole evacuation operation was organized roughly on three levels: first, establishing transit camps for the isolated pockets of refugees; second, transporting the refugees on foot, or by rail or motor transport; and third, settling them in refugee camps or shelters in their respective countries of destination. The two governments had exchanged chief liaison officers (CLOs) to coordinate the evacuation work with the local authorities. In turn, each district had a liaison officer who was responsible to the CLOs in Lahore and Amritsar. The district liaison officers informed the MEO about stranded refugees, abduction of women and children, and forcible conversions taking place in their areas. The MEO would, thereafter, organize rescue missions in coordination with local police and army units.

The basic presumption for success was state protection and availability of food and water for foot journeys, wherein the caravans could be as long as 240 kilometres with 50–60,000 refugees (Rao 1967: 16). But there was a lack of armed guards for protection, unavailability of food, and frequent attacks on the convoys, trains, and motor transport. The convoy commanders even complained of lack of arms and of having to issue Sten guns without ammunition.[11] In such circumstances, the fortunate ones who reached safety told of water wells and ponds en route that had been polluted with carcasses of slaughtered cows, of acute shortage of drinking water being sold at exorbitant prices, and of pregnant women giving birth on the roadside or on trucks proceeding to Amritsar (Chopra 1997: 11).

In an autobiographical note, the area commander of Amritsar region, Brigadier Mohinder Singh Chopra, later talked of long refugee columns that entered India from the Khem Karan sector into Amritsar district. Khem Karan (along with Ferozepur) was one of the popular entry points into India from West Punjab. These were also the sites of dispersal of outgoing Muslim refugees into Pakistan. Brigadier Chopra remembered that

exhausted refugees...sprawled everywhere, along the roads, in makeshift camps, in school buildings, in private houses, in fields and on the streets. They had trekked all the way from Multan and Montgomery. It was over these refugee columns coming on foot from Pakistan entering India at Khem Karan, that I undertook many air flights to assess the extent of the mass of humanity stretching unbroken for 15–20 miles [24–32 km]...Whenever possible, we dropped food parcels with cooked chapattis and vegetable in sealed bags (ibid.).

Such a humanitarian deed was clearly an individual act, and an erratic one at that. The organized state machinery is not as visible in personal accounts as in the official ones. If the refugees reached their destination safely despite all odds, it was because of their own ability to organize and persevere. 'Some convoys which came from Montgomery, for instance, were fairly well organized because they had amongst them a sprinkling of retired army personnel who provided safety and security with whatever means they had' (ibid.). That arrangements were far from adequate is clear from the casualties that such journeys entailed. The official sources, while telling a story of heroism, do admit a little reluctantly that 'often the sick and the feeble-bodied were abandoned by the roadside. So were the dead, with none to mourn them or perform obsequies. The living had no time for the dying and the dead' (Rao 1967: 17).

Even in retrospect, the mass migration does not cease to intrigue in terms of 'how people decided to leave their homes and lands for good' (Randhawa 1954: 25). After all, this

decision was only a matter of few hours everywhere. The fatal decision was not long delayed, as the ring of death and destruction from all sides. The hand that was sowing the seeds in the morning was hurriedly packing in the afternoon...There was nobody that they could turn to for help, nowhere that they could go for justice. Thus the only choice before them was to say goodbye to the land of their birth (ibid.).

Means of Transport

The reconstruction of the last journey in these different sources shows a class-divided process which could not be abridged even by as momentous an event as Partition migration. The duration of the journey and the means of transport used to undertake the journey are crucial indicators of the class differences that significantly altered the experience of displacement. The clusters of differing migration experiences can be built around the (1) foot columns (those who walked hundreds of miles over several days or weeks), (2) railway journeys (a shorter journey but undertaken in highly cramped and difficult conditions), (3) military trucks (used for short distance travel but not available easily), and finally, (4) air travel (swift and safe but available only to those who could pay the exorbitant price). The level of danger also decreased dramatically as the mode and duration of the journey became shorter.

A large part of the displaced population walked across the borders. The estimated number of people evacuated from West Punjab by organized caravans is given as 1,036,000, that is, roughly a third of the evacuated non-Muslim population. The foot columns of refugees were mostly of rural origin, whose prime possessions of cattle and farm equipments could not be carried on trains and motor transport. These caravans were vulnerable to attacks while passing hostile towns and villages, and a degree of organization was therefore necessary for survival. The caravans were organized with young women and children in the middle, and older men and women around them, with the last protective ring thrown around them by young men with crude weapons like *lathis* (heavy wooden sticks) or sometimes rifles.

Each looked to their own selves, as 'few showed pity for age or sex, and many aged or infirm persons who could not walk were deserted by their relations and left to die on the roadside. Mothers threw their newborn babies in bushes along the roadside and left them to die. The urge among the columns was to escape Pakistan and to cover the journey in the quickest possible time' (ibid.). Such a quick exit was possible only if one had the physical ability or the means to possess sturdy bullock carts. The ones who possessed bullock carts could place their bundles in the carts to gain speed, while 'others not so fortunate carried them on their heads. Among them were landless Harijans, and village workers, who did not possess any bullock carts of their own, and were accompanying their co-villagers' (Randhawa 1954: 28).

While foot columns were the preferred means of evacuation for the rural masses, the railways were deployed to ferry the urban populace. Over a million non-Muslims are estimated to have been evacuated by rail during the peak period from 27 August till the end of November 1947, and over 1.3 million Muslims in the opposite direction. The JEM Plan arranged for rail evacuation with contributions from India and Pakistan of 20 and 12 railway trains respectively to form a pool of stock for refugee movement. It was expected that 5–6 trains would run between East and West Punjab on a daily basis. A 'Refugee Rail' control was set up in Lahore with functions in respect to refugee movement 'similar to those of Mil Rail in respect of military movement' (K. Singh 1991: 548).

Table 3.2: Modes of transport employed during evacuation from West Punjab (mid-August till end-November)[12]

Modes of transportation	Number of people
Foot Columns	1,036,000
Special Trains	1,000,000
Motor Transport	313,4000
Air Transport	28,000

Source: Rao (1967) and Annual Report 1947-48.

These refugee trains were known as 'India Specials' or 'Pakistan Specials'. Due to their central role as a preferred means of urban evacuation, they have become symbolic of the last journeys of the masses. Some fictional works like *Train to Pakistan* by Khushwant Singh have immortalized the train journeys that carried millions of refugees to their new homelands. The special trains were frequently subjected to sabotage by ingenious methods, in order to waylay them and then massacre the refugees. In the novel *Train to Pakistan*, the saboteurs use a thick steel wire tied atop two poles across the railway track. The plan is to derail the train when it hits the steel wire and then kill all the passengers. In a poignant climax, the hero cuts the steel wire and falls on the tracks only to be crushed by the passing train that carries his beloved and their unborn child safely across the border.

Though the Refugee Special trains plan was started to evacuate the refugees en masse, it served an altogether different purpose for the attackers. Instead of launching random attacks, now one could indulge in 'wholesale slaughter' because these trains carried members of a single community (Aiyar 1994: 20). There were several methods besides derailment that were used to kill the refugees. For instance:

Sikhs on railway platforms would observe Muslims entraining, and enter the same carriages. After the train's departure, they would single out the Muslims and push them out of the carriages or throw them out of the windows, at pre-decided spots, like railside telegraph poles that were marked with a white flag. There gang of killers waited to complete the killing. Often the gangs conducting this operation had their couriers on trains who pulled the communication cord between stations, and then the killer gangs then operated throughout the train...The attacks were organised with military precision, with one half of the gang providing covering fire while the others entered the train to kill (Aiyar 1994: 20).

Another method was to throw crude bombs at the train or lay a boulder on the tracks. Sometimes the tracks were tampered with, pointing towards official complicity. An enquiry report about a train accident, for instance, points to the complicity of the lower railway staff:

Yesterday, at about 2 p.m., a Muslim refugee special (train) which left Ambala met with a serious accident at Shambhu railway station (Patiala state). Engine and three bogies derailed, resulting in 129 deaths and injuries to about 200 persons of whom nine died in the hospital...Train resumed its journey at 2.30 a.m. Accident [occurred] due to the train having been directed on to a deadline instead of the mainline, which is attributable either to gross negligence of railway staff or a deep-seated conspiracy. The station ASM, pointsman and the driver have been arrested ('Report of Shambhu Train Accident', quoted in K. Singh 1991: 565).

Often the trains would arrive at their destinations piled with dead bodies. Such 'ghost trains' would unleash another round of killings in order to send back an equal number of dead bodies on their return journeys. A personal account by Prakash Tandon, a Hindu Punjabi from Gujarat, states that:

one day, train crammed with two thousand refugees came from the more predominantly Muslim areas of Jhelum and beyond. At Gujrat station the train was stopped, and Muslims from the neighbourhood, excited by the news of violence in East Punjab, began to attack and loot. There was indescribable carnage. Several hours later the train moved on, filled with a bloody mess of corpses, without a soul alive. At Amritsar, when the train with its load of dead arrived, they took revenge on a trainload of Muslim refugees (Tandon 2000: 131).

Even though train journeys were fraught with danger, they were much in demand as a quick means to get away from 'risk-zones'. The 'Special Trains' were free for the refugees who could travel to any destination within the country of their choice.[13] But to get a place on the train was not that simple. The railway employees would normally be the first ones to find places for themselves and their families. A simple reason was that, as a safety precaution, the train timetables and their platforms would often not be revealed until about half an hour before departure. Through their networks, the railway employees could access that information more easily than anybody else. They could place themselves at the right time and place to board the train before the rush started. Many others would take to bribing the railway employees to gain this information. The refugees were sent out in batches following some sort of priority list maintained in the transit camps. Many refugees tried to get their names scaled up in priority through their personal connections or by bribing the officer-in-charge. Even an acquaintance in the railway department could prove to be valuable in such circumstances, as some refugees experienced. Shyam Lal Manchanda, a 16-year-old resident of village Peepal Sawan Kapur in district Multan was stranded in the Qila Multan camp, awaiting evacuation for several days along with his family.

It was the rainy month of September when we were waiting for the 'refugee special' train to evacuate us. Often the hostile Muslim groups attacked our camp. The arrangement for food and water was also not adequate. The only agency that fed and looked after the refugees actually was Multan Seva Samiti, a social service organisation started by some influential Hindus of Multan. The wait for evacuation seemed endless till we chanced upon a distant relative whose sons worked in the railways. He took pity on us and agreed to take us along on a goods train that had been arranged the next day especially for the railway employees. They were open carriages meant for transport of goods and animals. The journey was tough as we had no protection from rain, cold or hostile attacks. Many people fell sick on the way. But at least we were lucky to board the train.[14]

If it was important to get into the train, then it was even more vital to keep the engine driver in good humour. The driver could decide to stop the train at a hostile place or just abandon it midway. Shyam Lal Manchanda's train was similarly stopped at a station called Harbanspura near Lahore for two days.

As the train was open, the passengers, especially women, were jeered at by Muslims from the railway overhead bridge. We had collected stones to defend ourselves. Some people went to the driver and asked him to park the train either before or after the station and not at the platform itself. It was becoming dark and everyone was afraid of a possible attack. The driver agreed when he was paid some money at the rate of Rupees five per family. He pulled the train back away from the crowds. We passed the night with round-the-clock vigils. Next day we found out that our train had been stopped in exchange for another train at Amritsar which was full of Muslim refugees from Delhi. The reason was that an earlier train of Muslim refugees had arrived in Pakistan full of dead bodies. So our train was stopped as a guarantee for the Muslim special train from Delhi. Finally the two trains were exchanged at the border and we saw people from Delhi for the first time.

The 'Special Trains' were packed to capacity and the refugees had to fight their way in. This also meant that it was not possible to keep the customary distance between the two sexes. The usual separate compartments or exclusive spaces for women had no place in such an emergency. In a personal interview, a Sikh woman who was 10 years of age at the time of partition recounted this scene (her family was travelling from Sargodha to Amritsar in the month of August):

At the railway platform, there was a mad rush towards the train. My father was making sure that I and my siblings did not get lost in the crowd. The women of my family would normally never go out unaccompanied and without a head cover, dupatta. A sort of purdah was maintained in our house as far as outsiders were concerned. But now my mother was standing in the crowd trying to keep her head covered and observe all the customary niceties. It almost seemed impossible to get into the train till a complete stranger offered to help us. As the door was jam-packed, we had to be thrown in through the window. And then it was my mother's turn. The stranger and my father picked up my mother and pushed her in through the window. Nobody seemed to care at that time. It was important to save our lives. This incident, later though, made a big impact on my mother. She would often talk about it and the bad times when strangers could touch other people's women.[15]

The gender barriers were challenged in this scenario, though in a crude way. The liberty to touch female bodies is remembered by the narrator above as a demeaning incident that revealed the vulnerable position the women found themselves in. The inability of men to protect their women from the touch of strange men heightens this loss of power. While the immediate aim was to flee from violent situations and such incidents could definitely be overlooked, it did leave a lasting impact on the mother. The privacy she was used to had been violently intruded on. The memory of intrusion remained despite the fact that the family had escaped completely unharmed and that the stranger was merely trying to help.

The other form of popular transport—by military trucks—was used for short distances such as from Lahore to Amritsar or for transporting passengers from isolated locations to the railway stations for further journeys. Around 1200 military and civilian trucks were deployed by the MEO (India), with an additional pool of 1000 trucks at the peak period. By the middle of November around 313,400 non- Muslims and 209,440 Muslims had been transported in this way (Rao 1967: 18).

While all means of surface transport were prone to risks of one kind or another, air transport was free from all such dangers to life and property. The safest and quickest means of transport was also the least widespread. It was available exclusively to the upper crust of society, mainly high-ranking bureaucrats or rich people who could afford to pay their passage. Air transport was also meant to be for ordinary refugees from 'certain inaccessible points in Pakistan' (Rao 1967: 18), but this is rarely corroborated by testimonies of refugees, oral or otherwise. By the government's own admission:

air transport was both safe and speedy but could not be employed for mass evacuation. But this operation had a profound psychological effect on people living under a thickening pall of anxiety and terror. In the scale of air priorities, Government employees naturally came first. India was desperately short of technical personnel for the Railways, Posts and Telegraphs, and administrative, police and office personnel as well (Rao 1967: 18).

The government employees were clearly well looked after, as the above news report shows. The rehabilitation ministry had set up a Transfer Bureau, an agency specially created to cater to the state employees who were affected by the violence and population movement. The migration course followed by the government employees was different from ordinary people, as their travel, stay, and continued employment was arranged by the state.

Evidently, the government, as an efficient guardian of its employees, was able to transfer them out safely. For this purpose, as early as the end of August 1947, ten aircrafts were mobilized from various transport companies for six to seven daily trips between India and Pakistan. The scheduled flights between Delhi, Karachi, Quetta, Lahore, Rawalpindi, and Peshawar were increased (Rao 1967: 18). In addition, a fleet of British Overseas Airways Corporation (BOAC) aircraft was added to the available air resources. The BOAC fleet consisted of 18 Dakota and two York aircraft and could carry out 1962 flights at the height of evacuation between 15 September and 7 December. During this period it transported 28,000 people from Pakistan and 18,000 in the reverse direction. However, these official figures exclude large unaccounted estimates of passengers carried by companies such as Indian National Airways. The company announced two daily services between Delhi and Lahore in either direction, one daily service between Delhi and Rawalpindi, and day return service between Delhi and Peshawar via Lahore and Rawalpindi.[16] Although no concrete figures about the number of passengers ferried by this company and others like it are available, the extent of its services gives an approximate picture.

Those who flew to safety had a different view of Partition. They could witness the murderous events from safe distances, and, if cornered, could, more often than not, fly away without ever having to face the mob. Their stories about Partition were always about their hapless servants, cooks, and drivers who would go out to the city to run errands and quite often end up getting murdered. An influential Hindu 'refugee' who lived in the newly estab-lished rich quarters of Lahore called Model Town narrates one such story:

Lahore was rife with all sorts of rumours but father never told me anything. My only source of information was our chauffer Gulzara Singh, who would exaggerate everything he heard or witnessed. Every evening I had dinner with father without even exchanging a single word. His silence and a strange expression of sorrow stamped on his countenance disconcerted me greatly. I tossed in my bed at night, wondering what Independence would bring for us. Model Town, fortunately, was not touched by the massacres in the city...

'What has happened?' I asked in surprise. 'Your house has been attacked, he [a Muslim friend] replied with anxiety and panic writ large on his face. For me this was incredible. There had been no person in Model Town who had taken part in the rioting; even during the worst days the place remained peaceful...Hafeez Sahib made a hurried trip to our house to see the situation. He came back with the news that it was still dangerous for us to go back. Someone had told him in the neighbourhood had told him that Pathans were still keeping a watch on the area. What was to be done? Mr Bedi suggested that we should go to Delhi by air, leaving everything in Hafeez Sahib's charge. There seemed to be no other way, and father agreed to it. By the afternoon of that day, we were in Delhi telling my brother the story of our narrow escape (Anand 2001).

The import of this narrative is self-evident. The narrator positions himself in a newly developed upper-middle class locality of Lahore city. Information about the raging communal violence is gathered from the narrator's driver and servant who are depicted as friendly people. The gossipy portrait of the driver is drawn in a patronizing style, since nothing better could be expected anyway from people of that class. The violence and the gossip seem to belong to another world, to which the narrator is connected only through the his servants. When violence finally seems to come closer, the narrator's father compels him to seek safety in Delhi with his relatives. The fact that his experiences are far removed from what is popularly believed to have taken place is never seen as a complication worth exploring.

SPEED, CLASS, AND FORCED MIGRATION

The raging communal violence in Punjab made it imperative that the minorities flee the area as soon as possible to safe areas. Swiftness of movement was the key to ensure survival and protection of one's self and family. Each individual tried to get away from the danger zone with the fastest possible means of transport. Of the means available, like foot columns, military trucks, trains and airplanes, the last was the safest but also the most expensive, and therefore out of reach of most ordinary people. Following Virilio, the safety and swiftness can be measured on a scale of position in the class hierarchy. The *means of escape* employed are indicators of class and help us understand how different classes later related to the new nation and their former homeland. In population movements affected by genocidal violence and ethnic cleansing, not only is rapid movement essential for one's safety but also has repercussions later as to how one remembers the former homeland and how one formulates relationships with it. The speed at which one flees becomes essential to one's safety and very survival. However, the *swift escape route* cannot be opened without the means to afford prohibitively expensive advanced technology.

At every social-economic level across the rural–urban divide, a scale of speed and safety can be employed to measure how different classes experienced Partition migration. Those who flew across the turbulent borders had the shortest and safest journeys. This ensured that the entire violence-ridden stretch of the journey became no more than a brief leap of air travel. There was virtually no risk that air travellers would be attacked en route. Their memory of 'what happened during Partition' is therefore limited to the stories they had heard or news reports they had read. The events of violence do not figure large in such accounts, because the narrators had seldom themselves experienced them. The category of such migrants clearly belongs at the top of the class structure. Their experiences were quite different from other urban migrants who took to military motor vehicles and refugee special trains as a means of escape. A journey that would take an hour by air would take a couple of days, sometimes more, by train or truck.

The threat level increased with the increase in the total time of journey. Since train journeys were quicker and more affordable than air travel, there was a huge demand for them. While the journey became entirely free of cost with the introduction of 'refugee special' trains, the demand rose to previously unmatched levels. The special trains also became the target for concentrated killings where well-honed techniques were employed to first derail the train, and then kill its occupants. If one survived this organized massacre, then there was a greater possibility that the survivor could carry more belongings than the migrants who travelled on foot. Even though railway authorities fixed a limit on the luggage that could be carried on trains, it was always possible to find a way around such limitations. The mostly urban, lower-middle to middle class status of rail travellers is evident from their choice of means of escape.

The worst-off group on the scale of speed and safety was that of foot travellers. The bulk of this group was made up of rural inhabitants who would travel in village contingents led by the village headman. The columns were sometimes miles long, with thousands of migrants hurrying across the border for weeks on end. The safety of the foot columns was under threat most of the time from organized communal bands, highway robbers, petty thieves, and mischief-makers. They were subject to sudden and brutal attacks at all hours along the entire route. Those who could muster self-protection with assorted arms and weaponry had the best rate of survival. The differences within the foot columns were also apparent in whether people travelled on horses and bullock carts, or just walked. This difference also translated into how much of their belongings the foot travellers could bring along as compared to those on bullock carts.

Of all the above possible modes of travel, those that have become part of the popular imagery are the tightly packed trains and the foot columns of weary and traumatized travellers. Air travel has never been part of the national narrative of Partition, in which the birth of the nation is linked with traumatic territorial dismemberment and loss, followed later by rejuvenation attained through clear political vision, popular will, and perseverance displayed by the national leadership and the people. In this narrative, the new nation is built on struggle, sacrifice, and the indomitable spirit of the refugees who lost everything but succeeded in rebuilding their lives. The train journeys and foot columns fit this national narrative, where the loss and trauma can be witnessed through various media. Air travel, on the other hand, does not entail a similar sense of trauma or loss, and is therefore rarely mentioned in official accounts. The personal lives of the migrants are somehow linked with that of the modern Indian nation and it is the common story of endurance and success that has captivated the nation's imagination.

Notes

1. This pertains to some of the most popular photographs of train journeys during Partition migration that are widely used to 'show' the migration. The photos are available in the National Archives in Delhi as well as in the photo section of the Nehru Memorial Museum and Library, and are reproduced in history books as well as in some fictional work, e.g., the cover of Khushwant Singh's *Train to Pakistan* in its early editions.
2. Fortnightly Report (FR) second half of March 1947, India Office Library (IOL) quoted in Hansen (2002: 117).
3. AICC Instalment II, File no. G/34/1947.
4. AICC Instalment II, File no. G/34/1947.
5. Acharya J.B. Kriplani's report from Karachi city dated 27 September 1947 (AICC Records 1947–48, emphasis added).
6. See Acharya J.B. Kriplani's report from Karachi city dated 27 Septemebr 1947 (AICC Records 1947–48), where he mentions the plight of well-off merchants, and learned, professional Hindu and Sikh migrants.
7. This was narrated in a private interview with M.M. Chaddha, a refugee from Rawalpindi.
8. Editorial 'Rescue Them', *Hindustan Times*, 18 August 1947.
9. Nehru's speech reported in *The Times of India* dated 25 August 1947.
10. The figures are calculated from the district-wise population tables of the Census of India, 1941.
11. Convoy Commander JEM R. Krishna's Report; MEO Records No 10899/11 vol. II in Kirpal Singh (1991), p. 547.
12. These figures pertain only to migrants from the British West Punjab and exclude estimates from Punjab princely states, Sind, and NWFP. The figures were com-

piled from Rao (1967) and Annual Report 1947–48, Ministry of Relief and Rehabilitation.

13. This was testified to by most of the refugees during my survey. Moreover, no one was checking the tickets in such chaotic times.
14. Personal interview with Shyam Lal Manchanda, now a resident of Delhi, on 2 December 2000.
15. Personal interview with Mrs H. Kaur in Delhi dated 20 October 2001.
16. Advertisement in *Hindustan Times*, 29 August 1947, New Delhi.

4. Governmental Policies and Practices of Resettlement

In a scheme of rehabilitation and reconstruction planting of men is even more important than the planting of grain.[1]

—L.C. Jain

The governmental policies of resettlement can be condensed to show the repertoire of knowledge and action of the Indian state following the 1947 mass displacement. This chapter pursues a theme—of state participation in resettlement—that often remains absent in the narratives popularly told by the migrants. Therefore, the first task is to establish the active presence of the Indian state in the resettlement process. This not only draws the state into the referential frame of resettlement, but also helps to draw attention to the appearance of an ambiguous relationship between the migrants and the Indian state at a later stage. The second task is to follow the class divisions, apparent in the last journeys, into the transit refugee camps and the permanent housing projects that came to define the urban landscape of Delhi in the 1950s and 60s.

The mass movement from West Punjab and NWFP produced a large number of displaced people who needed to re-establish their homes, livelihoods, and kinship networks even while mourning traumatic deaths, sexual violence, missing family members, and the loss of accumulated material belongings. The immediate period following the migration represented a brief, nebulous moment where the ordinary business of life began competing with the extraordinary events of Partition. However, this nebulous space was soon overtaken by the compulsions of everyday life where both migrants and the state negotiated their claims to define the new urban landscape. This chapter focuses on the ensuing spatial competition between the state and the migrants. It is important to remember that it is the Indian state—and not international humanitarian organizations as is the contemporary norm—that appears as the main benefactor vis-à-vis migrants in the resettlement process. Hence the rationale behind the state efforts needs to be examined beyond the sphere of charity and humanitarian aid and within the terrain of *state formation*.

The primary suggestion offered here is that the resettlement process became a fertile formative ground on which the state moulded a modern citizenry while displaying and authenticating its fledgling legitimacy. The state was not alone in writing and performing the script of nation-building. The migrants actively defined their own role and space in this exercise through the formation of various interest groups—refugee relief organizations, social service groups, cooperative societies, pre-partition locality or caste based associations—that collectively bargained with the state for concessions, provisions, and even privileges.

A core area that compels attention, therefore, is the very nature of the Indian state. This study is located in a historical period when the Indian state changed from being colonial to post-colonial, with a brief transitional period between the two categorizations. The transfer of power from the British imperial government to the two dominions of India and Pakistan was preceded, actuated, and followed by unprecedented communal violence and population movement. The breakdown of law and order, and the state's inability to stop the population movement and restore peace is seen as an instance of its absence.[2] If the state authority is visibly experienced through its multifarious governmental functions, then the state functionality around the period of transfer of power needs to be explored as a whole, and not in chosen parts. The collapse of law and order must be collated and compared with the planned joint evacuation movement, the establishment of refugee camps, and the implementation of several resettlement schemes. The active presence of the state is easily established through these activities.

The class distinctions——and thereby the emerging social inequities—already visible among the fleeing migrants call for a closer look at the immanent response from the Indian state. The post-colonial state in India was the historic culmination of the decolonization process and of nationalist resurgence among the Indian elite.[3] Its origin within the anti-colonial freedom movement meant that the newly independent state departed from the popularly perceived repressive characteristics of the colonial state. For instance, in Punjab, the 1919 Jallianwala Bagh massacre in Amritsar (where hundreds of unarmed protestors in a political rally were shot dead in a single day) remains the core example of colonial injustice, inequality, and oppression. As an articulator of the Indian national movement, the Congress party had to contest the very culture of the colonial state (Kaviraj 1997: 223). This opens another significant issue vis-à-vis the state's role in the resettlement of forcibly moved population: that is, how radically did the independent Indian state depart from the colonial legacy of *inequity* while organizing resettlement? Such a question brings the state policies of compensation and housing under review, since the state, through a series of ordinances and legislative acts, not only became the largest owner of real estate in Delhi but also the prime authority actively engaged in the construction and planning of new townships.

These questions require an analysis that straddles a theoretical understanding of the Indian state and the empirical nuances that collectively seek to define the post-colonial state in India. The immediate period following Partition is extremely intriguing in terms of understanding the way in which the state performed within the public space. The very birth of the state on 15 August 1947 was accompanied by mass violence and unceasing population movement, which the state failed to counter effectively. But around the same time, between October–December 1947, the Indian state was engaged in a military operation in the Kashmir valley to ward off the Pakistan-supported tribal invasion threatening the region. The intricacy of the Kashmir case notwithstanding, it is important to note that the state that was unable to control one aspect of its governmental functions was fully active in another area that established its governmental authority. This suggests that the role of the state during the transitional period needs to be looked at in splintered forms: that is, the state at this stage cannot be evaluated as an aggregate whole. The agency of state alternates its role. Sometimes it is an active organizer, a partially functioning structure of authority. At other times it is a mere bystander in the entire process involving decisions to leave home, making the last journey, and resettling in a new place. It is essential, therefore, that the state and its processes are not looked upon as congruent, logical schemes but as often abrupt, improvised, and disjointed attempts at (re)claiming authority.

OFFICIAL MYTHOLOGY OF RESETTLEMENT

It is usually the task of researchers to construct official narratives out of everyday tools of bureaucratic functioning such as files, policy papers, minutes of meetings, and sometimes the lengthy notations in their margins. In this case however, the nature of the task is different. The government itself provides a running narrative in the form of a 230-page volume entitled *The Story of Rehabilitation* (Rao 1967). The document was issued by the Publications Division of the Government of India, in 1967 (that is, two years after the formal abolition of the Ministry of Relief and Rehabilitation when most of the rehabilitation work was deemed to have been completed). Though the volume is largely based on the annual reports of the ministry from 1947 onwards, it is more than a mere skeleton constructed by the annual reports. The series of events starting from the Partition of India, forced migration, and resettlement on an all-India level are woven into a single, unbroken story that has a definite beginning and an end. The composition is marked by a poetic flow and the roles of both narrator and central character are taken by the state.

The narrative can be read at two simultaneous levels. One level recapitulates the state encounter with the fleeing migrants; shows a prospering relationship between the state and the migrants that is established through resettlement schemes; and ends when migrants are finally deemed to have become citizens. At another level, the narrative directly appeals to the *reader of the text* through an emotive description of the events, the hurdles on the path, and the much-deserved celebration of success attained despite all odds. The twin levels work towards a single purpose: to garner sympathy, praise, and legitimacy for the state actions from the migrants on one hand, and from the readers of the text on the other. The actions and their narration take place with a time gap of two decades, yet the anticipated response (by the state) from the migrants and the readers does not seem very different. The entire narrative is built up on a range of emotions—of disbelief, helplessness, sense of loss, frustration, magnanimity, forgiveness, and finally, a calm resurgence of pride. Each of these emotions has a practical function in explaining the role of state in the events from migration till permanent resettlement. The narration begins with a dramatic prelude:

This is the story of a Ministry of the Government of India. A dull, uninspiring theme, you will exclaim. But it is a richly evocative saga. Here are drama and passion, illimitable human suffering, heroic endeavour. Within the confines of what a Ministry set out to do and what it accomplished, you find every element of a Greek tragedy. Only everything is multiplied a thousand fold. You have men whose reason is over thrown; men plunged into the depths of anguish. Impenetrable gloom shrouds the story of their purgatory. But, as in ancient legends, there is expiation and the slow return to blessedness. These, then, are the ingredients of our chronicle (Rao 1967: 3).

The official narrative is interspersed with expressions such as 'heroic endeavour', 'tragedy', 'pride', etc., routinely used to describe the circumstances and attributes of the state that helped turn around individual and collective mishaps. The author traces the cause of this tragedy in the partition of the country and hence to forces that are alleged to be outside the state's control.

It has its beginnings in the vivisection of our country, the rending asunder of territories in which people worshipping the one God under different names had lived in peace and amity as brothers, as all true religions teach them to do. A new and pernicious doctrine had come to poison men's minds—that religion divides instead of uniting. And men's minds were warped; they forgot their humanity and turned upon one another with the ferocity of jungle beasts. Arson, rapine and murder were let loose. People were uprooted from their homes and sent fleeing pell-mell for sanctuary. It was as if the lid had suddenly been ripped open from a boiling cauldron. Fear, suspicion and hatred came to dwell where there had been only friendship and common brotherhood (Rao 1967: 3).

On the one hand, the metaphor of people turning into 'jungle beasts' reiterates that there was 'peace and amity' and 'friendship and common brotherhood' before Partition, and on the other hand, lays the blame for violence and forced migration on the uncontrollable, though somewhat natural, human perversion that occasionally occurs. The hints at the 'naturalness' of Partition violence shift the focus away from the state and its inability to maintain law and order in all circumstances. The reference to 'peace and amity' makes Partition violence a kind of one-off event, thus rendering it unimaginable that the administration could have taken any pre-emptive counter measures. However, the frequent occurrence of communal violence is a fairly well-recorded phenomenon in colonial India and recent studies show that the violence during Partition was neither unprecedented nor unexpected by the colonial authorities (Hansen 2002: 80; Aiyar 1998: 81). The narrative, therefore, absolves the state of any responsibility in the turn of events that led to forced migration. On the contrary, the undisputed prevalence of violence serves as a preface to the coming events that makes them seem inevitable.

Once the inescapable course of violence and retaliation is established, the 'uprooting' of people from their homes seems an obvious consequence. It establishes the 'naturalness' of the Partition process, and a succession of events around violence and displacement becomes part of an unalterable script of Epicurean proportions. The affective description of the tragedy that befell ordinary people also provides a basis for the state to secure approval for its achievements that later make an appearance in the narrative. It helps generate compassion among the readers for ordinary people who were now assuming the category of refugees:

The story of the great migration has often been narrated in the white heat of passion. Its searing wounds, the immense pity of it, has been recorded in words that grip your heart and choke your throat. Your bowels of compassion are moved. Years after the immediacy of the events, their memories have been known to bring tears to one's eyes (Rao 1967: 4).

The natural accompaniment of this disrupton of faith was fear, and emotion that gripped men's mind insanely. It was fear hour of the day, and when one went to sleep fear was a screeching demon in one's nightmares. And one woke to reality, of which fear was the main component. This was the setting for the mass movements that followed the accomplishment of Partition (ibid.: 7).

The narrative dwells a great deal on the psychological fallout of violence and movement on the people. They are depicted as the lost, bewildered, and broken ones who cannot comprehend the breakdown of everything that was known to them. They sleep and wake up with demonic fears and are completely overwhelmed by the situation. The helplessness of the people also assigns a pro-active role to the state to take control of the situation. So far, a division has been successfully created between the role of the state in failing to control violence and its attempts to support the victims of violence whose only hope of survival is through migration. While the first situation is attributed to the inexplicable and uncontrollably natural spread of violence, the second is described as an outcome of human fears and fallacies. The successful intervention of state thus becomes possible in the latter situation in which fearful people are led by the state to safety. The inability of state to intervene in the former instance—to control violence because of its naturalness—becomes an illegitimate topic of debate. Thus, the ensuing account basically proceeds from the later situation, where the state had an opportunity to perform actively. The first step in the process was to evacuate refugees from the transit camps set up at various locations in Pakistan.

The task was far from easy, we are told. The enormity of the operations and the rather complicated nature of the tasks are two characteristics that are greatly emphasized. The comparisons of refugee evacuation with wartime activity highlight the looming emergency and the military precision with which the evacuation was required to be carried out. Once the readers are convinced of the gravity of the situation, it becomes easier to later have them appreciate the problems and to show overriding sympathy for state relief measures.

The key areas of state measures were shelter, food, clothing, and medical aid:

Some five million people crazed with fear, shattered in body and mind, most of them pitifully destitute, had come over, many lakhs more than had left the country. They had to be fed, clothed, protected from the ravages of disease, found shelter and homes, where they could be slowly nursed back to some semblance of lost dignity, and the spectre of fear driven from their hearts (Rao 1967: 36).

The official concerns expressed with regard to this task cover more ground than that of practical tasks to be performed. Various restorative techniques had to be employed on both body and mind.[4] While feeding and clothing was one part of the exercise, rehabilitating 'shattered', 'crazed with fear' destitute spirits was another focus. The state acts here as a kind parent under whose protection the refugees could hope to regain their 'lost dignity' and exorcize their ghosts of fear. The concrete measures of providing shelter, food, and medicines were then a dignified, carefully crafted route towards complete restoration. The magnanimity of various government agencies can be seen in organizing living space for the refugees in schools, army barracks, tents, etc., while any shortcomings could be attributed to the 'ever growing demand'. Bodily nourishment was secured with free rations that were calculated by per capita basic requirements, with liberal small additions for children (see Table 3.1). The uniform and fixed proportions of food, fuel, and clothing help depict a system that was well planned and functioned smoothly. Nursing back to health—of body and spirit—was an obvious goal towards which material reconstruction and fulfilment seemed a definite way.

One example of camp life described in great detail is that of the Kurukshetra camp, located 100 km outside Delhi. It was the largest camp in north India and later became the site for a whole new township. The camp is described as a success story that was hailed internationally.

The Kurukshetra camp quickly became the show-window of the Ministry's Herculean labours. It attracted observers from all over the country and quite a few from abroad as well. The United Nations Relief and Rehabilitation Agency (UNRRA) experts who visited it expressed the view that it was probably the biggest refugee camp anywhere in the world. They were unqualified in their praise for its administration. Following closely on their heels came a group of press correspondents to see things for themselves. The enthusiastic reports they dispatched to their newspapers showed how deeply they had been impressed by their observations. 'The camp is as clean morally as it is hygienically', wrote one of them. 'If there are no mosquitoes and flies, crime is also absent. The mortality rate is not above normal. All male and adults and children turn out for physical training every morning. In their spare time, women knit or spin. Life is orderly' (Rao 1967: 46).

Table 4.1: Rations distributed in camps[5]

Per family/adult	Ration
Fuel wood/coal	1 *seer* daily
Washing soap	3 oz per head per month
Matches	1 box (50 sticks)
Per head (Adult)	*Ration*
Atta or rice	10 oz
Dal (lentils)	1 oz
Ghee or oil	½ oz
Salt/Masala	½ oz
Gur/Sugar	½ oz
Per adult	
1 *Razai* (quilt) or 1 blanket	
2½ yards of cloth for pyjamas	
4 yards for *salwar*	
1 *Dupatta* or 1 *pagdi* (turban)	
1 *Bundi* or 1 Jersey	

Source: GOI 1947-48.
Note: 1 seer roughly equals 2 lb and 2 oz. 1 seer equals 1 kilogram, 1 pound equals 0.453 grams.

Though we are not told the particulars of which international newspapers reported the above-mentioned news, the emphasis on morality and hygiene is noteworthy. The descriptions of an orderly camp life seem almost idyllic. Refugees are well looked after and well nourished; women knit and spin while their children participate in routine physical training. This description of camp life finds little resonance in other descriptions such as oral histories.[6] However Kurukshetra was soon to become a 'laboratory for the experiments in abiding rehabilitation that were soon to be undertaken on a large scale' (Rao 1967: 47).

A supplementary objective pursued in the camps was to create a modern citizenry that was physically and mentally agile. This was an opportunity to *produce* a class of citizens that befitted the new nation. Such an opportunity to influence and 'correct' citizens did not exist in other parts of the country to the same extent that it did in the refugee camps. The camp residents were under direct state supervision; people outside the camps were not. This allowed the state to intervene more profoundly in the everyday lives of camp inhabitants. Corrective measures could include imparting simple habits like washing hands and the more complicated task of restoring moral fibre. The allusion to 'laboratory' in the above passage is not just a figure of speech, but rather a clear indicator of the larger idea behind these efforts. The camps sound like factories where migrants were turned from destitute refugees to self-respecting citizens: '...refugee was sent back ... restored and refreshed ... discarding the crutches ... just another happy useful citizen'.

The entire stay in the camp was structured to inculcate ideas of hygiene and cleanliness. The camp authorities paid specific attention to sanitary arrangements and the need to train people accordingly. But efforts were probably found lacking, since refugees were routinely exhorted to maintain standards of cleanliness in the camps by none other than Gandhi:

I have no doubt whatsoever that the refugees should look after complete sanitation, including latrine cleaning in their own camps. The camps should be models of cleanliness, simplicity and industry. I understand from Rajkumari [Amrit Kaur] that it was well nigh impossible to supply refugee camps with Bhangis for attending to the cleaning of latrines and general sanitation. Any infectious diseases like cholera might break out.[7]

Such public exhortation resulted in the appointment of welfare officers to refugee camps, mainly to look after the social and moral needs of the refugees. The stay in the camps was used to provide elementary education, vocational training to men and women, and on the whole, a 'comprehensive education in better citizenship' (Rao 1967: 47). The emphasis on 'right habits' was not limited to just personal and public hygiene but extended to other areas of citizenship as well, as will be discussed in Chapter 5. The significance of the state narratives lies in the cyclic process of (1) discursive distance that the state adopts when confronted with events of violence and disruption in public life, followed by (2) assuming responsibility in establishing routine and useful life in the refugee camps. While the eruption of violence and forced migration is described as sudden, unexpected, and chaotic (and in which the state shirks its responsibility of maintaining law and order), in the case of resettlement, the state not only associates itself with the public events, but proudly takes the credit for successfully steering the process. This pattern of distance and responsibility is manifest throughout the early decades of independence.

EXPLORING 'POST' IN THE POST-COLONIAL STATE

The distance that separated the state from the tumultuous events happening around it is best illustrated through these two notices:

Are you leaving for Pakistan? If so, please do not forget to surrender your ration cards (food and clothing) at your Circle Rationing Office or at the Delhi Railway Station. Issued by Delhi Rationing (Notice printed in the *Hindustan Times*, 10 August 1947).

When you come to Delhi...After alighting at the Delhi Railway Station, go to the Rationing Establishment there and fill in your particulars in the appropriate form. This will eliminate delay and botheration, for your Ration Card will be delivered to you automatically through the Circle Rationing Office of your area. Issued by Delhi Rationing (Notice printed in the *Hindustan Times*, 20 August 1947).

The first notice is addressed to the Muslim population of Delhi that was apparently expected to leave for Pakistan. In very people-friendly language, the Muslims are told to surrender their ration cards before they leave Delhi. This appeal would in itself not evoke any comment but for the time and circumstances in which it was issued: five days before the British were to officially hand over power to the Congress party. The unceasing communal violence so rampant in Punjab was yet to engulf Delhi.[8] The public stand taken by the Congress at that time was against migration of Muslims to Pakistan, as that would have amounted to acceptance of Jinnah's two-nation theory. As early as 1945, when the idea of population transfer was mooted by the Muslim League,[9] Gandhi unequivocally rejected it.

It [exchange of population] is unthinkable and impracticable. Every province is of Indian, be he Hindu, Muslim or of any other faith. It won't be otherwise, even if Pakistan came in full. For me any such thing will spell bankruptcy of Indian wisdom or statesmanship, or both. The logical consequence of any such step is too dreadful to contemplate. Is it not bad enough that India should be artificially divided into so many religious zones?.[10]

After the transfer of power, Nehru made his views against population movement very clear. A newspaper reported:

Referring to people rendered homeless, Mr Nehru promised all assistance but said that he was not in favour of wholesale migration of population. He said 'it was not in the interest of the majority of people to be uprooted from the soil. The lives and interests had to be protected by both the Governments who were responsible for the minority well being'.[11]

Needless to say, opinion at the high political level was against mass population movement and that makes the appearance of the first notice noteworthy.

Was the notice meant to encourage Muslims to leave or was it simply an example of a government agency (Delhi Rationing) working overtime? The advice to return ration cards cannot be treated as innocuous, since ration cards are ordinarily not only used to draw rations but are also used as identity documents while dealing with state agencies. The return of this document can be seen as a symbolic withdrawal from the Indian state.

The second notice was issued a week later to advise the incoming Hindu and Sikh refugees to fill in the appropriate forms after alighting at the Delhi railway station in order to receive their ration cards. The notice helps the readers conjure up refugees who, as the first act after reaching Delhi, would form long, orderly queues to fill in forms to receive their ration cards. In ordinary circumstances, these notices would read as perfectly ordinary information issued by a government agency. It is only when one looks at the rest of the newspaper pages that one realizes the extraordinary events happening in and around Delhi. For instance, the news headlines variously report 'Eye-witness account of Punjab carnage' (*The Times of India*, Delhi, 20 August 1947); 'Besieged families escorted to safety' (*Hindustan Times*, 21 August 1947); 'Riot destruction in Punjab' (*Hindustan Times*, 22 August 1947); '40,000 refugees in Delhi: Grave housing problem' (*The Times of India*, Delhi 25 August 1947); 'Situation in West Punjab grave' and 'Nehru's warning against competition in retaliation'.[12] So how did the Delhi rationing office decide that Muslims of Delhi trying to fight for their lives would/should remember to surrender their ration cards, or that the Hindu and Sikh refugees from West Punjab should, as their first act after escape, 'alight at the Delhi railway station and fill in the appropriate forms'? Was the rationing office so distanced from the chaos all around? Whom were they taking away 'from' or issuing the ration cards 'to', when the question of citizenship itself was not decided? There were many people moving to and fro, sometimes unable to decide whether to opt for India or Pakistan.[13]

The point here is not so much to illustrate the malfunctioning of the government agencies but rather to point out that the colonial apparatus used to govern populations remained unaltered in its post-colonial incarnation as well. The office of Delhi rationing did not cease or alter its functioning when the state became a post-colonial state. As a public office it responded to the growing violence in Punjab, the anticipated migration of Muslims from Delhi and the influx of Hindu and Sikh refugees in Delhi. The response—issuance of two notices—in itself shows how different government departments worked in isolation and distanced from the social-political churnings around them. Such departments/agencies, which had a continued existence after the withdrawal of British authority, looked upon the Partition-related upheavals quite differently from the institutions created especially at the time of, or after the Partition. The agencies specifically established to control refugee relief operations had a sense of emergency that was lacking in the existing institutions.

A significant legacy of the colonial state that remained intact and continuous was the idea of distance and impartiality that helped keep the rulers and the ruled at separate levels of the hierarchy. Sudipta Sen, while focusing on the period beginning in the late 18th century when the colonial state expanded and consolidated its power in India, suggests that the rule of the Company-state was based on 'the idea of custodianship of a vast, new and alien subject body' (Sen 2002: xxix). This required understanding the alien body, its contours, intricacies, symbols, and language, that is, creating a knowledge body that contained an inventory of 'facts' about the ruled territory and its inhabitants. Bernard Cohn (1996: 5) lays out an entire range of 'investigative modalities'—such as historiography, survey, surveillance, population censa, command of language—that the colonial state employed, first to gather and classify information and then to transform it into usable forms. James Scott (1998: 2) identifies 'legibility as a central problem in statecraft' since modern states in large territories could only be governed with a panoptic vision garnered through detailed standardized knowledge of the subjects like last names, age, medical records, population registers, etc., and through simplified language and legal discourse, legible city designs and organization of traffic.

In colonial India, this project of codifying populations and territory for administrative needs was juxtaposed with the role the state had assigned to itself as the custodian and moral protector of its subjects. The early historians recording India were influenced by the Scottish moral enlightenment that reinforced the role of the state as a moral protector, particularly of an ancient and glorious civilization that was seen as being on the brink of collapse (Sen 2002: xxix). In practical terms, this meant that the local customs and social order as understood by the colonial historians and ethnographers had to be, if not preserved, left undisturbed. If this was in part an ideological compulsion, it also made good administrative sense to avoid intervening in any local issue that would cause problems of law and order. The post-colonial state too maintained this kind of distance, expressed in observance of what administrators believed to be local order. A good example is the way in which the camps were organized, with low caste refugees in separate camps so as not to offend the sensibilities of upper caste refugees, and, similarly, with single women kept in seclusion so as not to disturb the prevalent gender order.

Another gap that marked state–refugee relations lay at the operative level where the refugees had to actually confront the state administrators.

Stephen Keller, a historian who conducted an in-depth study of Punjabi refugees in and around Delhi in the early 1970s, noted that

... the performance of the government employees and the social workers suffered from one of the chronic problems of a transitional society—how to bridge the gap between the semi-elite bureaucrat and the rural, or even urban, traditional member of the public. While to outsiders, and to the elite and bureaucrats themselves, all the [resettlement] efforts being made at the time are clearly beneficial, the refugee finds the tight-fisted, impersonal bureaucrat no substitute for the benevolent traditional methods of welfare to which he is accustomed. Here is no *biradari* offering a loan because of its obligations to its members; here is no landlord giving food or clothing to its constituents. Instead there is a man who dresses and speaks differently that the refugees and almost invariably conveys to him a sense of suspicion at stories of badly off he is and how much he has lost. That the individual who is supposed to maintain him is called a 'Refugee Administrator' (*sic*) or bears a similar title reinforces the refugee's suspicion that help emanating from his office is counterfeit nurturance. The man helps refugees because they are helpless. To get this they must display their helplessness and show how incapable they are of taking care of themselves. One cannot concede to all demands; he must shield himself from emotional involvement inherent in such a nurturance role. But such an attitude almost inevitably conveys to the refugee a sense of suspicion of the truthfulness of refugee's stories of how much they have lost. If he [the administrator] will not believe the truth, the only solution for the refugee is to inflate the story of his losses. By doing so he must not only confirm his actual weakness but accentuate it (Keller 1975: 74–5).

The unsettled relationship between administrators and refugees is quite accurately conveyed in this observation. It points to the dilemmas faced by both administrators and refugees in a situation that demanded humanitarian consideration. While the maintenance of an impersonal and distant approach was considered crucial by the administrators, it also conveyed a sense of mistrust of the refugees. The mistrust worked both ways, as the refugees felt that their claims were not taken seriously and therefore inflated them. However, the most significant portion of Keller's observations is with respect to the bureaucrat 'who dresses and speaks differently than the refugees'. This implies that administrators and refugees necessarily belonged to different levels in the social hierarchy since their manner, speech, and visible appearance separated them. While appearance points to the social class one hails from, speech points to more than social background. It refers to the entire body of language that the bureaucracy draws on to conduct its everyday business. It encompasses legal vocabulary, patterns of writing applications, letters, memoranda, and notices issued to the public.

This specialized language separates the administrators from the subjects who are governed through that language. But what of those refugees who do not look and speak differently from the administrators? What of those members of the public who themselves had been part of the state administration or were deeply familiar with it and understood the official language? Did the state–refugee relationship, involving suspicion and a sense of mistrust, operate for them too? This complicates the state–refugee relationship in a way that can only be understood with a thorough survey of the activities of the state and the response of the refugees in the first two decades of resettlement.

TECHNIQUES OF RESETTLEMENT

The entire exercise of the resettlement process can be broadly grouped into two fundamental categories: temporary and permanent measures. The temporary category covers all short-term activities of humanitarian emergency relief that ensured food, shelter, and medical attention. The relief agencies were thus engaged in the distribution of food, setting up tent colonies, and ensuring medical facilities for the newly arrived migrants. The permanent resettlement measures allude to state-led attempts to revive pre-Partition institutions such as schools, colleges, and hospitals and to create permanent housing and job opportunities for the migrants.

The role of the state in steering these resettlement measures is phenomenal, basically on account of two reasons. One was the lack of intervention by international relief agencies[14] and the other was that the state became the sole agency to control resources. Any evidence of involvement of international agencies was ruled out in a debate in the Constituent Assembly, where the Rehabilitation Minister K.C. Neogy categorically stated that no international missions had sent any aid workers to India. However, he does mention the British Red Cross Society for having sent 'considerable quantities of urgently needed medical and other supplies to the Indian Red Cross Society for relief work among refugees'.[15] Even in this case the relief resources were transferred from one agency to another agency and there is little evidence to suggest that there was direct involvement of international agencies in the relief work.

This created a dialectic arrangement whereby the displaced population was confronted with the agency of state. The Indian state came to own, in trust, a variety of abandoned properties belonging to fleeing refugees. The refugees on both sides left behind substantial immovable assets like houses, workshops, factories, shops, and farmlands. These assets were declared state property under the East Punjab Evacuee (Administration Property) Ordinance of 1947, whereby the state was proclaimed to be the guardian of the assets until the original owner reclaimed them.[16] The ordinance was amended a number of times before it was passed as a parliamentary act as The Administration of Evacuee Property Act, 1950. Under this law, an office of the Custodian General of Evacuee Property in India was created with the proclaimed object of providing for the 'administration of evacuee property and that this property has to be ultimately used for compensating the refugees who had lost their property in Pakistan.'[17] An 'evacuee' was defined as a person who 'on account of the setting up of the dominions of India and Pakistan or on account of civil disturbances, leaves or has, on or after the 1st day of March 1947, left any place outside the territories now forming part of India.'[18] The evacuees seldom came back[19] and the property effectively came to belong to the state. The state through the custodian's office could use, rent or allot it to incoming refugees. In effect, the state came to own the property since it could put it to any use that it deemed fit.

The most interesting aspect of these ordinances and administrative acts is the extent to which they allow us to see how parts of the state were working overtime to draw intricate legal documents to define who was a citizen or a refugee; which property must be deemed as evacuee property; how the property should be administered; and how the claims of lost property must be dealt with. The very first document was the East Punjab Evacuee (Administration of Property) Ordinance, which was issued as early as 14 September 1947 when the communal violence had still not subsided and forced migration was in full swing. It was extended a week later to Delhi where the violence was showing no signs of subsiding. The ordinance was 17 paragraphs long, each made up of several clauses that vested complete power in the state to take control of the evacuated property and to re-allot it to the incoming migrants. This was reinforced by a supplementary act a few weeks later, while new clauses vesting additional powers were issued as a full parliamentary act on 12 December called The East Punjab Evacuees (Administration of Property) Act, XIV of 1947. An entire legal framework was being developed by the state even when faced with an emergency political situation. This way, the failure to control law and order was balanced by the simultaneous creation of complicated administrative procedures. This again points to the fragmented way the state functions, wherein each part can only be assessed separately. The state does not appear as a well-structured monolith working with centrally determined goals, but rather as an entity whose separate parts do not necessarily work in tandem, and some of which obviously perform better than others.

Among the principal indicators of successful resettlement, as understood by the government, were access to a place to live and opportunities to establish one's livelihood. This can be deduced from the additional clauses attached to the definition of the term 'evacuee' (that is, those who were leaving India) provided for in the list of rules for compensation:

the following shall be deemed to constitute a preparation for migration for Pakistan, (I) disposal of bulk of one's household affects, (II) disposal of assets essential to one's profession, practise or calling a trade such as disposal of medical books and equipment by a doctor, (III) the disposal of law books by a practising lawyer and the disposal of his stock-in-trade by a trader, and disposal of tools and instruments by which a person earns a livelihood.

The loss, or deliberate transfer of these articles, was deemed, in a legal sense, to be a precursor to migration. The migrants were described as evacuees if they were leaving India, and as displaced persons, if they were coming from Pakistan. The legal parlance was obviously derived from a common sense approach that equated ownership of assets—like houses and the household effects therein—and the tools necessary for a livelihood as pointers of settlement. Thus, the idea of resettlement was formed around granting or making available such resources that could undo the act of homelessness. The state apparatus specifically geared to resettlement work had grown considerably within a few months, with the establishment of a full-time ministry and many specialized agencies staffed by hundreds of permanent employees.

Table 4.2: Names of the attached and subordinate offices under the Ministry of Relief and Rehabilitation and the details of gazetted and non-gazetted staff employed therein (located in New Delhi)[20]

	Offices	*Gazetted Officers*	*Non-Gazetted Officers*
1.	Director General, Evacuation, New Delhi	9	22
2.	Custodian of Evacuee Property, New Delhi	31	342
3.	Registrar of Claims, New Delhi	8	47
4.	Information Bureau, New Delhi	3	44
5.	Rehabilitation and Development Board, Delhi	15	94
6.	Fact Finding Office, Delhi	2	28
7.	Missing Persons Enquiry and Search Services	2	38
8.	Registration of Refugees, Delhi	None	24
9.	Advisory Committee, New Delhi	2 (1 Honorary)	14
10.	Special Employment Bureau, New Delhi	3	18
11.	Director, Harijan Section, New Delhi	1 (Honorary)	14
12.	Director, Women's Section, New Delhi	5 (Honorary)	13
	Total number of employees	81	698

Source: Constituent Assembly Debates 1948.

An intricate bureaucratic system and official hierarchy responsible for the administration of resettlement work was in place by March 1948. The categories of gazetted and non-gazetted staff point to the orderly manner in which the bureaucracy was organized by the post-colonial state. This order continued in the new apparatus, in the very first organ of the national state—resettlement administration—to be established in post-colonial India. While the non-gazetted staff refers to the lower levels of bureaucracy, the higher officials are annually registered in a state gazette of employees. Besides their official functions, the gazetted officers are publicly recognized as the bearers of state authority. Often the seal and signature of a gazetted officer is required to verify a document, a person, or copies of diplomas for routine matters like admission to school or issuance of ration cards. It is evident that an elaborate bureaucratic system to govern displaced populations had been set up quite early.

The role of the state in the urban expansion of Delhi became more pronounced when it embarked on its project of providing permanent resettlement to the refugees. The acquisition of evacuee houses provided accommodation that was far from adequate, since for every two Muslims who left India, at least three Hindus and Sikhs came in from Pakistan (Rao 1967: 56). The proportion was worse in Delhi, where for every outgoing Muslim refugee there were three Hindu and Sikh refugees who sought shelter.[21] The options available were, one, to distribute evacuee accommodation and, two, to create new housing colonies for the ones without a roof over their heads. Both these options were exercised at different levels but both were preceded by similar administrative processes. This process started with the arrival of the refugees at the Old Delhi railway station where a refugee reception centre was opened. All the disembarking refugees were registered and given a number and a card. They were then directed to refugee camps if they had nowhere to go. There were four big camps in the city: at Kingsway, Rajinder Nagar, Purana Qila and Pul Bangash.[22] The biggest camp was the Kingsway Camp comprising an estimated 30,000 refugees[23] spread over and around the old British barracks called Hudson, Reeds, Edward, and Outram Lines. One vital detail here was the manner in which camp allotments were made to the refugees:

On arrival at Delhi railway station,[24] refugees would go to Refugee registration office situated in a nearby building called Wavell Canteen. They would be given refugee registration numbers and asked if they needed food and clothing rations from the state. The answer, yes or no, would then form basis for the allotment of barracks or cloth tents in various camps. The ones who could afford their own rations would be allotted Hudson and Reeds Lines barracks while those who could not would be sent to Edward and Outram Lines. The latter would be housed in cloth tents from World War II while the former were settled in concrete barracks.[25]

Though this is a small detail, it is informative about those refugees who had their own means of survival, that is, those who had brought along some capital. At the very moment of arrival one can see how one's possession of various capitals, in the sense Bourdieu describes, determined how social class was immediately reorganized in the refugee camps. The financial means—measured in terms of affordability of food—was the first step in how the state authorities evaluated displaced individuals. This early categorization would later help the state in recreating social boxes in which to place the new arrivals.

The separation of refugees on the basis of class was visible within the camps as well. The camps were usually located in vast empty grounds, either around existing urban settlements or within the compounds of old historical monuments. The camps were dotted with green military tents left over from World War II campaigns in which the British Indian army had participated. Each camp location would have facilities for medical care and food ration depots. Savitri Puri, an 80-year-old refugee from Chakwal, recounted her stay in the Kingsway Camp in an unusual way.[26] It is unusual because her experience in the camp seemed to be far removed from the experience usually narrated, of poor living conditions, scarcity of food, and the lack of medical help. This account describes a satisfactory stay, sometimes even portrayed in glowing terms.

My family was from Cambellpur and I got married into a wealthy family in Chakwal. They were all officers and important people in the area. Puris were very famous in the area. There was even a Puri *mohalla* (neighbourhood) named after them. Then there was a *ladai* (war or violence) between India and Pakistan. We were living in Sialkot at that time. Everyone was leaving Pakistan. But our family kept on staying there because they had authority in the area. When the trouble grew, some people convinced us that we should go away for sometime and then come back. We came to Delhi where one of my brothers-in-law was a big officer. He was in charge of a camp. He arranged a tent for us that covered an area of more than 200 square yards (167 square meters). Our family lived there very comfortably. While others' families had very small tents we had the biggest one. All the camp inmates knew that we were related to the officer. We never had to go to the ration depot to get food. They would bring it to us in our tent. We never had to go and fill up water either. Some camp inmates would do that. When it was clear that we could not go back to Pakistan we moved into a rented house in the old city.[27]

This story differs from the usual accounts one gets to hear about the refugees on the move. A single camp area came to be divided into two different zones: a privileged zone and an ordinary one. The privileged refugees did not have to go through the same routine as the others. The prestige and rank afforded by family wealth became more useful with the networks and easy access to official machinery. Savitri Puri recalled her stay in the camp in positive terms, though few others did so. There was even a hint of pride in this recollection, since her family's experience set it apart from the ordinary refugees. Her family was able to sail through adversity in a far better manner than others they were acquainted with, and this strengthened their social rank and standing even further. It seemed like a test of their social standing that they had passed with enormous success. The sadness, disillusionment, and anger that one associates with the refugees who are forced to leave their homes is understandably missing here.

COMPENSATION AS A POLICY

The second step in the process of resettlement was to submit one's claims for compensation of loss in property left behind in West Punjab. The most vital pre-requisite for compensation was that the refugees should have owned some form of property. This pre-requisite straightaway barred the homeless and poor migrants from staking any claim in the new scheme of nation-building. They could continue to live on the margins just as before, while new territories were being carved out for the middle class refugees. For those who had owned some property previously, they required another set of capitals here while furnishing their claim for compensation. This was because of the extremely lengthy and complicated process one had to go through to actually receive compensation. The official language used to process the applications had created its own intricate terminology and codes that meant nothing to those outside the discourse of compensation. The office for filing compensation applications was located within the buildings of the Ministry of Relief and Rehabilitation in the British-built new part of Delhi. The entire process was administratively divided into three stages that could in reality sometimes take as many as 10–15 years to be completed.[28]

At the time of my fieldwork in 2000–1, the dilapidated record room at the now abandoned ministry premises reportedly housed more than 500,000 individual files pertaining to compensation claims in Delhi and surrounding areas. Since its closure as a full ministry in 1965, the Department of Resettlement had lost its immediate importance to the migrants and was no longer as crowded as it was earlier said to be. By the time I visited the premises it had three clerks who bide their time, waiting to be transferred to some other government department. I was told that the records were still in use occasionally because many cases of compensation were still to be fully closed. This was one of the reasons why the files had not become part of the National Archives. I asked the clerks if they understood how the files were archived and retrieved when required since there seemed to be a specific coded language that governed their existence. I found that these records were spread over five levels of an old building and there were only two peons at the office who were fully familiar with the way files were archived. It had been their job for more than 35 years to fetch a file when the clerks and officers needed it.

The minor bureaucratic rituals—of how the files were obtained and brought to the settlement table—are a pointer to the way in which the process of compensation claims actually worked outside the legal–administrative order. The terms of compensation were quite clearly laid out in the Displaced Persons (Compensation and Rehabilitation) Act, 1954, to be read together with an accompanying set of detailed rules issued in May 1955. The implementation of the Act meant an extended creation of resettlement bureaucracy in the form of a settlement office that handled the claim applications. The claimant had to fill more than 20 forms, many of which ran to five pages, before compensation could really be granted. The procedure was very detailed and made use of mathematical formulae to determine the extent of compensation deemed sufficient.

The type of claims entertained in Delhi were mostly in the urban category since a majority of the refugees came from small and big towns of West Punjab. The applications were to be accompanied by a series of affidavits duly signed, witnessed, and attested by a 'competent authority' that included a variety of high official ranks. The details to be furnished included identity card numbers of refugee registration, the nature of family organization in Pakistan (joint or nuclear), receipt of refugee maintenance allowance from the state, any debts owed to the state before migration, date of arrival, proof of residence in refugee camp, any independent exchange of property in Pakistan with that in India, claim to ownership of property, type and description of property, and location of the property in Pakistan. The information regarding exchange of property was considered necessary since there were commercial firms that specially dealt with exchange of property between India and Pakistan and also undertook to transport household articles from Pakistan to India for a price.[29] This general form was supplemented by special questionnaires meant for those already occupying government accommodation (mostly government employees) or evacuee property left behind by Muslim refugees.

Besides the specific property-related questions, there were separate columns that sought information about caste, sub-caste, names, and total number of male members in the family, and father's and grandfather's names in case of men and unmarried women applicants. Widows and married women had to furnish details about their husbands, husband's father, and husband's grandfather. While these questions do not have a clear function essential to determining the compensation claim, they reveal the attempts of the state to obtain information about the displaced society. This also points to the nature of the state as a social being inhabiting a space where state/society distinctions become obscure. The information about caste and family names often indicates one's class position and allows the state agencies to reify the disrupted social order. In the case of female applicants, their identity as claimants was accepted only when details of their male guardians—father, husband, father-in-law, grandfather-in-law—were furnished. The appearance of single women (unmarried or widowed women) after the violence and displacement was not uncommon. But any possibility of single women establishing a legally acceptable independent existence was denied by the state agencies through such official procedures. This is not completely unexpected since a substantial focus of the compensation policy was on the joint Hindu family unit, where the *karta* or the patriarch was deemed the rightful recipient of the compensation.[30]

This bureaucratic rigmarole led to the second stage in the claim process, known by its acronym CAFC, that is, Compensation Against Final Claim. The application was then assessed, the claims were verified by 'competent authorities', and a certificate of final claim was ready to be issued. At this stage mathematical equations and detailed charts of property value of houses, factories, and shops left behind in Pakistan were employed to arrive at the final figure. The belief among the government officials was that the claims were inflated at the time of application and needed to be curtailed accordingly. H.K. Dhawan, a retired officer (also a migrant from Punjab), engaged in the assessment of claim applications, recounted that in his experience a vast number of the claims were deliberately inflated by those who saw a money-making opportunity in the claim business.[31] There were professional advisors—lawyers or middlemen—who advised applicants to increase their claims. The inflated claims could be verified by equally dubious means through a pliable government official.

The interesting aspect of the claim procedure was that many individuals involved across the state/non-state divide were migrants. Most retired officers and employees at the rehabilitation ministry turned out to be former migrants or their descendants. During my daily visits to the ministry's now-redundant offices, I often met retired employees, themselves migrants, who came frequently to their old workplace to drink a cup of tea or play a game of cards with their former colleagues. Most had tales to tell of rampant corruption and most of the stories were about cunning individuals who cheated the state system to earn assets to which they were not entitled. While it is obvious that none of them would directly own up to having been party to fraudulent gains, it is difficult to believe that fraud could be enacted without official connivance, since so many watertight rules existed to control the claims.

The final stage was when the property file was issued to the claimant, wherein a suitable property was allotted in Delhi against the claim. Upon reaching this stage there were three options for the claimant as to the way compensation could be realized. The first was through allotment of a shop, house, or a vacant plot in a newly developed refugee colony; the second through cash payment of the assessed property value; and the third by selling the final claim certificate to another individual. Each of these options left scope for manipulative practices where the actual value of the compensation could be tampered with. For instance, with a number of refugee colonies being developed in Delhi, the officials-in-charge could alter one's fortunes by allocating property in some remote unattractive location. The cash payment could be calculated at a much lower value than the actual value of real estate on offer in Delhi. If the claimants exercised the third option to realize immediate cash against the claim certificate, then quite possibly they would undersell their claim. Many instances were recounted to me by the retired officials where gullible claimants, mostly women, were duped by crafty middlemen.

With a claim certificate in hand, the migrants reached another level of permanent resettlement: the construction of housing colonies. These were for those refugees who had found no place in evacuee houses, vacant military barracks, and other available *pucca* buildings. The ministry constituted the Rehabilitation and Development Board under the chairmanship of Aftab Rai in 1948.[32] The Board proposed a number of sites on the periphery of Delhi city for the rehabilitation colonies and preliminary planning work was started right away. As a precaution, preparations were made to stockpile building materials like cement, steel, and bricks that were apparently in short supply. The government set the monsoon season of 1951 as the target date for completion of the first phase of construction (Rao 1967: 59). The target was to construct dwellings for the top-priority group, that is, those who lived on roadside pavements, tents or in schools and temple buildings. The accommodation was to be a 'modest affair with one living room (14 ft x 10 ft), a verandah with an improvised kitchen, a bathroom and a lavatory' (ibid.: 60). This would cost between Rs 2400 to Rs 3500 in a city like Delhi. But there were many who could not even afford this amount. For them the 'Ministry developed certain sites on an austerity basis, parcelled them out into 100 square yards plots to be given away on a nominal lease. With each of these plots went a building grant of up to Rs 500 to enable the refugees to construct houses' (ibid.). Such measures meant that the government was only building on a small scale for less well-off people. But the official account suggests that

it would be a great mistake to imagine that putting up of cheap tenements and the development of building plots represented the sum total of the Ministry's housing effort. Government's planning was more ambitious, comprehending every aspect of the urban refugee's needs...Government's aim was not merely to set up a conglomeration of houses, but to assist with everything that goes to make community life happy and purposeful (ibid.: 61).

The government's intentions were obviously not fulfilled, as further evidence will suggest. Most of the resettlement colonies have come to symbolize the 'disorder' of urban living, with cramped living spaces, lack of water and electricity, filth and squalor, and the accompanying lack of social status for the residents. Nevertheless, it was declared that by the end of 1954, one was conscious of the change that was rapidly coming over the capital. The city seemed to be spreading out endlessly, new colonies were springing up everywhere, each one equipped with a market or shopping centre and provided with ample civic amenities. To a visitor who had last witnessed the Delhi landscape in the dark days of 1949 the transformation must have had a breath-taking quality. Few of the ugly patches of squatters that disfigured the Old city remained. Instead, wherever he wandered, he beheld new house, modest may be, but neat and comfortable. New colonies throbbed with a vigorous life. The misery and the squalor of the early days of migration had been all but erased from the memory (ibid.: 62).

A document entitled 'Policy Regarding Provision of Various Services in the Rehabilitation Colonies'[33] reveals the differing standards that the government adopted right at the beginning when creating housing for people of different economic levels. The document refers to these colonies as DP (Displaced Persons) colonies and sometimes alternates this with the term Cheap Colonies. Each area earmarked for construction could have more than one type of housing that fell into A, B or C category. Some colonies like Tehar and Ramesh Nagar were completely categorized as cheap colonies. The essential difference in the categorization, besides quality and area of construction, was the provision of civic services such as water, electricity, sewerage, garbage disposal, drainage, etc. The document as a matter of fact states that

the ministry of rehabilitation has developed certain cheap colonies, Ramesh Nagar and Tehar. The Ministry decided that services in such cheap colonies are to be provided on *austerity standards*, viz., there will be no provision for under-ground sewerage and street lighting and water supply will be by means of hand-pumps. Other colonies in this area will have normal standards subject to the availability of out-fall sewers and water main on the Nazafgarh Road.[34]

The rehabilitation ministry, however, received an opinion from the ministry of health that 'services in the cheap colonies should also be brought up to the same standard as in the other colonies'.[35] It was also pointed out to the policy makers that 'no local body will be in a position to take over and maintain these colonies unless the services are brought to the proper standards.'[36] The cautious advice from the health ministry points to the poor level of civic facilities offered in these colonies. The services like sanitation, street lighting, and water supply seem rather basic in nature, merely essential pre-requisites for a residential locality to be set up. The fact that the rehabilitation ministry was trying to cut corners in an area of essential civic facilities points to the inherent social bias of the authorities. Clearly, the poorer migrants were expected to be content with the bare minimum facilities. The document then goes on to detail the various conflicts and negotiations that the ministry had with different governmental bodies, especially municipalities, in order to convince them to take over the resettlement colonies, DP colonies, and cheap colonies. The fragile in-frastructure of these colonies must have been a deterrent to most authorities because of the costs involved. Therefore, the ministry even suggests that it 'will consider representations from the local bodies for tapering grants to them for a period of six months for running essential services like sanitation after which they must be able to tax the inhabitants, if they have already not done so'.[37]

The dismal condition of the colonies described in this report authenticates the residents' view that these colonies were located out in the wilderness, far away from the populated areas of Delhi city.[38] Essential services like sanitation, sewerage disposal, water, and electricity supply were not available regularly until some years after they had moved into the apartments. Many government-built apartments did not have a toilet and bathroom attached to them. For example, in Lajpat Nagar the apartments were built in gallery style, with a set of four apartments opening out into a common passage. Each set of such apartments shared toilet/bath space located at the corner of the building. It was only in the early 1970s that the municipality built a toilet and bathroom within each individual apartment.

Clearly, a toilet/bathroom in each apartment was seen more as a luxury rather than as a basic requirement since it was outside the primary model of government constructions that had one room and one verandah in each unit. However, water supply, effective sewage, and electricity are bare essentials and can by no means be considered luxuries. The reasons for delay in providing these services lay in the bureaucratic disagreements among various government agencies. While the rehabilitation ministry was responsible for developing the colonies and constructing the housing units, it had to hand over the routine administration of these colonies to some municipal authority. Since the basic infrastructure developed by the ministry was far from satisfactory, none of the authorities were willing to take charge of them. The decrepit and inconsiderate planning defines both the processes and the products that resulted from the ministry's efforts. The following example shows how the ministry came to be at loggerheads with the very constituency—refugees—that it had been established to serve.

Purana Qila

The ancient dilapidated fort called Purana Qila was one of the major transit campsites for both Hindu and Muslim refugees. When the Muslim emigration subsided around the end of 1947, the camp no longer remained a transit point for refugees, but became a temporary halting place for Hindu and Sikh refugees till they had found a permanent alternative for housing. However, for a long time to come, temporary residence in the camp became a permanent reality for the refugees who were constantly engaged in negotiations with the ministry. A document entitled 'Settlement of Claims of quarters at Purana Qila' reveals conflict of another kind that the ministry was engaged in.[39] A series of letters were exchanged between the rehabilitation branch of the ministry and Nanak Singh, the president of the Purana Qila Congress Committee. The distrustful and patronizing posture adopted by the ministry officials was in conflict with the disillusionment confronting the refugees. The various facets of the conflict are best represented through the actual correspondence between the two parties. The following letter to the AICC president gives a thorough description of the problem as the residents of the camp saw it. The entire letter is reproduced below verbatim to introduce the conflict, as it presented itself half a century ago.

Box 4.1

To
The President AICC
Sir,
Most respectfully I, as a Representative of the residents of Purana Qila Refugee camp lay down the following few facts for your kind and sympathetic consideration:-
The refugee camp in Purana Qila was established in January 1948 and at that time the Government declared that those who could afford to live at their own expenses were eligible to stay in the camp. Necessary tents would be provided for the occupants. We all agreed to the above proposal and shifted to the camp after obtaining the necessary permits from Delhi Municipal Committee. At the time of occupation the local officers helped us a lot and for which we are very thankful to them. They further suggested us to form a committee of all the residents to enable them to hear our grievances and suggestions through the committee. The suggestion was warmly welcomed by all of us and accordingly we formed a committee. On occupation of these tents we found that tents were not safe against fire and theft and therefore we suggested to the authorities concerned that some pucca rooms should be built for all of us. But it was pointed out by the officials that our proposal was not acceptable as the necessary funds were not available with the authorities since all the expenditure to be incurred during the year had already been catered for in the budget that year. Realizing the difficulties put forward by the officials we further proposed that since enough building material was available with the Government the same may be utilized for building of the rooms. The charges for the labour would of course be paid by the individuals concerned. This proposal was accepted by the officials and it was estimated that a room will cost about Rs 750 including Rs 150 a labour charges. We are NOT aware as to what transpired between the officials and the higher authorities concerned. It was also decided that a sum of Rs 750 should be paid in 5 yearly instalments of Rs 150 each. It was further decided that those who could not afford to pay Rs 150 at a stretch may pay it in 12 monthly instalments of Rs 15 each. We were made to understand that after paying the above amount the rooms would belong to the individual concerned and that Government would have nothing to do with it. The last date for depositing this amount was fixed as 15 May 1949. We accordingly

paid the amount and obtained the necessary receipts, a copy of which is attached for your information please. Necessary rooms were built and were allotted to us after a period of 4 or 5 months. Necessary receipt is attached.

After a period of two years we were surprised to see the authorities concerned forwarded us the bills as rent for those rooms which was NOT justified as we were the owners of the rooms according to the previous decision. Members of the Committee have approached the authorities concerned several times and every time the reply was 'something is being done very soon'. Instead of giving us a satisfactory reply and a final decision they have started evicting some of us which is NOT reasonable on the part of the authorities concerned.

Since we are unable to get a satisfactory reply from the authorities concerned we approach your honour to please mediate in our case and give your personal attention to our grievances which are quite reasonable. We do not want that our Government should suffer due to our account but at the same time we too do not want to suffer for no fault of ours.

In the circumstances explained above we hope that your honour will kindly take personal interest in our case and will approach the authorities concerned at an early date to meet our demands which are apparently very reasonable.

Thanking you,

NEW DELHI   Yours faithfully
Dated the 25 Mar 1954   NANAK SINGH
                                 (President, Congress Committee, Purana Qila)[40]

Source: Ministry of Relief and Rehabilitation

This letter was clearly written with a strong hint of disappointment and a feeling of having been left out in the larger schemes of development in the city. The writer begs that his prayers be read with 'kind sympathetic consideration' since appeal to human compassion seems to be the only mode in which their complaints will be heard. The writing style, forms of address, and the signature in the letter suggests that the writer had adopted the 'official language' since matters of state are deemed to be intelligibly expressed and understood only in the specific language of the state. The adoption of the official letter-writing style is significant since the letter is addressed to the president of the AICC and the ministry. The inherent class stratification in resettlement can clearly be observed in the founding principle of the Purana Qila camp settlement where only those refugees were allowed who could afford their living costs. The state-led class division continued later as the camp residents of a single camp were moved together to another location of permanent housing.

At the beginning, the letter suggests that the relationship between the state and the migrants had started amidst mutual cordiality and warmth, as the writer recalls that 'at the time of occupation the local officials had helped us a lot and for which we are very thankful to them' and also that 'the [officers'] suggestion was warmly welcomed by us all.' The local administration was suggesting new ways of community living through formation of resident associations that in a way promoted micro-level democracy. A little further on in the letter the tone changes to one of frustration and anger where the refugees level accusations at the administration for not having fulfilled their promises. This suggests that between the occupation of the camp settlement in 1948 and the time when the letter was written in 1954, the state–refugee relationship had undergone a dramatic overhaul. The cordial tone of 1948, had in 1954, become bitter and angry. The letter narrates a series of events, starting from the move into the camp, tent homes, leaking roofs, lack of ventilation, and constant negotiations with the officials that eventually led to the construction of concrete rooms. The residents continued to believe that they would be allowed to build permanent homes at their present location or a location nearby. It seems that any such promise made by the state was oral and publicly offered, without any detailed consideration at that time. There was a precedent for such an option since most camp homes in Kingsway Camp in north Delhi were allowed to be converted into permanent homes. The ministry denied any promises of ownership and noted that 'it has been explained to the displaced persons on (*sic*) Purana Qila on more than one occasion that Government cannot accept the position that the tenements were constructed there as a relief measure.'[41]

This answer is accompanied by a quick handwritten note in the margin that shows a deeper belief held by the administration about the refugees than was visible in the official answers delivered in the Parliament or those sent to Nanak Singh. It outlines a strategy vis-à-vis the answer that should be sent to Purana Qila residents:

As suggested [that Rupees 150 was towards advance rent] but the answer should be as brief as possible. Representations have been received in the past and disposed off. Questions have also been asked in the Parliament and State Assembly. There is nothing new that the residents of Purana Qila wish to know. It is merely a question of pressure tactics.[42]

The lack of trust between the authorities and the refugees is clearly demonstrated in this note. It was hardly surprising therefore, that the Purana Qila residents continued their battle with the ministry. In the meanwhile, Nanak Singh had been replaced by S.K. Saluja. The new president also complained that the 'tenements are without any cross-ventilation, without a kitchen, without a bathroom and without a latrine.'[43] He alleged that the refugees had

contributed a sum of Rs 60,000 in cash to cover the construction charges of these tenements, thereby giving an excellent and unique example of co-operation with the Government. Apart from the above sum of Rs 60,000, we have paid other amounts also from time to time. We had also volunteered our services for levelling the site where the present Nizamuddin Extension Area houses stand, on a call by the then Rehabilitation minister, Shri Mohan Lal Saxena who had promised that houses would be built there to settle us permanently, and then the Government would not charge anything from us for the tenements. We toiled there free of any charge, but we were not rehabilitated at the Nizamuddin site.[44]

The class tensions are obvious here, as the camp residents feel cheated at having been denied access to the spacious, well laid-out colony developed in their neighbourhood. Nizamuddin was one of the state-developed colonies where open plots for private construction were publicly auctioned. Upper-middle class refugees from West Punjab who had higher claims to compensation bought most of the plots.

Table 4.3: Population density in selected refugee colonies in the 1950s[45]

	Name of the colony	Area (acres)[46]	Population	Density
1.	Rajendra Nagar	255	22,000	86
2.	Patel Nagar (East and West)	400	24,000	60
3.	Malkaganj	28	2,500	89
4.	Kingsway	151.3	18,000	118
5.	Vijaya Nagar	40	3,000	75
6.	Nizamuddin	33	2,500	75
7.	Nizamuddin Extension	64	4,000	62
8.	Jangpura	130	7,000	53
9.	Jangpura Neighbourhood	26	1,500	57
10.	Lajpat Nagar (East and West)	750	45,000	60
11.	Kalkaji	355	17,000	47
12.	Malviya Nagar	400	24,000	60
13.	Bharat Nagar	14	1,500	107
14.	Tilak Nagar	266	15,000	56
15.	*Purana Qila*	20	6,000	*300*
16.	Kotla Ferozeshah	7	1,500	214
17.	Azadpur	9.2	1,500	163
18.	*Rehgar Pura*	7.5	2,500	*333*
	Total	2956	198,500	67

Source: Bopegamage (1957: 82–3).

The contrast can also be seen in the differences in population densities of the different refugee colonies planned by the administration (see Table 4.3). The localities can be roughly classified on the basis of density into three groups: (1) lower: with 200 and above persons per acre, (2) middle: between 80 and 200, and (3) upper-middle: with less than 80 persons. These categories have to be interpreted very cautiously because many of the newly planned colonies were not fully populated by the mid-1950s, which is why localities around Old Delhi (like Malkaganj) appear to have taken in a larger intake of population while a lower-middle class colony like Tilak Nagar jumps into the upper category. The location of these colonies which were very far away from the old city (for example, Tilak

Nagar), has to be borne in mind since their distance from commercial area made them less attractive and therefore sparsely populated. It was only later, in the 1960s, that these areas started gaining population. Another anomaly is the reporting of collective figures based on a single local administrative division and not on the basis of smaller units within the same locality. These may differ dramatically. For example, the two subdivisions in Patel Nagar area (East and West) are reported as one unit where no more than 60 people live in each acre. But the areas are vastly different in their layout, size of houses, size of streets, and availability of municipal facilities. While East Patel Nagar has large bungalow-type houses built on plots ranging in area between 300–1000 square yards (250–836 sq m) with backyard extensions called 'servant quarters' to house the family servants, its counterpart in the West has accommodations built on plots of 100 square yards (83.6 sq m).[47] The concentration of population and the individual access to shared facilities also differs vastly in the two areas. The combined figures from the two areas, however, give a very misleading image. Similarly, Lajpat Nagar area houses a number of divergent classes and the different layers can be observed when one moves from one small sub-division within one area to another. Likewise, each settlement in different parts of Delhi has at least two versions of localities, one that is planned with larger plot sizes and spacious streets, and the other with cramped accommodations set close to one another.

However, interesting comparisons between two settlements—Purana Qila and Nizamuddin—can already be made at this stage. While Purana Qila has a very high density of 300 persons per acre, the neighbouring Nizamuddin has on average 68 persons per acre. While the letter from Nanak Singh quoted earlier tells us about the conflicts the residents were engaged in, it does not fully inform us of the living conditions therein. A study conducted in mid-1950 describes Purana Qila as a colony that

lies about three miles away to the south of Old Delhi. Once upon a time it was a fortress. All the poorest among the displaced persons live there. The majority of the houses in this colony are one floor single-room tenements. There are about 800 tenements in total. However, some have taken shelter in the old stony barracks or alcoves in the wall. Many of these single room tenements are overcrowded. In some about two to three families, mostly those of relatives, live together by using the two side rooms and the common verandah. The lavatories are communal lavatories. The occupants of these houses belong to the middle and low income groups. Teachers, clerks, peons, carpenters, bus drivers and conductors live here (Bopegamage 1957: 85).

The observations about the living standards of the residents made by the author, roughly 5–6 years after the establishment of the colony, are remarkable considering Purana Qila was one of those areas where refugees who could afford their own living expenses had been settled. The author, who must have witnessed the colony after some years, described them as the 'poorest among the displaced persons'. The living standards of the residents obviously fell during those years. The overall picture presented in this study is rather depressing and stands in clear contrast to how the conditions in these colonies are described in the government's official report (discussed above). The author, having described a number of different refugee settlements in Delhi, finally comments that:

> The general observation we make is that the conditions obtaining in these colonies are deplorable. Many of them lack the basic amenities of life. Some have no filtered water, no electricity, no drains and no proper roads. The rent of some of the houses built for the displaced persons are so high that they lie vacant now (ibid.).

The refugees from Purana Qila camp were eventually resettled in several different DP colonies, but most of them came to live in Lajpat Nagar area.[48] This area is now the hub of 'illegal construction', as few can afford to move out to better localities. The children and grandchildren of the Purana Qila camp residents are now engaged in a different battle with the authorities. The housing sites in Lajpat Nagar now stand in stark contrast to Nizamuddin, where the streets are wider, well-lit, with spacious houses and parks for the children. The refugee colonies in Lajpat Nagar, on the other hand, have narrow streets, small cramped apartments, open garbage lots, and unauthorized additions to the apartments for extra space. It is paradoxical that while refugees are blamed for the 'urban disorder', the authorities remain beyond scrutiny. These conflicts and negotiations that the ministry was engaged in show that ugly buildings and filthy streets did not emerge from nowhere but were produced by the new state. While a sort of 'official sympathy' existed for the refugees and their plight, its translation into reality was seldom smooth.

WHO EMBODIES THE STATE?

Nanak Singh's letter also points to the ambiguity in the public perception as to *who* represented the state authority—government officials and the cabinet of ministers, or the leadership of the Congress party. The letter is addressed to the president of the AICC, pleading with him to intervene in a matter that is technically outside the jurisdiction of a political party. Both the Congress and the Congress-led government were actively engaged in resettlement work and each had its own organizational fronts operating in the public sphere. This is a significant point at which to explore the process of state formation and the efforts to induce public recognition of state authority. The dividing line between the two, it seems, lay in its approach to the resettlement work. While the state approached it as a matter of making administrative decisions and laying out effective policies, the party work, mostly led by women activists, approached it with an idealistic compassion that aimed at keeping the promises made to the people during the freedom struggle.

The 1947 Partition was a critical moment, not only in terms of altering the political geography of South Asia, but also in terms of state formation. The withdrawal of British administration saw the demise of the colonial state, following which the functions and power of the state were transferred to the dominions of India and Pakistan. The transfer can be seen at two levels: one, to take over administrative responsibilities and, two, to assume authority and legitimacy in the eyes of the subjects. The administration and day-to-day functioning of the government basically involved continuation of the colonial system, complete with its hierarchy, codes, and ideas of governance. The assumption of authority, on the other hand, involved 'performance of power' in the public sphere where it could be seen and then verified by the subjects. The authority was thus performed through public activities: for example the political leaders' visits (to the refugee camps, slums, residential colonies, factories, etc.) to hear the grievances of their constituents, addressing public gatherings, receiving petitions from the citizens during certain 'open hours',[49] writing recommendations to the bureaucrats to expedite certain pending matters of the petitioner, etc. If the officer concerned received a petitioner with a recommendation from a political leader favourably, the act amounted to acknowledgement of the leadership's authority. Such acts of authority had to be performed everyday by a number of actors, the sum of which translated into 'transfer of power'. While the first step was easy to climb, the second was an intricate web of negotiations between the ruler and the ruled.

If it is established that power is performed through public actions, then who performs it on behalf of the state? In other words, who inherited the power transferred from the colonial state? Was it the Indian National Congress (INC) or the cabinet of ministers, collective constituents of the Government of India (GOI)? Here the picture becomes blurred as far as refugee resettlement is concerned. The first body to be instituted specially for the 'riot sufferers and refugees from Pakistan'[50] was not the Ministry of Rehabilitation but the Central Relief Committee (CRC), which was founded by the All India Congress Committee (AICC) President, Acharya Kriplani, as early as 25 July 1947. Interestingly, the organization had two distinguished women leaders during the early years of resettlement. Sucheta Kriplani was its first organizing secretary in the period 1947–51 and she played a dominant role in the establishment and management of refugee camps. She was succeeded by Mridula Sarabhai, who was then leading a campaign to 'restore' abducted Hindu and Sikh women from Pakistan to India. The female leadership of the CRC testified to the common belief that links women with social work, that is, mothering the destitute and orphans, providing food and shelter. The relief activities and refugee camps became institutionalized symbols of traditional feminine functions—caring, nurturing, and managing private homes. Women, as camp leaders, primary-level teachers and first aid workers among others, fulfilled many functions in the refugee camps.

The ministry, on the other hand, was a male bastion even though it had similar functions to that of CRC in the early years. Later its functions got diversified while planning and developing refugee townships as part of the permanent rehabilitation efforts. The ministry controlled the purse strings to the funds earmarked for refugee welfare. The financial and policy making was, thus, an important characteristic of the ministry that set it apart from the CRC. But to a large extent, the activities of the ministry and the CRC frequently overlapped. Both these bodies worked so closely together that the differences were invisible to a layperson.

While the camps were officially established by the ministry, the CRC was responsible for organizing a number of programmes within the camps. The programmes included distribution of food, clothing and cash payments, and vocational training for the refugees, besides launching searches for missing persons in collaboration with the ministry. Of all these CRC activities, the best organized were the work centres set up in the four big camps in Delhi: Kingsway, Purana Qila, Pul Bangash, and Rajinder Nagar. The target group of these centres was refugee women who were taught embroidery, stitching, and tailoring among other skills. The skills were also used commercially to earn money for the upkeep of the women workers as well as the centre. Besides private buyers, the newly established 'Central Cottage Industries Emporium' in New Delhi was the main outlet for the articles produced at the refugee work centres. At Kingsway, the CRC established an industrial home[51] where refugees were trained in mechanical skills and also a production centre for sports goods.[52] The sports goods centre was closed in 1952, while the industrial home was handed over to the Indian Co-operative Union Limited in the same year.

That the relationship between CRC and the ministry was rather ambiguous is elucidated by a dispute concerning payment of dues in the years 1952–3. The claimant was a man called Ram Rakha, who described himself as a 'displaced person deserving sympathetic consideration'.[53] The dispute was with CRC over the construction of bathrooms and latrines in Purana Qila. Ram Rakha claimed a sum of Rs 12,600 while the CRC put the amount down to Rs 1967. To complicate the picture, there was another claimant, Kartar Singh, who had supplied construction material worth Rs 200 to Ram Rakha and had not been paid so far. While the parties concerned traded their respective claims through letters, notices and petitions, their correspondence also reveals the functioning of the administration. It turns out that there was more than one agency involved in this case, creating a situation where multiple authorities existed but each shirked the responsibility.

This dispute shows, on a different level, that the ministry often entrusted its work contracts to the CRC, thus bypassing the official state construction agency, the Public Works Department (PWD). As most of the work done by CRC was directed towards providing relief to the refugees, its construction projects were dealt with similarly. The recruitment or selection for such jobs was often arbitrary and based on personal connections. Ram Rakha was given the contract on compassionate grounds as this seemingly innocuous quarrel shows. A note prepared by CRC presents the arrangement as follows:

Under an agreement executed between the CRC and Lok Seva Sangh (LSS), all construction work for which the CRC secured contracts from the Ministry of Rehabilitation was passed to LSS for execution. LSS, in turn, engaged contractors for carrying out the work. So that the CRC is not bound to any claim or compose disputes of any contractor.[54]

As Sucheta Kriplani explains in a letter to Mridula Sarabhai:

Shri Ramadhar as secretary of LSS gave them (Ram Rakha) certain amount of work on an abatement as supervision charges. Out of this 10% abatement, 5% was to remain with CRC and 5% with LSS. Shri Ram Rakha later complained that he was suffering great loss and relief should be given to him. Shri Ramadhar being the then in-charge of the construction department recommended this case for reducing the abatement by 5½% amounting to a total of Rs 2200. Thus we sacrificed our share of the abatement plus 1½% and above it.[55]

When the CRC became irked by the pressure from Ram Rakha for further favourable allowances, Ramadhar reminded the committee, 'Ram Rakha is a refugee and that the main idea of giving him this contract was to enable him to earn something thereby. But actually he suffered a loss.'[56]

Ram Rakha not only got the contract on sympathetic grounds but continued to bargain, using his situation as a refugee, to gain more concessions from CRC. Nowhere in this correspondence is there any reference to any past experience or training that qualified him to fulfil the given contract. Clearly he approached the secretary of the Lok Sevak Sangh through personal connections and landed the contract without any competition from either refugee or non-refugee construction firms. Ram Rakha was not the only one who benefited from such arrangements. Sardar Kartar Singh, a Congress MLA from Delhi state and a 'refugee' from Lahore, supplied building material to Ram Rakha in this project. When Ram Rakha got embroiled in this feud with CRC and failed to pay his supplier, Kartar Singh used his influence with Congress committee and got the amount due to Ram Rakha stopped till he was paid off. Nevertheless Ram Rakha was recommended a final settlement of Rs 562 (in addition to the earlier offer of Rs 1967) in October 1953, even though his 'claim was found to be without any foundation.'[57]

It is fair to assume that Ram Rakha accepted the final offer because the matter, as far as the documentation was concerned, was closed after this date.

At a cursory glance, one could argue that ministry was the state agency while the CRC and its offshoots were the non-state actors. But the fact that both the state and non-state agencies had sprung from the Indian National Congress bridges this apparent gap. An exclusive Ministry for Relief and Rehabilitation was formed at the initiative of Jawaharlal Nehru, the indisputable leader of the Congress party and the new Prime Minister. The CRC had been formed by the Congress party president well before the Congress government had come into existence. Similarly, organizations like the Bharat Sevak Samaj[58] and the Punjab Relief Committee[59] were formed by Congressmen or their families. Both official and unofficial organizations facilitated each other's functioning as they were threaded together by the Congress link.

Though it is easy to establish this common link, it cannot be simply assumed that both the ministry and the non-state agencies were mirror images of each other. They duplicated many of their relief functions, but vastly differed in the matter of appearance. While the ministry provided the funds, planning and liaison with other government departments, and was answerable to the Parliament, the CRC and other such organizations actually 'performed' those functions in the refugee camps and the newly settled colonies. The CRC took on the role of a 'catalyst' that provoked the ministry on behalf of the refugees. It came to embody the 'official compassion' that became the hallmark of refugee resettlement. In Ram Rakha's case, it acted with compassion even when it was clear that he had made undue claims. The ordinary bureaucratic procedures were given short shrift at the CRC as the aim was to help the refugees.

The ministry also functioned with the same mandate but was open to scrutiny by Parliament and was bound by well-precedented bureaucratic practices. CRC had none of these constraints and thus presided over the resettlement process as the 'soul' of the state. In a number of cases it intervened on behalf of the refugees and insisted that the ministry look at the matter 'compassionately'. This amounted to the 'public performance' that suited both the state and the Congress party. The petitioners knew the leaders of CRC as highly respected Congressmen and women who then approached the government as representatives of the refugees. The ministry could seldom refuse the request that was forwarded by individuals, like Sucheta Kriplani, who had an impeccable reputation earned through the freedom struggle and public service. So, the rest of the 'Story of Rehabilitation' is a story of the various state agencies which looked upon refugees and their rehabilitation as an administrative task, and non-state agencies like CRC who became the conscience of the state in terms of refugee rehabilitation.

CONCLUSION

The prime outcome of this chapter is the establishment of active state involvement in the resettlement process. The evolving narrative in the following chapters is no longer centred around the refugees alone but also brings in the state as a major player in the process. The evidence of state participation is largely gained from official sources, particularly because the state remains curiously absent in the personal narratives of resettlement. The Indian state itself emerges as an intriguing theme of enquiry since the Partition migration and resettlement happened in the shadow of decolonization and the successful Indian freedom struggle. In mid-August 1947, the state moved from being 'colonial' to 'post-colonial'. The change therein was not limited merely to nomenclature but was also manifested in the reformist zeal with which the business of state was conducted henceforth. However, the enthusiasm visible among social workers and freedom fighters did not alter the fundamental structure of the Indian state. The basic structures of the colonial state remained largely intact in its post-colonial incarnation.

The discussion in this chapter also shows that state apparatus is not necessarily a congruent and coordinated unit but rather a conglomeration of various governmental agencies working autonomously towards common goals. The establishment of the Ministry of Relief and Rehabilitation was meant as an effort to centrally coordinate the resettlement process, but clearly the anticipated coordination did not always take place. Outside its own immediate jurisdiction, the ministry had to appeal to other ministries and government agencies to cooperate on the resettlement issues. The various circulars to the state governments and other ministries to, for example, give preference to refugees for employment, were issued as advice that these bodies were not bound to follow. The fact that these directives were followed is more due to the sympathy the refugees had gained and the influence of Jawaharlal Nehru, rather than the coordinative powers of the ministry. The presence of multiple state or state-sponsored agencies engaged in resettlement work and the frequent rehabilitation ministry–CRC negotiations also point to the diffused character of the state. Thus, an understanding of state as a seamless monolith is considerably misleading as shown through the policies and actions on resettlement.

The resettlement of the Partition refugees was the first challenge before the newly independent state. Many of the institutions engaged in the resettlement work were colonial entities that did not alter their outlook after the colonial withdrawal. The new institutions and organizations like the rehabilitation ministry and CRC, however, were different from their colonial counterparts. They displayed reformist zeal and an urgency to set the disorder right. This again was not a complete departure from the colonial legacy, where the administration would try and raise the local society to better moral standards.

Such an extraordinary event as Partition did not collapse the previous categories of class, caste and gender, since the principle of resettlement was compensation. The experiences of Savitri Puri compared to the witness of the Purana Qila conflict tell two completely different stories. One can safely surmise that the resettlement process separated the owners of capital (of any kind) from the non-owners. The class differences visible during the population movement became further entrenched when permanent housing projects were undertaken on such a basis. This ensured that refugees were reinvented in their old class order of social classification.

NOTES

1. Quoted from 'Some Thoughts on the Problems of Rehabilitation of Displaced Persons from Pakistan' drafted by L.C. Jain on 7 February 1948. Diwan Chaman Lall Private Paper Collection. NMML, New Delhi.
2. See Kamtekar's (1989) argument on breakdown of law and order during the communal violence.
3. This is a contested argument since nationalist historians like Nanda (1998) and Bipan Chandra et al. (1983) see the Congress-led anti-colonial movement as a mass-based popular resurgence of nationalist sentiment. The subaltern historians like Partha Chatterjee (1994), on the other hand, view the emergence of Indian nationalism vis-à-vis creation of a new national elite exposed to English education and western intellectual discourses.
4. This paternalistic approach to refugee resettlement is visible in contemporary instances as well. See for example Simon Turner's (2001) study on camp life in the UNHCR-run refugee camps for Burundian refugees in Tanzania, where the stay in the camp was used to experiment with new social arrangements.
5. The tables are constructed from the various figures given in the Annual Report 1947–48, Ministry of Relief and Rehabilitation (GOI 1947–48).
6. In most of the oral histories that I collected during my fieldwork, camp life was not described in such illuminating terms. The complexities involved in the organization, establishment, and management of the camps are far too lengthy to be discussed here.
7. 'Refugees should do useful work in camps', *Hindustan Times*, 12 September 1947.
8. It was not till after 15 August that any noticeable incidents of violence were reported in Delhi city. A detailed logbook was maintained from 21 August onwards, when an explosion took place in Shahdara due to a student trying to assemble a bomb at home. The massacre of Muslim labourers in Delhi Cloth Mills in Sadar Bazar took place in the first week of September. Nehru undertook a tour of the city on 6 September especially in Karol Bagh area following which a 24-hour curfew was imposed in Delhi (for details, see 'A day to day narrative of the disturbances which took place in Delhi in August and September 1947', File no. 21, G.D. Khosla Papers; and 'Nehru Tours City Riot Areas' main report in *Hindustan Times*, New Delhi, 7 September 1947.
9. See Raja Ghazanfar Ali's statement quoted in Rai (1965: 72).
10. M.K. Gandhi (1947) 'To the Protagonists of Pakistan', reproduced in Rai (1965: 73).

11. Front-page report in *The Times of India*, New Delhi, 25 August 1947.
12. Headlines cited from *Hindustan Times* (HT) and *The Times of India* (TOI), both published from New Delhi.
13. There are a number of cases where the Muslim citizens of Delhi moved to Pakistan only to return in a few weeks or months. Refer to cases like *Mohammad Din Chatriwala* v. *Custodian East Punjab, case no 46, CGR; Hasan Mian kala Sultan* v. *Additional Custodian, case no 51 CGR.* These cases pertained to the Muslims properties being declared abandoned and therefore liable for being taken over by Custodian General of Evacuee Property. Many people came back to find their properties confiscated, which resulted in court battles with the Custodian's office. In other cases, only one member of the family, mostly the male head, went to Pakistan to survey the place before migration. During his absence his property was declared 'evacuee property'. In such cases the wife and other dependants had to either vacate the house or contest the government notification. For an example, refer to *Ghulam Fatima* v. *Amar Singh*, decided by the Custodian General on 1 May 1949.
14. This excludes the activities of Red Cross volunteers who actively participated in the emergency relief distribution.
15. Constituent Assembly Debates, 7 February 1948, Question no. 149 placed by R.K. Sidhva to the Minister of Relief and Rehabilitation, page 375.
16. Syed Mohammad Husain (1954), 'The Laws and Practice Relating to Evacuee Property in India being Commentaries on the Administration of Evacuee Property Act, 1950 and Allied Acts' p. ix.
17. Administration of Evacuee Property Act, 1950, Ch. 1 (para1).
18. Ibid. Ch. 1 (para 2).
19. A few evacuees, though, did come back, as the records in the office of Custodian General suggest. There were several cases where litigation was taken course to for the restoration of property. For example, see *Mohammad Habibudin* vs *Government of Hyderabad, 1953, Hyderabad 157.*
20. Sourced from Constituent Assembly Debates, 30 March 1948, Question no. 1058 placed by Giani Gurmukh Singh Musafar to the Minister of Relief and Rehabilitation, p. 2739.
21. Derived from the population proportions.
22. All India Congress Committee (AICC) Records (2nd Instalment) File no. 3(XV).
23. Personal interview with H.K. Dhawan, a retired Assistant Custodian at the Minsitry of Relief and Rehabilitation on 15 December 2000.
24. This station is now called Old Delhi railway station near Kashmere Gate.
25. Personal interview with Kataria, a refugee from Dera Ismail Khan, conducted in December 2000.
26. Name changed.
27. Personal interview with Savitri Puri, 20 January 2002.
28. It could take longer than 15 years as I found during my fieldwork. In 2000 and 2001, I met several old refugee men and women who routinely came to the claim office to recover their dues. Most were not certain that their applications would succeed even after half a century but they continued their visits since it had become part of their routine.
29. See announcement from L. Durga Dass and Sons, File no. 73, Diwan Chaman Lall Papers, NMML.
30. See Rule 19 (2&3) of the Displaced Persons (Compensation and Rehabilitation) Rules 1955, by Dina Nath Nijhawan, New Delhi.
31. Personal interview with H.K. Dhawan, retired Assistant Custodian, conducted on 15 December 2000, New Delhi.

32. See Annual Report 1947–48, Ministry of Relief and Rehabilitation (GOI 1947–48: 33–4).
33. File no. 90(1) 54 -H1 (A) Ministry of Relief and Rehabilitation, 1954.
34. Ibid., emphasis added.
35. Ibid.
36. Ibid.
37. Ibid.
38. Several original allottees in the areas like Lajpat Nagar and Kingsway spoke of the poor conditions—lack of water and electricity supply—in the new colonies both during the survey and the interviews.
39. 'Settlement of Claims of Quarters at Purana Qila', File no RHB/122(2)/54, Ministry of Relief and Rehabilitation.
40. Ministry of Relief and Rehabilitation, letter dated 25 March 1954 in File no RHB/122(2)/54.
41. File no RHB/122(2)/54, letter dated 21 July 1954.
42. Note dated 11 August 1954.
43. File no RHB/122(2)/54, letter dated December 1955.
44. File no RHB /122(2)/54, letter dated December 1954.
45. The population density figures are calculated on the basis of data sourced from A. Bopegamage (1957: 82–3). The date of the compilation of data is not mentioned in the source but from the date of publication it can be deduced that the figures pertain to the mid-1950s situation in Delhi city.
46. One acre is equal to 4046 square meters.
47. The size pertains to the total plot area while the legally allowed built-up portion on each plot is no more than 60 per cent of the total area. Therefore, a plot of 100 square yards canr.ot have covered area of more than 60 square yards (50 sq m).
48. During my fieldwork survey, I met several refugees in various colonies of Lajpat Nagar who had lived in Purana Qila camp since 1948.
49. This practice of 'open hours' also known as 'morning *darshan*' was popularized by Jawaharlal Nehru where any member of the public could hand over a petition explaining his grievance against any office or person. The petitioners hoped for quick redress, having drawn the personal attention of the Prime Minister. The lawns of Teen Murti House in 1947 were thronged by hundreds of refugees every day, as recalled by many surviving refugees during my fieldwork.
50. AICC Records (Instalment II) 3 (XV) dated 4 September 1954.
51. AICC (Instalment II) File no. 3 (IV) dated 17 June 1952.
52. AICC (Instalment II) File no. G-38 (1) dated 1 July 1952.
53. From Ram Rakha to Mridula Sarabhai dated 1 April 1952: AICC (Instalment II) File 1A (Part IV)/1951–54.
54. 'Claims of Shri Ram Rakha, Contractor, against the Central Relief Committee', undated, File 1A (Part IV) 1951–54.
55. From Sucheta Kriplani to Mridula Sarabhai, dated 4 June 1952. Ibid.
56. 'Claim of Shri Ram Rakha, Contractor, against the Central Relief Committee', undated, ibid.
57. From Sucheta Kriplani to Balwantray Mehta, dated 22 October 1953, ibid.
58. Bharat Sevak Samaj, India Service Society was formed in 1952 by some Delhi Congressmen with Indira Gandhi as its Chairperson. The organization worked in the camps, slums, and the new resettlement colonies in Delhi.
59. Punjab Relief Committee was formed in 1948 for the benefit of Punjabi refugees in Delhi by Bhim Sen Sachar's wife.

5. Restoration of Loss

The narration of everyday past is enveloped in *moral evaluation*—that is, past events do not get narrated in isolation, but are constantly evaluated in terms of normative 'good' and 'bad' depending upon their outcome. The presentation and analysis of the narratives in this chapter operates within this invisible grid of morality and restoration. The theme of active state involvement in post-Partition resettlement continues in this chapter. While Chapter 4 established the state presence in the entire process of evacuating and housing the refugees, this chapter focuses on the social aspects of the state, as visible in the way refugees were separated, categorized, and then housed in Delhi by the government. The task of reordering the mass of refugees was guided by the prevalent social norms which the state authorities reproduced in their policies. It is only when the state is accepted as a social being that one can understand the different policy approaches that the state adopted towards widows and single women as compared to family units headed by patriarchs. Such multi-levelled approaches appear, however, as part of a single project that sought restoration of loss incurred during Partition.

This chapter concerns the multiple levels of *loss* experienced during the cataclysmic events of Partition and the state and non-state attempts towards *restoration* of such loss. The process of post-colonial state-formation in India was accompanied by an abrupt partition of territory, unprecedented inter-communal violence, loss of life/property, and mass displacement of people. The loss thus experienced must variously extend to the post-colonial state through loss of territory, inability to protect its subjects, and consequently loss of its claim to sovereignty. To the fleeing masses though, the loss was of homes, immovable property, and lives, as well as the loss of a familiar lifestyle. The sexual violence against women and abduction of 'our' women represents another sort of perceived intangible loss of honour—of the family, community, and the nation—seemingly considered irreparable.[1] The loss is experienced both at material and emotive levels that may or may not be publicly acknowledged by the victims.

Since *loss* dominates the violent upheavals of partition and migration, the policies and efforts towards resettlement can be seen as attempts towards *restoration of loss*. It can be seen as a 'coming to terms' strategy, whereby preoccupation with the *present* allows one to push back the traumatic *past*. Such a project of restoration can therefore be witnessed at differing levels of state, communities, families, and individuals. Each of these levels requires a multiple range of objectives and motivations, and each of them is complicated by conflicts around gender, class, and caste. The four levels are not necessarily isolated from one another; rather, they are interconnected through masculine notions of family, honour, and morality. It is in the multi-levelled and multi-propelled restorative project to check the displacement that we can see the subjective and value-based norms and traditions of social behaviour entering the lexicon of state policies. The 'social' being in the state becomes more pronounced and visible in the campsites and newly established colonies for migrants than in its official premises. It is not just the state intervening in private lives but also the private ideas of social organization and behaviour also influencing the response of the state.

While efforts at restoration by the state—through production of modern citizenship among the displaced population—have been explored in Chapter 4, this chapter focuses on the social, familial, and personal attempts at restoration. The state nevertheless continues to be a part of the narratives about to be told, especially through its non-recognition and discursive absence. There remains a curious gap in the narratives of resettlement told by the state and those recounted by the migrants: the state-run projects of resettlement appear prominently in the official accounts but rarely appear in the discourse of resettlement widespread among the migrants. The denial of state participation in the resettlement work is a popular theme among refugees, according to which 'they had not only (not) received a *pie* (1/256 of an old rupee) but had even refused it' (Keller 1975: 75). The quantitative survey conducted during fieldwork in this project, however, showed otherwise. More than 40 per cent of the respondents recalled having lived in a state-sponsored refugee camp and having received occupational support in terms of jobs and financial loans. In a survey conducted in the early 1970s in Delhi, four-fifths (79.7 per cent) of the respondents felt that the Government had helped them upon their arrival (ibid.). There is a lapse of more than 25 years between that survey and this one, and changed results show that the belief—of lack of state help—has gained wider currency over the years. This tension between the state and the refugees is one area of exploration in this chapter.

The second area hinges on the underlying basis of restoration where both the popularly acknowledged and unacknowledged attempts at restoration are shaped by a shared moral code derived from the prevalent social norms. The applicability of moral ideas is not uniform and visibly shifts around variables of gender, class, and caste. It will be argued here that it is moral codes and social norms that influenced both the state and the non-state attempts at resettlement of displaced population during Partition. The purpose of this chapter is not to use morality as a yardstick for making historical judgements, but rather to see how human moral codes are put to use and vigorously or cleverly circumvented while socially reordering the displaced people. Three narratives from different parts of Delhi will be used to show how single women on the one hand, and well-knit middle class families on the other, restored order to their lives. The state agency was present in all the cases but the power relation of the migrants with the state varied significantly. The outcomes of each of the three resettlement courses also differed dramatically.

Punjabi Pride and the 'Moral' Grid of Resettlement

The main argument that frames the following narratives is that the state and migrants were attempting to recreate, at different levels, 'the universe of moral obligation'[2] that was seemingly destroyed during the internecine violence and the unexpected movement during Partition. The mass of human refugees produced in the process needed to restore their losses in a manageable social order, and this is where the prevalent moral codes of social behaviour and organization crept silently into state policies. In the resettlement accounts told by the migrants, morality as a theme forms a permanent background against which all individual and collective actions are measured in hindsight. At an everyday normative level, subjective distinction between 'right' and 'wrong' form a moral grid that influences routine ordinary decisions. It is not surprising, therefore, that this moral grid appears even more prominently in the extraordinary event of displacement. Whether normative morals guided individual decisions in the immediate circumstances of displacement can be debated, but the following narratives will show that the flashback into one's personal history rests upon a kind of moral evaluation, wherein individuals often tend to debate with themselves about the rightness or wrongness of their actions at that time. In the Partition displacement of Punjabis, the most significant feature is the strong will to collect and restore the interruptions in their personal and familial lives. And more importantly, the restoration must take place in a just manner befitting Punjabi tradition. This belief is best articulated in a speech written by a Punjabi leader, Diwan Chaman Lall, who upon displacement made Delhi his home. The speech is called 'The Fate of the Punjabi Nation' and amply brings out the pride, a sense of injustice rendered to Punjabis, and a forward-looking attitude.

I heard one man say to another the other day: 'My friend, the Punjab deserves your sympathy.' As a Punjabee who witnessed the tragic horrors of Partition and the terror as well as bravery, dastardly acts and acts of heroism, a remark of this nature nauseated me. No Punjabee worth his salt wants anyone's sympathy. What the Punjabee wants is justice. We have not only been uprooted—seven million of us—but all that we cherished has been destroyed, the sanctity and refuge of our homes, the little soil most of us owned, whitened in the past with the sacred bones of our ancestors, the tradition of *mohalla*, the city, the village, the *biradari* and the leadership—all things which were part and parcel of our existence, nay, which made our existence endurable and pleasant and happy—all that is finished for us...The gravest problem of all is not to seek and obtain sympathy. The gravest problem is to reinstate the brave Punjabi nation as an integrated nation, restore it to its traditional ways of family and community life and make it once again the most prosperous and happy people they once were in their original homes. I am convinced that this is possible.[3]

This speech represents a defining feature of the ideas behind resettlement envisaged by the Punjabis themselves. First, there is a belief that injustice has been done to the community through forced displacement and, second, there exists a deep opposition to acceptance of charity or sympathy since it challenges the characteristic Punjabi pride. The destruction of homes, village life, traditions of mohalla and biradari exchanges are recounted as loss: 'all that is finished for us'. Despite the loss, Punjabis do not look for sympathy from others but look to their own resources to 'restore it [nation] to its traditional ways of family and community life'. At once, a range of losses become integrated with one another; personal loss contributes to the larger community loss, which is why restoration of personal loss becomes restoration of the lost community way of life. The evocation of 'justice' as a primary goal rather than achievement of sympathy underscores the moral uprightness the Punjabis have been elevated to through the experience of 'tragic horrors of Partition'. Experiences of injustice become a basis of moral elevation, and strategies towards restoration, an act of justice in themselves. Thus, even if they differ from the normative standards, restorative practices become a rendition of circumstantial morality.

Perplexing moral considerations often grow within an individual human sphere, but extend to organizational entities like the state as well. The public actions of the state are swathed in basic moral categories of vice and virtue. For example, the institution of the social welfare system that seeks to protect and enhance individual rights and public goods, provision of fair justice that punishes criminals and rewards law-abiding citizens, encouragement of public charity through tax exemption of charitable contributions, and active policing of activities deemed nefarious. The moral authority of the state is established through actions that prove it to be impartial, just, and even-handed. It is worth pondering why the single most publicly expressed complaint against the Indian state is set around allegations of corruption. An entire discourse of corruption and corrupting practices plaguing the Indian state has been noted in the recent writings on state in the India (Gupta 1995; Fuller and Benei 2000). The role of the Indian state during the 1993 riots in Mumbai and the investigations undertaken later stand as clear examples of vice/virtue, like the dual quality of the state or 'a deep and marked constitutive split between its sublime and profane dimensions' (Hansen 2000: 35). The significant point here is that the entity of the state not only makes a distinction between vice/virtue, but also visibly carries both value systems within itself. To establish and consolidate its public authority, it frequently travels between the two polarized values. As has been argued in the previous chapter, the distinct bodies of authority engaged in the resettlement work—the Indian government and the CRC—fulfilled dual versions of the same task of resettlement. At a popular perceptive level, the CRC showed the sublime face of governmental authority that allowed the gov-ernmental agencies to carry out profane activities.

The continuous flux inhabiting the modern Indian state derives much from the conceptual moments when the idea of a sovereign independent India was being formed. Partha Chatterjee (1986) has shown the constant tensions between the two moments in Indian national history: the moment of anticipation, when the nation was growing in its yet embryonic state, and the moment of arrival, when the actual birth of the nation took place. The anticipatory moment contained the vision of how the independent nation must be and the methods required to achieve it. Gandhi led an idealistic struggle against colonialism while awaiting the arrival of the nation. His ideas of social and state organization were built around the traditional Indian village model defined by self-contained rural economies that just produced enough for their local requirements. He was strongly opposed to machinery and saw the overall mechanization of the society as an evil of mass production, amassment of wealth, and a source of corruption in humankind. In the ideal society, the citizens produced and consumed locally and, as far as possible, practised ahimsa or non-violence in their everyday life at both structural and personal levels. The business of ordinary life in such a society was guided by the principle of satyagraha, or the pursuit of eternal truth where one's own conscience was the judge of one's actions. The ideal state envisioned by Gandhi was a revived version of 'Rama Rajya', the much revered mythical state led by the Hindu god-king, Rama, who was renowned for his exemplary moral conduct and just rule. The new state was to preside over such a society and would actively facilitate its existence.

The moment of arrival steered by Jawaharlal Nehru somehow altered this social vision and thus the role of state in social organization. The reality of governance was far different from imagining how governmental matters must be dealt with. The resulting tension becomes apparent in the way state decisions veered between attempts to erect the ideal nation-state and the immediate administrative demands that constantly challenged it. The stern and swift military action in 1947–8 undertaken by the Indian state against the princely states of Hyderabad and Kashmir, as part of territorial consolidation, clearly does not adhere to the ideals of non-violence and truthful pursuit. The recurring moral questions of right and wrong did not figure high on the agenda of the independent Indian state as they did when the acquisition of state power was a mere possibility. The strenuous struggle between Gandhi's moral politics and Nehru's pragmatic vision becomes a defining characteristic of the post-colonial Indian state. This inconsistency is revealed very prominently during the resettlement work, where the state frequently attempted a balancing act between morality and pragmatism in its policy decisions and their implementation. The same dichotomy between the moral and pragmatic approach becomes visible in family and community restorative efforts as well. The entire restoration—both state and non-state—is conducted on the moral grid of mythical traditions, normative beliefs, and the legacy of an ethically waged struggle for sovereign nationhood.

Three distinct narratives are constructed below around the theme of restoration to show the different strategies employed to make a home again in Delhi. The narratives accrue from the experiences of (1) the joint Hindu family, (2) the Arora biradari from Dera Ismail Khan, and (3) a widow with young children. Each account tries to reveal the intricacies and personal compulsions that led the individuals and groups to take the paths they did. The state is involved in each instance but the modes of involvement depart from each other, pointing to the dissimilar relationships the state had with different social groups.

'WITH THE WILL AND GRACE OF GOD'

Karol Bagh is one of the largest, unplanned commercial areas that took shape soon after 1947. Till the time of Partition it used to be a quiet suburban extension to the south-west of the walled city centre, mainly inhabited by middle class Muslim families.[4] The central artery of the area is called Hakim Ajmal Khan Road, named after one of the distinguished physicians of Delhi. This is now overpopulated with shops, impromptu bazaars on the sidewalks, and illegally parked vehicles in every nook and corner. The bazaar has spread in all directions and has become one of the biggest shopping sites in Delhi. The elegant 1930s-style bungalows have given way to large showrooms while many others have been carved up into several tiny shops. The teeming shoppers and the seasoned shopkeepers have together erased whatever past history the area may have had. The evidence of its past history, however small, hangs on the billboards of old shop fronts. If one walks around the area, one can still find several shops that have a sign saying 'established 1947'. Many businesses like Punjab Jewellers, [Rawal] Pindi restaurant, and Lahore Marts also give a clue through their names that their origin is somehow linked with Pakistan.

This is the only inkling that survives in visible terms, but otherwise everyone knows that the market was born after the Punjabi refugees started putting up random stalls in the area, selling anything. There are also many shops that were successful concerns in West Punjab but were shut down during Partition and were set up again in Karol Bagh.

One such well-known shop in the area is 'Krishan Lal Mehar Chand'[5] that sells silk materials and traditional wedding dresses for women. It is not unusual for middle class women in Delhi to advise the uninitiated to visit KLMC to buy silk saris and lengths of salwar kameez. The business in the shop is still conducted in the old style, where, customers, seated on an upraised platform, are shown delicately embroidered silk pieces. The sales-man has a couple of helpers who bring the wares to the exhibition space, fold the material again after it has been seen, return the rejected ones back to the neat shelves, and then take the selected pieces to an old wooden cash counter. The counter is placed next to a small shrine built in the wall housing Lakshmi and Ganesh, the Hindu deities of wealth and prosperity, as is customary in most shops. The old patriarch of the family, who is otherwise physically assisted everyday in his most simple activities, sits at the cash counter. He does not transact any business but ethics demand that he, as head of the family and the business, retain that position as long as he wishes. His oldest son and grandson sit in other parts of the shop and personally show material to long-standing customers or to those who look distinguished in some way.

The shop began figuring in my mind for more than its silk saris when I saw its old advertisement issued in a Lahore newspaper at the turn of the last century. Its reprint accompanied a nostalgic account written by an old Lahore resident who had moved to Delhi after Partition (see Neville 1998).[6] There was an entire story waiting to be told about a family business establishment that, just like millions of people, was displaced and successfully re-invented. It seemed part of the master narrative wherein displaced people had fought a variety of adversity and risks but had, through sheer hard work and persistence, found success. But the more I delved into the family story, the more it parted ways with the master narrative.

I began by directly approaching the old patriarch at the cash counter with the question that had been lurking in my mind: is this shop the same KLMC that had existed in the old city bazaar of Lahore? I received a very pleasant welcome since it is not uncommon that many third-generation customers, whose grandparents/parents had migrated to Delhi, also drop in for purchases. But my purpose was different. Nevertheless I was invited next morning, when customers are few, to talk to the oldest son who actually ran the business. Narayan Lal told me that he was six years old during Partition, and all that he knew was based on the family stories that are regularly recounted.

The business, now more than 160 years old, had achieved a good reputation in Lahore for selling imported luxury and Indian goods for women. The old patriarch, his father, was the oldest of five sons, and headed the business at the time of Partition, and the entire move had taken place under his guidance. His four other brothers had parted ways due to family disputes and set up separate enterprises in Delhi and Benaras after Partition. His family, mainly the women and children, had moved away from Lahore and to Benaras and Delhi long before the declaration of transfer of power was made on 3 June. He himself stayed behind to look after the property and retrieve their valuables. They were able to remove their entire belongings from the shop godown as well from their family house safely across what later became the border. They had received compensation for the immovable property that they had left behind and their bank accounts had also been transferred. Having given me a preliminary outline, he invited me home the following day when the shop was closed for the weekly off. When we met again, he began, to my surprise, with a series of complaints against the state and the unjust administrative 'system' that had made them suffer during Partition. From our previous day's conversation I had the impression that their story was not the same as told by many others who claimed that they came empty-handed in dangerous circumstances. So what was the complaint about? I was told that the family had to fight a legal battle in Delhi over its property in Lahore. It was not a story that I had come across before.

Our house was located in the city in Babian di Gali, a Hindu locality very close to Mochi Darwaza, a completely Muslim area. Our *haveli* [large house] had an internal corridor that connected the two areas but we kept it locked all the time. During riots, Muslim mischief-makers would throw bricks and sometimes tried to break in. I remember playing in that corridor. Our shop was very close by in the *bazaar*. Sometimes before Partition we bought a big house in Model Town area that had been newly developed; a lot of rich people from the city were buying houses there. I can't remember the number of rooms there but I could run there from room to room all day. It was a big house. But communal violence had started growing in the city and there were fierce debates in the family as what to do. My father's younger brother wanted to claim his share and move to Benaras, which is the big centre of silk *sari* weaving. But my father, as head of the family, decided that we would all move together. The question was how to move the huge stock lying in the shop safely without attracting too much public attention. So over several trips the most expensive stock was transferred in several instalments. When we moved out of the house we got police protection because we had several customers who were political leaders, like Khizar Hayat's (Tiwana) family. When the violence began in Lahore we always had protection, at least 12 police constables posted outside our house round the clock. My family knew some politicians. Then three months before we moved out we sold the house in Model Town and received an advance sum. But when we came to Delhi the buyer from Lahore made a legal claim to recover the advance amount. We said that we were refugees and had left everything behind, but the court in Delhi ruled that we had to return the amount.

The house in Model Town had been claimed as evacuated refugee property in Pakistan, and the transaction with the buyer had therefore never been fulfilled. It was not unfair that the buyer asked for the advance sum to be returned. But the movement from Lahore had created the idea that injustice had been meted out to those who were fleeing, and that somehow seemed to justify the claim to retain the advance sum. It was an ordinary sale of a house that took place during Partition. The argument put forward by the seller that 'they were now refugees' allowed them, in their view, to opt out of their ordinary universe of obligation. In this claim, the family had invoked the popular discourse associated with refugees of being with-out shelter, destitute, and incapable of looking after themselves. Their claim circumvented critical self-reflection that would easily distinguish them from the mass of refugees living in state-run campsites around Delhi. There was a clear expectation of special consideration on account of the circumstances. The fact that the court in Delhi took no note of it and ordered them to return the amount was interpreted as an act of injustice inflicted on them by the authorities. As this case shows, ideas of perceived injustice clearly differed depending on one's individual experiences during Partition.

The interviews were conducted at the family house located not very far from Karol Bagh in one of the post-Partition 'refugee' colonies called Rajinder Nagar. The area has two parts, called 'old' and 'new'. The old part is a former campsite where temporary sheds with one room and bathroom were constructed by the state for quick allotment in 1947–8. The houses here are cramped in narrow streets, each built over an area of no more than 100 square yards and shared by large families. Now the temporary sheds have been replaced by very narrow three-storeyed buildings by the successful second generation of migrants. The 'new' area was added in the 1950s and was obviously better planned. The land was developed here by the state and auctioned openly, where the migrants eligible for larger compensation could bid for them against the state-issued certificates of compensation. The houses here are spaciously built around public parks and well-lit broad streets. The two areas bearing the same name stand in contrast to each other. The Lal family lived in 'new' Rajinder Nagar in two large three-storeyed houses built wall-to-wall with each other, and occupied by the immediate members of the joint family. After an initial introduction to the family history by Narayan Lal, I was allowed to meet his father (88) and his uncle (82), who sat together during the day talking about the family and business affairs. The two families, as I had found out from Narayan, were not on the most cordial terms due to their differences in sharing the family inheritance. But a strong sense of traditional hierarchy meant that the father was still considered head of the joint family and given ritualised respect by both the families. This was obviously more pronounced in front of a stranger, when I met them together. The anger and sense of injustice felt by Narayan and expressed to me in private was conspicuously missing now. The focus was now on the commonly shared family story that had led them to Delhi.

A sort of mythical past narrated by the family elders created a collective space where nostalgia mixed with pride overrode the inner family differences. The story narrated had all the elements of a drama, a misty beginning roughly 160 years ago, followed by smooth sailing with the climax reached during Partition. The connecting thread running through the narration of a number of different events was the description of the extraordinary personal qualities of the forefathers and the older generation that had seen the entire family through various crises. The various events were recounted with a common preface in which the forefathers were praised repeatedly. I was told that the family was blessed for generations through the good karma earned by their ancestors. The third and fourth generation of sons had also imbibed the ritualized references to God and their ancestors and often repeated that it was 'with the grace of God' and the karma of their forefathers that they were successful.

With his older brother's permission. Narayan's elderly uncle Swaraj Ram repeated what I had already found out from Narayan earlier in the day. The family story began in Lahore city, where one of the ancestors, Krishan Lal, had a successful business in luxury clothing for women. He was described as being a kind, merciful, courageous, and morally upright man who helped the poor generously. He was known to have many times given away expensive shawls and woollen sweaters to beggars freezing in the winter cold during his daily morning walk on the banks of the river Ravi. His adopted son Mehar Chand was similarly a charitable person, who through his keen business sense brought further success. The establishment came to be known as Krishan Lal Mehar Chand after them. Narayan's father succeeded his own father, Mehar Chand, upon his death, some time before Partition. He had led the entire family through that transitional period from Pakistan to India.

It was interesting to find that between the two generations the crux of the narrative had not changed considerably: the account was not very dissimilar from what had been recounted earlier in the day. The only difference was in the details that decreased down the generations in naming the places in Pakistan, exact dates, or the relationships within the extended family. While the story line retained its original form, the place where the migration took place started appearing as an alien place as the events became more hurried when passed down from the first to fourth generation. It is not surprising that the descending generational difference produced sketchy accounts, since only those parts of oral histories remain intact that are repeatedly refreshed. In this case, the family success formed the repeated theme, not the description of the place where they came from. The larger events of Partition merely formed the background against which the older generation had displayed their political and commercial skill. The arrival in Delhi and the resettlement remained a question that was frequently avoided when it came to the issue of state compensation. The position maintained was that they never took anything from the state, but achieved material success through sheer hard work, skill, and vision. Swaraj Ram recounted the success story in the first-person narrative as an eyewitness and participant in the events.

We never took anything from the government. It is because God has always been kind to us. We bought a shop here and in Benaras and our business took off very well. It was due to the grace of God. We met kind people and everything became alright. Our ancestors' good *karma* kept us going. They were religious and charitable like Lala Mehar Chand. Whatever we have today is because of them. We are grateful to them. Their good deeds benefited us later. There was a movement started by the Congress to boycott foreign-made goods. And our shop only sold foreign products from England, Japan, China and all over. It was all imported. And the Congress said that Indians must boycott imported goods. The ladies [customers] had also started boycotting the shops selling foreign goods. And some were even setting the foreign goods on fire. Lala Mehar Chand was very religious and would say his prayers everyday and go to river Ravi every morning at 5.00. We have got this prosperity because of them. The money earned honestly always multiplies and doesn't vanish overnight. There is clear proof. Lala Mehar Chand was a very clever businessman so he decided not to offend the Congress and not lose his other customers at the same time. The shop had a front room and additional rooms in the basement for storage of extra stock. He instructed the servants to store the foreign-made stock in the basement, while the shop front was stocked with Indian goods. There was therefore no protest against our shop. The customers who wanted to buy foreign goods could ask in confidence and the goods from the basement were brought to them. If Lala Mehar Chand did not have this clever arrangement, then we would have suffered loss in business. It was all because of his clever business practices that we are here today.

The boycott movement that Swaraj Ram referred to was part of the Civil Disobedience movement pursued by the Congress under the leadership of Gandhi. In 1930, Gandhi called for a complete boycott of foreign goods in favour of homespun cotton cloth (khadi). He especially appealed to the women not only to reject foreign clothes but to actively campaign against them. Women did play a leading role in the campaign by organizing day-long vigils and protests outside shops selling foreign cloth. The campaign eventually became a mobilizational tool for women's participation in the larger national struggle for freedom, to the extent that 'women who had never stepped outside their homes, women who had stayed in *purdah*, young mothers, widows and unmarried girls became a familiar sight outside the…stores selling foreign cloth quietly but firmly persuading the customers to change their ways' (see Chandra et al. 1989: 276).[7]

A clear observation from this account would be that businessmen and shopkeepers kept a variety of political interests in good humour by not directly offending or challenging popular campaigns. It is not unusual for businesses to keep their direct commercial interests free from ideological constraints and to adopt a non-committal stance. What is more interesting is the constant invocation of a set of moral values like charity, kindness, and fairness against deliberate circumvention of another set of honest business practices and pursuit of truth in everyday transactions. The actions of an individual are weighed in moral terms that display positive qualities or a virtuous disposition, while those values that point to lack of honesty in public dealings are seen as astute business sense and not vice. The varied representations notwithstanding, the principal actor in the story is placed on elevated moral ground. It is clear that determination of moral rightfulness of an action is a regular part of everyday life, that is, all actions are viewed through normative moral lenses. The uncomfortable aspects that show moral failings may be cleverly skipped in narration, but they retain their space in the evaluation of daily life.

The interaction of the Lal family with the Indian state—both colonial and post-colonial—takes place in similar ways, that is, on a corresponding level where citizens are defined not through subjection but rather through negotiations. The uneven power equation between the state and the refugees in this case never appears, chiefly because the refugees concerned never attained a position of helplessness that defined a host of other refugees. The family was able to steer its assets and belongings through critical moments of history. This ensured that they never had to seek shelter, food, and other basic necessities from the state. This does not mean that the family did not take advantage of the governmental schemes of compensation, subsidized plots of land, etc. But its lack of helplessness allowed it to negotiate with the state from a power of strength. Such social groups were treated with much more dignity and respect by the state authorities than underprivileged groups. The process by which the family gained the present shop in Karol Bagh is an example of how influential migrants could turn adversity into profit. As Narayan Lal recounted,

Karol Bagh was a residential area where no commercial businesses were allowed. My father came to Karol Bagh in 1947 and saw that some refugees had already started selling merchandise on the pavements. Many refugee families were settling in this area since the Muslim inhabitants of the area had emigrated to Pakistan. My father saw big potential in the area and decided to set up shop here. He found a big house (where the shop is now located) owned by an old widow and he persuaded her to sell the house. She was reluctant but he somehow succeeded in convincing her to sell. The shop was established on the ground floor, while the first floor was rented out to a bank. The rents were very low in those days. Now the problem was that the municipality would not accept the shop as an authorized business because the area was residential. But one day, the wife of an officer (they were Bengalis) came to buy *saris* here and my father complained to the officer about his problem with the municipality. After all, we were refugees trying to set up our business again after all the disruptions. The government officials had been troubling us and were not being helpful. The officer said that it was very simple because he could get the area declared as commercial and that should solve the problem. The conversion charges would be around Rs 16000, but that would take care of the matter. He turned out to be an influential officer who could actually get this done without much delay. The property prices in the area shot up as soon as the area was declared commercial. We had bought it as a residential property, so we gained immensely from the conversion. The only problem is that the bank refuses to vacate the first floor even after fifty years of stay. And they still pay the same petty rent settled in 1948.

The process of establishing the shop shows that on the one hand the KLMC family had enough capital to allow them to purchase property in the city, and that they, on the other hand, invoked their refugee status, if required, to gain sympathetic consideration for their case. They were not dependent on the state for their daily subsistence but nevertheless used their refugee identity to extract concessions from it. Their acquaintance with state author-ity was not in the state/refugee dialectic; rather, they came across as being different from those refugees who lived under state protection in the refu-gee camps. Through such strategies—of establishing an independent livelihood—they were distancing themselves from the mass of refugees, yet becoming one of them, whenever strategically required. This allowed such migrants to approach the state from a position of power. The moral assessments tend to appear more prominently in the 'success' stories where the migrants not only regained the pre-Partition standards of living but also surpassed them considerably. A painful story of displacement has a curious happy ending that does not conform to the public and historical memory of trauma associated with Partition. This route of deviation—from alleged trauma to a normal happy life—needs to be explained not only to others, but also to oneself. The ethical correctness when inserted in the narrative becomes an effective tool capable for bridging the deviations. The point of the narrative then becomes twofold: one, to lay out the personal journeys travelled, in often distressing, extraordinary circumstances, and, two, to insist that the 'success' was achieved through virtuous means capable of standing public scrutiny even after half-a-century. The invocation of 'God' and his kindness becomes an encrypted explanation that places family success as being well-deserved and therefore not open to uncomfort-able enquiries. Any embarrassing details can, thus, be circumvented with a spiritual shield.

A similar 'blessed' instance of displacement is that of Diwan Chaman Lall, an influential Punjab politician and member of the Constituent Assembly, who was actively involved in the resettlement politics in Delhi. Upon his arrival in Delhi, he along with several other influential Punjabi refugees formed several associations such as the Refugee Protection Society and the Refugee Cooperative Housing Society. He was the patron of a multitude of organizations like the Federation of Displaced Persons Association, the Refugees Old Motor Parts Dealers Association, and the Punjab Refugee Society among others. At times, these associations were formed in conjunction with Punjabis established in Delhi long before Partition, like Sir Sobha Singh, the noted building contractor of Imperial New Delhi, who had little to do with the vagaries of Partition but was made the president of the Refugee Cooperative Housing Society.

A fresh wave of Punjabi migrants in Delhi had ensured a strong Punjabi presence in Delhi politics. As early as the 1951 elections, Punjabi refugee candidates were lobbying for seats as a group. Chaman Lall, who had been appointed as India's ambassador to Turkey, was unable to contest elections himself but lobbied hard within the Congress party to allocate a certain number of seats to Punjabi refugees. He submitted a list of 23 names, most of whom were from his own social class, and whose personal descriptions hardly fitted the archetypal refugees in the refugee camps because, first, most of them lived in non-refugee areas of New Delhi, and, second, many among them, like Sardar Ujjal Singh, were well-established political leaders from East Punjab, or well-established professionals and industrialists. Their descriptions included remarks like 'important refugee leader', 'refugee business magnate', 'important refugee industrialist', and 'refugee merchant from Sind'. Very few of them had a history of refugee-related direct experience in the refugee camps or otherwise, and their claim to the candidature accrued from 'the complete confidence' the refugees had in them.[8]

Diwan Chaman Lall, however, could hardly claim to have experienced what the common refugees were facing at that time. His entire movable property was retrieved from Pakistan through the offices of the Deputy High Commissioner for India and Pakistan, for which services he paid Rs 114 in all.[9] His immovable residential and agricultural properties in Lahore, Murree, and Bhera were negotiated for sale by a professional company that specialized in exchange and sale of refugee evacuee properties in India and Pakistan.[10] The firm was called Durga Dass and Sons, and it had offices both in India and Pakistan in the major cities. It seemed that this firm had steady business and a loyal clientele among the upper class Hindu, Muslim, and Sikh refugees. They had ready and fixed terms of commission in organizing such an exchange.

The terms and rates of commission clearly show that these property exchanges took place among an upper section of the pre-Partition Punjabi society. The rates were fixed with an authoritative knowledge of the ground realities and difficulties in making such deals. This indicates the experience and reputation the firm had acquired over just a few years since it was being patronized by well-established rich Punjabi families. The value of the properties considered for transaction, in hundreds of thousands of rupees, points to a wealthy clientele which had circumvented the route of obtaining compensation against lost property in Pakistan. The state compensation was likely to be far lower than the market value of the lost properties. Therefore, the most profitable strategy was to sell or exchange one's property through private firms outside the state apparatus. The trauma of displacement, thus, had to be confronted by the elite on a far different level than the ordinary refugees who had to come to terms with the material losses as well as emotional setbacks.

WRITING THE STATE OUT OF COMMUNITY HISTORY

While it was quite usual for refugees from big cities—Lahore, Rawalpindi, Peshawar, etc.—to make their life choices at an individual or familial level, those from small towns articulated their interests collectively, as formally organized communities. Two such examples of currently functioning community organizations that I followed in Delhi are Dera Ismail Khan Seva Samiti (DIKSS) and Jampur Welfare Association (JWA).[11] Besides the similarities in the goals and structures of the two organizations, the fundamental difference that makes them good examples for comparative analysis was that DIKSS was established in 1914 (that is, more than two decades before Partition), whereas JWA was formed just after Partition. The pre-history of DIKSS (that is, dating before Partition) makes it possible to follow the process of *community relocation*, while the formation of JWA is significant as a process of *community mobilization*. The difference in descriptive nomenclature—*seva samiti* and welfare organization—itself points to the differing characters of the two organizations. The name 'Seva Samiti' clearly refers to the organization's long-term orientation towards social service, while 'welfare association' suggests aggregation and articulation of immediate interests of the community. Through the first few decades after Partition, both the organizations were actively involved in enunciation of problems faced by the refugees from their respective towns. Since refugee resettlement is no longer an issue, current activities are geared towards consolidation of the community through intra-community marriages, celebration of religious rituals/fairs, and support to charitable causes.

Most introductions to hometown associations begin with the description of the place, the people, and the things/customs that people think make those places special. When I met Sushil Chaudhry, the president of the JWA, he described Jampur as a big bustling city in Pakistan. Like him, most other members of the association compared Jampur to other big cities like Lahore. The fact that I could not place Jampur in the map of big cities in Pakistan did not help either. It was only after poring through the volumes of the 'Imperial Gazetteer of India' that I could identify Jampur as a little known sub-division in district Dera Ghazi Khan in south-west Punjab. The Gazetteer describes the town of Jampur as

situated 32 miles south of Dera Ghazi Khan town. Population (1901) 5928. There is a considerable export of indigo to Multan and Sukkur and a good deal of lac turnery is carried on. The municipality was created in 1873. The income and expenditure during the ten years ending 1902–3 averaged Rs 10100 and Rs 9600 respectively. In 1903–4 the income was Rs 11500, chiefly from octroi; and the expenditure was Rs 12500. The town has an Anglo-vernacular middle school, maintained by the municipality, and a dispensary.[12]

The figures mentioned here are far from how a big city can be described. To make a quick comparison with Lahore, the population of Jampur in 1901 was 5928 (Lahore 186,884), the income of the town in 1902–3 was Rs 10,100 (Lahore average Rs 530,000), and expenditure in 1902–3 was Rs 9600 (Lahore Rs 510,000).[13] The point, however, is not about factual inaccuracy but about how people remember places. For the association members, Jampur remains a large, populous, and commercially active place. Though the memories of the town have ceased half-a-century later, to be the focal point of association, the younger generation is occasionally reminded of the place their grandparents/parents left behind. In their monthly newsletter, *Jampuri Patrika*, an occasional poem or article with reminiscences of Jampur is printed. The interesting feature of such articles is that they are reproduced from the old issues of the magazine dating back to the 1970s, since hardly any new pieces are written anymore. One such informative article is called 'O Children! Let me tell you the story of Jampur', originally printed in 1973 but reproduced in the 1998 annual number of the newsletter. In one-and-a-half pages, the writer tells the entire story of the town, the movement of Hindus, and resettlement.

The intriguing characteristic of this memoir is that while the town is described quite vividly, the events that led to the departure of Hindu residents are quickly skimmed over. In no more than four lines, the author informs the readers that 'we had to leave our province' and have since acquired respectability through jobs and houses. There is no mention of the Muslim residents of the 'province', though the 1941 population census reports record the majority of the population in district Dera Ghazi Khan as Muslims (88.1 per cent). In the sub-division of Jampur the total population in 1941 was 11,862 of which 7975 (67.23 per cent) were Muslims.[14]

The figure of 4000 for the Hindu population mentioned in the story comes close to the census figures, since there were hardly any other religious communities noted in the survey.[15] The Hindus are described as brothers who were united as a community with common social norms. They were knit together not only through kinship arrangements but also in business initiatives. They were enterprising, adventurous, and upwardly mobile people who did not give up hope in the face of adversity. Any remorse and bitterness at the turn of events in 1947 is glossed over rapidly and the focus is on becoming good citizens of the country.

The decision to migrate from places that had a minority Hindu/Sikh population was a common decision rather than an individual one. In Jampur, the decisive instant was when the influential men began leaving the town. There were reports of violent attacks but it was the departure of known families that spurred on the decision to leave. Once the decision to leave was made, traditional community leadership took over in making arrangements. In November 1947, many families took the refugee special train and finally arrived in early 1949 in Delhi. In between there were brief halts at Ferozepur, Bhiwani, and Panipat in Punjab, after which lack of opportunities brought them to Delhi.

Though the personal stories of hardship and moments of introspection are missing in the collective narratives, they do exist in private discourses that are not accessible to the public. Making inroads into that closed sphere is a challenge, requiring not only persistence but also at times confrontation with those seeking refuge behind the public discourse.

The north Delhi residential colony of Derawal Nagar is inhabited by refugees from Dera Ismail Khan (DI Khan) in NWFP in Pakistan. The colony was created as a cooperative housing scheme sanctioned by the government for the refugees from DI Khan in the late 1950s. The land here, as in many other group housing schemes like Gujranwala Town, was developed by the state and sold at nominal rates to the members of the DI Khan Sewa Samiti (DI Khan welfare society). Both the organization and the colony are named after the town from which the refugees hailed in Pakistan. In the middle of the colony, a temple has been built on the lines of the temple left behind in DI Khan. A community centre, a homeopathic dispensary, and a small library are attached to the temple where prominent members of the society gather every Sunday and on other days of religious importance. The society consists of upper caste Khatri families with a common descent in DI Khan, where most members are part of the same kinship networks. Though organized as an open, democratic organization with a working committee, executive committee, a written constitution with aims and objectives, and a periodic newsletter for its members, it is obvious that membership is bound together by caste and religious norms that go beyond the prime condition of past domicile in DI Khan. The collective narration that follows was presided over by Leela Ram Wadhwa (b. 1919) and K.K. Pahwa (b. 1926),[16] the patriarchs who spoke for everyone else. Their voices were supplemented by others but never contradicted or challenged. Leela Ram as president and Pahwa as his deputy set the parameters in terms of tone, forms of address, and the body of thought meant to be conveyed, not only to me as the interviewer, but also to the younger members of the society who had only heard of these stories as children. The field of enquiry covered the familiar ground of the last journey from Pakistan and the rebuilding of homes and lives in this north Delhi suburb.

One of the first popular beliefs that was challenged with this narrative was the ethnic description of refugees as 'Punjabis'. Leela Ram described himself and the group as Hindu Pathans with a distinct Derawali/Frontier identity. But curiously, this was not a kind of initial definition that preceded the rest of the account, but rather an insistence that they were Punjabis just like everybody else even though they spoke a different language/dialect from the Punjabis from the plains. The issue was skirted for quite a long time, till he started talking about the allotment of land to refugee housing societies, wherein he felt that 'Punjabis' had got prime tracts of land while the refugees from DI Khan had to make do with left-over wasteland in north Delhi. This, he continued, happened despite the fact that the Rehabilitation Minister at the time of allotment was Mehar Chand Khanna from DI Khan. At some level, the discontent simmers but the wider identity of being a Punjabi refugee has been accommodated, though efforts to educate the younger generations about their special history have been renewed by the society through various community activities.

The recollections were peppered with a nostalgic tour of district DI Khan where Hindus formed no more than 10 per cent of the total population of 298,131.[17] The town of DI Khan was described as the town of temples, the 'Kashi of Frontier'[18] where Hindus lived respectably in one half of the town while Muslims occupied the rest. The town was a trading junction and the last point of transit for goods on the way to Afghanistan and Central Asia. Most Hindus and Sikhs were traders by professions and had substantial landholdings; almost all of them vaguely described their families as being 'well-to-do'. This self-perception about their socio-economic profile in pre-Partition Punjab and NWFP is echoed elsewhere as well (Randhawa 1954; Fox 1985), where they are described as 'urban, lower/middle class whose main occupations were that of merchants, bankers, moneylenders, professionals and teachers' (Fox 1985).[19] The urban-middle class profile of the incoming refugees is further confirmed in a number of quantitative studies conducted later in Delhi city (Rao and Desai 1965).

It is clear that the community networks, whether formally organized like the DI Khan Seva Samiti or loosely structured like the JWA, were well-knit social bodies organized around caste and class lines much before Partition. The community leaders, mostly well-off traders or traditional wealthy men exclusively classed as '*rais*' (Jaffrelot 2000), led the movement by organizing relief measures during evacuation and later organized the community members upon their arrival in Delhi. The reorganization of the community was effected through the modern terminology and mechanism of 'cooperatives' that the Indian state was pursuing vigorously at that time.[20] As a collective body, a group of migrants hailing from a specific place in Pakistan were eligible to apply for land at nominal rates. A quick glance around Delhi shows a list of residential localities named after towns left behind in Pakistan: Gujranwala Town, Multan Nagar, Kohat Enclave, Derawal Nagar, and Punjabi Bagh, to name a few. The last-named colony, however, does not relate to any place but assumes the identity label describing ethnicity. This too began as a society with membership of migrants from a variety of places in West Punjab. While resettlement became easier for individuals as a collective body, it was restrictive in many ways. Only those migrants were allowed 'in' that fitted the description class- and caste-wise.

While the background of the community and its glorious past in DI Khan was illustrated with examples from Leela Ram's and Pahwa's family histories, they turned to P.L. Kataria (b. 1934) to describe their struggle after forced migration from DI Khan. Kataria told me that he had travelled in a crowded train along with his family and arrived at Delhi railway station where his family was given refugee registration numbers and a place to live in Hudson Lines barracks in Kingsway Camp. He had to do odd jobs for survival, like selling vegetables, manual labour, or filling up ration forms for illiterate refugees upon their arrival in Delhi. Then Kataria got a job in the army, and later in a government department as a clerk, from where he had recently retired. All this was told without any vivid recollections or silent pauses that are so closely associated with narration of personal histories.[21] One could perhaps consider it as an example of the gendered mode of narration of personal histories. Or was it an inevitable pitfall of collective narration presided over by community patriarchs, where the narratives become repetitive, well-rehearsed, and ritualized? In any case, vivid details were considered irrelevant by the group, where the idea seemed to be to construct an account that reiterated the earlier stated unique characteristics of the community such as *gairat* (pride or self-respect), ability to work hard, and loyalty (like their Muslim Pathan counterparts). But an insistence on hearing the irrelevant details produced confusion and impatience and even friendly warnings of failing to see the wood for the trees. .

Kataria's story was one of the oft-heard stories about the refugees who came empty-handed and rebuilt their lives from scratch. This was the celebration of the true human spirit embodied in the refugees and enacted a million times after Partition. While it is not always possible to challenge stereotypes, it is possible to construct a fuller and a unique individual account by asking for finer details. Kataria's family was settled in Hudson Lines, an area reserved for self-supporting refugees, suggesting that they did not come entirely empty handed and had some means to fall back upon. It was still not clear as to why Pahwa and Leela Ram turned away from their personal life stories to fill in the last journey from DI Khan to Delhi. How did they experience that mythical journey and why were they reluctant to narrate it?

Leela Ram described his story as irrelevant, in no way connected with my research on refugees. The prime reason was that he had migrated to Delhi in 1946, long before the Partition occurred. He further narrated that his

family was long established in trading business in DI Khan. In 1936 some British officers distributed a pamphlet asking the Hindus in DI Khan to choose a place where they would like to migrate in the event of Partition between India and Pakistan. So, my father chose Delhi while many others chose other Hindu cities like Lahore and Amritsar in Punjab. Finally, in 1946 my father sent me to Delhi to purchase a shop and establish independent business. When the trouble started in Punjab, the rest of my family moved here as well. We later helped many others from DI Khan to move here and organized relief for them.

Surely, Leela Ram's experience was quite different from Kataria's in that he had made that journey long before anyone else had anticipated Partition. Even though it is difficult to locate the 'pamphlet distributed by British officers' along with any such known historical event, it is clear that some people were definitely entertaining the thought of leaving for perceived safer areas. The date ascribed to the distribution of the pamphlet is historically inaccurate because it was in 1936 that the idea of Pakistan was first generated by a group of Indian Muslim students at Oxford. The idea was never taken seriously until Jinnah reincarnated it as the famous 'two nation theory' in 1940 at Lahore. So the question of making a choice between India and Pakistan in 1936 simply does not arise. Pahwa, on the other hand, recalled the efforts that he undertook to locate his younger brother in DI Khan, while most of his family had already moved to Alwar and Delhi in the month of April 1947. He was 21 years old at that time and had to stay behind to look after the family property and to evacuate his brother.

The superintendent of police was a Muslim officer who would not allow us to take anything away. I had to negotiate with him for everything and we were not feeling safe even in our own house. As the situation worsened we decided to leave. We bought two plane tickets and flew to Delhi where we already had family.

Pahwa's story was also 'different' in that he flew down to safety and did not intimately know the perils of travelling on trains or other more common modes of travel. When asked about the 'Partition journey', he would normally refer to widespread narratives but never his own. Both he and Leela Ram described their migratory experiences as irrelevant and then pointed to others who had experienced the more popular modes of journey. In a way, they seemed compelled to attune their experiences to the better-known ones, as if they had been robbed of the glory attached to the popular narratives.

From these narratives, it is clear that there was more than one form of capital that the refugees had accumulated and transplanted to Delhi. If one proceeds with Bourdieu's (1984) identification of types of capitals (as described earlier) and the process by which they are obtained, then one can understand why some refugees needed state support while others did not. This means that personal wealth when combined with education and networks of social-political influence in most circumstances afforded the bearer of capitals immense power of negotiation. Even for someone like Kataria, whose personal narrative came closest to the popular ones, the journey to resettlement was more complicated than the popular accounts. From his account, one can hazard a guess that his family belonged to the latter group not only in terms of some savings transformed as financial capital, but also in terms of capital gained through education which enabled him to earn a living and maintain his self-supporting status. The profits earned from such in/visible capital enabled many like him to retain their self-respect and male pride that later formed the basis for some of the mythical accounts about refugees.

Another finer detail that challenged the popular refugee perception was the account of his efforts at gaining employment. The initial phase, where he had attempted odd jobs, was full of minor anecdotes and related episodes, whereas the latter part where he gained a permanent job was bereft of any description. It was presumed to be too ordinary to mention, as it had little to do with the general theme of struggle successfully waged by the refugees. The details of state assistance could tarnish the long-established glory since Kataria had benefited from the relaxed rules and employment policy practices of the government. The government had announced a number of provisions concerning refugee employment as early as 1948 (see GOI 1947–48).[22] These included an increase in age limit for application to state jobs from 25 to 40 for the refugees, and a lenient view of educational qualifications. The latter included treating a candidate who had failed Class 10 or passed Class 8 as equivalent of a matriculate; the creation of employment exchanges or job data banks for the refugees; work training centres within refugee camps, for example in Kingsway and Arab-ki-Sarai;[23] exemption of training requirements for teachers (Saxena 1950: 51);[24] and the establishment of transfer bureaus for refugees who were previously employed by the state and were now displaced from Pakistan and sought new jobs. Those students who could not sit for their exams due to violent disturbances were given certificates in lieu of social service rendered in refugee camps. These certificates could then be used to strengthen claims for employment or admission to educational institutions. In April 1948, the Ministry of Rehabilitation asked the state governments to reserve all the vacancies created by the displacement of Muslims for displaced persons (Saxena 1950: 51). The Ministry of Railways even agreed to reserve 15,000 vacancies in grades III–IV for displaced people, while the Ministry of Industry and Supply agreed to allot additional quotas of steel to create greater employment opportunities for them (ibid.: 42).

For displaced teachers there were ample employment opportunities in schools being established for refugee children. For purposes of recruitment by the Union and State Public Service Commissions, the prescribed age-limits were invariably relaxed in favour of refugee candidates. The total number displaced persons thus absorbed in the different services have been placed in the neighbourhood of 80,000 (up till end 1948) (Rao 1967: 64).

Even the provincial governments had agreed to give job preference to displaced persons.

Two observations can be made: first, that those narratives which do not adhere to the master narrative seldom get offered in public and, second, the former refugees are reluctant to recognize the state efforts to afford them privileges in jobs and other such opportunities. Both these tendencies help construct a larger-than-life persona of the Punjabi refugee who travelled a self-instructed arduous path towards resettlement. The distinctions between the personal accounts told by Leela Ram and Kataria, for instance, point to such pervasive dichotomy, where Leela Ram felt constrained in fully narrating his own experience and had to turn to Kataria to tell the 'authentic' story. It seems that the accounts (such as Leela Ram's) are not that exceptional after all, because for every 'authentic' story, an exception also makes an appearance. Such appearances are more frequent than possibly acknowledged before. Similarly, state intervention in securing jobs and other opportunities is not reflected in the popular accounts, though there is plenty of evidence in official records that points to the aid offered by the government.

Encamping Widows

The intricacies of camp establishment can hardly be judged from the official narrative that presents the layout and functioning of the camps in uncomplicated terms. To begin with, the camps were not established on a single all-purpose format, even though the Kurukshetra camp is described as the model for all other camp establishments. The popular alternate model was the self-supporting type where those refugees who could support themselves financially were housed. As mentioned earlier, the distinction between the state-dependent and self-supporting types was made right from the beginning, when the refugees arrived in Delhi. At the refugee registration centre near Delhi railway station, the refugees would be asked if they needed free rations from the government or whether they had their own means of support.[25] This classification had an administratively convenient logic: the distribution of rations could be organized more easily if the targeted recipients were housed together. Both these arrangements— state-dependence and self-support—worked in a familial framework wherein nuclear/joint units were either headed by male members or at least had adult male members. As will follow below, a separate arrangement was devised by the state authorities for the female-headed households, basically families looked after by young widows with small children.

The class-based distinction afforded by such early compartmentalization was further fine-tuned when the gender-based classification was introduced around the same time. A large number of women had been widowed, orphaned, or separated from their families during the violence. This stratum of refugees was different from other young female refugees variously noted in recent studies of women victims of the Partition who appear as 'abducted women' whose fate was constantly negotiated between the two governments (Major 1998; Menon 1998; Butalia 1998). Many such women—who had nowhere else to go—were upon their official 'recovery' sent to state-run homes where they could lead quiet lives. Unlike the abducted women, the widows could not be put up in state-run homes with other abducted and now 'restored' women since they often had small children to support. While their families did not, for reasons of social ignominy and stigma, easily accept the abducted women, the widows often had no family left to support them. But the treatment of these two types of displaced women by the authorities was not that different, though care was taken not to house them together.

A novel way was found to settle the widows by establishing a whole separate refugee colony with detached one-room houses in south Delhi. It was neither a camp nor an independent residential area but a secluded and protected space created as a temporary arrangement where young refugee women and their children came to live. The obvious question to ask is what rationalities prompted the government to separate widows and other single women from the rest of the refugee population? The frail administrative ground—of separating state dependants and self-supporting refugees for easier ration distribution—hardly explains why women had to be separated from men in similar circumstances. The plausible answer seems more to do with normative ideas of gender positions in society that could not be altered even in the cataclysmic event of displacement.

It was while conducting a door-to-door survey in Lajpat Nagar area that I heard of this unique 'widow colony' as it is known locally. The localities in the area—Nirmal Puri, Old Double Storey quarters—that became my field site for many months, are some of the several lower-middle class colonies built by the government through the 1950s for allotment to refugee families. Most refugees in this area had moved into the state-built one/two room apartments directly from the camps. The families living there had either one grandparent or sometimes both, who would be the spokesperson(s) to tell the family story.

I heard about the allotments to families headed by widows for the first time when I talked to Yashwanti Mehta's family.[26] The present head of the family, a 50-year-old man, told me that the apartment had been allotted to his mother in the 'widow quota'. When I spoke to 76-year-old Yashwanti, she told me about the unique colony for widows where she had lived for 20 years after moving from Lahore. When her son grew up he refused to live in the colony any more because there was stigma attached to the place, since widowhood is a fate often considered worse than death.[27] The marriage rituals in Punjab require that widows be kept away, failing which a similar fate (of widowhood) would befall the newly wed bride. One consequence of living there was that her son could not find a bride for himself, as no one would marry their daughter into a location where she had to live in the shadow of collective widowhood. At the same time the government was willing to offer alternative accommodation to those widow-headed families where male children had grown up and taken charge of the household. So Yashwanti's family was allotted this apartment in an ordinary refugee colony, her son got married, and he now had grown-up children himself.

Soon the story told by Yashwanti became a sort of pattern as I went around in the area. There were a number of families where either mothers or mothers-in-law had been instrumental in getting the apartment for the family when the male children in the family had grown up. But an obvious concern that followed was about those families where there was no male child. What sort of movement pattern did they follow? I was told that those families did not move out at all because the daughters would grow up, get married, and go away. Did the mothers follow them? No, they did not. It was not often that sons-in-law would want to have them stay with the family. This meant that the temporary housing arrangement from 1947 still existed half-a-century later. I now had a matchless opportunity to actually 'see' a campsite in its living form, since most other sites had been rebuilt over the decades as private houses or as apartment buildings by the government. But this colony, I was told, was still undeveloped and therefore retained its original contours. It had, however, acquired an official name as a colony—Kasturba Niketan[28]—so that the residents could be listed on the municipal electoral rolls of the area.

I was told that reaching the place would not be difficult at all, as everyone in the area knew it well. It was then that I discovered the unofficial name of the colony, that is, *vidhwa colony*, or 'widow colony'. While no one could point out Kasturba Niketan, I was easily led there when I explained that it is a place where widows were settled after the Partition of India. It was a vast open space dotted with several one-room accommodations painted in a light yellow colour that usually marks most government properties in India. What separated this colony from the rest of the crowded Lajpat Nagar area was the high boundary wall topped with barbed wire. Several parts of the wall had crumbled over the years, and barbed wire could barely shield the place any more. But it still served its purpose as a visible marker that separated this colony from the 'ordinary' residential spaces in the area.

Once in the colony, the task was to approach the residents and hear about their experience of movement and their lives in this open barricaded space. The entire process of approaching them, explaining the purpose of my visit, gaining their confidence and gathering stories and accounts was cut short considerably, as I found to my surprise. I approached a group of elderly women in white[29] sitting outside in the warm November sun and introduced myself. They did not need to be persuaded to speak, unlike the residents in the 'normal' colonies, and they readily agreed to talk to me. This response was quite different from what I had experienced in the last four months, where most of the time prospective respondents had be convinced of the credentials of the interviewers and the usefulness of the project. It was only towards the end of the day that I realized that these women were quite used to interventions from strangers like government officials, surveyors, social workers, and political activists. My position as a stranger seeking clues to their life experiences and journeys was not extraordinary. They were used to it, as their everyday lives had been linked for the last five decades with such strangers.

I was invited the next day again for a lengthy session, when Rajrani told me her personal story.[30] She lived in Lahore city with her husband who worked as a rail mechanic at the time of Partition. She belonged to a family of cloth sellers in Gujranwala, was married off at the age of 16 and had two daughters by the age of 21. In 1947, her husband died of a sudden heart attack and she was left to fend for herself with very little savings to rely upon. As the summer violence spread in Lahore and surrounding areas, she decided to leave the city along with some of her relatives. After a short stay in Amritsar, their first destination, the family left for Delhi, which was rumoured to be full of a variety of opportunities. She lived along with her daughters in a house rented by her relatives. But after a couple of months she felt unwelcome in the house, as she and her daughters were considered a source of trouble by both the male and female members of the family. The male relatives looked upon them as liabilities since they had to 'protect' additional number of females in these chaotic times, while the female relatives found problems at the household level—sharing of daily chores, distribution of food among children, and a burden on the meagre resources. In November, her uncle found out that the government had started a housing scheme for widows and suggested to Rajrani that she apply for separate housing. The problem was that the death of her husband was not directly related to the communal violence and she was therefore not really eligible for that scheme. But her uncle insisted that she should suppress the cause of her husband's death and make an application.

Soon it became clear that waiting for the processing of applications in ordinary bureaucratic course was a futile course. An alternative option was found, as Rajrani told me:

My uncle had heard that every morning Nehru held a public *durbar* [audience] where he listened to complaints and received petitions from ordinary people. Next morning he took me to Nehru's house and we sat along with hundreds of other refugees on the lawns. Nehru was known for his compassion and sense of justice and that is why all the people were there to present their appeals. He never sent back any refugee empty-handed from his door. When I saw Nehru I went up to him with folded hands and told him that I was a widow with two daughters to take care of. I had nowhere to go and my relatives did not want me any longer. He asked me if I was literate and could work. I said I had been to primary school and the only work I could do was tailoring, embroidery and knitting. He told me not to worry and right there told an officer to allot me accommodation in Kasturba Niketan. Now the officers could not refuse because they had Nehru's orders. I moved to this house that winter and I got employment as an apprentice tailor like other young widows. My uncle and his family were only too relieved that I along with my daughters was not their responsibility any more.

The establishment of independent widow-headed households was a bold venture but what made it exceptional was that the state was actively encouraging it. There was a reformist streak in the way the state encouraged women to explore livelihood strategies and lead independent lives. But what did this state-induced autonomy mean in social terms? Did it mean that the state sought to reverse gender relations within the families and society? The difference between the symbolism of independent female-headed households and its translation into concrete social terms lay in the organization of the colony.

The colony was not like one can see today. It was like an *ashram* [retreat for ascetics] with a central building that had a common kitchen, school for children, work centre and office. The houses were built around it. Widows with less than five children got one-room accommodation, while those with more than five children got two rooms. We were not allowed to cook separately. Three times a day, a bell would ring to announce meals and we would all run and queue up with our plates in the kitchen. The residents took turns in cooking and serving week by week. In the morning the children would go to the school while the mothers would go to the work centre for stitching, knitting, etc. We could not go out of the colony without the permission of the *Behenjis* (female social workers). The whole area was barricaded with high walls and barbed wires for the protection of women. No men were allowed in at all. We could receive visitors in the main visiting room, where a guard and a *Behenji* would make sure that no mischief took place. Over the years some rules changed, like we were allowed to cook and go out in groups on our own. A food and cloth ration shop was established within the colony so that we did not have to go out. It was very convenient for the women. But when the children grew up and boys became men, the rules for male visitors had to be changed. We could not have thrown out our grown-up sons. And if they could live here, then why could our male relatives not come in? My daughters went to school here and learnt to cook and sew. They were beautiful and well brought-up so they got married in good families. One lives in Delhi and the other lives in the USA. They are well-off and happy in their homes.[31]

It is clear that the protective features of the Hindu joint family organization formed the basis of this colony set-up. The difference here was that the state authority determined and enforced the norms in the colony, rather than the dominant male members who usually lay down terms in families. The defining characteristic was the physical and normative *protective seclusion* of widows, concretized by walled boundaries, restricted movement, and a strictly enforced personal code of conduct. Such an arrangement is not unusual within families where the conduct and movement of unattached female members is constantly monitored and controlled. A large part of the family rules are aimed at establishing control of female sexuality, which is inevitably linked to issues of reproduction, family honour, and social stigma. Reproductivity is strategically governed through marriage alliances within the community, and female sexuality therefore needs to be kept under social gaze to avoid any unintended and socially unsanctioned reproduction. While their families guard unmarried women till they are given away in marriage, the rules become more complicated for the young widows. It is no longer a question of sexual control. Widowhood suggests inauspicious womanhood that other female members of the family need to be warned against, and kept away from.[32] Besides the need for protection that applies to all women in their fertile years, seclusion needs to be additionally enforced on the widows. Not only are they unattached, but they are also considered symbols of misfortune from whose shadow other women must keep away.

It is quite significant that here the state agency appropriates the task of enforcement which otherwise lies in the domain of families. The agenda of social reforms in the state policies of resettlement, if any, is limited to bringing women within the labour-intensive, income-generating sphere. The basis of social organization not only remains the same, but becomes institutionalized through state policies. The social policing is conducted by state agencies and social workers instead of family members. The creation of such a landscape in the colony points to the state-performed *restoration of social routines* that had been disrupted or threatened during the violent upheavals.

NEGOTIATING WITH THE STATE—FAMILY, BIRADARI, AND WOMEN

The three cases discussed here should be seen in a comparative frame and not in isolation from one another. At a broader level, the stories told in individual instances are quite similar: they talk about the circumstances that led to their displacement and their separate journeys to Delhi which led to their inhabitation in a single city. At deeper levels, however, the stories appear far removed from each other in their circumstances, strategies and subsequent outcomes. What simultaneously distinguishes and unites the three accounts are the techniques of negotiation vis-à-vis the state that individuals, families, and groups could employ to restore their ordinary lives. In some cases, these even turn the project of restoration into a considerable social profit, meaning the acquisition of a better social status than the one held before Partition.

The different social positions held—by the KLMC family, the DI Khan Society, and Rajrani—determined their power of negotiation with the state authorities. It may be surmised that the level of independence from the state in socio-economic terms determined their negotiating power vis-à-vis the state. Such independence was, in turn, entwined with the pre-Partition social positions held by the migrants. The wealthy, the educated middle classes, and government employees had better prospects of being self-supporting migrants. Those migrants whose source of income was disrupted during movement had to depend on state support till they could re-establish their means of livelihood. And last of all, there were those who had no prospects of gaining any income or wealth to support them. These migrants had to depend entirely upon state largesse to subsist. In all circumstances, there remained a possibility of gaining compensation against the immovable property left in Pakistan, which could free the state-dependent migrants and enable them to gain their independence. In Rajrani's case, this did not seem like a possibility because she lived in a rented house with her husband and this did not make her eligible for any substantial compensation.

The power to negotiate with the state seemingly accrues from (1) personal wealth and social prestige held in pre-Partition days and transferred upon migration, and (2) aggregation and articulation of collective community interest. Most members of the government and the institutions of state came from the wealthy or educated middle class, which made the task of negotiations between migrants and the various state authorities easier. Since the negotiating parties were more or less equal, the outcome was much more profitable for the migrants. The techniques of negotiations between equal parties are different from those where one party is beholden or indebted to the other. The techniques of appeals and prayers do not figure here prominently to bring about concessions and privileges from the state. The demands are seen as obvious and just, ones that should be met. The process by which the KLMC family set up their business in Karol Bagh is a case in point. The shop needed to be authorized by the municipality as a legitimate commercial venture, failing which the business had to be relocated in a recognized commercial area. Since this would have been bad for business, they chose to negotiate with the state authorities to declare the entire area as commercial. This allowed them to make huge profits since they had bought the property at low residential rates instead of investing huge sums of money in buying property in a regular commercial area. This could not have been attained without them invoking their refugee status.

Another good example is a scheme of loans provided to those students who were studying in foreign countries and whose parents had become refugees. This category of students is a minor one in sheer numbers, because not many families could afford to send their children for studies abroad. It was only the wealthy and the educated upper-middle class families who could afford to do this. However, the government agreed to set up a loan scheme whereby children of refugee parents could borrow money from the Indian state repayable within four years (GOI 1947–48: 23).[33] No interest was levied on the loan in the first year, while the last three years were assessed at a low rate of 2 per cent. That this scheme was not aimed at a broad section of the migrants is clear from the number of students who applied for the loan. Till March 1948, only 26 Indian students residing in the UK had applied for the loan and all of them were accepted as being eligible. A total sum of £7171 was distributed among them. Similarly, 22 students applied for studies in the US in the same period and they received a sum of $39,710 in all. The idea of 'greater public good' is simply absent in this scheme. It is clear that large sums of money were earmarked for a section of the population who most likely did not even need these funds. This seems extravagant when one compares the education grants being made to other middle class refugee children in India. One scheme earmarked an expenditure of Rs 200 per refugee student in the schools and colleges to finance extra shifts to teach an additional number of students (GOI 1947–48: 22).[34] The exact amount of money used or the number of beneficiaries of this scheme is not mentioned in the report. Another allocated Rs 40,000 as an interim relief to 607 refugee students for college and technical education (GOI 1947–48: 23).[35] A comparison of the amount of money in relation to the number of beneficiaries shows that the loan scheme to the students studying abroad had considerably lower and limited returns than the other schemes. The scheme was granted because it seemed 'natural' that the educational career of these upper class students should not be disturbed and that the state must facilitate its continuance in all circumstances.

The negotiating power generated through collective interest articulation is visible in the way the DI Khan society got land sanctioned for a new housing colony. The authorities could not alienate such a group because it represented an enterprising trading community that was in the course of establishing successful business ventures. Their demands were not ignored because they were not only well knit as a group but also had the patronage of wealthy men like Leela Ram and Pahwa. To add to this, Mehar Chand Khanna, a refugee from NWFP, was a member of the Congress government and later became the rehabilitation minister. Such political influence and patronage of wealthy men was crucial in gaining land at low concessional rates from the authorities. These two factors were absent in the collective struggle launched by the Purana Qila residents, who were neither patronized by wealthy distinguished men nor had any substantial political influence. Their collective demands could therefore easily be ignored without upsetting any configuration of power.

The widows in this scenario had no possibility of conducting profitable negotiations with the state authorities. To begin with, they were rejected by their own families, who entrusted their social obligations to the state. The social stigma attached to widowhood ensured that they led a secluded life where they could not legitimately express their desire for anything— for example, better housing, better education for their children—considered to be more than basic needs. They were expected to be content and grateful for everything they received from the authorities. This skewed their relationship with the state authorities and made them incapable of any negotiations. To this day, a battle to retain their homes on the government land continues, as they refuse to move out of the place where they have lived for more than 50 years. They do not really hope to win this battle either. In a way, they remain imprisoned in their past. For them, any chance of gaining personal independence and social prestige has continued to diminish because of their unprivileged social position. This does not mean that 'success' has completely eluded individuals. Rajrani has spent most of her life as a social outcast, but her two daughters have found success through marriage. One of them lives in US with her husband, who is reported to be a successful engineering professional, while the other lives in a middle class Delhi locality far away from the widow colony. It is not surprising therefore that Rajrani does not talk much about her pre-Partition experience, as there is nothing particularly illustrious to be narrated. The KLMC patriarch and the members of DI Khan society, by comparison, frequently invoke the glorious past of their families.

The KLMC family departs from the master narrative from the very moment of their departure: that is, they 'plan' their movement even before the actual Partition took place. Their departure is not situated in chaos and any 'unexpected' turmoil around them. This is the first challenge to the belief that Partition movement took place amidst turmoil and chaos. The turmoil is indeed expected and confronted with minute planning in terms of business and personal relocation in areas that were not deemed threatened by any eventuality of territorial partition. The family looks for alternate safer business locations—Banaras and Delhi—and begins transferring its stock-in-trade. The movement, therefore, does not entail either any material loss or loss of lives in the family. The safe outcome of movement (that is, devoid of major losses) is the second challenge to the popular accounts, which depict Partition as an event of destruction and bloodbath. This observation must not be understood as a *denial* of trauma, loss, and violence that took place during Partition, but rather as an indicator that no single path to population movement can be identified as the overwhelming truth of Partition migration.

The president of the DI Khan society, Leela Ram, and his family similarly migrated at least a year before Partition took place. Leela Ram was entrusted with the job of establishing business and home in case the family had to suddenly migrate. Pahwa, the vice-president, and his family did not migrate at the same time as Leela Ram, and were thus confronted with the dangers associated with Partition movement at a much closer level. To escape these purported dangers, they flew out of Pakistan. The mode of travel presents the third challenge to the master narrative. The presence of Kataria, like many other members of DI Khan society, however, seems to have a representative role when the personal accounts need to be presented to strangers or newcomers to the group.

The experiences of the widows, by comparison, stand in sharp contrast to those of the KLMC family and the DI Khan society members. The planned, and largely unhindered, familial movement in the former instance and the planned collective efforts towards resettlement in the latter are conspicuously absent in this case. The widows had no such support and advantage that could alleviate their circumstances from abject helplessness and dependence on authorities. They were beholden to the state for even the very basic provisions that their male counterparts were usually not. Rajrani was sent to the widow colony not because she lacked a family (she had her children and an extended circle of relatives), but because her uncle and his family refused to support her for long. It was a social rejection since she, as a youthful widow, was seen as a possible sexual threat to the other female members of the family. She was also an economic liability since she, together with her children, had to be supported on her uncle's income. In ordinary circumstances, the relatives would feel socially pressurized to look after Rajrani after her husband's death. Any failure to do so would mean collective shame for the male relatives because they would not be fulfilling an accepted social obligation. Such social niceties, however, became meaningless in the face of as cataclysmic an event as Partition since it was not only Rajrani who was experiencing loss but millions of other people as well. With Partition, she ceased to be the sole recipient of sympathy and support within her extended family. Her relatives had also experienced loss, though of a different kind, and could no longer attend solely to her needs.

To her uncle, the possibility of gaining a state-supported home for Rajrani seemed to be the logical and convenient thing to do. This would not have been possible in Lahore where the family resided at the time of Partition. A state-run home would not present itself as an option. She was *entrusted* to the state to provide for material needs as well as the social protection that was otherwise her family's responsibility. It seemed as if her uncle expected the state to make similar provisions for female protection as he would have done within his own house. The widow colony indeed seems like an oversized version of 'widow quarters' within an ordinary household dating half-a-century back. The widows would often live secluded lives, making an appearance only when strictly required. They were not expected to have any contact with male strangers, and, in a way, to delegate their previous social powers and obligations to the next in line married women within the family. In the case of elderly women, the successor would normally be the daughter-in-law, or in the case of younger women, like Rajrani, it would be the mother-in-law or a married and experienced aunt. Rajrani had thus been attached to the family of her uncle where her aunt looked after the social and familial matters. The widow colony represented the social norms that governed the lives of widows within a Punjabi society. The high barricaded walls, guards at the entry door, and restrictions upon male visitors magnify the invisible barriers that 'protect' widows in ordinary households. The state was in this way fulfilling the function of a resourceful family patriarch. Such adequate arrangement for the widows would earn social accolades, prestige, and approval for the family. Such behaviour by the state, emulating a patriarch, was expected to earn similar approval for its actions and arrangements from the larger migrant society. The state clearly emerges as a social being, not governing society in a detached way, but doing so by appropriating social functions that have great symbolic value in establishing its legitimacy.

CONCLUSION

The centrality of moral restoration is visible in the three different narratives of resettlement. The highly legal–technical matters of obtaining resettlement land for community housing, movement of business, and acquisition of one-room accommodation were not entirely devoid of the normative moral grid. At times, individuals and families had to detach themselves from moral expectations since they impeded personal growth and opportunities. Multiple losses during displacement could not be restored in keeping with the usual ideals. It is clear from the three accounts discussed here that measurement and reiteration of one's personal journey of migration and resettlement vis-à-vis this moral grid is more important now than before. The story of comparatively successful resettlement cannot be marred by the acknowledgement of normative immorality practised during the thick of Partition events, like, for example, filing false compensation claims and furnishing incorrect details to get accommodation, employment, and grants. Thus, the narratives are laced half-a-century later with remarks and conclusions where the *end* (successful resettlement) is expected to justify the *means* (morally questionable resettlement practices).

The three accounts also suggest that the state was deliberately written out of the community and personal familial history. While evidence exists aplenty to show the extent of the state involvement in the resettlement exercise, it never gets mentioned in these instances of personal or collective success. It is only in the case of Rajrani that the state is depicted as a role player in her personal story of resettlement. Her continued residence in the state-owned housing colony remains a fact that cannot be stated otherwise. In the other two cases, state involvement challenges their personal struggle and robs the glory therein. It is not surprising that the state never enters the success stories.

These narratives bring out the multiple levels of resettlement and the state appropriation of social norms therein. The multiple levels are bound, however, by a common quest for restoration of loss and disruption suffered during the migration. It also meant that the mass of the refugees passed through a social sieve which determined the mode of their restoration. This should not be taken as a socially deterministic argument, since migrants took their own routes to resettlement based on their exclusive idea of what restoration should be. The refugees at all levels, across class and gender, took the matter of resettlement in their own hands and used the various offers made by the state as opportunities to re-establish themselves. This challenges the idea of refugees as victims and shows that the refugees did make use of whatever little room there was to manoeuvre. However, the middle class/middle caste male population seems to be the main beneficiary of state largesse. The master narrative tends to cover up all these different migrants and the divergent resettlement routes they had travelled, and therefore needs to be challenged.

NOTES

1. See Urvashi Butalia's (1998) account of sexual violence and abduction of women during the Partition upheaval in her *The Other Side of Silence: Voices from the Partition of India.*

2. I have paraphrased Helen Fein, who described the perpetrators in a genocide as being 'outside the universe of obligation' that allows them to exonerate themselves from their actions. See Fein (1984) 'Scenarios of Genocide: Models of Genocide and Critical Responses' in Israel Charny edited Towards the Understanding and Prevention of Genocide: Proceedings of the International Conference on the Holocaust and Genocide, pp. 4–5.

3. Speeches written by Diwan Chaman Lall, Section no. 32, Chaman Lall papers, NMML, New Delhi, emphasis added.

4. See Narayani Gupta's (1999) account of the planning and extension of Delhi city during the colonial period in her *Delhi Between the Two Empires, 1803– 1931.*

5. Name changed.

6. See Pran Neville (1997) *Lahore: A Sentimental Journey.*

7. See Bipan Chandra's description of the Civil Disobedience Movement in Chandra et al. (1989: 276).

8. A letter dated 2 October 1951, File number 1444, Diwan Chaman Lall papers, NMML, New Delhi.

9. Letter dated 4 May 1954 from Property Field Officer in Lahore to Diwan Chaman Lall. File number 74, Chaman Lall papers, NMML, New Delhi.

10. Letter dated 8 April 1953 from Durga Dass and Sons to Diwan Chaman Lall. File number 73, Chaman Lall papers, NMML, New Delhi.

11. 'Seva Samiti' simply means service organization.

12. Imperial Gazetteer of India (Provincial Series) vol. II, The Lahore, Rawalpindi, and Multan Divisions; and Native States, p. 270.

13. All comparable figures from the Imperial Gazetteer, vol. 11, p. 30–8.

14. Census of India 1941, Table V, 'Towns arranged territorially with population by community', pp. 36–7.

15. The census records no Scheduled Castes, Jain or Adi-Dharmi residents, though there were three Indian Christians and 24 Sikhs in the sub-division of Jampur.
16. Group interview with the members of Working Committee, Dera Ismail Khan Sewa Samiti, Derawal Nagar, on 7 December 2000.
17. See District Population in NWFP, Census of India, 1941.
18. Kashi is the ancient holy city of the Hindus, located in the present north-central state of Uttar Pradesh. 'Frontier' refers to NWFP.
19. See Richard Fox's (1985) description of Punjabi Hindus in the 'Introduction' to his *Lions of Punjab: Culture in the Making*.
20. A comprehensive study of cooperatives in India after 1947 is Eleanor M. Hough's (1966), *The Cooperative Movement in India*
21. For example, see Urvashi Butalia's (1998) account of her interviews with female survivors of Partition in her book *The Other Side of Silence: Voices from the Partition of India*.
22. See Annual Report 1947–48, Ministry of Relief and Rehabilitation, Government of India.
23. See AICC Papers (II Instalment) about various work training centres run separately for men and women.
24. M.L. Saxena was the Minister for Relief and Rehabilitation from 1948–1950.
25. Personal interview with P.L. Kataria (b. 1934) conducted in December 2000 in Delhi. He arrived as a refugee from Dera Ismail Khan in August 1947 and found temporary employment at the refugee registration office to fill up registration forms for the incoming refugees for a small fee.
26. Yashwanti Mehta (b. 1926) migrated to Delhi in September 1947 from Lahore. All male members of her family including her husband had been killed in communal violence, following which she left along with her three daughters and one son. Personal interview conducted at her residence in Nirmal Puri, New Delhi, in October 2002.
27. The family and social politics around widowhood have been looked at in great detail in, for example, Kumkum Sangari and Sudesh Vaid (1996), 'Institutions, Beliefs, Ideologies: Widow Immolation in Contemporary Rajasthan' in Kumari Jayawardena and Malathi de Alwis (eds), *Embodied Violence: Communalising Women's Sexuality in South Asia;* R.N. Saksena (1975), *Social Reform: Infanticide and Sati;* V.N. Dutta (1988), *Sati: Widow Burning in India*.
28. It was named after M.K. Gandhi's wife, Kasturba Gandhi, like many other state-run women's homes.
29. The colour white is worn in widowhood.
30. Personal interview with Rajrani (b. 1926) in November 2001.
31. Ibid.
32. Besides a number of apparent reasons like loss of social status and impending conflicts over property,widowhood also has mythical shadows wherein the widow herself is considered a cause of her misfortune. An example is the Hindu legend of Savitri, who has foreknowledge of her husband's death. She is shown as strong-willed, clever, and determined to keep her husband alive and she persists with Yama, the god of death, till he gives back her husband's life as a boon to her. Savitri is seen as an ideal wife for she has the preservative attributes. This suggests that a wife through faith and devotion can bring alive the dead husband, while the lack of these qualities may result in widowhood. The ability to keep the husband, and in the process decide her fate, therefore lies with the woman.

33. Annual Report 1947–48, Ministry of Relief and Rehabilitation, p. 23.
34. Annual Report 1947–48, Ministry of Relief and Rehabilitation, New Delhi.
35. Annual Report 1947–48, Ministry of Relief and Rehabilitation, New Delhi.

6. Missing Fields
The 'Untouchable' Migrants of Partition

The conspicuous absence of *achhut* ('untouchable') refugees in the popular narratives of Partition presents a barely touched theme within modern Indian history. This *discursive absence* emerges not only from a particular tradition of historiography that aims to construct authoritative accounts of political events, personal lives, and social shifts from an elite (as opposed to subaltern) perspective, but also from an assimilative common Hindu identity which has been increasingly acquired by these untouchable migrant groups. They have rarely been represented in Partition accounts, and least of all, as a separate people.

The discursive absence does not mean that they were *physically* absent from the Partition drama, but that they were not included in the stories of injustices meted out to 'Hindus' by the Muslims during the Partition violence. Their numbers were sometimes included in the government statistics to show the size of the non-Muslim population that needed to be evacuated from Pakistan, but the statistical category of 'non-Muslim' did not make them full Hindus, even though many had taken to Hindu reform sects like the Arya Samaj since the late 19th century. The government set up separate refugee camps, separate mass housing schemes, and separate job arrangements for them, mostly as sweepers in the city municipality. This spatial and occupational separation was much in accordance with the upper caste Hindu ideal of keeping the polluted castes in isolation, in order that their shadow or touch would not pollute others. Thus, what emerges is a somewhat tragic account of untouchable migrants from West Punjab who have been kept out of the Hindu upper caste and middle class narratives of Partition. It is not only the fear of contamination at a physical or social level that seems to be of importance to the upper caste Hindus but also the wish to keep the Partition narratives sacred and protected from contact with the 'untouchables'.

ABSENCES AND OTHER RELATED QUESTIONS

The history of migration during Partition is popularly imagined as the history of upwardly mobile upper caste Hindus and Sikhs who were forced to move amidst chaos and violence. The emergent quintessential refugee in fictional,[1] autobiographical,[2] and official[3] accounts somehow 'restricts' the investigative field of resettlement to the middle class areas of Delhi where the upper-caste refugees were settled by the government. The almost complete absence of untouchable Hindu and Sikh castes, figuratively, as well as physically, in Partition migration accounts in the resettlement colonies[4] opens an unexplored area of Partition history. The emerging maze of unsolved puzzles is knotted together with a single question: did untouchable non-Muslims migrate at all from West Punjab during Partition? If they did, then where did they resettle?

This chapter is mainly concerned with the second question, which carries an inherent methodological problem: how to reach a group that is not part of the popular imagination and whose history of migration has, for some reason, never been recorded, and has been deemed irrelevant. The Partition migration story that we know so far is essentially the story of upper caste, middle class Punjabis who contributed to post-colonial Indian historiography in a number of ways.[5] This exercise, therefore, bears the twin burden of physically locating untouchable refugees in Delhi city and then reconstructing and telling this story of migration and resettlement that has remained untold and shielded from the popular discourse of Partition.

While looking for the untouchable groups, it is important to remember what names and terminologies they were identified with when the caste classifications became a part of the administrative framework. Once again the population censuses and ethnographic surveys conducted by the colonial state in the late 19th century assume significance because social distinctions of caste and religion became fixed in an official binding mode. Often the names and categories the groups use for them are influenced by the classifications derived from the colonial administration. A good example is a widely used reference volume on the Scheduled Castes in India that alphabetically lists all the untouchable castes and describes their origin, habits, rituals, etc. (K.S. Singh 2000). The description of untouchable groups in Punjab in this publication is largely based on the colonial accounts of G.W. Briggs, Denzil Ibbetson, and H.A. Rose, which are still considered the most authoritative ethnographic compilation of castes.[6] While the current caste categorization remains influenced by the colonial classification, new concepts claim to represent the untouchable groups. The contemporary terms like Dalits, Harijans, depressed classes and Scheduled Castes (SCs) were not even invented till the early to mid-20th century. Each of these terms carries a discursive baggage and a history of its own.

The category of 'depressed classes' was used extensively by Ambedkar to collectively describe the caste-based discrimination and oppression that kept a large section of the Indian population in social bondage. Such a description became the basis of a *legal expression*—Scheduled Castes—in the Government of India Act 1935, wherein untouchability was identified as a ground for affirmative action. Based on the above-mentioned ethnographic works, a list of untouchable castes requiring institutional support was incorporated in a schedule of the Constitution. Separate electorates were identified for the untouchables to gain them sufficient representation in the provincial assemblies as well as the Constituent Assembly. The term '*Harijan*' literally means 'God's own people' as used by Gandhi to describe the untouchables. It became a widely used term among the Congress activists and leadership during the freedom movement and was used quite commonly by the Congress governments after independence. The term retains a *patronizing element* of the upper castes and is often rejected by the untouchable groups. The Gandhi/Congress connection, however, means that it opens avenues for opportunities for houses, jobs, etc., through official patronage in a variety of ways. A preponderance of '*Harijan Bastis*' and 'Harijan welfare schemes' around the country testify to that ambiguity. The concept of Dalit stands in stark opposition to the other widely used patronizing or legal categories. Being a Dalit means being an oppressed entity since it describes the condition of caste-based subalternity. The word is used as a *political expression* and with pride, much the way the Black movements in the US use the word Black. The Dalit movements have a much more recent history than the other conceptual or legal categories defining untouchability. The usage of each of these terms, therefore, carries larger meanings and histories, rendering impossible substitution of one for another.

In this study, the English equivalent of the Sanskrit word *achhut*—untouchable—is used consistently for two reasons: one, to represent the condition of social untouchability as it presented itself at the time of Partition and, two, to circumvent deeper legal-political meanings attached with other terms that gained currency more recently. Untouchability literally depicts a known social practice wherein people outside the fourfold caste system are considered polluted and unfit for physical touch or social exchange.[7] These include castes that are traditionally associated with menial occupations: for example, Bhangis (the scavengers), Chuhras (the sweepers), or Chamars (the leather workers) among others, who collect and dispose human waste and garbage, cremate human dead bodies, and handle carcasses of dead animals. The untouchable castes also include the professions of Dhobi (washermen), Nai (barber), Mirasi (the entertainer) and Taili (masseur), each of which has had a traditional role in the Punjabi villages. These caste groups have been the prime human material available for conversion and sectarian recruitment, both among the Christian missionaries and the various religious reform movements like the Arya Samaj and Khalsa in Punjab from the late 19th century onwards.

Table 6.1: Percentages of various untouchable caste
populations in West Punjab, 1881

	Carriers/ Hawkers	Nomads/ Criminals	Gypsies	Scavengers	Leather workers	Washermen
Lahore	1.1	1.3	0.2	10.7	6.4	1.9
Sialkot	0.7	1.1	0.1	7.8	5.3	2.0
Gujranwalla	–	0.7	0.2	9.4	7.9	2.0
Gujarat	0.8	0.2	0.1	5.6	8.3	1.6
Shahpur	–	0.1	0.2	6.7	8.9	1.4
Jhelum	–	–	–	4.2	8.6	1.7
Rawalpindi	0.1	0.1	0.2	2.7	7.3	1.6
Montgomery	0.1	0.4	0.8	6.8	8.2	1.8
Jhang	–	–	0.1	5.3	9.7	1.4
Multan	0.3	1.0	0.1	5.3	7.7	2.4
Muzzafargarh	0.7	1.2	–	3.3	7.4	1.9
DG Khan	–	0.4	–	1.3	0.5	0.2
DI Khan	0.1	0.1	–	2.0	2.4	0.6
Peshawar	0.1	–	–	1.3	3.9	1.1
Hazara	0.1	–	–	0.6	4.5	1.0
Kohat	0.3	–	–	0.7	2.1	0.7

Total Population in British Punjab: 18,850,437 (actual figure)

Source: Ibbetson (1916: 256–7, 292–3, 298–9).

Reading the caste statistics at the turn of the 19th century, it must be noted that untouchable groups are not clubbed together as a separate category on their own but rather clustered around their occupational characteristics. The ethnographic studies of caste (for example, Ibbetson 1916), are based on the categories of landed peasantry, commercial moneylenders, artisans, vagrants, menials, and nomads among others. Thus, Chamars (leather workers) and Chuhras (scavengers), the two largest Punjabi untouchable groups (see Table 6.1), appear in the menial/artisan section, where not all the castes mentioned (for example, Sunar or goldsmiths) are considered untouchable. This shows that an independent category of untouchables, wherein an array of untouchable groups could be collapsed, was yet to be conceptualized, even though the status of certain castes was recognized as being that of outcastes. The castes are mentioned by their specific names and separated according to their professional categories, which later became the basis of the legal and political categories of SCs, Harijans, and Dalits.

A quick survey of Punjab social history would suggest that untouchable caste groups were present in sufficient numbers in Punjab, long before Partition took place. They often belonged to various religions and popular sects of Punjab, but their social status and traditional occupation rarely changed as a result. The presence of untouchable caste groups in Punjab was recorded in a systematic manner soon after the 1849 British annexation of Punjab. Population censuses were undertaken in Punjab as early as 1861 to plot the ethnographic map of the region. The untouchable groups gained prominence in the various mid- and late 19th-century historical accounts mainly as the source material from which religious converts could be recruited. The Christian missionaries followed the British administrators in Punjab and targeted the untouchables for conversion once they realized it was almost impossible to convert caste Hindus. The Arya Samaj and Khalsa reform movements saw Christian conversions as a provocation and began a *Shuddhi* or purification programme to reconvert untouchable Christian converts to the Hindu or Sikh fold as the case may be. This means, in statistical terms, that untouchable groups were classified into their post-conversion religious denominations. Conversion to casteless religions like Islam, Christianity, and caste-opposed religions like Sikhism did not however mean that caste distinctions had been successfully removed. It simply meant that broad religious categories became approximate pointers to social structures. Thus, it is difficult to determine what proportion of untouchables existed within the Muslim, Hindu, Sikh, or Christian folds. The 1881 census compiles proportional figures of untouchable castes in Punjab outside the religious categories. Table 6.1 shows a vast array of individual untouchable castes grouped under their traditional occupations and deemed roles in the districts of West Punjab districts that came to constitute a part of Pakistan after 1947.[8] The Muslim and non-Muslim categories are not included in these figures, since they did not matter much in terms of caste behaviour, and occupations.

A useful clue may lie in the historical confluence of religions that took place in Punjab due to frequent incursions in the region from West and Central Asia. Islam was introduced in Punjab by adventurers, conquerors, and Sufi saints around the same time in the 9th century that the Crusades began making headway in West Asia. Through large-scale conversions, voluntary or involuntary, Islam became one of the dominant religions in the region. The areas in the western part, which lie closer to Central Asia, proved to be more receptive to the new religion than the eastern part. As a result, the Muslim population in the Punjab, particularly West Punjab, was far greater than the Hindu or Sikh population. This also suggests that the untouchable and other menial groups would have taken to Islam as well in far greater numbers than their counterparts in East Punjab.

Table 6.2: Statistical population enumeration of religions in Punjab, 1881[9]

Muslims	Hindus	Sikhs	Christians	Jains	Buddhists	Parsis	Others
11.662.434	9.252.295	1.716.114	33.690	42.678	3251	465	1184

Source: Census of India 1881.

Table 6.3: Scheduled Caste population in West Punjab districts, 1941[10]

District	Population	Percentage
Lahore	32,735	1.9
Sialkot	65,354	5.5
Gujranwalla	7485	0.8
Sheikhupura	22,438	2.6
Gujarat	4621	0.4
Shahpur	9693	1.0
Jhelum	771	0.1
Rawalpindi	4233	0.5
Attock	1015	0.1
Mianwali	1008	0.2
Montgomery	43,456	3.2
Lyallpore	68,222	4.9
Jhang	1943	0.2
Multan	24,530	1.7
Muzzafargarh	2691	0.4
Dera Gazhi Khan	1059	0.2
Transfrontier Tract	Nil	Nil
Total	291,254	1.4
Total West Punjab Population	15,717,390	–

Source: Census of India 1941.

Table 6.2 shows the population strength of various religious denominations in actual numbers. Muslims emerge as the largest group followed by the Hindus and then the Sikhs. The caste specifications are subsumed in these larger figures and do not indicate the proportion of untouchable groups within each religion. Within the first half of the 20th century, untouchable groups had become a separate legal category and the occupational distinctions were not clearly visible in the population computations. A comparison of the 1881 census of castes when compared to the 1941 census shows that a single expansive category—SCs—had emerged in administrative terms. This category was set apart from Hindus, Muslims, Christians, and Sikhs, which would make it safe to presume that in this table SCs referred to those who still remained in the Hindu fold and had not converted to other religions. This would then be the approximate figure of Hindu untouchables who could migrate to India along with upper caste Hindus during Partition. Such an assumption excludes possibilities of conversion to Islam during the riots to escape violence and a personal unwillingness to migrate. What would make this assumption plausible is that throughout the late 19th century and early 20th century, these groups were vigorously wooed by anti-caste Hindu reform sects like the Arya Samaj in Punjab. Also, these groups had followed Hindu and Sikh cultivators to the West Punjab colonies during the canal colony movement from East Punjab. Thus, their migratory pattern could be expected to be the same as that of the upper caste Hindu.

DRAWING BLANKS, FINDING CLUES

The colonial premises of the now abolished Ministry of Rehabilitation in Delhi proved to be an exceptionally fruitful field site. I would go there daily to gain access to the various documents, policy handbooks, and annual reports of the ministry dating back to 1947 and onwards to find out what kind of work it was engaged in at that time. The building was in shambles and the entire place was either being torn down or rebuilt in parts. The only part that remained intact was the 'Record Room', a five-storeyed house where the entire records including the personal files of the refugees and their compensation claims were preserved. The records had never made it to the National Archive for preservation since they were technically still active, that is, they were used everyday because some of the claims and disputes from 1947 were still in the process of being settled. The daily queue of old men and women sitting patiently outside the offices of the settlement officer was a testimony to that. The episode of Partition in their personal lives was not yet over, even after half a century.

In terms of documentary material, I did not gain much, as most of the material, other than personal files, was in disarray lying amidst heavy dust and being eaten away by pests. Heavy rains some years ago had flooded the lower level of the building and most of the material there was rotting because no one had retrieved it. I was told that I could pick up from the dust anything that I found useful. What I lost in documents was made up by the exceptional interaction I would have everyday with one of the lower-level employees. His name was Sham Singh and he worked there as a peon whose duties included fetching files and serving tea to the officers and clerks. He told me one day that he was born in Lahore and had come to Delhi during the Partition riots. He did not remember exactly when he was born but he described himself as being *jawaan* (in his youth) when he came to Delhi.[11] He had come along with millions of other refugees who were crossing over the border to escape the violence. He and his family had found protection in a church and were later evacuated by the Indian military. They travelled to Delhi in a special train and began living in a refugee camp. He had done basic schooling in Lahore at an Arya Samaj school, and after doing a variety of odd jobs he got permanent employment at the Ministry of Rehabilitation.

There is nothing unusual in this story and it appears much like the stories one hears all the time about Partition migration. What made this story special was that Sham Singh was a Chamar, a leather worker by caste. Chamar is an untouchable caste group spread all over Punjab in large numbers. It is often clubbed together with Chuhras (the sweepers), in Punjab, Rajasthan, and Delhi, for the purposes of population computation. Rarely does one come across a personal or an official narrative of untouchable groups or individuals in the popular discourses around Partition. If one hears about these groups, it is often in the forms of jokes that on the one hand ridicule, and on the other, present the tragic position of untouchables during the Partition. In a popular joke, one is told of two Chuhras who were busy sweeping the roads of Lahore during the Hindu–Muslim violence. While Hindus were trying to flee from the violence, Muslims were pouring into the city from India. One sweeper asked another if he knew why people were running here and there. The other answered, 'Hindus are running to India while Muslims are looking for Pakistan. But look at us, we are the kings of both India and Pakistan. We don't need to escape to another place and nobody is going to touch us.' And they continued sweeping the empty streets afterwards.'[12]

This joke may not invoke very much laughter but it makes a significant point: untouchable groups were not in the communal scheme of things. They were neither Hindus nor Muslims and therefore were not fit even for communally charged killings. The story is meant to highlight the untouchable status of these caste groups since the very condition of untouchability becomes a potent defence mechanism against mass violence. The sympathetic message, if any, is that these people did not need to escape from the impending violence that threatened Hindus and Muslims, but needed to escape from their everyday servitude. The joke ends with the two Chuhras sweeping the street long after everyone has left. It marks the circumstantial irony, in that the sweepers did not attempt to change their ordinary role even in such a cataclysmic situation. They remained impervious to it. Listeners are expected to laugh at this punch line because the irony and the stupidity of the Chuhras should be apparent to the audience. It is incomprehensible wonder for the Hindus and Muslims alike that there were some groups who could remain isolated during the Partition from the events happening around them. Thus untouchables are not a part of the mainstream accounts of Partition, though they appear occasionally as caricatures.

My encounter with Sham Singh, however, made me realize that untouchable groups were neither untouched by nor isolated from the

Partition-related events. Sham Singh happened to be just the first untouchable migrant I had met. He told me that he lived in a Harijan Basti (Harijan settlement) around Lajpat Nagar, where most of his neighbours were also untouchable migrants from West Punjab. They had the same stories that he and millions of other Partition migrants had, but they lived together and in isolation from the upper caste refugees. I immediately decided to expand my original fieldwork plan and to include the untouchable refugee settlements in the survey and interview schedules.

However, I was soon to realize why these stories had never become part of the mainstream in the first place. My daily routine at the ministry was laced with frequent heated discussions and endless cups of tea. While I would wait for the documents and reports to be produced, the head clerk and the section officer, both upper caste and middle class, would often provoke a discussion as to why some of the Partition claim settlements were still pending. They would tell stories of false claims filed for higher compensation and disputes that arose among different family members once compensation was obtained. Significantly, like most of the other staff, both had parents who had migrated during Partition from West Punjab. Through their personal family histories they were inextricably linked with the history of Partition, which explained their extraordinary interest in my research. Each day they would tell me their family stories and small related anecdotes. This would often be linked with the exceptional work the ministry did for the refugees at an all-India level and how the Punjabis did justice to the state support by turning self-reliant and successful, while the Bengali refugees continued to be dependent on the state for a very long time. An ethnic explanation of Punjabi willpower versus the Bengali laid-back attitude was frequently offered. They volunteered their personal examples of how hard they had worked to reach where they were today, displaying the same determination their parents had shown after Partition.

Sham Singh was never a part of these discussions, even though he would regularly supply us with tea. He would sit down on the ground some distance away from us. He was always there listening to what was being said but never intervening with his own stories. His low rank in the official hierarchy did not allow him to participate in such seemingly informed and authoritative debates. When one day I expressed my wish to interview Sham Singh and possibly visit his neighbourhood, I encountered clear disapproval and animosity from within the regular discussion group. The reaction was not completely unsurprising because my talks with Sham Singh threatened to raise him to the same level as them.

Sham Singh could sense the disapproval and was hesitant to talk to me. On my part, I decided not to pursue the matter any further so as to prevent any complications that could arise for him at his workplace. We kept a distance from each other from then on. As a result I could never gain any information about the location of the untouchable refugee colony where he lived. A vital clue was gained and immediately lost. The most positive outcome was that Sham Singh's presence and silence pointed to the gaping blanks in the popular Partition history. These blanks needed to be filled in immediately if one were ever going to sketch the full canvas of Partition movement and resettlement.

SEARCH FOR THE FIELD IN DELHI

In this project, the absence of clear clues to the resettlement locations of untouchable refugees in Delhi meant that the methodological equivalent of a fine toothcomb had to be used to sift through the known areas of refugee resettlement in search of low caste refugees. I began with a quantitative survey in the resettlement areas of Lajpat Nagar, Amar Colony, Nirmal Puri, Old Double Storey, Reeds Lines, Outram Lines, Edward Lines, and Hudson Lines in Kingsway Camp. These areas when put together encompass various levels of the middle classes as well as some poor sections. The reason that I chose Kingsway Camp and Nirmal Puri was that one would be more likely to find low caste settlers in these lower-middle class colonies than in affluent locations. These locations were developed and allotted by the government, unlike places similar to Nizamuddin where land was developed and sold to refugees for private constructions. There was more likelihood that low caste refugees had been granted residential space in the cheaper and more densely populated Government Built Property (GBP) areas by the state because of state policies.[13]

However, the outcome of the survey posed more questions than it solved. A part of the questionnaire pertained to personal information about individuals: levels of education, occupation, income, religious practices, caste affiliations, and inter-communal interaction at the time of Partition. One of the objectives was to see whether the socio-economic background of the migrants in West Punjab had an impact on the localities that they resettled in upon movement. The specific query on caste coupled with other information on education, income, and locality of residence would help in determining the class and caste dynamics operational in migration and resettlement. These hypotheses were not proved by the survey. Of the 454 individuals interviewed, over 80 per cent belonged to various denominations of upper castes. The breakdown of the compiled data was as follows: Arora (36 per cent), Khatri (32 per cent), Brahmins (7 per cent), Bania (4 per cent), Others (10 per cent), Ravidasi and Kabirpanthi (4.6 per cent). The remaining respondents turned out be non-Hindus, mainly Sikhs, while a few others refused to answer this question.

The interpretation of these figures needs to be pursued with caution since caste is an everyday reality, a signifier of one's place in the social hierarchy, and therefore often a cause of personal and social conflicts. The responses to queries on caste in quantitative surveys are not merely a matter of offering choices and then ticking columns. While posing questions and receiving answers from those who decidedly belong to upper caste groups is easy, the raw edges appear when responses are sought from members of intermediate or low caste groups. In Punjabi social hierarchy, it is the intermediate castes like Arora, Khatri, Bania and Jat that dominate the urban and rural economies. While Brahmins remain on top of the caste hierarchy in many parts of India, it is the intermediate castes that top the social hierarchy in Punjab. The widespread appeal of religious reform movements like Arya Samaj in Punjab meant that the traditional Brahmin-dominated caste hierarchy went through a change in favour of those castes that controlled the economic structures. The backbone of the agrarian economy was controlled by the moneylenders, shopkeepers, and traders, comprising urban mercantile castes like Arora, Khatri, and Bania, together with the landowning Jat caste groups who dominated agrarian production. Brahmins did not have any direct role in this economic cycle and their traditional role as priests and intellectuals was undermined by reform movements that opposed rituals and hierarchies.

In the sample, a majority of the Punjabi Hindus belonged to these dominant castes: less than 5 per cent claimed low caste origins. The options in the questionnaire offered for low castes were Ravidasi and Kabirpanthi, which are actually not caste names but names of the anti-Brahminical religious sects, popular among the low castes. The preliminary test survey conducted in December 2000 showed that the simple use of low caste names was problematic since caste names are often used as abuses or insults.[14] This created a methodological problem for the interviewer who had to read aloud out all the options to the respondents (all aged over 70 years and often in need of assistance). The upper castes felt insulted that they were offered the option of low castes among others, since they clearly 'looked upper caste and of noble origin'.[15] The respondents who belonged to castes considered low in the hierarchy found questions about their caste status offensive. Since the aim was to find the approximate caste affiliations and not the exact sub-categories, the refurbished option of low caste names as religious sects was devised to serve as an indicator of the marginalized caste origins.

The category 'others' also needs to be explained since it includes a variety of people who refused to spell out their caste status. Some respondents who wanted to establish their progressive credentials said that they did not believe in the institution of caste and therefore would not identify themselves with any caste group. Several others did not wish to reveal their caste affiliation to complete strangers. The reluctance does not necessarily stem from reasons of personal privacy, since exchanging information about one's caste when introducing oneself is not uncommon. For one, it is fairly common that groups and individuals who gain class power often attempt to reinvent their caste status. Since a disputed caste status is better than being relegated to low castes, the category 'others' provides a suitable space for such uncertain instances. Second, state policy is another factor. Since the provision to reserve 22.5 per cent seats for Scheduled Castes and Tribes in jobs, academic institutions and at all levels of state infrastructure as part of affirmative action was introduced, this often becomes a ground for rivalry, jealousy, and conflict. The upper castes feel that they have been cheated of jobs, which on the basis of merit should belong to them, while low castes see it as a rightful means of reversal in caste domination. This conflict is played out in daily life as well, for example, when state employees appointed through the reserved quota want to live in 'respectable' middle class areas. The knowledge of their caste status often means diminished social interaction in the neighbourhood. It is not surprising therefore, that many want to disassociate from their low caste identities once they have acquired other symbols of middle class life.

The marginal appearance of low caste respondents in the resettlement areas suggests two possibilities: one, that the untouchable castes in West Punjab did not migrate in large numbers, and two, that they did not resettle in the middle or lower-middle class areas of Delhi. The second option seems more likely, considering that there is definite evidence of untouchable migration in various accounts. While the survey firmly established which resettlement areas did not have untouchable residents, the search in the official archives pointed to the actual locations where untouchable settlements were developed in 1947.

EXPERIENCING 'DIFFERENCES' OF CASTE

It was in the second phase of my fieldwork that I finally began locating the missing pieces of the resettlement puzzle. The archive of official files and documents at the Ministry of Rehabilitation contained brief mentions of low caste migrants, officially termed Harijan refugees. The Annual Report mentions that a Harijan section of the ministry was established on 15 February 1948 to 'settle uprooted Harijans' (GOI 1947–48: 24).[16] The projects accomplished through this section included, (1) allotment of 50,000 acres in 570 villages in East Punjab to 570 Harijan families in Karnal and 4000 in Gang colony in Bikaner from Bahawalpur, (2) construction of 301 houses for Harijans in Ahmedabad, (3) securing employment for

407 Harijan refugees as sweepers and for 70 Sindhi Oades as construction workers, and (4) a housing society for Harijans in Delhi.[17] On the Delhi resettlement, the report further mentions that 'at the end of August 1948, Rehgarpura scheme was almost completed. Two co-operative housing societies for Harijans were formed, and a share capital worth Rupees 4000 was subscribed till 31st August 1948. The Harijan families also secured tarpaulins to cover their roofless huts' (GOI 1947–48: 68).[18]

The cooperative societies mentioned here are the Rameshwari Nehru cooperative housing societies[19] that were allotted land to build housing facilities for the Dalit refugees in the Rehgar Pura area of Karol Bagh. This little piece of information in the ministry's annual report (ibid.) allowed me to associate the well-known untouchable colony in Karol Bagh with the untouchable refugees of Partition. The settlement is located in central Delhi, next to the now-sprawling commercial area of Karol Bagh. This is where a large number of Punjabi upper caste refugees had set up their commercial enterprises as well as their homes. The place had been a middle class Muslim locality built a few decades before the Partition to relieve the congestion in the walled city area. Rehgar Pura, an untouchable colony, was located a bit further south of Karol Bagh where many Muslim sweepers and leather workers resided. The non-Muslim sweepers also resided in the area, especially after the Delhi municipality started large-scale recruitments from among Punjabi Chuhra communities to keep the clean.[20]

During the Partition riots, both upper caste and untouchable Muslims fled the Karol Bagh and Rehgar Pura areas since it was one of the sites in the city where maximum violence took place. The untouchable non-Muslim refugees were resettled in the same locality where fresh mud huts were constructed for them. Many years later, concrete sheds were constructed by the government, called *Sau Quarter* or literally one hundred quarters. Within the locality these are known as Partition housing, as distinct from the houses occupied by those who settled there before Partition. The area is now relatively prosperous when compared to other untouchable colonies located in east and north Delhi. The main reason is its proximity to the commercial activity in Karol Bagh. Skinning, tanning, and shoe manufacturing have emerged as major cottage industries in Rehgar Pura, where most houses are sites of the leather trade in one way or the other. Many upper caste traders from Karol Bagh have purchased property here to use cheaper real estate in Rehgar Pura for manufacturing units or storage sites. The property prices have as a result gone up dramatically, many times over their original value of a few hundred rupees in 1947. The tall four-storeyed newly constructed buildings and painted houses are evidence of capital earned on property rent by the original owners.

It was with some difficulty that I 'found' the untouchable refugees since it was not a field site that could be physically identified through popular accounts. Having located it through documentary evidence, I found that I could not follow the same procedure I follow when I interviewed 'ordinary' refugee families. To begin with, I knew no one who could personally introduce me to the residents, since most people I knew had never been to that colony. In Delhi Rehgar Pura is known as a place where Chuhra, Chamar and Bhangi communities live, manufacture, and trade in leather products. It is a different world for most middle class people in Delhi, who might, venture into the colony for commercial reasons but never for social intermingling. It was, therefore, not surprising that during my fieldwork no one in other refugee colonies ever mentioned having friends or acquaintances in Rehgar Pura.

It was through a network of Dalit activists that I gained contact with the members of the Rehgar Mahasabha residing in Rehgar Pura.[21] Once in the locality, with newly acquired personal contacts, this previously missing field site became as 'normal' as the other refugee colonies. There were old men who had migrated from Lahore, Sialkot or other places in West Punjab sitting in the public park talking about local neighbourhood politics. Women were as usual less visible, audible, and accessible in public spaces, but I was allowed inside the homes to talk to the women as well. The marked difference was that people were more receptive to my queries than in the other colonies since no one had ever visited them to talk about their past. It was clear that my questions about their migration journey came as a surprise to them and that they had never considered themselves a part of the larger Partition discourse even though they had gone through, more or less, the same political circumstances as others had. They were now a part of current Dalit politics in a variety of ways. Rehgar Pura had been a place where Kanshi Ram, the founder of Bahujan Samaj Party (BSP), had started the Bahujan movement in early 1970s.[22] As a result, most residents were deeply involved in local- and national-level politics. However, not everyone was involved in BSP politics, though they were connected to it from its inception.

A temple dedicated to the Hindu goddess Ashthbhuja located in the centre of *Sau Quarter* (literally one hundred quarters) told a different story: of how the untouchable migrants groups had taken to Hindutva politics. Most of the homes I visited were not very different from the upper caste Hindu homes I had been to in the way they displayed the statues and photos of the goddess. At a purely theoretical level, this was a contradictory symbolism to be kept on the display mantle in an untouchable home. The idea of purity and pollution had ensured that untouchables were not allowed to enter Hindu temples, draw water from the same source, or come in physical contact in any way with other castes. Thus a physical and spiritual separation was considered essential by the Brahmins to maintain caste purity. The symbol of this goddess was a symbol that did not actually belong to the untouchables. The untouchables had taken to a number of other forms of worship that tended to speak for them instead of the upper castes. The religious sects of Balmiki, Ravidas, and Bala Shah gained popularity among the untouchables, built as they were around the ideals of a casteless society, equality, and non-discrimination, woven with different stories of origins of the untouchable castes. These sects on the one hand presented a non-Hindu spiritual avenue for the untouchables who had not converted to Islam or Christianity, and on the other, became symbols of protest against the oppressive Brahminical system. Thus, a Balmiki temple in the locality would be an expected sight, going by the social-historical developments in the Chuhra and Chamar communities in north India. The presence of a Hindu temple presided over by a goddess who is popular among the Punjabi Hindu refugees revealed new social-political sides of the untouchable migrants.

The personal histories of the residents in Rehgar Pura gave some clues of this unexpected feature. One of the regulars in the municipal park was Sewa Ram, who was born in 1920 in Lahore to a Chamar family engaged in the business of shoemaking. He would sit everyday in the park with other men, most of them refugees like him. They spoke in Punjabi, alternating it with Marwari Hindi, and while speaking to me, would try and switch over to ordinary spoken Hindi. Sewa Ram told me his account of the journey he undertook along with his family at the time of Partition.

I lived in Mohalla Mishri Shah close to Delhi Gate in Lahore. I lived at least the first 30–35 years of my life in Lahore. My father had migrated to Lahore from Rajasthan for better employment opportunities. We originally come from Rajasthan. We had done very well for ourselves. We had built a whole *basti*, a colony called Mishri Shah where more than 60–70 families of 2000 or more people lived. They all came from our Rehgar *biradari* originating in Rajasthan. We had proper mud houses. The mud was as good as the cement you use here in Delhi. We had a Rehgar *Sabha* which would organize community functions and gatherings regularly. During summers when it was very hot we would gather in the morning to drink sherbet, eat food together and talk. Our children went to DAV schools and got education. We had an Arya temple in the locality. We were into social service. On 11 August 1947, I remember, we had to leave all that. There was an old Muslim man who knew us and he came to our colony. He said that we should leave. He had seen a group of Muslims who had sworn with their hands on the Quran that they would create *jihad* by killing all the Hindus they would encounter that day. Our *Mussalman* friends helped us by transporting us in their *tongas* (most were *tonga* drivers).

The account told by Sewa Ram is again not very 'different' from the accounts of upper caste Hindu refugees. They were threatened with Muslim violence just like the other Hindus were. Their stories of helpful or villainous Muslims are quite like those of other Hindu and Sikh refugees. They took almost the same routes and resources as many others and arrived in Delhi for similar reasons: they either had previous contacts living in Delhi or expected to gain better economic opportunities. Their entry into the Hindu religion had already begun when the Arya Samaj movement gained ground in Punjab. The untouchable groups were among the main targets since they had to be protected from conversion to Islam and Christianity. The extent of Arya Samaj involvement is evident by the fact that the children of Rehgar community were admitted into Dayanand Anglo-Vedic (DAV) schools. Arya temples had been introduced in various places and Lahore was one of the places where Arya organizations had successfully taken root. They had, in a way, begun entering the category of non-Muslims from then on. The association must have become strong enough for the Rehgar community to be threatened with attack by the local Muslims. Thus their departure took place in similar circumstances to those of the upper caste Hindus.

The divergence from the accounts of middle class upper caste Hindus occurs in three ways: first, unlike the upper caste migrants, the untouchable migrants did not move away from the violence-prone areas before the actual Partition; second, their differing experiences of resettlement once they arrived in Delhi; and third, their full acknowledgement of government support in resettlement. Once the migrants arrived in Delhi, they were inevitably separated on a caste basis. The untouchables were helped by the government in different ways, which may be deemed discriminatory, from the non-untouchable migrants. Yet, among the untouchables, the credit for their social and economic success is duly given to the government. This is something that is often avoided by the upper caste Hindus since it challenges the myth of their own role in successful refugee resettlement. The untouchable refugees remain beholden to the Congress government, whose policies of rehabilitation had dramatically transformed their lives. Most of them said that they could have never dreamed of making such economic gains in their lifetimes had they remained in Lahore. The rupture in their lives had proven to be a positive turning point. They received systematic support from the state that would have never happened in ordinary circumstances.

Such an account of resettlement was hardly what I had expected to hear, given the level of paltry governmental support provided to the untouchables. The Indian state was planning at different levels for refugees, wherein the level of support was determined by their class and caste. This was not a stated policy, but the existence of multi-layered schemes shows that each such scheme was aimed at different sections of society. The hallmark of resettlement policy was compensation, that is, the level of support depended on what one had lost in Pakistan. The aim of the state was to compensate that loss and no more. This left people like Sewa Ram out of that compensation loop since they did not own much. The colony described by him consisted of mud huts, which in retrospect seemed to him better than cement concrete. (Such mud huts are often unplanned or makeshift settlements that are usually inhabited by untouchable or other menial social groups. Provision of housing for the poor has rarely been a serious agenda for the colonial as well as post-colonial state in India. Thus, the lack of proper housing forces such groups to inhabit such 'illegal' colonies.)

Upon their migration to Delhi, the Chamar communities, like all other untouchables, were provided with mud huts in a location that was already inhabited by untouchable groups in Delhi. In a way, they were located by the government in a place that was already 'polluted' by their fellow caste members. They were, as was the norm, given jobs as sweepers with the municipality or encouraged to set up shop as shoemakers. Their traditional caste occupations were the basis of the facilities they would receive from the state. Clearly, the events of Partition migration and resettlement were experienced *differently* by the untouchable migrants in terms of skewed governmental support and the resultant socio-spatial exclusion. The experiences were, nevertheless, congruous with the systematic marginalization—social, political, and economic—that they were faced with on an everyday basis in pre-Partition Punjab.

It must be noted that a large number of untouchable migrants in Delhi who migrated from Punjab actually locate their origins outside British Punjab. The earlier generations had travelled to Punjab as menial employees of the colonial administrators. The frequent movement they undertook along with their British employers every now and again also facilitated their encounters with the Arya Samaj. P.L. Kanojia, a retired section officer with the Indian government, told me his personal story where this linkage of travel and openness to new Hindu reforms becomes clear. Kanojia belongs to the Dhobi (washerman) caste and he was born in Lahore from where he migrated to Delhi after Partition. He differs considerably from Sewa Ram, in that he lives in a residential colony in outer Delhi that is unmarked by caste distinctions. His house is modern two-storeyed and seems like a commonplace listless middle class home equipped with modern electronic gadgets, a young male house help, and plenty of security arrangements to guard the possessions from criminals. It is the knowledge of his low caste that makes him different, since he represents one of those who have broken out of their caste barriers. He also differs from Sewa Ram in his political preferences: he is an RSS supporter while Sewa Ram is a firm Congress loyalist.

My father had a small shop to wash and iron clothes in Lahore city outside the Lahore railway station. There was an Australian building on McLeod Road, I think. It was close to that. On one extreme corner, there was a Hindu *mohalla* where the entire population was Hindu. Sanatan Dharam Sabha also had property there. There was a big temple and a Sanatan Dharam College. It was the first college established in Punjab. We lived there. I was born there. My father was uneducated but his ambition was to educate his son an education. He got me admitted to the DAV school which was an organ of the Arya Samaj. It was a very powerful organization in those days, first socially and then politically. I had the privilege of meeting many big people like Mahatma Hans Raj. We had very good time in those days. DAV was the best institution in those days.

Hindu leaders were afraid that Christian missionaries would want to convert us. We had seen the British from close quarters. They were more than just rich Indians, but they were our enemies who had made us their slaves. The Arya Samaj did the right thing by opening schools that gave an Indian education. They also taught us English. Poor and low-caste people like us could study at these schools for free. I had the fortune of having Pandit Jagannath and Pandit Vishwanath as our history teachers. They taught us about the golden history of India and also the history of England. Such books were selling like hot cakes in those days. The school was established in 1926 or 27. I could have never got that quality education elsewhere.

These narratives clearly show that untouchables groups who frequently moved in the Punjab region had already come into contact with the Arya Samaj and, thus, a new Hindu identification. Their close interaction with the British had somehow disillusioned them enough to respond favourably to the Aryas. The events of Partition gave them similar opportunities and threats of violence put them on par with their upper caste counterparts. The physical separation of the camps and housing for upper castes and untouchables failed to foment any discontent among them. The repeated stress on DAV school and the level of education therein showed that Kanojia was deeply beholden to the education and subsequent opportunities that Arya Samaj membership had provided him. He was able to separate himself from the other untouchables to carve out an indistinct middle class for himself and his family. However, this did not mean that Kanojia was easily accepted by his upper caste colleagues even when he accepted a Hindu education and way of life.

After I had joined government service, I became a member and office bearer of the SC/ST employees union. We had separate unions for upper-caste and untouchable employees. I was a Grade II officer and yet they did not allow me to join the officers' union. The SC/ST union was full of Grade IV employees, mainly employed as sweepers, peons and office boys. I was instead asked to become their office-bearer, as I was one of the few who could speak English. I often wondered why I had to join the SC/ST union. My colleagues were polite and respectful but they were resentful of the SC quotas in jobs. I was well qualified and hardworking so I always got respect from them (personal interview, January 2002).

Kanojia was clearly reluctant to voice his discontent fully since that would immediately detach him from his upper caste colleagues. He drew solace and legitimacy from the fact that he had been asked to lead the the SC/ST union since he was one of the few untouchable employees who were well educated. His status as an office-bearer set him apart from the ordinary members who belonged to the lowest rung in the official hierarchy called grade IV. Any hint of resentment was absolved through the behaviour of his colleagues who were personally 'polite and respectful' towards him. While he narrated his life as a government employee, it constantly shifted between personal pride at having gained this official position and silent umbrage at caste barriers and discriminations that prevented him from realizing his full potential.

However, Sewa Ram and Kanojia were bound together even in their different narratives through the acknowledgement of the state's role in resettlement. There was an absence of the kind of critique that I routinely faced with upper caste Hindus; in fact, Sewa Ram's and Kanojia's tale was actually leavened with fulsome praise for the state. The explanation for this seemed twofold. First, as untouchables they had learnt not to expect any just distribution of wealth, resources, or opportunities from those above them in caste, class, or social-political power. The little they got from the state was seemingly unexpected and was therefore more appreciated than it would otherwise be. Second, property prices had risen enormously in the commercial areas of Delhi, including Rehgar Pura, as a result of which they had gained far more economically than they could have ever hoped for.

This seemed to be a constant theme that was brought up every now and then to prove their contentment in life. The tiny plots of land where their mud huts stood in the late 1940s were now sites of multi-storeyed houses. The arrangement for most plot owners was to contract a private builder who would build the entire house with his own investment. The builder and the owner would come to own two floors each in the house. The owner could reside in one apartment while the spare one could be rented out. This gave them a modern apartment to live in and also ensured a fixed income from rent that would support them in their old age. This strategy of building and renting out is being used all over Delhi since the late 1980s, when certain restrictions in the building bye-laws were removed. The rising population in Delhi meant a severe shortage of residential and commercial space, which made such private arrangements highly lucrative. The limited social parity that economic success provided them led them to be more grateful to the authorities than their upper caste counterparts. Moreover, there were no tales of personal or collective heroism—during violence and migration—in circulation that had to be safeguarded from state intervention.

It is intriguing that the complaints against the state authorities are far and few among the untouchable migrants. On a comparative level, the untouchable migrants did not get even a small pittance when compared with the various grants and loan schemes earmarked for the upper caste refugees. In the period April–August 1948, the rehabilitation ministry spent Rs 2000 on Harijan relief and formed two cooperative societies with a share capital worth 4000 rupees to construct mud huts. When compared with the figures of £7171 and $39,710 given out as low interest loans to children of refugee parents studying abroad, the amounts given to the untouchables were just a pittance (GOI 1947–48: 23).[23] The discrimination by upper caste refugees against the untouchables does not seem to be a big issue for the government-established agency, the Harijan Sevak Sangh (HSS), which that worked specifically for the untouchables. Its offices were situated in Kingsway where a large majority of refugees resided in the camps. Its monthly letter of February 1948 gives an interesting glimpse into its main priorities.

The main highlight of the letter is an item about Orissa where at the Jagannath temple in Puri 'following the refusal of entry to Harijans by the priests and temple authorities, a batch of Harijans and caste Hindu volunteers offered *Satyagraha* at the temple. After two days the district magistrate had the temple doors opened and the Harijans are now entering the temple and worshipping without obstruction'.[24] Similarly, in Assam, temples were reportedly thrown open to Harijans.[25] In East Punjab, the newsletter reported, the government had announced two constitutional acts for the betterment of Harijans at a Harijan conference held in Adampur near Jalandhar.[26] It is clear that the HSS had other agendas that had larger implications for the untouchable population. The untouchable refugees figure only in one instance in this newsletter. where the general secretary of the HSS is mentioned as submitting a report on the plight of Harijan refugees from Sind. This shows that the discrimination against the untouchable refugees— in distribution of relief funds and opportunities—was never considered a priority even by an organization created for the benefit of untouchables.

A single complaint of discrimination is voiced in a letter from B.R. Ambedkar to Jawaharlal Nehru, wherein the situation of untouchable refugees is highlighted. This is the only instance where the word 'discrimination' is clearly used to describe their plight:

(1) The SC (Scheduled Castes) who have come to East Punjab are not living in refugee camp established by the Government of India (GOI). The reason is that officer in charge of these refugee camps discriminate between caste Hindu refugees and SC refugees.

(2) It appears that relief and rehabilitation department has made rule that it is only refugees who are staying in relief camp can receive ration, clothing etc. on account

of their not staying in the refugee camp for reason mentioned above the SC refugee are not getting any relief. This is a great hardship.[27]

The discrimination mentioned here did not however get thorough redress, even though the letter was written as early as 18 December 1947. The mud huts in Rehgar Pura appeared a few months later under the aegis of Rameshwari Nehru cooperative society. The caste discrimination among the refugees hardly arises as a major source of concern among the political parties, ministry officials or even organizations like the HSS.

ABERRATIONS IN THE MASTER NARRATIVE

The entire episode at the ministry appears as a compact version of the various processes that lead to the creation of *master narratives*, that is, how some accounts gain widespread acceptance while others are silent. The upper caste middle class Punjabis, in a way, claim the Partition narratives as their own and are reluctant to allow others to share the limelight with them. The head clerk and the section officer symbolically represented the highly vocal groups that tell their version of the Partition events publicly and repeatedly. They told me stories like the ones I heard over and over again from the hundreds of survivors that I would meet formally and informally during my fieldwork. An entire discourse about brave, hardworking Punjabis was reproduced everyday at the ministry's almost abandoned offices.

On the other hand, Sham Singh symbolized the silent *aberration* within that master narrative, which was always present but never publicly visible or audible. The silent figure in the background was now threatening the grand narrative itself, by merely suggesting that its story too be heard by others. The story was never heard because the dominant figures in this drama expressed their disapproval at the proposed intrusion. Sham Singh continued to be an aberration whose experiences had to be kept out of 'their' story. It had never belonged to him and he had obviously never offered to participate in it. He withdrew his offer to take me to his neighbourhood just as silently. Now the task before me was harder than before because, on the one hand, I had become aware of Sham Singh's presence in the events of Partition migration, and, on the other, I had no clue how to trace an entire group of people in a burgeoning city like Delhi which was home to at least 14 million people at the time of my fieldwork. Ironically, it was the documents from the ministry that I was originally seeking that gave me a clue to the possibility of finding the untouchable refugee settlements in Delhi.

It became clear later that there were many untouchable groups who had settled in Delhi but whose narratives had failed to become popular or known to others. The untouchable migrants had been previously engaged with the reformist Hindu movements, and the events of Partition made that Hindu identity concrete since they were faced with the same threats as upper caste Hindus. This did not mean that untouchables were accepted by the upper caste Hindus. The government-organized schemes and housing facilities set them physically apart from the other refugees, according to prevalent caste norms.

CONCLUSIONS

A major task of this chapter has been to piece together the missing parts—the untouchable refugees—in the Partition resettlement puzzle. Though the untouchable refugees remain discursively absent in the popular narratives of the Partition, they did physically migrate to India. Their experiences, losses, and journeys do not appear to be particularly different, yet they constitute highly divergent experiences from those of the upper caste Hindu migrants. Like their upper caste counterparts, the untouchable migrants in Delhi had an urban, mobile background that made them migrate from place to place as the service class attached to the British colonial administration. Almost a century-long interaction with the colonial Empire meant that the socio-economic conditions and personal aspirations of the untouchable service class had been considerably raised. The influence of the late 19th century social reform movements brought the untouchables into focus primarily for recruitment to the reformed religious groups like the Arya Samaj.

The untouchables were clearly seen as 'empty' in their own identity and therefore objects over which Hindu, Sikh, and Christian missionaries competed for conversion. This trend continued during Partition as well, when India and Pakistan evidently competed to gain the untouchables on their side. While Pakistan wanted to retain untouchables to avoid loss of traditional menial labour, the Indian liaison officers lobbied hard to make them leave their homes so as to emphasize Pakistani aggression. The untouchables who would, otherwise, remain socially marginalized were nationalized in this process.

The Indian national claim upon the non-Muslim untouchables did not, however, improve their conditions. Upon their arrival, they faced discrimination and separation from their upper caste brethren. They were housed separately from the upper caste migrants in the transit camps as well as in the permanent housing. They were settled in the existing untouchable housing colony on the margins of the city. The financial assistance provided to the individuals and groups was pitiful and meagre in comparison to the state schemes for assistance to the upper caste migrants.

Interestingly, caste discrimination was never a stated government policy, but the creation of a separate agency for the untouchables meant that they were no longer included in the general category. The separation from the upper caste groups led to the integration of untouchable migrants with the existing untouchable groups in Delhi. This integration also served to diminish their distinctive experiences of Partition.

NOTES

1. See, for example, *Azadi* by Chaman Nahal, *Tamas* by Bhisham Sahni, and *Train to Pakistan* by Khushwant Singh, where all the main characters—who later become refugees—come from upper caste, middle class families.
2. See O.P. Narula (2002) *I Still Remember a Small Town in Punjab*; Prakash Tandon (2000); Som Anand (2001); and Pran Neville (2001).
3. See M.S. Randhawa(1954*).*
4. An exception is the life story of Maya, a Punjabi Dalit woman, narrated in Urvashi Butalia (1998).
5. The upper caste Punjabis not only dominated the political-administrative infrastructure but also academia as historians of the partition process. An example along with works and authors cited in notes 1–3 is the work produced by well-known historian B.R. Nanda under the pseudonym J. Nanda (1948), *Punjab Uprooted: A Survey of the Punjab Riots and Rehabilitation Problems.* The authorship of this work was acknowledged by B.R. Nanda, a Punjabi Khatri refugee from Lahore, at a public lecture on 11 February 2002 at India International Centre, Delhi.
6. See H.A. Rose (1911); Denzil Ibbetson (1916); and G.W. Briggs (1920).
7. For a good discussion on untouchability, see Mendelsohn and Vicziany (2000); Kancha Illaiah (1996), *Why I am Not a Hindu: A Sudra Critique of Hindutva Philosophy, Culture and Political Economy.*
8. NWFP was still an administrative part of Punjab at that time.
9. Compiled from the population tables, Census of India, 17 February 1881.
10. Compiled from the Punjab province population tables, Census of India, 1941.
11. As a government employee, Sham Singh had official records according to which he had two years more of full service, which made him 58 years old in 2000. But this he described as a formality, since hardly anybody kept records of birth at that time and while filling up forms people would just put an approximate date. Often when getting employment with the government, people would fill in a lower age so that they could have a longer span of employment and a higher pension. Among an older generation it is not uncommon to find that people have two dates of birth, one which they call the real birth date and another which is the official one on the school leaving certificate. This practice is becoming less common now, especially in the cities, where more and more births take place in clinics where records are regularly maintained.
12. I have heard this joke many times over especially from my Pakistani Punjabi friends, with the Chuhras in the joke described as Christian converts. This may have to do with the isolated position Christian minority groups have within Pakistan.
13. The reference here is not to any specific policy document but rather to the affirmation against caste-based discrimination made by Gandhi and the Congress

leadership. The preamble of the 1950 Constitution clearly articulates an egalitarian state and society, irrespective of the biases of caste, religion and gender. Therefore, equality in allotment schemes for refugees would be a logical culmination of this ideology in the resettlement process.

14. For example, it is quite common among middle class Punjabis in Delhi to use low caste names like Chuhra, Chamar and Bhangi as insults, implying someone who is unhygienic, engaged in unclean, dirty work, or has inferior social origins.

15. Personal interview with Kedarnath Sachdeva, a Hindu Arora refugee from Sialkot, in October 2001.

16. Annual Report 1947–48, Ministry of Relief and Rehabilitation, Government of India, p. 24.

17. Annual Report 1947–48, ibid., pp. 24, 68.

18. Annual Report 1947–48, ibid., p. 68.

19. It is named after the social activist Rameshwari Nehru, who was actively involved in the freedom struggle as well as later in refugee resettlement work.

20. For a description of the migration of Chuhras from Punjab to Delhi city, see Vijay Prashad (2000), *Untouchable Freedom: A Social History of a Dalit Community*.

21. A number of people helped me reach Rehgar Pura and its residents. Among them are Umakant and Arun Chaudhary, Dalit activists who provided me with crucial clues and contacts during my fieldwork.

22. The BSP is a Dalit political party with pockets of influence in Delhi, Uttar Pradesh, and Punjab. It is the first Dalit party to have gained political power in Uttar Pradesh.

23. Annual Report 1947–48, Ministry of Relief and Rehabilitation, p. 23.

24. AICC Papers File no. G-24/1947–8.

25. Ibid.

26. Ibid.

27. Dr B.R. Ambedkar Papers, File no 1–3, R–2922, Nehru Memorial Museum and Library, Delhi.

7. Claims of Locality
At Home in Delhi

This chapter aims to show the intricacies and challenges involved in claiming a new place as one's own. Any claim to locality by newcomers involves two distinct processes: One is to create an existential space for themselves in the new place, and the other is to bring the relationship with the old place to a conclusion. For the Punjabi refugees this involved, one, contesting and negotiating for social, political, and economic space with the local Delhi residents, and two, coming to terms with the loss of homeland which is now subsumed by the 'enemy' state of Pakistan. These two processes work simultaneously when a new place becomes the location of one's 'home'.

One of the most remarkable characteristics of the refugee resettlement process in Delhi is the absence of any noticeable local–refugee conflicts. This is especially interesting when compared with the resettlement of Muslim Partition refugees in Karachi, which has resulted in violent conflict between locals (ethnic Sindhis) and refugees (Muhajirs). The roots of Muhajir separatism are often located in the political processes and official policies of ethnic polarisation pursued by the Pakistani state in the early decades after Partition, leading to alienation of the Urdu-speaking migrants.[1] The emergence of a separatist identity among Muslim refugees in Karachi stands in sharp contrast to the Hindu and Sikh refugees in Delhi, who, in comparison, effortlessly claimed membership among the Indian citizenry. In each instance of population movement and resettlement, the migrants had to compete with the local residents to create a space for themselves. However in Delhi, as we shall see, the migrants not only created a niche for themselves but also successfully edged out the local residents. It is the local–refugee dialectic and the entire process of refugees successfully claiming the locality which forms the core of this chapter.

It must be clearly stated that the aim of this chapter is *not* to make a comparative analysis of the contrasting outcomes of refugee resettlement processes in Delhi and Karachi; rather, it is to delve in the highly emotive issues of belonging and deprivation that characterise these processes. The central question is: when do refugees begin feeling at home? Two main sources will be used to further the enquiry: archived private letters[2] and personal interviews with the refugees conducted during the fieldwork, and archived correspondence[3] between a Delhi resident and the then Prime Minister, Jawaharlal Nehru. Interestingly the private letters are mostly addressed to Nehru and rarely to the local Congress leaders or government officials. While the archives from the early years show how refugees responded immediately to the rupture in their lives, the personal testimonies half-a-century later point to the accumulated experiences and journeys of the individuals. The correspondence, on the other hand, reveals the concerns of the local residents who felt deprived in the new scheme of things in Delhi, where the highest priority was given to the refugee resettlement. In both instances, letters from refugees as well as locals are addressed to the president of AICC or directly to Nehru, in whom the political legacy of freedom struggle was combined with the executive authority of the office of Prime Minister.

The theme of refugee resettlement reflected in the content of these letters—ranging from complaints, appeals, and requests to letters that express sheer anguish and frustration—presents research material in a highly emotive context where the state figures as a principal actor. It is not surprising that such material evokes an equally emotive reading. Urvashi Butalia describes the relationship between the refugees and the state authority as that of parent–child, where the children (refugees) appeal for their simple needs to be provided for by the parent (state) (Butalia 2001). The state, then, becomes a compassionate listener, a provider, a protector, whose authority must be invoked to relieve oneself from suffering. Similarly, the response of the Bengali refugees in demanding compensation in West Bengal is framed as a passionate debate on 'right or charity', where the apathy of the state forced the Bengali refugees to politically organize themselves (Chatterji 2001: 76). The comparative yardstick brings Punjabi refugees into this debate to show how the central government favoured Punjabi refugees over their Bengali counterparts while distributing relief funds. In either argument, the state is seen as the final arbiter and main organizer of resettlement, while the refugees are simultaneously shorn of their agency.

The relationship of the refugees with the state seems to be the primary concern in these studies. Butalia believes that the relationship was reciprocal in nature: 'If the refugee, then, looked upon the state as its parent, the state equally looked upon the refugee as its child'(Butalia 2001: 215). However, the state–refugee interaction was not that uncomplicated, as this chapter will show. The *mai-baap* (parental) approach, with a subordinate position adopted by the refugees towards the state, cannot be taken at face value as it is a well-known strategy employed by ordinary people when confronting state authorities. The pleading tone in the private letters as described by Butalia has another face that sarcastically mocks the authorities and frequently challenges them. The challenge, therefore, is to sift through this emotive material and separate, if possible, some concrete denominators of feeling at home that help conceive refugees as their own *agents*.

'REFUGEE' AS A POTENT LABEL

Among Partition refugees, it is the label 'refugee' that tends to define the social positioning of individuals and groups. The label was extensively used by the migrants as well as by the state for its own administrative purposes. Interestingly, the legal documents used terms like 'displaced persons' or 'evacuees', while the official writings use the tem 'refugees' to describe the plight of migrants.[4] In non-legal description, Partition migrants were described as refugees, in order to convey a specific implication of their displacement. But in the mid-1960s, this usage became less popular and has finally ceased to exist in active memory in the last couple of decades. The use and withdrawal of the term 'refugee' offers us a valuable opportunity to discern the reasons and circumstances that led to its employment and then withdrawal. It calls for a wide range of explanations beginning with the meanings of the term both locally and within the lexicon of international aid agencies. We also need to find which identities replaced 'refugee' once it was out of vogue.

The term 'refugee' denotes widely acknowledged meanings, legal implications, and instant associations with the popular images of refugees around the world. Since World War II there has been a dramatic expansion in the literature related to 'refugee problems' that has led to the formation of a whole field of study—refugee studies—that is kept alive by regular university courses, research papers, academic journals, newsletters, etc., that provide a platform for the refugee researchers to interact on common ground (Lippert 1999). While most concepts come packed with inherent scholarly debates and disagreements, a problem area crucial to this study needs to be specifically mentioned here: the wide gaps in the local understanding of concepts that are otherwise globally created, understood, and applied. This problem is not necessarily legal–technical in nature, but relates rather to how local people understand and then use such conceptual categories to alter or expand their own social vocabulary and distinctions. This is why it becomes imperative to compare and contrast the meanings invested in terms like 'refugees' in their local immediate context of application. The local meanings offer useful clues not only as to how refugees were perceived at the time of crisis, but also how the usage influenced the integration and identification process later on.

To conceptualize the forced migrants of Partition, we need to look for the nearest equivalent of the term refugee in the three main local languages: Hindi, Urdu, and Punjabi. The expressions that are sometimes used in lieu of refugees are *panahgeer, sharnarthi,* and Muhajir. While both panahgeer and sharnarthi are used interchangeably in Hindi and Punjabi,[5] Muhajir is used in Urdu with connotations that pre-date Partition, and are linked to the Islamic tradition of migratory journeys. The Hindi/Punjabi terms suggest someone who seeks shelter, protection, and support. Such a need is of an immediate nature and does not necessarily entail acts of charity. It may simply suggest a break in one's journey for a shorter/longer period where one is seeking a place to rest for a while. It is quite common to find *panah-ghar* and *sharnarthi-grah*, both meaning shelter-homes, all over India, particularly around the religious shrines. These places offer very basic facilities for travellers and pilgrims at very nominal prices.

On the other hand, the term Muhajir is derived from the Islamic tradition, when Prophet Mohammad fled from Mecca to Medina to escape religious persecution in 622 AD. The idea of undertaking journeys to realize a true Islamic society is, therefore, inherent in the Muslim belief and the expression Muhajir includes suggestions of persecution, escape, and periods of temporary shelter before the ideal society is achieved.[6] The Urdu expression is markedly different from the Hindi/Punjabi term, and the contrast is realized later when one looks at the way both ordinary people and the governments of India and Pakistan viewed refugees in their respective countries.

The Muslim migrants from India with their labels as Muhajirs came to Pakistan feeling that they had sacrificed their homes and livelihood to facilitate the making of a Muslim state. Their migratory status later became the rallying point for creating a separate Muhajir political identity and demands for provincial autonomy.[7] On the other hand, the usage of common terminology normally employed to describe travellers to describe Partition migrants in India failed to become a rallying point for a separate identity for the Hindu and Sikh migrants. It must be noted that all three expressions are devoid of the legal and administrative implications associated with the term 'refugee'. They do evoke empathy, concern, and charity but do not necessarily call for an organized legal response. As such, outside the bureaucratic policy frames, refugees in India need to be understood more as a social category rather than a legal one in the way it is locally understood. Having brought the local terminology into this discussion, it needs to be stated that the term 'refugee' does not as a consequence become redundant for us, since it was singularly used by the Indian state to describe the Partition migrants. It may not translate all the meanings ascribed to the local term but it is important because it becomes the facilitator through which the panahgeer, sharnarthi, and muhajirs become part of a global discourse of forced migration. The category of refugees comes complete with its discursive meanings and its specific historical development after the two world wars.

RAGE IN LETTER-WRITING

The letters written by private individuals during and immediately following Partition comprise a rich source in which personal accounts, comments on the political situation, and stories of individual struggle come alive. Letter-writing to authorities with prayers, requests, grievances, and appeals is an established tradition in India even today. Political leaders routinely hold public sessions where members of the public submit their pleas and petitions. Often the letters are not written by the petitioners themselves, because they are either illiterate or are not adept at letter-writing. It is not very difficult to distinguish the letters written by proxies, as they have a dispassionate tone and a concrete subject matter. The letters written by the petitioners themselves often display an emotional tone and verbosity that betray their amateur skills. However, the letters are mostly written by individuals who have some connection with the state as well as the local communities, that is, they are either retired or currently employed government officials, or had been involved in the national freedom struggle.

The letters are also interesting because they contain evidence that is not revised or polished. The accounts tell a story of 'here and now' as it was experienced in 1947 and without the benefit of hindsight. There is no systematic collection of private letters to be found in any public archive, though there are innumerable letters written to various authorities around that time. The letters are scattered throughout the archives of the political parties, political leaders, and refugee organizations.

Though most of the letters are quite long, with strong emphasis on an official letter-writing style, they are best read *in toto* in their original form. Since many letters are written in longhand, it is difficult at times to read them properly.[8] Most of the letters are written in English, pointing to the literate middle class origins of the letter-writers. Many letters are incomplete: for example, the writers forget to identify themselves while they take pains to introduce their situation. In other cases, the letters are neatly typed on official letterheads that clearly state the position of the writer and the capacity in which he is writing.

The following letter is an example from among the hundreds of letters written by private individuals to take up issues related to their personal situation with the state. This letter was chosen because it is one of the few letters which is followed by a sequel, suggesting that the writer interacted with the state officials on more than one occasion. The changed context— from personal to public/political—offers a deep insight into how ordinary people made sense of the events unfolding around them.

Box 7.1

41, Arambagh Lane, New Delhi,
28th October 1947.
Shri Acharay Jee,
Sadar Namaskar. I am quite a stranger to you but before encroaching on your busy time [I] will try to introduce myself. I am an unfortunate resident of Campbellpur district (Punjab) and was living in Quetta. Formerly a follower of Bapoo Jee [Gandhi] but now have lost my way. The Independence in Pakistan came to me as follows:- On 22.08.1947, my son 30 years old with his wife and daughter were killed at Bostan station when undauntedly defying mob attack and their all belongings looted. I was made to move out of Quetta, after loading all my belongings under pressure into a wagon. I with five dependent members succeeded in getting into Delhi and the wagon is still in Pakistan. My inherited as well as own collections in all kinds and shapes in Punjab has changed hands against my will. My strength is failing in reducing the personal and family needs to MINIMUM because no means exist. The hunger and winter are not co-operating. How to fit youngsters in the society remains a problem. Now, I with my dependants, am a complete destitute but not CALM. I do not know what is coming next.
In studying the leading papers, the trend and tone of articles and general treatment being met adds everyday to my fretting and chaffing – thus I am compelled to write to you. Acharya Ji, request you to kindly excuse me for addressing you and mistakes in my language. No disrespect to any personality is meant.[9]

Source: AICC Instalment II.

The letter-writer never identifies himself but a handwritten clerical note on the margin says 'A letter from an old Congressman, Mangal Sain who has lost much in Pakistan and complains of appeasement of Muslims (last few words unreadable)'. The clerk recommends the letter be sent to the Ministry of Relief and Rehabilitation for further action.

The letter quite clearly lays out the compelling circumstances in which the writer was involuntarily 'made to move out of' Quetta. He emphasizes again the forced nature of his movement that took place 'against my will' when he was made to load his belongings 'under pressure into a wagon' and on the losses when he mentions that the wagon was left behind in Quetta. The material loss is preceded by the irreplaceable loss of the lives of his young son, his wife, and their daughter. The only solace, if it could be so called, seems to be the fact that the deceased 'undauntedly defied the mob'. He hints at the scarce resources the family is left with and writes in bold letters that his central concern is to keep their personal needs at a minimum. The cold winter has begun setting in when he writes in late October and it seems to him that even nature has turned against him by 'not cooperating'. He makes a cryptic remark about the problems the young people faced in the new circumstances, though we are never told what these problems are. A strong likelihood is that parents, especially middle class parents, were worried about the rupture in their children's education and their lack of prospects. He doesn't specify whether the youngsters are male or female, though the parental concerns differed according to the gender of their children. The daughters had to be married off suitably, a project that became difficult in the new situation. The loss of material wealth and status combined with the lack of reliable kinship networks upon made finding suitable spouses difficult.

The primary concern on behalf of male children was to ensure that they did not mix in what is popularly called 'bad company', that is, to keep them away from bad influences. It must have been a tough task considering that the young men's normal routines like going to school/ college or helping their fathers with the family business were disrupted. The dilemmas of the young men were not only about their personal development but also about their inability to rescue their families from newfound misery. During my fieldwork, a peculiar incident that hinted at these dilemmas was recounted to me by a refugee from Malkwal in Punjab. At the time Partition took place, he was 21 years old, single, and had acquired pre-university education. He came from a fairly well-off middle class family, and when the violence broke out in Punjab the whole family migrated to Delhi. They came to live in Kingsway Camp and were together with their relatives (around 35 people) allotted a small army barrack unit measuring approximately 50 square metres. This was a sudden and dramatic reversal in their living conditions and overall family status.

I wanted to help my family financially but there were no jobs to be found. And I was young, strong and enthusiastic. It was difficult for me sit in the camp and do nothing. So finally I, along with my cousins, who were in the same age group and same conditions, tried many different things. We even went to the extent of going to the railway platform in the main station everyday and spotting a long-distance train that was scheduled to depart in the next half hour or so. We would occupy a sleeper berth or two in the reserved compartment and wait for the rightful passengers to arrive. People were eager to leave for wherever they had to in those days and were in no mood to argue over this irregularity. We would refuse to vacate the seats till they paid us Rs 10–15 per berth. The passengers who were already afraid and just waiting to get away feared us even more when 7–8 strong young men sat together and blocked the seat. In this way we could earn a bit so as not to become burdens on our families. We did this for a very long time for months at end. But the circumstances were such that we could have tried anything in those days. Soon I found a job in Connaught Place as a shop assistant and later I got this shop in Khan Market.[10]

This incident was described to me as an example of desperation. This plan of occupying berths to demand small amounts of money seems innocent but I was told later by Balraj Malhotra that he considered himself fortunate for having got out of that phase. One of his relatives, an officer in the municipality, helped him in getting a licence to ply a cycle-rickshaw in Delhi. Later he was introduced to a shopkeeper in Connaught Place, who gave him valuable training and contacts to get his own shop. In each phase of his story, there is an older male figure who guided him on to a successful path, at the end of which he established his own business, got married to a girl whose family had also migrated to Delhi, and had children of his own. He now leads a regular life in Delhi, the life of an elderly patriarch who is at peace with the paths he has travelled so far.

It is these possibilities for young people to get engaged in nefarious activities that the letter-writer probably hints at. There is a latent rage in his writing that becomes obvious when he refers to his present position that he may be 'a complete destitute but not CALM'. In bold letters he recounts the state of agitation he finds himself. One can clearly see the underlying anger even when he makes excuses for his writing style and the very fact that he wrote that letter. Finally he insists that 'no disrespect to any personality is meant', suggesting that his anger is not personally directed at anyone in particular. He is writing to express the rage he felt at the circumstances that forced him to leave his home, lose precious lives in his family and lose his life savings to reach a destitute state.

Another letter that is machine-typed and six full pages long follows this letter. The second letter is undated but the order in which it is filed suggests that it was no more than a month or so after the first letter that it was received at the AICC office. Now the contents of the letter are no longer personal but respond to the general political situation that forced millions to become refugees. The rage that was earlier expressed in negative terms as absence of CALM now becomes more direct in pointing out the failure of the political leadership to protect the populace.

The Congress has made a bargain to satisfy the Muslim greed by offering minorities in 'Pakistan' with their honour and properties. Shree Santhanam while sitting in a castle like office and living in a palace of Royal City, cannot go into the depth of suffering to gauge them that is why he calls it a 'lesser evil'.[11] Whatever has happened is due to the weak and yielding policy of the Congress which is lost in only building Constitution and preaching theories to Hindus who are already peace loving, non-violent and law abiding. The entire EVIL lies in the separation theories (i.e., communal award, vivisection of country on religion basis, exchange of population, and accepting religion as the base for Nation etc.) agreed to on one hand and now when the tree has grown and started to bloom now lesser evils and bigger evils are being differentiated.[12]

The Congress leadership is directly held culpable for the current situation, in which minorities have lost their bearings. The writer now boldly uses his identity as a Hindu and speaks for all the Hindus who are described as naturally being 'peace loving, non-violent and law abiding'. The Congress on the other hand is seen as appeasing the Muslims who got Pakistan uncontested, with their 'honour and properties' intact. The contrast is obviously with the Hindu minorities from Pakistan, who were denied their honour and property. The writer accuses the politicians of refusing to appreciate the sufferings of the Hindus. One can hazard a guess as to what the writer means by 'lesser evil' when he mocks K. Santhanam for being cocooned in luxury and therefore divorced from reality. The writer refers to some studies of 'Shree Santhanam' that unjustly compare European conditions with Indian conditions. It is highly probable that Santhanam referred to the population transfers that took place between World War I and World War II under international treaties. The policy papers from the ministry of rehabilitation contain several references to the situation in Europe that tended to serve as a precedent for the population exchange in India. The prevailing view at that time favoured separation of diverse ethnic groups as a way of pre-empting ethnic conflict. It was, therefore, considered a lesser evil than outright strife and annihilation of populations. The writer sees the acceptance of these principles—of separating nations on the basis of religion—as the root cause of this collective evil, which the politicians were trying to justify by distinguishing between lesser and greater evils. He further elaborates on the plight of ordinary people who are now refugees:

When the exchange of population was agreed to arrangements should have been made well ahead for accommodation before immigrants arrived in the UNION [refers to the Indian Union]. Instead of bridging the gap Refugees are expected to manifest their further patience and tolerance. If they had not the courtesy or forethought, they should have asked 'Pakistan' to lend them a helping hand who have so successfully screened out all non-Muslim elements stark-naked, scrapped their belongings and passed to Muslims. In foreign press and before UNO they have placed the whole blame on the Hindus and Indian UNION (sic). Shree Acharya Jee (AICC President) your sermon is really out of tune song when winter is setting in, the limitations of administrators which actually have no bounds are being considered to be overcome. The material needs of the time cannot be met with words only. The wrecked refugees are being treated like wooden stock which can undergo seasonal changes, without bodily needs as lifeless material with no loss to State, Nation or individuals. Would those talking so high try to fit the Refugees shoe on their own feet for a while and then express how comfortable they are? I have gained an experience during past 6 weeks that narrations of Refugees about their sufferings and actions of Muslims are taken lightly and not more than a cinema screen. A humiliating propaganda against Punjab refugees has been started recently. This is because they are weighing Muslims with themselves who have achieved success through violence and the later are trying to win them since 1919 through AHIMSA and conventional actions.

A continuous feature of these letters is the use of capital letters each time the writer wants to emphasize his feelings—absence of CALM; his helplessness, with resources at MINIMUM—and entities or ideologies significant to him, namely, UNION and AHIMSA. Each formulation points to feelings of frustration and anger that he has felt and identifies the objects against which the anger is directed. Another development is

that he no longer views his misfortune as a private matter but as part of
the wider circumstances beyond his control. He separates Hindus as a
distinct group who have on the one hand been victimized by Muslims
and the Pakistani state, and on the other left unprotected by the Congress
leadership that should logically protect their interests. Hindus emerge as
non-violent and tolerant people, whereas Muslims are by nature violent
and untrustworthy, who are being inconsequentially sought to be won
over through ahimsa (policy of non-violence propounded by Gandhi).

Another prominent feature is that the word refugee is spelt with a capital
'R', which marks them out as a separate category. One can infer from the
letter that the refugees in question are Hindus and these identities shape
up simultaneously and frequently overlap one another. What binds these
two identities together is the insensitivity and thoughtlessness that both
are subjected to by the Muslims, the Pakistani state and the Indian state
under Congress leadership. While Muslims and Pakistan are held responsible
for driving minorities (that is, Hindus) out of Pakistani territory, the Indian
state is blamed for not having made appropriate arrangements when an
agreement on population exchange was reached with Pakistan. The conduct
of the Indian state is compared with that of the Pakistani state and the
results seem rather unfavourable for India since Pakistan had been successful
in 'screening' non-Muslims (that is, stripping them of their belongings),
whereas the Indian state had allowed the Muslims to leave with their
belongings.

In a sarcastic phrase, he reminds the AICC President Jugal Kishore
Acharya that his advice to refugees (probably to bear with the situation)
was inconsonant with the practical and climatic realities. In a number of
places the writer literally translates popular Punjabi proverbs and expressions
to describe the situation of refugees. For example, he compares refugees
with a piece of wood that is traditionally left outside by carpenters to
expose it to all the seasons before it is put to use as raw material for furniture.
The comparison turns highly rhetorical when he describes refugees as
lifeless material, like wood left outdoors that causes no sense of loss to
anyone including the state and the nation. What he seems to reinforce is
the dual feeling of being rejected—both by Pakistan and now by the Indian
state. It is also a feeling of alienation, where the writer feels that policy-
makers are far removed from the sufferings of the refugees and do not
therefore take their situation seriously. Thus he provocatively challenges
'those talking so high' to actually try living in the same conditions as the
refugees.

Further on, he makes an orderly list of developments that he thinks
indicate a 'bigger evil' looming large over Hindus and India. These include
possession of arms among Muslims in India; Muslim plans to sabotage

India from within; state protection that Muslims receive from Pakistan to enact a well-thought-out plan, probably to ethnically cleanse Pakistan of Hindus; Muslims allowed to sell their property in India before leaving and the ultimate realization of the goal of '*Jihad*', to get gold, land and beautiful girls; and finally the excessive trust imposed by Gandhi in Muslims. The result of this coming evil can already be seen in the Congress leadership's response to the crisis.

Before the transfer of Power, Shree Pandit Jee showed his helplessness in saving the East Bengal and Punjab Hindus as actual Power was in some other hands, but now when the Power has come the song of Nationalism is being harped. The parting Muslims in camps are being served with milk, sugar and other needs while those having arrived from Pakistan are not getting sufficient cereals to keep on. This is either to please the Muslims or their masters in Pakistan. The Congress has made innumerable sacrifices no doubt but it was all due to the Hindus who, forgetting their self, kept it feeding with men, money and thought without making any reservations. On the other hand, Muslims who contributed the least got the best of it. Now Hindus have no home or protection in either of the dominions both look only to the interests of Muslims only.

The constant themes repeated in this letter are those of anger, disappointment, and a feeling of having been cheated by the new regime in India. The disappointment grows bigger because earlier the administrative power lay with the British and the Congress could express its inability to effectively act in favour of native population. But after the transfer of power, nothing changed significantly for ordinary people. Then the writer invokes another familiar comparison with Muslim refugees who, in his view, got a better deal from both India and Pakistan.

The disappointment with the Congress-led government in India needs to be put in a larger context. It is quite understandable that the immediate hardship faced by the refugees alienated them from the authorities, but the picture painted by the letter-writer about the Muslims is far from true. Their situation was not very different from their Hindu and Sikh counterparts, especially when one considers the approximate period when this letter was written. In the preceding couple of months (August–September), some of the worst massacres of Muslims took place in Delhi. Richard Symonds, an English relief worker touring Delhi, describes the scene in Purana Qila, which had been converted into a transit camp for the Delhi Muslims leaving for Pakistan.

The Muslim population of Delhi of all classes—civil servants, businessmen, artisans, *tongawallahs*, and bearers—had fled to a few natural strongholds, including the Purana Qila (an impregnable Mogul fort), Humayun's tomb and the quarries on the Ridge. At the time of my arrival, the Indian government regarded these camps as the responsibility of the Pakistan High Commissioner who was, however, hardly in a position to move out of his house. There was scarcely any communication between the camps and the outside world except through Europeans, who were able to move safely in both directions. I joined [Alexander] Horace[13] in the largest camp, the Purana Qila which was sheltering 60,000 refugees in tents, in corners of battlements and in the open, together with their camels and *tongas* and ponies, battered old taxis and luxury limousines. There were orderly rows of tents which organised bodies of college students had put up. You might meet anyone from a *nawab* to a professor. Rich men offered thousands of rupees if we could hire them an aeroplane to Karachi. It seems possible to buy anything, from taxi to the hawkers boxes of matches, which were the only ones available in Delhi. From time to time Europeans hurried through looking for their bearers who had fled from their houses. Though it was four weeks since Independence Day, it was British troops who were manning the narrow gate and directing traffic through the lanes and tracks. Three tents were occupied by harassed Pakistan officials, making lists of other officials for evacuation, though risks of being massacred on the special trains to Pakistan were so great that most of those who were not officials preferred to wait and see how things turned up (Symonds 2001: 34).

The scene depicted here is not very different from the condition of Hindu refugees as reported at that time. On each side, the Muslim, Hindu, and Sikh refugees underwent similar agonies, anxieties, and fears when forced to leave their homes. The profile of the Muslim refugees from Delhi is quite remarkable though, since Delhi was a political and commercial centre. The outgoing Muslim population was on average better off as this passage shows. It reports a fair mix of differing social classes: from *tongawallahs* (horse carriage-drivers) to lowly bearers to *Nawabs* (feudal rich men). The proportional change in religious composition of Delhi was rather momentous. The 1941 census recorded 53.2 per cent Hindus, 40.5 per cent Muslims, and 2.3 per cent Sikhs residing in the city. This approximate proportion had been recorded and maintained in the city since the first decadal census conducted in 1881. The 1947 mass migration changed this traditional communal balance. The 1951 census found 82.1 per cent Hindus, 6.6 per cent Muslims, and 8.6 per cent Sikhs in the city. While the Hindu population had greatly increased, the Muslim population was tremendously reduced in numbers, as a majority of the Muslim residents were either annihilated in the massacres or had chosen to leave the city. The preferred destination for Delhi emigrants was Karachi, another sprawling cosmopolitan city that was the commercial centre outside Punjab province. The fact that these diametrically different social classes were forced to take shelter collectively in Purana Qila points to the gravity of the circumstances in which minorities in Delhi were compelled to leave.

This is far from how the condition of Muslim refugees is described in the above letters. While the anger felt by the Hindu refugees is understandable, the dramatic comparison with Muslim refugees—'they are being served with milk and sugar'—was far from true. But this anger, based on exaggerated reports, can be seen as a reason for the increased communal violence in Delhi. In some incidents incoming refugees were directly accused of instigating riots in Delhi. On 26 August a newspaper headline read, 'Refugees warned against breach of peace'. The report read as follows:

After over three months of quiet, the peaceful life of Delhi was disturbed on Sunday evening when there was a case of arson in Subzi Mandi area. The trouble began when a few refugees forcibly occupied vacant houses on the refusal of landlords to rent them. Before the police arrived the trouble developed into a clash leading to arson and looting. The refugees in Delhi have been warned by the local administration to abstain from doing anything which may disturb the peace of the city. Delhi has given shelter and relief to refugees belonging to all communities pouring in from all parts of India. The refugees are in a desperate mood and have not appreciated the hospitality given. They should not forget that they should not indulge in and encourage lawlessness and incite other people by circulating harrowing news of mob fury to their co-religionist here. They would only help to disrupt the peaceful life of refugees, causing hardship not only to the local citizens but to themselves.[14]

This news report contains a few clues as to how identities were being shaped at this stage. First, within two weeks of Independence, refugees had emerged as a separate category in the public discourse. They are identified as a separate group by a Delhi newspaper. Second, the report is written in a way that speaks for the local Delhi citizens whose peace is being disturbed by the incoming miscreants. The local Delhi administration similarly warns the refugees to refrain from creating such trouble as may cause hardship for them and the local citizens. By now two distinct groups have emerged in the city: the refugees and the local citizens. The use of the term 'citizen' is not strictly correct since all, refugees and residents alike, were legal citizens of India. The refugees had at no point been deprived of citizenship rights. The choice of the term 'citizen' somehow emphasizes the deeper claim to locality that the residents had acquired, having lived in the city over generations. This distinction made by the local newspaper is much like the differing ethnic/civic basis for citizenship in contemporary Africa.[15]

In India, the differences between residents and the refugees were never jurisdictional, as citizenship was claimed both on legal grounds and by virtue of a shared history. The claim of a distinction is more based at the social level where refugees were seen to have brought in different cultural norms and values. The incitement of violence in the city was, for instance, seen as a proof of different values that had accompanied the refugee influx. The warnings issued to the refugees point to the magnanimous stance adopted by the residents, which the refugees had seemingly failed to appreciate and reciprocate. Such warnings also helped the residents to state what they stood for—peace—which allowed them to reiterate their claim on the city, especially when their claim to the city was being contested by the newcomers. The refugees were, in this way, told that they could not act as they pleased and that they must observe the collective norms of the city residents.

AT HOME IN THE NEW HOME

A significant focus of the open-ended interviews during the fieldwork was on how the refugees described their association with Delhi city. In other words, how did their migrant status affect their claim to locality? They had made their *new homes* in Delhi but did they feel *at home* in the new place? If so, then what constitutes the state of being at home? The expression 'home' is used in a dual mode, first as a noun and then as an adverb. The grammatical shift indicates the shift in focus from a concrete object to a qualitative state of being. The shift does not travel in one direction, but rather in a pendulum mode; it swings back and forth between the visible concrete and the intangible. The swing allows one to explore the complexities of association with places and the feelings of belonging.

Such associations become especially intricate when the movement from one place to another is mired in imprints of violence, fear, and loss. It involves, on the one hand, coming to terms with past events, and, on the other, creating new support structures. As Chapter 5 has shown, past and present are never really disrupted on a linear scale. The way one remembers the past depends much on one's present circumstances while the present is often an outcome of past events. Thus, the nature of relationship with the new place is intensely linked to the evolving relationship with the original homeland that one was forced to leave. It is a web of spatial associations that influences the transition in identity labels—from refugee to local—accompanying the spatial movement.

The president of the DI Khan Society made a revealing remark that the locals had by the 1960s stopped calling them refugees.

The locals had never supported us. They used to call us *Sharnarthi*, the refugees. It sounded like a term of abuse because we were used to giving charity to others not receiving it. All of us had big businesses in Dera Ismail Khan. And we had self-respect and pride just like the Pathans. We worked hard to get rid of this 'refugee' title. Some of us got small jobs, others became hawkers or traders buying and selling on a day-to-day basis. But we never begged from anybody and never sat down to lament our fate. It was God's will that we were displaced. Later, some big officers came to visit us and said we were not *Sharnarthi* but *Purusharthi*, able-bodied men capable of achieving the impossible. Earlier we had to write 'refugee' in every official document but in the 1960s we refused to be so described. We had shops, houses, jobs and a lifestyle better than the locals, so why should we accept being called the refugees?[16]

Two strands of discussion emerge from this account. The first is the approximate date mentioned—the 1960s—after which the narrator recalls a movement away from refugee status. It is quite significant that a date is attached to this transition. The important feature of this approximate date is that it was around this time, that the Indian state decided to formally stop the resettlement schemes. The change was evident in 1965, when the

Ministry of Relief and Rehabilitation closed down and all the residual resettlement work was transferred to the Ministry of Home Affairs. There is a symbolic message in the closure of the ministry and the transfer of the remaining work to the home ministry. The refugees no longer needed a separate governmental agency to specifically look after their affairs. They had integrated with the local populace over the two decades and therefore could now be governed by the home office just like everyone else. This official closure appears in the personal account later as a determined refusal to be called a refugee. The refugees were no longer required to fill out separate forms or state their refugee status, which had earlier differentiated them from the local populace. These administrative changes had profound implications for the social identification process whereby the refugees felt more integrated.

The second is the emphasis on acquisition and ownership of immovable assets like houses and shops, and on means of livelihood. The argument seems to be that the ownership of property allows one to contest the notion of being a refugee. It again retains a symbolic aspect—the claim to a piece of land helps one concretize the relationship with that place. A piece of land, an apartment or a similar type of asset that cannot be moved from a place seems to form an association of belonging. It must be mentioned here that the fieldwork I conducted took place in the erstwhile refugee colonies where refugees were settled permanently by the state. This meant that all the people interviewed at various class/caste levels were, in essence, property owners. The method of acquisition of this property varied considerably and was largely based on the compensation policy of the state (Chapter 4). Even though the allotted property varied hugely in actual size and value, it can be deduced that there were no homeless people among those who were officially registered as refugees. Thus a claim to an immovable resource seemed to link them to the new place.

Similarly, sources of livelihood—jobs/private businesses—emerge as another form of association that ties people with places. While the state had offered a place to live in the refugee camps, schemes for financial loans and liberal terms of employment in the state departments, it did not offer a scheme of regular financial support. In the case of widows, physically handicapped and incapacitated individuals, a small amount, ranging between Rs 10 and Rs 40, was allowed. For others, especially the male refugees, such schemes were not available since the belief was that 'rehabilitation is incomplete so long as the refugee is unable to support himself and his family through his own efforts. Only when the displaced person has shed his dependence on government or private doles has he been fully rehabilitated' (Rao 1967: 62). The use of the masculine pronoun clearly suggests that the focus of the government was on male refugees, while the female members of the family were automatically seen as included in any such scheme. The disruption in private employment and businesses meant that the refugees were deprived of the regular income they were used to. To reach even the bare minimum level of lifestyle they were used to, they had no choice but to find work. The government was equally clear that 'every grown up and able-bodied refugee had to be found gainful employment. No one willing to work could be denied an opportunity to earn a living' (ibid.: 63). Thus both the state and the refugees made employment and self-support their priorities. While the state chose this path for administrative and financial reasons, the refugees had no alternative but to find work to support themselves and their families. Thus accounts like the one that follows are an integral part of the migration stories in every family.

My father came a little later than us as he was looking for my elder brother in Dera Ismail Khan. The train that he took stopped at Samalkha [around 100 km from Delhi] and was not allowed any further. We were jewellers by profession. My father had his professional tools along with him, which he had carried all the way on his head. Ha walked along the rail line to Delhi with his meagre belongings and somehow reached Kingsway camp. We had got a place to stay in Edward Lane and later we moved into a quarter in Hudson Lane where we had a big room and a verandah. There was no electricity. It came in October 1958 in the whole camp. Meanwhile we had got a small space in a shop in Kinari Bazaar in Chandni Chowk. Somebody helped us in getting us that place. All the shops belonged to the Delhi residents. But someone just offered that we use that space to start our work. May father worked there for 5–6 years, after which we were allotted a shop on rent basis in Kamala Nagar at the rate of Rs 16 a month. There was no rooftop, but my father kept on working there. In 1980 we purchased that shop through the savings we made with our income. My father married off my sisters and fulfilled all his familial duties.[17]

The insistence in this account is on respect for one's profession, ability, and the will to work hard in all circumstances. From the very beginning, the narrator's father began looking for a place to set up his shop. He managed to get a small space in an established shop belonging to a Delhi resident and worked hard to make enough savings. He got a shop allotted in a newly established commercial area called Kamala Nagar (named after Jawaharlal Nehru's wife Kamala Nehru). He worked in adverse conditions—no rooftop on the shop—but was never deterred by the lack of basic facilities. Later he was able to purchase the shop from the concerned government agency, adding to his assets. His son, the narrator, took on responsibility for the seemingly successful family business after the death of his father. He told me that they were 'well-settled' now, just like everyone else in the group had said. They had houses, shops, jobs, and a respectable status in society. In the narrator's view, the final act of his father to marry off his daughters suitably in the same city was what truly joined him to the place.

This is where he was able to fulfil his paternal obligations, which are within Hindu tradition considered a fairly significant aspect of life. An individual's life span is considered complete when he—that is, especially the father, has fulfilled his duties that include supporting and protecting the family and marrying off his daughters honourably. It often has to do with the control of female sexuality, failing which the family honour risks being sullied. The daughters have to be guarded till they mature for marriage, after which their sexuality is controlled by their husbands. A father who fails to fulfil this contract loses honour even in death. Therefore, fulfilment of such obligations is a major part of the evaluation of one's life.

This also shows how establishment and extension of familial and kinship networks is considered highly important. Marriages also open possibilities for extending one's social relations. The event of marriage itself is important in establishing one's status through the extent of expenditure incurred and the social status of the family to which one's son/daughter is contracted. For the refugees therefore, marriage contracts held an array of social possibilities from where they could re/create their social networks. This added another significant possibility of settling down or being at home. Most of the accounts contained such an element where the marriage of one's self, siblings, and that of one's children were narrated as milestones in the process of settling down and forming greater associations with the place.

Within the two decades after Partition, the refugees considered that they had settled, and they were considered settled by others as well. They had succeeded in reaching the standard of living of the residents and in some cases even surpassed them. In 1956, a study of immigration in Delhi city was conducted at the initiative of the newly established Planning Commission of India.[18] The survey was carried out among a sample of 5956 households comprising a total of 80,278 persons of which 35.9 per cent were refugee-headed households; 33.6 per cent 'normal' immigrants, and the rest (around 30 per cent), were local households.[19] In terms of actual numbers, more than half the population comprised immigrants, refugees, or otherwise. However, this statistical evidence needs to be evaluated cautiously. While the scope and scale of this survey was extensive, it is quite unclear as to the kind of questions asked in gathering this data. The object of the survey was to examine the immigration that occurred as 'a natural process of urbanisation and economic development' (Rao and Desai 1965: vii). Difficulties in making these sharp cleavages are well recognized by the author, as he accepts that the Partition exodus was accompanied simultaneously by an even larger immigration, that is, the Partition migration became a catalyst to migration from the areas surrounding Delhi, to Delhi city. The separation of the resident population from the migrant population was easy, by measuring the extent of remittances sent back home and kinship networks outside the city. It was far more difficult to separate Partition migrants from other migrants. This was because there were 'a number of persons born in Delhi during the reference period who had, therefore, acquired the personal status of residents' (ibid.). Moreover, it was difficult to make clear distinctions between the migrants and the refugees, as there were several families from Punjab who had residence in Delhi prior to Partition due to employment-related transfers. These families gave shelter to their relatives and friends who were forced to leave Punjab during Partition. The distinction was even fuzzier in the case of those refugees who had moved to Delhi after having lived in two or more places within India.

The refugees also had considerable political influence and showed great initiative in organizing politically. A social-behavioural study conducted in the early 1970s showed that the refugees were politically more astute than the locals in Delhi (Keller 1975: 178). It was found that wherever the refugees settled in large numbers they succeeded in gaining political power. It was particularly the high caste refugees who controlled local bodies, cooperatives, panchayats, and town councils. The refugees had closer ties to politicians. More than 60 per cent of the refugees in the survey claimed to have regular contact with politicians that ranged from at least once a month to several times a year, while less than 40 per cent of non-refugees made similar claims. While more than 40 per cent of non-refugees claimed to have never met a politician, only 15 per cent of the refugees made this claim. It is not certain whether it was their refugee status that made them approach politicians, but it is clear that the refugees displayed better ability in organizing themselves and bartering their vote blocks for further political influence.

Significantly the study also showed that within the last two decades, the refugee responses to the government had become moderate and not different from those of non-refugees. The hostility and rage evident in letters written in the late 1940s immediately after Partition seems to have dissipated. Among the refugees, disillusionment with the government was on very similar grounds to that of the residents. The responses were 'neutral' on average, that is, little intensity or extreme views were expressed while narrating their disappointment. There were common issues that concerned both the refugees and non-refugees: government corruption and lack of trust in the government, particularly with respect to the five-year plans and foreign policy vis-à-vis China and Pakistan among others. In the last decade, India had been engaged in full-scale wars with China (1962) and Pakistan (1965 and 1971) and the seemingly troubled relations with India's neighbours were very much in focus when the survey was conducted. The importance of this survey lies in the similarity of the responses of residents and non-residents. The fact that they had found common issues shows that their separate spaces within the locality were slowly merging into one.

PUSHING THE BOUNDARIES

While the story has so far been constructed on the basis of 'refugee' sources—letters, oral testimonies, and surveys—it is important to see the other side. How did the residents perceive the entire in-migration and the gradual breakdown of the refugee–local boundaries? As shown earlier, the refugees did succeed in creating a space for themselves while pushing the locals to the city's economic, political, and social margins. The residents never retaliated for the loss in influence they suffered, and hardly any open clashes have been reported between locals and refugees. Yet there remains an underlying animosity between them that is publicly expressed in a cultural frame: the alleged loss of the city's culture after 1947. This is usually conveyed in carefully worded phrases but the uneasiness can always be felt. Post-Partition Delhi is described as a place where 'Tilak Nagars and Nehru Roads proliferate, and hardly anyone knows of the poetry of Mir and Zauq, the humour of Ghalib, and the quality of life that Chandani Chowk once symbolised' (Gupta 1999: 'Preface' to 1981 edition).[20] The reference is to the numerous refugee colonies that sprang up as part of permanent resettlement. Most of them were named after prominent national leaders like Bal Gangadhar Tilak (Tilak Nagar), Jawaharlal Nehru (Nehru Enclave), and Vallabhbhai Patel (Patel Nagar), to name a few. Therefore, this cultural nostalgia is not devoid of territorial or latent social biases, as most of the reminiscences are located around the walled city, British-built New Delhi, or the spacious residential areas of south Delhi.[21] The urban expansion that took place post-Partition has now come to symbolize the loss of high culture and nobility that Delhi once stood for. The other reference is to poets like Mir Taqi Mir, Zauq, and Ghalib, who symbolized the high point of the cultural renaissance that the city experienced in the later Mughal period.

However, one needs to exercise caution before accusing the residents and their successors of harbouring an elitist bias against the refugees. A part of this critique emerges from an ideological opposition to right-wing Hindu dominance in Delhi. The religious identities have gained significant ground in the last five decades and the city's former cultural symbols (like the poets mentioned above) who happen to be Muslims by religion have been marginalized. The history of the city is popularly associated with the Mughals, but the right-wing Hindu groups have tried to resurrect a Hindu history of the city. This is evident in the way a part of the city has been named as Indraprastha, the mythical capital of the epicurean Hindu Pandava dynasty.

Among the city's architectural symbols like Red Fort, Qutub Minar, and Purana Qila (Old Fort), the Old Fort happens to be the only Hindu structure said to be built by Pandavas. The right-wing Hindu groups have often demanded that the state change the city's symbolic representation from Red Fort/Qutub Minar to the Old Fort. In 2000, the Union Minister for Tourism in the BJP-led central government, Jagmohan, announced a large-scale plan to create a theme park in Delhi to show the Hindu past of the city. Purana Qila was the chosen site, where elaborate homes of the five Pandavas, complete with mythological artefacts, were to be created to 'inculcate right "values" and *samskaras* (traditions) especially among children.'[22] The progressive intellectuals and collective bodies in Delhi see this as an attempt to distort and impose upon the representation of the historical path the city has travelled over centuries. Though it is necessary to separate the opposition to right-wing Hindu politics from the overall contempt for cultural degeneration identified with Punjabi refugees in Delhi, it becomes a rather complicated task when the Punjabi refugees emerge as the key proponents of Hindutva politics in the city. Most of the influential politicians in Delhi, both in the Congress party and the BJP, have a background in Pakistan.[23] A powerful 'Punjabi lobby', as it is popularly referred to, emerged in city politics soon after Partition, to the extent that the local Delhi politicians felt increasingly marginalized.

Brij Krishan Chandiwala, who had played a significant role in organizing the Congress party in the city, led the local Delhi politicians. The seething indignation felt by the local politicians is voiced in a letter Chandiwala wrote to Jawaharlal Nehru to draw his attention towards Delhi's rapid degeneration. Incidentally, he signed himself off as a local resident, a *Delhiwala*, rather than as a Congress functionary.

The people of Delhi are living a life of helplessness. Their greatest crime, perhaps, is that they do not have any feeling of provincial unity and that they readily accept everyone as their own. That is why, except late Hakim (Ajmal Khan) Sahib and Asaf (Ali) Sahib, the leadership of Delhi has always been in the hands of outsiders. The Delhi residents have never complained against it and the result is that they are considered aliens in their own home. There is no one to look after their interests. Can the legislative bodies in Delhi, Municipal Corporation and the Delhi state Congress really claim to have spoken on the residents behalf? They do not share the interests of the residents. The residents are fast becoming a minority. I will rather call them the *adi nivasi* [native residents] of Delhi who have been denied their rights completely. All the opportunities and the avenues in the city have been closed for them. There are neither any houses available for them nor any vacant land to construct suitable houses. There are no possibilities for employment for them. There is neither salvation nor culture and art any more. In just a few years they have lost almost everything.[24]

The letter reads essentially as an emergency plea made in a moment of desperation. The territory that marked off local residents from the rest was now being usurped by the Punjabi refugees. Not only were the locals losing their rightful base, they were further being pushed away—spatially, economically, and politically—to make way for the refugees. Thus, the prime purpose of this letter was (1) to establish the Marwari Hindu trading community as the rightful natives of the city, (2) to protest over their newfound marginalized status in every sphere, and finally, (3) to express their disillusionment with the present political leadership that had failed to represent their interests. While the dissatisfaction is clearly articulated, it is guarded enough not to lay the blame directly on the refugees. The veiled indications, however, allow one to witness the disillusionment with post-Partition developments and the influx of refugees. The dissatisfaction clearly arises from the state's patronization of the newcomers through various government schemes of employment, avenues for political organization through cooperative bodies and welfare societies, and the elaborate mass-housing projects for the refugees. In the mid-1950s, when the letter was written, one could clearly see the results of the state efforts. The state support had contributed to a considerable improvement in the general living conditions of the migrants, whereas the situation of the residents remained more or less static.

The Delhi residents appear as cosmopolitan in their approach since they are found lacking in the provincial feelings of unity. This openness towards 'outsiders', about whom the city's residents have never complained, is held responsible for the increasing influence of these 'outsiders' within city politics. The outsiders seemingly took over the city's affairs once again. The political bodies also took up the concerns of these newcomers while the residents felt completely ignored. The theme of insiders/outsiders becomes particularly paradoxical since most of the population settled in Delhi city has emigrated from the neighbouring regions. As the political centre of north India, Delhi attracted a variety of adventurers, fortune-seekers, traders, and invaders. The long line of Muslim rulers in the region came from West and Central Asia, including the Mughal dynasty itself. More than three centuries of uninterrupted and politically stable Mughal rule attracted a large number of traders from the Marwar region of Rajasthan to its political seat in Delhi.[25] Thus, the Hindu traders cohabited with the Mughal retinue of skilled administrators and artists in the city.

There has never been an ethnic group in Delhi city that could claim deep ancestral roots and long historical associations. This is so because the inhabited urban areas of Delhi have historically moved at least seven times: that is, seven urban locations are known to have existed at different historical periods. The British-built New Delhi around the Raisina Hill is the eighth site on which the city was founded afresh. The post-Partition expansion of the city took place to accommodate migrants who came in dramatically different circumstances from the earlier migrants like the Marwari traders. This ambiguity in the description of who is an insider or outsider is clearly acknowledged in the further correspondence between Chandiwala and Nehru. While Chandiwala had been guarded vis-à-vis the Punjabi refugees in his first letter, Nehru clearly points to the events of Partition as a possible cause of his worries while replying.

Some of the complaints you make are the unfortunate consequences of the Partition and of course, the rapid growth of Delhi. Also Delhi has become a rather cosmopolitan city with large number of foreigners here, in addition of course to a very large number of displaced people.[26]

In a crisp and a matter-of-fact way, Nehru states the reality of Partition and its unavoidable consequences that have led to the present scenario. He reminds Chandiwala that the recent turn of events has changed the city-scape in many ways. In the early- and mid-1950s, many countries were establishing their diplomatic missions in the city, and Nehru sees the presence of many foreigners as a sign of cosmopolitanism. In addition to the foreigners he mentions the presence of 'a very large number of displaced people', who have in his view contributed to the city's transformation into a cosmopolitan place. The reply ends without Nehru commenting on the lamentable situation that the city has come to. Probably the reply was not what Chandiwala had expected, as it failed to assuage his disillusionment. The cautionary mode evident in the first letter by Chandiwala becomes conspicuously absent and is replaced by a more forthright and direct tone in his next letter.

In 1947, when the refugees from Punjab started pouring in, every province tried to stop their entry whereas Delhi welcomed them with open arms. As a result, of the 3,000,000 strong population of Delhi, the local residents account for no more than 400,000 or 500,000. The sacrifies made by the Delhi residents are not minor. That have on their own wiped out their exclusive identity forever. None remains, neither their language nor their attire and tradition. The Delhi residents have become strangers in their own house. Let us not forget that in this city everyone who resides has come from somewhere else. And over the years they became part of this city. I believe even these people (Punjbai refugees) will one day start identifying their selves as belonging to the city.[27]

For the first time, Chandiwala specifically points to the event of Partition, which brought Punjabi refugees to Delhi, whereas in his earlier letters he made general remarks about the 'outsiders' without naming them. Much of the letter is a repetition of the earlier one but the description of loss and marginalization felt by the local residents has become more elaborate.

The acute feeling of marginalization can be seen in the statistical comparison that he makes between the refugees and the locals. He calculates the total population of Delhi at 3 million, while pegging the locals at less than a sixth of the total. The figures are far from accurate, since the 1951 census enumerated a total of 1.7 million inhabitants in the city. Even a decade later, in the 1961 census, the figures did not exceed 1.6 million. It was only in the mid-1960s that the population of Delhi crossed the 3 million mark. The figures for the local population can be similarly derived from the 1941 census, that is, before the arrival of Punjabi refugees. There were less than 1 million people residing in Delhi before Partition, of which approximately 300,000 Muslims left for Pakistan in 1947. This still leaves over 600,000 local residents in the city after Partition, even when natural population growth is not taken into account. The significant feature, therefore, is not the inaccuracy of figures but the unrealistic difference between the refugee and the local populations that helped show the dominance of 'outsiders' in the city. It points to the level of inferiority that the locals felt when they compared themselves to the newcomers. Chandiwala follows these figures by asserting that the sacrifices made by the local residents 'are not minor'. Their lack of numerical strength is contrasted with their major contribution to the freedom struggle.

Interestingly, the letter never adopts a vituperative tone towards the refugees. It only highlights the cultural losses—in terms of attire, speech, and traditions—suffered by the locals without directly accusing the refugees. It completely circumvents the issue of political and economic gains made by the refugees. The even-handed approach that is so characteristic of both the letters enables the writer not to breach etiquette even while lamenting the cultural degeneration. In the second letter his tone becomes more forthright when he openly describes the marginalized state of the local residents, but this openness does not enable him to remark or speculate on the cultural values that the refugees represent. So one never hears any partisan value judgements about Punjabi refugee culture. It needs to be kept in mind that the writer is a responsible leader of the Congress party and would be expected to refrain from making unmeasured remarks, especially in a letter to the prime minister. But this partial silence is symbolic of the relationship that refugees and locals had come to share. The popular discourses about Punjabi refugee culture are far from charitable, with Punjabis depicted as ostentatious and devoid of cultural sophistication.[28] However, it is not very often that one hears these views in politically correct situations where the commentator risks being publicly quoted. The only narrative that I have come across in print that assumes an unrestrained tone is the following:

Punjabis started selling meat out in the open in push carts. Even the Muslims would never do such a thing. It was nauseating. Then they set up stalls where they cooked meat, fish and boiled eggs in the open. That was not all. The people of Delhi were not the kind that would let their women folk freely, but the Punjabi refugee women did so. They did not suffer from any inhibitions on this account. Punjabi women also went along in the *baraat* (wedding procession) during the wedding ceremonies. In Delhi women were strictly prohibited from joining *baraat*. The only women who were occasionally taken along were the dancing girls or prostitutes, never respectable women(Gupta 1997: 31–2).

These are the views of an anonymous local Delhi resident as quoted by Gupta (1997). It seems that the possibility of anonymity is what allows such popular beliefs to appear in print. During my fieldwork, I never came across any local resident expressing such views openly. They would cleverly circumvent this by saying that everything indeed changed after 1947 and Delhi lost its exclusive culture. The only people who publicly bemoaned the cultural degeneration of the city were upper class Punjabis who had themselves migrated to Delhi in 1947. This public critique of the ostentatious and unsophisticated cultural bearings of the Punjabi refugees served as a class marker that separated the elite among them from the rest. It had a locality bias as well, since most well-off individuals among them lived in exclusive zones located in south, central, and New Delhi while the rest were confined to the over-populated areas of east, west and south Delhi.

Even while the underlying animosity played on the cultural aspects, there were far better-defined economic reasons that fuelled the differences. The refugees were fast gaining economic self-reliance through state-aided job opportunities and easily available loans to start business enterprises. A clear indicator was the comparative level of income between the refugees and the residents. By 1957, the refugee households had already reached an average monthly income of Rs 177, compared to the Rs 178 available to the resident households.[29] The annual per capita income of the refugees was Rs 408 as against Rs 404 for the residents. These figures contain a proportion of income earned from property that was higher in the case of residents since they owned considerable real estate in the city. The net income figures excluding income from property put the refugee income higher than the residents, that is, refugees earned an average monthly income of Rs 130 from work, whereas the residents earned only Rs 117. Thus, it was the ownership of property by the residents that kept the economic balance in their favour.

But this was to change as well during the decades of the 1950s and 60s, because the government was developing new residential and commercial areas as part of the refugee rehabilitation schemes. The residents could not directly stake a claim to this newly opened-up land except by bidding for it on the open market. Here they could not compete with the refugees since the refugees received the land as part of the compensation scheme, which meant that they did not have to raise fresh capital to buy it in the open market. The housing situation, as noted in the 1957 survey, had become sufficiently similar between the refugees and the residents. The survey made a detailed enquiry into the size and overall housing conditions as well as the rents paid by the occupants. The ideal housing facilities described in the survey included a living room, a verandah, and an open space for the family.[30] The results were separated according to the availability of these facilities to the refugee and the resident families (see Table 7.1).

Table 7.1: Distribution of households according to availability of living space[31]

Accommodation	Residents (%)	Refugees (%)
Living room only	20.5	20.6
Living room and verandah only	17.3	18.0
Living room and open space only	33.6	29.6
No living room and both open space and verandah	28.4	31.7
No living room but verandah	0.1	0.1
No living room but verandah and open space	0.1	0.0
Total	100.0	100.0

Source: Rao and Desai (1965: 294)

The first possibility of accommodation enumerated those who had access only to a living room. In the survey results, both refugees and residents were placed at almost similar levels in this category. The second possibility was to have a verandah in addition to the living room, in which category the refugees fared marginally better than the residents. The third possibility was to have access to both a verandah as well as an open space. Here too the refugees were placed far better than the residents. The results depicted the patterns of urbanization that had emerged as a consequence of the state's permanent resettlement policies. The standard model adopted in the refugee housing colonies was to build one large concrete room on a 100-square yard plot. Of the total area in a given plot, only 60 square yards could be built up, which left 40 square yards open for a verandah. Often the kitchen would be located in the verandah as a temporary structure or within the living room. The original design can still be seen in the buildings that have been left unaltered in areas like Kasturba Niketan in Lajpat Nagar. Typically the living room contained a large bed, a sofa or some chairs, and a stack of multi-sized steel trunks containing valuables, clothes and other personal items. Only the women and children would use the room for sleeping at night, while the men slept outside. It was only in winter that the men would sleep indoors. The verandah was used as much as the living room for daily chores, especially if a water tap—for washing clothes, etc.—was connected therein. The verandah also served as a common space where the neighbours dropped in frequently to chat and drink tea. This created a daily life that was lived as much outdoors as indoors in these colonies. The accommodation in the newly developed colonies was much more widely spaced when compared to the residential spaces in the old city. The emphasis on the open space along with the verandah is therefore understandable, since both these features were not very frequently available in the narrow by-lanes of the old city. The survey shows that while 28.4 per cent of the residents had access to both open space and a verandah, a larger number of refugees (31.7 per cent) had access to the same facilities. In a few years, the refugees had surpassed the housing level attained by the residents over many generations. The refugees also had an edge over the residents in terms of internal facilities—such as kitchens, baths, and toilets—available within the accommodation. On most variables, refugees in the upper classes seemed to do better than their counterparts among the residents (see Table 7.2).

Table 7.2: Percentage distribution of households according to internal facilities[32]

Facility	Residents	Refugees
Nil	23.8	28.4
Kitchen only	6.4	6.0
Toilet only	26.7	14.7
Bath only	0.2	1.0
Kitchen and Toilet	8.9	5.0
Kitchen and Bath	1.2	1.2
Toilet and Bath	6.4	11.3
Kitchen, Toilet and Bath	26.4	32.4
Total	100	100

Source: Rao and Desai (1965: 302)

The level of facilities being considered here is quite basic, as is evident in the sample proportions above. More than a fifth of the people surveyed, both among the residents as well as the refugees, did not have access to a constructed kitchen, toilet or a bath. In any case, such facilities were not the essential focus of the planners responsible for the construction of refugee housing. The basic model consisted of a large room, a small kitchen, and a common set of bathroom and toilet for every four apartments. This kind of construction can be seen in the Old Double Storey quarters area of Lajpat Nagar.

In the mid-1970s, modern flush toilets and baths were constructed in individual apartments at a cost shared between the residents and the municipality. This left the common set of toilet and bath located at the building corners as a site of conflict among the residents on one hand and between the residents and the municipality on the other. The influential residents attempted to occupy the vacant space to build shops or to sell it off to real-estate agents for commercial use. The problem remained as to who among them should claim ownership to the spare land in question. This has become a prime cause for litigation among the residents as well as against the municipality. Another model, for example, in Old Rajinder Nagar area, was to construct a concrete room with a temporary asbestos roof, with an adjoining open verandah and a small kitchen on a 100-square-yard plot. The provision of toilets and bathrooms was at a very basic level, though each unit would have such separate facilities. A better model of government constructions can be seen in colonies like Ramesh Nagar, where the apartments were constructed on either single or double levels; they contained a small kitchen, a functional toilet, and a bath as well as a fenced verandah.

At a comparative level, the refugees had acquired as good, if not better, facilities as the local residents. The class variation is also visible in the possession of facilities, that is, many more refugees (32.4 per cent) have access to all the basic facilities—of kitchen, toilet, and bath--compared to the residents (26.4 per cent). This is not necessarily true in other categories down the scale, for example, more residents (26.7 per cent) have access to toilets than refugees, of whom only 14.7 per cent have such a facility. This shows that the higher the level of facilities, the better the conditions enjoyed by the refugees. Two explanations for this outcome can be: (1) a modern and uniform urban planning pursued by the state and (2) a better-off class of refugees who migrated to Delhi and could claim and obtain better civic facilities. The likely answer lies between these two possibilities, that is, the government was indeed following a functional model which was far closer to the aesthetics adhered to in British New Delhi than the Mughal style of housing visible in the old city. But the government was far from uniform in providing sufficient civic facilities in all the colonies (see Chapter 5) developed by it, since allocation was based on the principle of compensation. Thus, different class groups had access to different levels of facilities and seemingly there were far better-off refugees than residents. It is clearly evident that the refugees had, in a couple of decades, created a distinct urban space for themselves.

'WOULD YOU LIKE TO VISIT PAKISTAN?'

While successfully competing for the space in Delhi was one part of claiming locality, the other, equally important, part was to conclude the relationship with their former homeland. This conclusion does not necessarily involve bringing the relationship to an end; rather, it suggests a coming to terms with the past. An important aspect to emerge during the interviews was about the significant influence that the government's stance had on personal views. It was not just personal aspirations that framed the responses; the very aspirations were framed vis-à-vis the given situation of Indo-Pak relations. The first set of interviews was conducted after the 1999 Kargil conflict, when *Pakistan allegedly initiated the fourth 'war' between* India and Pakistan while the peace talks was still going on. The immediate background of the interviews was framed by the 2001 terrorist attack on the Indian Parliament building in New Delhi.[33] The follow-up interviews took place in the shadow of thawing Indo–Pak relations in 2004–5, when the cricket teams from both countries visited each other on goodwill tours, bus services through the Wagah border were resumed, and several entry points on the line of control (LOC) in Kashmir were opened in a historic breakthrough, following the earthquake affecting both sides. The responses differed in these contrasting political scenarios, particularly with respect to how freely the respondents could express themselves without conjoining the issues of patriotism and nationalism with their remembrance of homeland.

A question I repeatedly posed was, 'Would you like to visit Pakistan?'. My purpose was to find out if there were any emotional nostalgic ties that bound the refugees with their former homelands. It was a double-edged question that expressed a historical reality: that the former homelands were no longer situated in an accessible territory but were sovereign parts of an enemy country. I often asked the same question in another way: 'Would you like to visit your ancestral village/town?' This would invariably lead to a deeply felt affirmative and a sense of nostalgia when a number of happy anecdotes from childhood or youth would be recounted.

But presenting these places as Pakistan changed the response considerably. At once those places stopped being the 'home' that the narrators fondly remembered. The word 'Pakistan' encompassed the entire chain of events— of violence, loss, and forced movement—that had brought them to Delhi in the first place. It also evoked a popular discourse about Hindu–Muslim polarity and the unbridgeable gaps that led to a Muslim Pakistan and Hindu India. Right-wing Hindu politics is based on an imagery of Muslims as violent, untrustworthy, and domineering males, who have for centuries tried to suppress and alter the Hindu way of life. The territorial break-up of British India and the emergence of Pakistan are seen as an assault on the sacred body of Mother India, the imagined female goddess representing the Indian nation. These encapsulated beliefs were invoked when Pakistan was mentioned rather than specific names of ancestral places.

In the survey format, this question was posed in two parts, neither of which mentioned the name of any place. The place was substituted by the word 'home', indicating a habitual space delinked from any specific territory.

The first question simply asked if the respondents had visited their homes since Partition. Over 80 per cent responded that they had not. The second question asked if they would like to visit their home in the near future. The answer was mixed, with 60 per cent saying that they did not want to go, while the rest expressed a hesitant affirmation. Though the possibility of answers in the survey questionnaire was limited to two choices—yes or no—the answer was reached with plenty of debate not just about one's personal wishes but about Hindu–Muslim relations in general, the political situation between India and Pakistan, the injustices and crimes committed during Partition, perceived betrayals by their Muslim neighbours or friends, etc. The answer, therefore, was never an either/or and most people took a long time to arrive at either of these conclusions. Many questioned whether it was 'correct' to visit Pakistan as it was an enemy country now. And for many others it was a question of economics and accessibility, which is why they had not even considered the possibility.

This leads us to dual levels of analysis. One is about the collective memories of Partition where the Muslims had 'betrayed' the Hindus and carved out a territory for themselves. The other is about the differences in the social class of the refugees that influenced their decision to travel. The master narrative of Partition resulting from the collective mind became a source of conflict, since the refugees had to choose between conforming to the widespread belief—that Pakistan was an enemy and therefore a visit there would be taboo—or saying aloud what they personally wished. They risked disapproval with the second choice. This inner conflict became clear when people thought aloud about the rightness or wrongness of visiting their former homes. The open-ended interviews brought out this conflict more openly, as in this example:

The place has been defiled by the Muslims. We cannot have a good relationship with them until they change their ways of living. They are dirty and untrustworthy. They are just opposite to everything Hindus stand for. We worship the sun rising in the east, but they worship Mecca in the west. We wash down from head to toe, but they wash their feet first. We eat individually with ritual purification, but they eat together from the common platter. There is nothing for us to go back to. It is not the same anymore. Everything has changed. No Hindus live there anymore. We have brought the tree and the statue from the local temple in Dera Ismail Khan to create our place of worship here.[34]

Evidently, the question is not just about the belonging to the place that was once their homeland: it is also about the defilement of that place. While the place remains where it was, it no longer represents the pure space that the Hindus had once inhabited. It is now occupied by the Muslims who are impure and untrustworthy. The spatial purity and, therefore, a natural sense of belonging no longer exists. Mary Douglas (2002: 9) suggests that '...sacred things and places are to be protected from defilement' and such a distinction can be made visible on the grounds of hygiene and cleanliness. Thus, a clear diametrical opposition between Hindus and Muslims exists, which can be demonstrated in the everyday practices related to food, personal hygiene, and rituals of worship. The Hindu exodus from that place somehow emptied it of the purified space which they had constructed and maintained through their continued presence. Such practices were no longer a part of that abandoned physical geography.

But there were sacred objects, like the tree in the temple and the statue, which were an integral part of their lifestyle and could not therefore be left behind. The tree was uprooted and the idol dismantled to be taken along for the long journey. This was not done till it became certain that the movement was permanent and there was no possibility of return. A new sacred space was constructed in Delhi where the tree was replanted and the idol ritually reinstalled. In this way, the sacred was partially protected through movement, though the sacredness of the place could not be similarly ensured. Following Douglas, a correlation between sacredness and belonging can be constructed: that is, identifiable objects that could be protected from defilement remained symbols of belonging within the community. On the other hand, the place could not be protected from defilement at the hands of the Muslim occupants, and was thus considered unfit for any further association. There was a sense of pride at having saved the tree and the idol from 'Muslim touch', which also allowed them to be the symbols of collective belonging, whereas this pride was completely absent because of the failure to protect their right for continued existence in their ancestral land. This failure had, in a way, made the association with the place difficult, of which a Muslim-dominated DI Khan remained as living proof.

This ambivalent relationship with the former homeland does not hold for the second-generation Punjabis in Delhi. There is often a sense of curiosity to see the place where their parents once lived. This feeling abounds even in the face of tragedy as recounted by a 40-year-old man. A part of the curiosity was the fact that Pakistan was never discussed in their home and their father rarely talked about his own family or life in Pakistan.

My father lived in Sargodha district of Pakistan and was the only son in the family. He had seven sisters before him and was much pampered by his parents. My grandfather was a trader and a stockist of sugar and blankets. At the time of the Partition, my father was 13 years old and four of his older sisters had been married off. When the violence started in their locality, my grandmother ran away with him as she wanted to save her only son. My grandfather was killed while trying to save his three unmarried daughters. He did not succeed. They were raped and then murdered. My grandmother and my father joined a refugee caravan and reached Delhi. She had managed to bring half a kilo of gold along. She rented a room in Paharganj and they lived off the gold for a while. She was very afraid. She never went to any government agency for compensation or help. She was uneducated and terrified of the events that had taken place. She just wanted to live a low-profile life. My father started going to a school and started working part-time after Class 10. He was married off to my mother, who also came from a refugee family.

My father would never talk about his past life. He had some fears and would not allow us to go too far off. Fate has been good to him. We are seven brothers and one sister, but my father would never tell anyone how many of us there are. He fears 'evil spirits'. I came to know all this from my mother and grandmother. She never met her four married daughters. Nobody knows what happened to them. My father has emotional attachment to his place. He says if he is taken there, he will recognise everything. I want to go to Pakistan to see how it is. Perhaps even to my father's old home. When I applied for a visa I was denied, so I could not go.[35]

This narrative contains some typical characteristics that may define the response of the refugees upon movement. Life in Pakistan was comfortable since his grandfather was a successful trader. The grandmother took grave risks to save her son as he was the one who would continue the family in future. She had some assets to bring along—half a kilogram of gold—which saw them through hard times. As an uneducated widow, and thus a powerless person, she was afraid to approach any strangers including government officials. There was a clear breach of trust that made her wary of unknown people. Her sole focus was on her son, his education and later his marriage, which was solemnized with a girl also from a refugee family. Some of these features appear in most of the personal stories in a variety of ways.

The narrative also contains some untypical characteristics like open admission of rape of young daughters that took place during the violence. Such episodes are often hidden and rarely spoken of in public: even more so when the grandfather, the chief male figure, fails to protect his daughters from such humiliation. There is no heroism attached to this male figure and therefore there are no fond anecdotes attached to his persona. He is narrated as the one who fought but was killed in the process. The focus turns to the grandmother, who takes grave risks to secure her son's life and his future. She has rarely encountered government officials as she did not make any claim for compensation. Most of the people I came across during my fieldwork had staked their claim for compensation in one way or the other. This woman though had not even registered herself as a refugee and therefore she never figured in the refugee-related statistics. This shows that there may be far more individuals and families which never followed the route of refugee registration and the long arduous wait for compensation.

Another unusual aspect in this narrative is that the events related to violence and migration are rarely told in the family. The father, who as a young child was rescued instead of his sisters by their mother, remains quiet and stoic about this side of his personal history. The silence is broken only when he inexplicably stops his children from going far away from the house. His past experiences become visible in his protective behaviour when he zealously shields his children from any possible dangers. He refrains from counting their number in public for he fears that his personal and his family's happiness would be endangered. This is an unusual account because most narratives aim at establishing the heroic aspects of one's personal experiences. Such publicly acknowledged fears show a fragile human being who is vulnerable and not always in control of the situation. This is far from how most of the Punjabi men like to depict themselves and their forefathers.

What makes this narrative most interesting is the explicit lack of hostility to Pakistan, especially since the narrator belongs to an upper caste, middle class Hindu background. This average profile would ordinarily be associated with supporters of the right-wing Hindu political groups that profess hatred towards Pakistan. The narrator does not disclaim his Hindu origins and is far from agnostic. The journey he wants to make to Pakistan is a religious one, even though it is a Sikh shrine that he intends to visit. There remains a profound level of curiosity to see the place his father came from. It is only the inaccessibility—through denial of a visa—that stops him from pursuing this goal.

There are some for whom travel documents and resources are not a problem. Such practical hurdles are of no consequence for the rich or the upper-middle classes among the migrants. Their responses also vary considerably. Kuldip Nayar, born in 1924, is a migrant from Sialkot in Pakistan. He is an acclaimed author and journalist, having edited one of India's biggest newspapers, *The Indian Express*. He has maintained his links with Pakistan through continued relationships and routine visits. He has been actively pursuing the peace dialogue between India and Pakistan and routinely organizes visits to Pakistan by Indians and vice versa. He aims to end the hostilities between the two countries through 'people to people contact' or what is popularly called the track II diplomacy, wherein ordinary people communicate instead of government officials of the two sides. As he says, 'We are one people. We eat the same food, wear same clothes and have similar culture. The Partition was political and did not have people's support. The people still have links with each other and visit when possible.'[36]

This view is poles apart from that expressed by the members of the DI Khan Society, where Muslims are seen as an impure opposite of their pure ritualized selves. It is remarkable that the Hindu–Muslim relationship is viewed in such opposing ways, where, on one side the Muslims appear as the irreconcilable Other to the Hindus, while on the other Hindus and Muslims are seen as a single being with more commonalities than differences.

What differentiates these two beliefs is the class background that plays a significant role in enabling continuity of contact with the former homelands. While for one class technical difficulties like obtaining visas and financial support for travel pose no problem, for the other this often emerges as the chief hurdle.

There are a small number of organizations in South Asia that have a stated objective of peace between India and Pakistan and demand open borders. The 'Pakistan India People's Forum for Peace and Democracy' (PIPFPD) has been the most active and has members on both sides of the border among intellectuals, authors, journalists, academicians, retired bureaucrats, artistes, political activists, etc. The members of this organization belong to the elite sections of Indian and Pakistani society, for whom active peaceful engagement with Pakistan is a political goal. Easy accessibility to a popularly perceived enemy territory, Pakistan, allows them to view it differently than those who cannot visit the place as smoothly.

These differing stances—on visiting the homeland in Pakistan—found a common ground in 2004–5 when the two inimical states decided to allow greater access to ordinary people to visit the other country. The governmental sanction to visit the erstwhile enemy changed the popular discourse considerably, even though people in Delhi still expressed mistrust of the Pakistani government on security issues. Those respondents who were reluctant to claim their lost linkages with Pakistan, like the members of the DI Khan Society, were now less guarded in the changed political circumstances. The government-sponsored peace initiative had overnight elevated Indo-Pak peace from fringe dream to actual reality. This impacted the relationship of Punjabi migrants with their former homeland in two ways: one, easier accessibility to Pakistani visa enabled many, for the first time, to seriously probe possibilities of visiting Pakistan, and two, there was little political risk attached to visiting or even publicly discussing the wish to visit Pakistan once the Indian government was seen as supportive. The prospect of travelling across the Indo-Pak border was now open to a larger section of society rather than being limited to the well-placed, elite social segment. The only deterrent now was the travel cost that, needless to add, few among the lower middle class could actually afford.[37] The dramatically changed discourse on Pakistan, most importantly, points to the power of state or state-like authorities in determining the nature of such discourses.

Conclusions

The above discussions have shown the subtle and at times invisible processes that transform refugees into locals. Forced displacement means that the migrants have to engage themselves not only with home-making in the new place, but that they also have to come to terms with their departure from the former place. For the Partition migrants, their ties with the former place are impeded due to the inimical relationship India and Pakistan share. Their former homes are now located in enemy territory. The business of the state is clearly not delinked from the ordinary lives of people. This helps explain the dilemma and discomfort people express when faced with the choice of visiting their former homelands. It also suggests that a positive change in the India–Pakistan relationship would allow the former Partition migrants to deal with their personal loss better. The closure of borders between the two countries, four wars and continued low-intensity conflict have influenced, so far, the way Punjabi migrants view Pakistan.

This chapter also shows that the Punjabi migrants have been able to resettle themselves in Delhi successfully. A clear explanation is the multi-level support received from the state and the widespread sympathy from the local Delhi residents. Another explanation is the efforts made by the migrants themselves to ingratiate themselves with the local milieu and feel at home in the new place. The meaning of being 'at home', even in the maze of emotional turmoil, seems to have three concrete manifestations: one, ownership of fixed property that helped establish a personal stake in the locality; two, establishment of means of livelihood in the locality; and entrenchment of social and familial networks that brought individuals closer to the locality.

The discussions also point to the resentment of the local Delhi residents at the changing physical and cultural contours of the city. The resentment, however, never develops into open violent conflict since refugees are not a marginal entity but an increasingly successful group poised to take over the city. Towards the mid-1960s the question of locality seems to have been resolved in favour of the refugees-turned-locals.

NOTES

1. A full description of the causes and processes behind the ethnic strife in Karachi are beyond the purview of this chapter. The theme is dealt with at length in Feroz Ahmad (1988); Farhqat Haq (1995); and Moonis Ahmar (1996).
2. Urvashi Butalia (2001) has successfully pointed to an archive of private letters. However, this gives a misleading picture to the reader that there exists a systematic collection of private letters written to political leaders by the Partition refugees. The letters in question are randomly scattered throughout the records of the All India Congress Committee as well as the private-papers collection of Jawaharlal Nehru. Therefore, it is difficult to claim a systematic survey of such an archive. My use of the phrase 'archived private letters' pertains to those letters that I found in the files of the AICC (1947–48) and the private-papers collections.
3. Henceforth 'correspondence'.
4. See 'Administration of Evacuee Property Act, 1950' and 'Displaced Persons (Compensation and Rehabilitation) Act, 1954' where the terms 'evacuees' and

'displaced persons' are used. The official pieces of writing, e.g., *The Story of Rehabilitation* (Rao 1967), use the term 'refugee'.

5. Both Punjabi and Hindi are derived from Sanskrit and are therefore closely related. They follow different scripts based on the common Devnagari system.

6. For an interesting insight into Islam and migration, see Seteney Shami (1996), where he clearly demonstrates the use of Islamic tradition as a means to interpret transnational lives lived in an increasingly globalized world.

7. The Muhajir question in Pakistan is fully dealt in J. Rehman (1994), Imtiaz Ahmad (1994); Shahid Javed Burki (1999) *Pakistan: Fifty Years of Nationhood*; Subrata Mitra and R. Alison Lewis (1996) *Subnational Movements in South Asia* and Ali Bauazizi and Myron Weiner (1986) *The State, Religion and Ethnic Politics*.

8. I will mention, wherever appropriate, if the letter was handwritten or machine-typed.

9. AICC II Instalment File no. G/24/1947–8.

10. Personal interview with Balraj Malhotra, born 1928 in Kadranbad, Malkwal, district Gujrat in Punjab province. He owns a successful bookselling business in Khan Market in Delhi. This market, named after Khan Abdul Ghaffar Khan, was established in 1950 for allotment to Partition refugees.

11. The writer most likely refers to K. Santhanam, a member of the Constituent Assembly from Madras. He was very actively involved in the Assembly debates on refugee-related issues, particularly when financial bills on the issue were brought up for discussion. See Constituent Assembly Debates 1947–8. Elsewhere in the letter, the writer directly refers to an article that K. Santhanam wrote in the *Hindustan Times*, though we are not told about the contents of that article.

12. AICC II Instalment, File no. G/24/1947–8.

13. Alexander Horace was a fellow relief worker.

14. 'Refugees warned against breach of peace', *Hindustan Times*, 26 August 1947.

15. Mahmood Mamdani (1996) has pointed to the opposing modes of determining citizenship, where ethnic roots in the locality become a stronger and more legitimate ground for citizenship vis-à-vis incoming migrants whose ethnic roots lie outside the locality. The differences can be seen in the way laws of governance and rights to ownership of property are defined for two such groups.

16. Personal interview with Leela Ram Wadhwa, December 2000.

17. Personal interview with Bhatia, member of the DI Khan Seva Samiti, in December 2000.

18. The study was conducted by V.K.R.V. Rao who taught economics at the University of Delhi. It was part of a series of such studies conducted in various newly settled refugee colonies. See Rao and Desai (1965).

19. The author distinguished between the natural reasons of migration that differed hugely from the 'abnormal' reasons of Partition migration. The natural reasons are explained as economic push and pull factors (Rao and Desai 1965: vii, viii).

20. Narayani Gupta (1999) *Delhi between the Two Empires 1803-1931: Society, Government and Urban Growth*, quoted from the preface of the first edition printed in 1981.

21. See for example the July 2002 issue of the monthly journal *Seminar*, entitled 'First City?' where most of the participants in their first-person memoirs narrate the idyll that Delhi was, the shaded boulevards of the new city, the lights, and bazaars of old Delhi and the upper class cosmopolitan life of South Delhi. There is no mention of the nondescript areas that were developed after Partition, except some areas of South Delhi, where the bulk of the population now lives.

22. Praful Bidwai, 'The Hindutva Offensive', *Frontline*, 10 November 2000.
23. This includes the Union Minister for Tourism, Jagmohan, the former Delhi Chief Minister, Madanlal Khurana, and Member of Parliament, Vijay Kumar Malhotra among others.
24. Correspondence from B.K. Chandiwala to Jawaharlal Nehru dated 1 May 1955, Chandiwala Papers, NMML, Delhi.
25. The foundations of the Mughal Empire were laid by Zahir-ud-Din Babar in 1526 and the empire was further consolidated by his successors, among whom Akbar is credited with establishing an elaborate administrative system. For further reading, see, Irfan Habib (1963), *The Agrarian System of Mughal India*; Irfan Habib (1982), *An Atlas of the Mughal Empire*; I.H. Qureshi (1966) *The Administration of the Mughal Empire*; John F. Richard, (1993), *The Mughal Empire*, vol. I, Part 5, of the New Cambridge History of India.
26. Correspondence from J. Nehru to B.K. Chandiwala, dated 26 May 1955.
27. Correspondence from Chandiwala to Nehru, undated, Chandiwala papers, Nehru Memorial Museum and Library, New Delhi.
28. There is a popular joke according to which the only form of culture visible in Punjab is agriculture. In a way that sums up how Punjabis are humorously perceived by non-Punjabis: that their only possessions are built on agriculture-based economic advantage brought in by the Green Revolution.
29. A household in this survey was defined just as in the 1951 census, that is, a group of persons living together and sharing the facilities of a common kitchen. This, however, does not include servants or paying guests. See Rao and Desai (1965: 5).
30. The living room is described as inclusive of a sitting room, a bedroom and a reading room: in short, all the space a family makes use of while at home. A verandah is a paved and fenced terrace that is usually considered an integral part of the house. See Rao and Desai (1965: 293–4).
31. The table is sourced from the 1957 Survey. See V.K.R.V. Rao and Desai (1965; 294).
32. Rao and Desai, Greater Delhi.
33. The Parliament building was attacked on 13 December 2001 by a terrorist squad suspected to have been sponsored by Pakistan. It caused widespread condemnation and led to a worsening of India–Pakistan relations. See news report, 'Suicide Squad storms Parliament; 5 militants killed; Army Deployed', *The Hindu* 14 December, 2001.
34. Personal interview, President, Dera Ismail Khan Seva Samiti, 2002.
35. Personal interview with Rajesh Babbar, 2002.
36. Personal interview, March 2002, New Delhi.
37. Among the respondents in Lajpat Nagar and Kingsway Camp who I approached the second time in 2005, very few had actually taken the opportunity to visit Pakistan. The ones who did travel belonged to the more affluent sections and mostly came from outside these localities. A large majority of the travellers were young second or third generation Punjabis who had combined their love for cricket with the curiosity to see the land of their ancestors.

8. Ethnic Amnesia
Identity Making among Punjabi Hindus

The popular cry in Delhi at the time of Partition was 'Hindus have come from Punjab, help them generously and welcome them with open arms.'[1]
We are first Indians and then Hindus, Muslims, Gujaratis or Punjabis.[2]

These two quotes together convey the complex identification process which accompanied the resettlement of the Partition migrants from Punjab. The migrants were initially received in Delhi as 'Hindus' who had sought refuge away from Muslim Pakistan. The Sikhs were included in this widely used general label to describe the victims of Muslim aggression during Partition. Once in Delhi, the Hindus and Sikhs together competed with the local Marwari Hindus in ways that highlighted their ethnic 'Punjabi' essence. The very raison d'être for migration—the event of territorial partition and post-colonial state formation—meant that a third significant identity of being 'Indian' was introduced. The third identity was popularized and reinforced through concerted campaigns towards national integration by the Indian state. The validity and popular currency of the three labels has often been contested, interrupted, and then revived.

How do migrants from Punjab imagine themselves more than half-a-century after Partition took place? The central argument of this chapter concerns Punjabi Hindus whose identification with the Indian nation-state has become inextricably deeper than that among their Sikh counterparts. Over the decades, the Hindus from Punjab have noticeably delinked themselves from their Punjabi ethnicity. This ethnic amnesia is linked to the post-Partition unfolding of tense Hindu–Sikh relations, creation of a separate Sikh-dominated Punjab province, and a wider acceptance of the right-wing Hindu organizations among Punjabi Hindus. The delinking from Punjabi ethnicity amidst Hindu–Sikh tension does not automatically entail open identification with being 'Hindu' in a religious sense; rather, the very definition of being Hindu is reworked into a nationalized context of being a patriotic Indian. In other words, withdrawal from Punjabi ethnicity has made the identities of Hindu and Indian compatible and often interchangeable. The previous chapter followed the twin-stretch journey from being ordinary people to refugees and from refugees to locals in the city. But becoming a local still did not resolve the other identity conflicts derived from ethnicity and nationalism. This chapter will follow the often discontinuous identification process wherein primordial identities—based on shared religion, language and region, and imagined ascriptions like nationality and citizenship—frequently competed for prominence, suffered interruptions, and were popularly revived.

GENERATION TO GENERATION

The instant pointer to ethnic amnesia—partial remembrance of one's ethnic history—is the language in which different generations of the Delhi Partition migrants speak to each other and to strangers. It is quite common to hear three languages—Punjabi, Hindi, and English—being spoken in the same conversation. The dividing line that separates the original migrants from their second and third generation descendants is the non-use of the Punjabi language among the latter. This dividing line became apparent when I met with the members of the DI Khan Society during my fieldwork. To begin with, I was greeted and introduced to all the members in Hindi. This was not unusual, since Hindi is the national language and the main form of communication in schools, colleges, offices, and other formal places. The fact that we were strangers to each other made it imperative that we communicate in a formal way despite the mutual knowledge that we were all ethnic Punjabi speakers. The members of the society would, however, confer among themselves in Punjabi or the local Derawali dialect and quickly revert to Hindi when addressing me. The language switch was obviously an instrument to distinguish the familiar from the unfamiliar. We continued speaking Hindi till the 12-year-old grandson of one of the members came to interrupt. He spoke to his grandfather in fluent Hindi with words interspersed in English. The grandfather replied to him in Hindi as well.

It was a very mundane conversation but what made it special was the language in which it took place. The grandfather, who seemingly preferred speaking Punjabi with his friends, chose to address his grandson in the national language, Hindi, rather than his mother tongue. Punjabi. Clearly, the mother tongue was no longer spoken between different generations of the same family. Upon further enquiries I found that the young boy could speak only Hindi or English and had no knowledge of his grandparents' mother tongue. The only two languages that were familiar to him were the official national languages. Most members agreed that they spoke their mother tongue only among people of their own generation. Their children could understand it but had taken fully to Hindi, while their grandchildren had been linguistically even further distanced from them. Most were not regretful about this, since they claimed that Derawali was of no use in Delhi. Everybody spoke Hindi or English and that is what helped one in education and jobs. As Hindi/English speakers, they were identifiable as full members of Indian nation-state rather than as migrants on the margins. In a way, the second and third generation Partition migrants had rejected their linguistic past. This rejection of one's mother tongue in favour of another language stands in contrast to the long-held belief that 'no individual "chooses" his or her mother tongue or can "change" it at will' (Balibar 1996: 166). The naturalness or primacy of the mother tongue is what is challenged in this case. The point is not just about appropriating new visible traits that distinguish one's ethnic identity, but rather about rejecting some of the earlier traits. It is about the amnesia that sets in about one's ethnic history which allows one to separate from a given identity.

Another, though less obvious, signifier was the statue of goddess Sheran Wali Mata installed in the DI Khan Society temple. So far, the worship rituals among Hindus in Dera Ismail Khan had been described as chiefly including the cult of Bohriwala Thala. The main object of worship was a tree which had been blessed by a Sufi saint and worshipped by Hindus and Muslims in the area alike. The belief in the sacred tree was clearly deeply felt, as the tree had been uprooted and brought along by the migrant Hindus during Partition. The sacred tree was replanted in a DI Khan society temple courtyard located in one of the resettlement areas in west Delhi. The temple in Derawal Nagar, however, did not have any distinct mark that separated it from ordinary Hindu temples in Delhi city. The place of pride did not belong to a tree but rather to the Hindu goddess Sheran Wali Mata, whose origin and popularity in the city roughly coincides with the Partition migration from West Punjab to Delhi. The pre-Partition syncretic cult around the tree seemed to have been circumvented in favour of a new religious cult. The story and significance of the sacred tree is known less among the younger generation who have fully appropriated the rituals of goddess worship. This change in preference—of symbols of worship—reveals the underlying identification process, especially when the appropriated symbol itself is of recent date. The meanings attached to the goddess speak much of the historical reality of her devotees, most of whom migrated to Delhi following Partition.

IDENTITY: LABELS AND PROCESSES

The final, and in many ways concluding, part of our analysis is the theme of identity-making among the Punjabi migrants. The identity debates arise on a similar exploratory plane like many other conceptual themes, for example, memory, that move constantly within and across multiple levels of individual, community, nation, and society.[3] While it is usually accepted that identities are multi-dimensional, it is still debatable as to what aspects of an individual's or a social group's life history constitute identities. Edward Shils (1957) and Clifford Geertz (1963) have both variously argued that primordial ties, or the givens of one's social existence (that is, the congruities of blood, speech, custom, religion, and territory), are the 'basic facts' (Geertz 1993) that determine the production of social identity. They also seek to establish that since these primordial identities pre-date national identities, they are far more authentic and true reflections of social relations. The primordialist approach points to the possible constituents that may become the basis of identity formation, but does little to explain why people or groups seek to actively withdraw from an ascribed identity.

This project is concerned not only with how certain identities are pursued but also *how some others are cast out of publicly displayed identity baggage*. A vital question that frequently remains unaddressed relates to how one given identity gains predominance over others, while the rest remain dormant or in relatively subsidiary positions.[4] It is commonly accepted these days that identities are multi-levelled, malleable and prone to interpolations, and therefore not fixed. What remains to be explained is why some identities tend to surpass others. Each individual or group derives from ascribed categories like caste, race, class, gender, locality, etc., conveyed through differences in language, customs, politics, religion, and cultural taboos. These different labels are carried and conveyed routinely, but all are not articulated in a single instance. For instance, the identity of being a forced migrant does not dissolve one's previous social identities of class, caste, and gender, but they do step back when interacting with the administrative agencies that advance emergency aid, loans, housing, etc., solely based on their evaluation of one's loss as a forced migrant.

Similarly, the markers that enable people access to wider and non-controversial identities tend to be flaunted more openly than the ones which lead to social reprisal and banishment. This could be seen in Delhi city, where speaking Hindi and not Punjabi became a common norm even among the Sikh population when Hindu–Sikh communal relations began worsening after the mid-1960s. The Sikhs who spoke Punjabi were immediately associated with the Sikh militant movement and were treated with suspicion. This meant that the Punjabi language increasingly became something that was used at home in private, while it was replaced by the national language Hindi within the public domain.

Three main identity labels—Hindu, Punjabi, and Indian—present themselves in this study as a result of the historical events leading to the partition of British India, communal violence and the accompanying mass migration. These three identity labels are important because they have become a contested turf over which political battles are fought in post-Partition Delhi. A part of the quantitative survey in this study was devoted to the identity aspect, wherein the respondents were asked to choose one from among these three identities that defined them the best. This was supplemented by two additional questions: one about the preferred language spoken at home (Hindi or Punjabi) and the other about the political parties they preferred voting for.[5] The latter question is important because of the stereotypical characterization of the Punjabi Hindus (associating them with Hindi and Hindutva politics) in Delhi, according to which they are considered the chief supporters of the right-wing Hindutva movement in the city. The survey results, as we will find, far from confirming the stereotype, instead confounded the entire understanding of the identity question among the Punjabi Hindu refugees in Delhi. Among the 454 respondents, a majority (64.8 per cent) described themselves as Indians, compared to 16.5 per cent who described themselves as Punjabis, and 13.2 per cent as Hindus. This clearly points to the following: (1) Hindu migrants have distanced themselves from their Punjabi identity, (2) their identification with Hindu identity is not as deep-rooted as is commonly believed, and, finally, (3) they associate themselves most with the national identity of being Indian. The survey results challenge the most commonly held beliefs and myths about Punjabi Hindus in Delhi and help establish an exploratory path for this chapter.

In this study, identity is seen as multi-dimensional and adaptable, but it is the dominant aspects of this multi-level identity that form the basis for analysis. Once the dominant identity associations are identified, there is a danger of leaving out the subsidiary aspects whose marginal position needs to be explored in order to understand why these aspects were discarded from public display. The preceding discussion allows us to summarize that it is those identities that tend to occupy dominant space which (1) enhance one's ability to strategically negotiate, and (2) lead to membership of exclusive groups and associations. This does not preclude identities that are constructed defiantly as symbols of protest—based on race and caste, for example—since these collective identities also open up space for negotiation and tactical advancement. The first step to unravel identity formation, then, is to isolate dominant identity markers used as social separators in a given context.

LANGUAGE: READING LABELS

How are identity labels displayed and read by others, or, in other words, how are identities manifested in public? The decrypting of identity labels calls for a knowledge of the historical processes and tools that produced them in the first place. It also requires an a priori acknowledgement that labels are constructs signifying given discursive positions. Tangible signifiers of identity, once isolated, allow one to follow the processual course that they travel. The signifiers can be organized around their audible characteristics like speech, music, and forms of greeting, and the visible ones like race, colour, clothing, and bodily markings representing religious or caste traditions. While these markers are readily discernible in public spaces, others, like food taboos, marriage rituals, religious practices, and personal hygiene practices, that mark finer differences, require an incursion into private spaces as well.

In this study, language, religion, and politics appear as the three prominent signifiers. Together they open the path to understanding the making of Indian citizenry from the mass of migrants from Punjab. The challenge is to follow these identity markers displayed on the surface along with the less obvious processes that shape them. A popular right-wing Hindu slogan used in the 1950s and 60s during the campaign against a separate Punjabi state—Hindi, Hindu, Hindustan—summed up the complex inter-relationship among language, religion, and politics. The territory of Hindustan was claimed to belong to those who practised the Hindu religion and spoke Hindi. This equated the territorial claim to nationhood with the practice and use of a complementary religion and language. The battle turf for this campaign was set in post-Partition Punjab, where Sikhs had demanded the creation of a separate Sikh homeland. During the Partition negotiations, the Sikhs, as a thinly scattered religious minority, found themselves compelled to make a choice between Pakistan and India. While Muslims had gained a homeland for themselves, the Hindus as a majority group had made a natural claim to India. The Sikhs, on the other hand, had no regional home where they could claim statehood. The demand for a separate Sikh state within the Indian federation became a major turning point in Hindu–Sikh relations.

In this quest for territorial demarcation and separate identity, language became the prime indicator of Hindu or Sikh identity: Hindus were those who spoke Hindi while Sikhs spoke Punjabi. As a corollary, the Hindi speakers became the authentic claimants to the territorial expanse of Hindustan. The Punjabi language, on the other hand, had to be rejected to reiterate the Hindi/Hindu identity, even though Punjabi was the acknowledged mother tongue of the natives of Punjab—Hindus, Sikhs, and Muslims alike. Paul Brass (1974: 294–7) has shown that Punjabi was the main spoken language in Punjab till language became a political issue in the late 1950s.[6] In 1921, the population of Punjab was 49.78 per cent Hindu, but only 13.16 per cent identified themselves as Hindi speakers. On the other hand, the Sikh population amounted to just 17.98 per cent, whereas 64.08 per cent of the population identified themselves as Punjabi speakers. Language and religion were clearly unconnected at this juncture. This changed when the 1961 census took place. Now there were 63.67 per cent Hindus and 55.64 per cent Hindi speakers, while the Sikh population had increased to 33.34 per cent but Punjabi speakers had reduced to 41.09 per cent. As a result, the Sikh/Punjabi identity gained prominence as the

Hindus retreated on their claims to Punjabi. The Hindu rejection of the Punjabi language shows that choice of language is a matter of personal will, motivated by larger social processes of identity remaking. It is indeed possible to disclaim one's mother tongue and introduce another language into one's daily life.

Such a change does not, however, necessarily take place in a single generation, as my own survey showed. A vast majority of original migrants (68 per cent) claimed Punjabi as their main form of communication. The multiple levels implicit in this answer could clearly not be received and comprehended through the question, 'What language do you speak at home?' The inherent levels of spoken language became apparent through personal interactions with the families of the individual respondents. The older generation migrants spoke Punjabi with their partners, relatives, and friends, while their children and grandchildren invariably spoke Hindi/English with them. Any discussion with the respondents and their families on the theme of everyday language would bring forth two reasons in favour of Hindi. First, Punjabi was considered a crude, vulgar, and unsophisticated language, best put to use during quarrels,[7] and, second, Hindi was the national language and it was felt that it should be a spoken by all patriotic Indians. There was a stigma of 'low culture' attached to the Punjabi language that the younger generation did not want to be a part of. Most considered it a language that was only spoken by their grandparents and therefore a language that belonged to the family closet.

The popularity of Hindi over Punjabi among Punjabi Hindus in Delhi remains a critical issue. A clear explanation is the official endorsement of Hindi by the Indian state in the state-run academic bodies and other institutions. However, this does not fully explain why Bengali migrants in Delhi, unlike Punjabi Hindus, have been able to maintain their mother tongue.[8] The probable answer may lie in what Erikson (1968) calls the 'critical social response' that makes individuals reconsider their publicly professed identities. The Hindu–Sikh rift and the demands for secession by the Sikh militant groups in the mid-1970s in Punjab can be seen as the basis of the critical response that led to the Hindu withdrawal from Punjabi identity.

A quick overview of the Punjab conflict will show how language, politics and religion became entangled in post-Partition Punjab. The Akali Sikh–Arya Hindu rivalry continued after Partition, even though Hindus and Sikhs had stood together in opposition to Muslims during the Partition violence. During the negotiations for territorial division between India and Pakistan, the Sikh vulnerability and insecurity as a minority community without a territorial base was exposed. This became the basis for the Akali demand to have a distinct Punjab state where Sikhs would be in a demographic majority. As early as 1947, Akali leaders had successfully negotiated the delineation of Punjab into Hindi and Punjabi linguistic regions in what came to be known as the 'Sachar Formula' (Nayar 1966). Though linguistic division was meant for educational purposes, it served to emphasize Punjabi, and not Hindi as the mother tongue of all those who originated from Punjab.

It was under such tense circumstances that the Bhartiya Jan Sangh (BJS) was formed in 1951 just before the first general elections in independent India (see Weiner 1957). The party propagated a 'revival of Hindu 'principles' (selectively chosen by the party's founders) as the proper basis for Indian nationalism and modernisation' (Heeger 1972: 865). The BJS also hosted the intermarriage of the Arya Samaj and RSS, which was welcomed by the Punjabi Hindus. The predominance of the Arya Samaj in Punjab opened a gateway for the more militant RSS ideology, and Arya Samaj activists would often become members of the RSS. Heeger calls the Punjab RSS a 'generational appendage of the Arya Samaj-Hindu Sabha movement', wherein the sons of the Arya Samaj leaders found the militant approach of RSS more appealing than the Arya Samaj (ibid.). The Arya–RSS connection becomes apparent with the knowledge that the very first RSS *shakha* in Punjab was inaugurated in an Arya Samaj-supported DAV college.

The import of this connection can be fully explained with a brief introduction to the RSS. This organization was formed in 1925 among the high caste Chitpavan Brahmin community in Pune (see Basu et al.1993; Anderson and Damle 1987). The social-reformist zeal of the Arya Samaj was offset by the RSS vision of a patriarchal hierarchy wherein the upper-caste Hindu male was situated at the core of society. The volunteers, *swayamsevaks* as they were called, were trained in spiritual and physical aspects to counter the insatiable Muslim greed for territory and resources that ideally belonged to Hindus. The Hindu women were seen as the chief victims of Muslim lust, to avoid which Hindu men had to prepare for retaliation. The central belief in this approach was that India was the land of Hindus, while Muslims were foreigners who had usurped and mutilated the Hindu motherland. The earliest definition of the term 'Hindu' was offered by V.D. Savarkar, a leading RSS icon and Hindu Mahasabha leader, in 1923 in a pamphlet called 'Hindutva/Who is a Hindu?' According to him, a Hindu was 'a person who regards the land of Bharatvarsha from Indus to the Seas as his Fatherland, as well as his Holy land—that is the cradle land of his religion.'[9] This definition names two important components—territory and religion—as essential to national belonging. Neither of the components exclusively makes a Hindu; rather, it is their inevitable combination that produces Hindus.

Over the years, Savarkar's tenets have been built upon to suggest that a Hindu is the one whose *janmabhoomi* (land of birth), *dharambhoomi* (land of worship), and *pitrabhoomi* (land of forefathers) is the one and same. The emphasis on the 'land of worship' as a necessary requirement becomes useful in excluding Muslims and Christians from Hindu nationhood since their land of worship is located outside India. This did not, however, exclude Buddhism, Jainism, and Sikhism from the Hindu fold, as these had grown in indigenous conditions as Hinduism had. To describe the national–political aspects of the Hindu religion, a new term—Hinduness or Hindutva—had to be created to clearly 'express totality of the cultural, historical and above all the national aspects along with the religious one, which mark out Hindu people as a whole' (Basu 1993: 8). Thus, Hindutva sought be an integrational project creating a singular identity that befitted Hindu nationhood.

The Hindu–Sikh cleavages in Punjab widened after Partition, since the earlier common inimical object, Muslims, had departed from Punjab. The BJS became the new platform for the Punjabi Hindus to voice their discontent. At this juncture, the language issue was the most critical and provocative issue confronting the Punjabis. In 1956, the BJS sponsored a Hindi Raksha Samiti ('Save Hindi Society') to campaign and agitate on behalf of Hindi, in opposition to the Akali argument that Punjabi was the primary tongue spoken in Punjab. The confrontation grew fierce since it was no longer the spoken language that was at stake, with the Akalis now having linked the Gurmukhi script with Punjabi instead of the Devnagari script which was more familiar to Punjabi Hindus. The concerted campaign to 'save Hindi' brought the BJS closer to their Hindu electorate and this was visible in the 1957 elections where the BJS won 9 seats where it had won none in 1952 (Heeger 1972: 870). In a short span of five years, the BJS had become an influential voice of the Punjabi Hindus. The language conflict between Hindi and Punjabi had a lasting impact on Hindu–Sikh relations. The agitation for Punjabi was now seen through the prism of nationalism, wherein Sikhs appeared as anti-national and unpatriotic. The use of Hindi became the benchmark for one's loyalty to the nation. This criterion was fulfilled by the Punjabi Hindus in Delhi in order to separate themselves from the Sikhs.

RELIGION: GODDESS OF THE DISPLACED

Anand Sharma, a 17-year-old third generation Punjabi Hindu is a devotee of Sheran Wali Mata, the most popular object of worship for Hindus in Delhi. He and his friends spend most of their spare time organizing the night-long worship sessions (called *Jagran*) to invoke the goddess. Their devotion is not merely a spiritual vocation; it also helps the young men to intermingle with the girls in their neighbourhood which they may not be able to do freely otherwise. Some months ago, Anand and his friends established a musical band specializing in devotional songs for the goddess. The band could be hired for Rs 5000 a night, and for an additional price the young men also promised to set up a colourful tent with a decorated platform for the goddess and also provide a statue of the goddess. Technical equipment and a good audio system was part of the deal. I met Anand at his family home in the widow colony in Lajpat Nagar (see Chapter 5), where he lived with eight other family members in a single-storey accommodation built over 100 square yards. His widowed grandmother Savita Devi had migrated from Lyallpur to Delhi during the Partition violence and had been allotted this accommodation by the government. His grandmother was very proud of him because 'unlike other young men, he did not chase girls or get into crime and instead devoted his free time to the goddess.'[10]

His lucrative part-time vocation as a singer of devotional songs and his spiritual belief in the goddess had earned him lavish praise from his family. He had told his grandmother all about the goddess, her powers to grant wishes, her various legends, and the rituals with which to please her. The last bit of information—that it was Anand who told his grandmother about the goddess—was a bit puzzling because I expected the grandmother to have handed over the ritual knowledge to her grandson. The cult of the eight-armed goddess is strongly linked with the coming of Punjabi Hindus to Delhi. His grandmother, however, insisted that she had never worshipped the goddess back in Lyallpur, though she had heard that worship of the goddess was associated with the hilly regions of Punjab. She did not know the rituals and had learnt them through her grandson. This generational gap suggested that the goddess worship had been introduced to the family much after they reached Delhi and they had not brought along this spiritual knowledge. The history of the goddess's origin in the city was of no importance to either Anand or his grandmother. Her presence and significance was profound and permanent in the Sharma household.

If one were to venture outside British-built New Delhi and the old walled area of the city into the post-Partition settlements, small festive tents housing colourful images of a young woman riding a tiger would become a rather common sight. Her attire, pose, and appearance are striking and unusual even for a Hindu goddess. She is draped in a bright red, decorative sari, is heavily ornamented and is always seen crowned with a golden diadem. Sheran Wali Mata has eight arms, with each hand holding either a prayer article or a mythical weapon associated with Hindu epicurean heroes. Five of her eight hands carry a sword, a trident, a bow and arrow, a club, and a *sudarshan chakra*[11] to symbolize her prowess and destructive abilities, the other three hands—with a conch shell, a lotus, and an open palm imprinted with *Om*, the ancient Hindu symbol for inner peace—celebrate her peaceful, preservative instincts. Her chosen vehicle, an ornamented tiger, always accompanies her in a fierce, combative and roaring posture. The eight-armed goddess is the most popular object of worship among the Punjabi Hindus in Delhi.

The cult of Sheran Wali Mata has no clear pre-Partition history either in Delhi or Punjab, but is somehow inextricably linked to the Punjabi Hindu migrants of 1947. The pre-Partition residents of Delhi link the arrival of this goddess with the arrival of Punjabi refugees after Partition. But surprisingly, the quantitative survey showed that none of the 454 respondents specifically mention the eight-armed goddess as the prime object of worship before Partition. A pantheon of Hindu gods and goddesses was subsumed in the majority reply (73 per cent) that 'we worship all deities'. 'All' included various incarnations of the Hindu trinity of Vishnu–Brahma–Shiva, their female counterparts, the eight-armed goddess and even the Sikh gurus. Essentially, it was an evasive, non-committal reply. Most, however, were certain that goddess worship was not popular in Punjab except for the hill regions (now Himachal Pradesh) and that they had been introduced to this practice after their arrival in Delhi. A quick survey of the late 19th-century religious history (see Chapter 6) shows that the traditional Brahminical forms of worship had been challenged by the popular religio-social reform movements in Punjab. The Arya Samaj, as a widely accepted religious institution, questioned the elaborate rituals, ceremonies, and taboos involved in the traditional forms of worship. Thus, goddess worship in elaborate rituals points to a new emergent symbolism among the Punjabi Hindus.

The presence of the eight-armed goddess can be both seen and heard in the city. The tents are dressed in eye-catching bright red and gold decorations, while taped devotional music is played over loudspeakers. The popularity and devotion of the goddess can be gauged from the fact that even the politically charged VHP-led Ram temple movement in the early 1990s, wherein Lord Ram was hailed as the prime Hindu divinity, failed to alter the devotional patterns in Delhi. Sheran Wali Mata continues to be omnipresent and the most worshipped Hindu divinity in Delhi. Each local temple in Delhi usually houses various idols of male and female divinities, but the biggest pedestal for worship is reserved for Sheran Wali Ma who sits atop her lion in the centre of the temple. The idol size and placement distinguish her in the Hindu divine hierarchy as practised by Punjabi Hindus in Delhi. The scale and extent of devotion places her almost on par with the cult festivals of Ganesh Chaturthi in Mumbai and Durga Puja in Kolkata. The goddess worship is not remarkable in itself, since the worship of Shakti, the female divine principle, or Durga, the fearful incarnate of Lord Shiva's consort Parvati, is well known in different parts of South Asia. The relative absence of goddess worship in pre-Partition West Punjab is what makes her post-Partition popularity in Delhi even more significant. Such significance can be best understood both through the tales of origin that are believed and told by her devotees as well as her identification (which is not often publicized) with the Rashtra Sevika Samiti, the women's wing of the RSS. Both attempt at ascertaining her divine genealogy and help understand the magnitude, historicity, and import of her widespread devotion among Punjabi Hindu migrants.

The commonly told tale of her appearance is not very different from that of many other goddesses. To begin with, this story is located in distant antiquity when Mahashakti, the female divine principle, was called upon to protect the gods from the onslaught of demons. She took the form of a beautiful young girl who combined the divine qualities of Mahakali (Strength), Mahalakshmi (Wealth), and Mahasaraswati (Intellect). She vowed to vanquish the demons to protect the gods and the human race. She was armed for the battle but she was benevolent by nature and ready to forgive those who sought her protection. Her beauty, however, attracted the demon king who followed her through forests and mountains. The goddess hid herself in a cave for nine months. When the demon king did not cease his pursuit even after that period, she took the form of Mahakali the vanquisher and killed him with her trident. An era of peace and tranquillity was established thereafter. This story is ritually narrated at each worship session.

The other story places the origin of this goddess less than seven decades ago. In 1936, Lakshmibai Kelkar, the mother of an RSS activist, persuaded the RSS founder K.B. Hedgewar to form a women's wing called the Rashtra Sevika Samiti. Her original plea was to get the RSS—an upper caste Hindu male preserve—to open itself to female membership. This was refused by Hedgewar and instead the Samiti was offered as a compromise gesture. The women activists were mostly recruited from among the families of RSS members since they already had their family's approval. The Samiti was to become a facilitator for the production of ideal Hindu women befitting the membership of the extended Hindu family envisaged by the RSS. As a symbol around which to mobilize Hindu women, a new goddess was created as the bearer of the Samiti's values and philosophy. The new goddess was a combination of the three main Hindu female divinities—Mahakali, Mahasaraswati, and Mahalakshmi—bringing together intellect, prowess, and prosperity that an ideal Hindu woman was expected to emulate.

The Samiti literature introduces the goddess as 'coordination of Strength, Intellect and Wealth (that) elevates the nation to a higher plane ... (she carries) weapons in all eight hands symbolizing the qualities necessary for an ideal Hindu woman' (Bacchetta 1997: 137). An icon of the deity is installed at the first Samiti headquarters in Wardha (ibid.). At the shakha gatherings, the members offer the Samiti prayer that invokes her as the 'eight-armed goddess who rides the lion'. The goddess was multifaceted and gifted in more than one arena, just as the Hindu women members of Samiti were encouraged to be. The emphasis in the Samiti, like in the RSS, was on both intellectual and physical training of its members. However, unlike Hindu men who had been 'seduced by the western power and knowledge', the Hindu women were seen as 'a pure space that [had] escaped the transformative effects of colonisation' (Sarkar 1996: 186). The body and mind of Hindu women had to be therefore kept free of polluting influences through ritualized intellectual and physical training (see Sarkar 2001). While the Hindu men fought battles in the public space, the Hindu women had to manage and secure the home from outside influences.[12]

This connection between Sheran Wali Mata and the Samiti has rarely been made, especially because the cult has become popularly attached to the Punjabi Hindus in Delhi. The Delhi incarnation of the mother goddess comes closest to the Samiti's goddess and distinguishes itself from other prevalent female Hindu divinities. To begin with, she is a single unattached female person who results from the confluence of the Hindu female trinity of Kali, Saraswati, and Lakshmi. She combines the qualities of the three main Hindu goddesses and is therefore an ideal feminine persona. Second, she is mobile, that is, the benedictory spaces she occupies are mobile and makeshift, and the devotees can install a temporary altar for worship. This is an unusual characteristic, since the Hindu form worship takes place in temple-like spaces marked for spiritual practice. Hindu idols are installed with certain rituals of purification and are therefore generally fixed. In this case, however, Sheran Wali Mata is mobile and her idol or framed photo can be installed in either public or private spaces with minimal rituals. Though the sites include regular concrete buildings perceived as Hindu temples, the worship rituals are largely conducted in festive, makeshift, and mobile temples shaped out of small colourful tents. These tents can be found all over the city's residential and commercial areas, set up in crowded market squares, on busy side streets, or even traffic intersections.

The goddess is invoked by individual devotees in private celebrations or collectively sponsored by various trader federations or shopkeepers' associations in the city. The usual spectacle involves a dais set up in the tent where a number of framed photos and idols of the goddess are installed. Besides incense sticks and other paraphernalia of rituals, a cash-box marked with a swastika symbol for donations is displayed prominently that passers-by are expected to contribute to. The colourful tents as her temporary home highlight her unusual mobile character.

Third, the rituals of her worship are rather flexible, that is, they are marked by a lack of pre-ordained prescriptions. The uncomplicated worship rituals can be performed by anyone and the services of priests are therefore hardly required. The final, and the most telling, characteristic is the unusually high audio levels associated with the worship practices. Both private and public ceremonies are conducted on loudspeakers, to the extent that the noise level has itself become a worship essential. The special songs composed to invoke the goddess are played constantly during the day and late into the night. The songs themselves have no origin in any known tradition of worship. The lyrics are often quick, easy and uncomplicated compositions fitted to the lates popular Hindi films songs or Punjabi folk songs. The singers are seldom trained in any particular tradition of Indian vocal rendition, but this genre of spiritual singing has now acquired its own style marked by high pitch and simple delivery.

Two arguments can further the above discussion about audio levels and about the mobility of the goddess. The high audio levels are an essential feature of the rituals and a connection can be made between the level of volume and corresponding levels of assertion made by a group. The 'noise' created by a religious group was often a cause for communal violence in the colonial period: for example, the muezzin's call to the Muslim believers to join the prayers was sometimes seen as a provocation by the Hindus and Sikhs.[13] The colonial administration spent much of its time regulating such audible and visible provocations to avoid violence.

However, the high audio levels in goddess worship are not seen as a provocation in Delhi. After Partition, Muslims became a minority in the city. Goddess worship became popular among the small-time Hindu traders and merchants who patronized it as a spiritual and recreational ritual.[14] The traditional late evening hour associated with the worship is entwined with the business hours of the shopkeepers who could devote time to it only after business hours were over. The entire ritual became a way to assert their presence in and claim to the city. They were no longer a minority in West Punjab who had to worship in whispers to avoid conflict. It must be pointed out that the audio levels were not raised to the maximum immediately after their arrival in the city.[15] They were raised gradually, especially 'during Indira Gandhi's time', as Anand's grandmother remembers. This is when she had begun noticing this colourful and energetic form of worship. This rough date—the late 1960s onwards—was proposed by many other interviewees as well. The significance of this period is twofold: first, the resettlement efforts were officially concluded by this time and, second, after India's victory in the 1971 India–Pakistan war, Indira Gandhi was hailed as an incarnation of the Hindu goddess, Durga. This seemingly contributed to the boldness required to raise the volume of the rituals in goddess worship.

The shifting places of goddess worship, on the other hand, point to the mobile character of the goddess who accompanies her devotees in this unusual way. This strikes a familiar chord with the history of Punjabi migrants, who have a long history of migration predating Partition. The fact that the goddess is not rooted in a single sacred ritualized place means that sacred space can be created at multiple locations through prescribed rituals. The collapsible tents and portable idols mean that a place of worship can be erected and dismantled as and when required. This reflects the routine her devotees have had, of moving and resettling and then moving again to other places. These two features associated with Sheran Wali Mata help understand why and how she became a divine cult among the Punjabi Hindus in Delhi.

POLITICS: THE HINDU VOTE?

A popular method to gauge identification at a mass level is to correlate people with the political ideologies they support. This means reading the electoral results in a way that links the vote share of a given political party to a similar composition among the electorate. This derivative of population should logically bear the ideological imprint of the party it voted for. While it is true that electoral participation offers individual voters an opportunity to identify themselves with the political ideologies they support, one should be cautious against stretching this simplistic correlation too far. As we will find, the Punjabi Hindus offer their electoral support for far more deep-seated strategic reasons than are visible in the voting patterns. It is not the electoral affiliation but rather the community-based associations and networks that need to be explored.

It is commonly believed that Punjabi Hindus in Delhi support the extreme right-wing BJP. In support of this belief, the 1951 elections to the municipal elections in Delhi are treated as evidence of the support that the BJS, a predecessor of BJP, had received from the Punjabi Hindus. The BJS had emerged as a main rival to the Congress party with 25 per cent of the total valid votes cast, compared to 33 per cent votes won by the Congress (Jaffrelot 2001).[16] This was considered a big feat, given that the Congress represented the glory inherited from the entire freedom struggle that led to independence. Of the 15 states in which it contested elections in 1951, the BJS performed best in Delhi with a vote share of 25.92 per cent or 169,997 actual votes.[17]

The quantitative survey showed that while 40 per cent of the respondents preferred voting for BJP, 26 per cent still voted for the Congress. An equally large number (26 per cent) of respondents refused to answer this question because it was considered a politically sensitive question. Such a question is considered sensitive because most voters in Delhi refuse to ally themselves with either the BJP or the Congress unless they are members or recognized political activists committed to a given party. It is not unusual that members of a single family vote together for the BJP or the Congress as a strategic choice. It is less an individual exercise of political expression and more of a strategy. This again is a pragmatic Punjabi idea of keeping options open since no one knows which party will sweep to power. So there is always some member of the family who remains close to the powers-to-be. The members of DI Khan Seva Samiti explained this commonly used far-sighted strategy clearly to me.

When we were in Pakistan the Muslims used to ridicule a Hindu devotional song, *Mujhe le chal Ganga paar* (take me across the Ganga river). The song was very special for the Hindus in the Frontier and Punjab as it expressed the need to see the Hindu pilgrimages situated across the Ganga. At the time of Partition, the Muslims said that the time has now come to fulfil your wishes: we will send you across Ganga very soon. When we came to Delhi, we came to our *Dharambhoomi*, or the sacred land of Hindus. We have connected with our scattered *biradari* again and we live here as a family. Most of us are related to each other through marriage in one way or the other. Some of us vote for the BJP while others vote for the Congress. But different voting choices do not come in our way because we agree on the same ideals. We are Hindus. Many of us have been associated with the RSS even though the RSS did not help us a lot during Partition. Whichever party comes to power, we always have a member of the DI Khan *biradari* in some position of influence or the other. For example, Mehar Chand Khanna from DI Khan was a member of Hindu Mahasabha and he worked a lot for the Hindus in the Frontier. Later he joined the Congress and became the Minister for Refugee Rehabilitation. He worked for his community. He was very firm with Muslims, just like Sardar Patel. Its not the Congress or the BJP we vote for; we vote for those who can solve our problems.[18]

Permanent representation and influence in the political structure is, thus, the key to voting patterns among biradaris and families. The voting decisions are made on far more pragmatic grounds than the authentication of a given political party. The same electorate may vote alternately for the Congress or the BJP, based on an assessment of their contribution to the community welfare, the larger Hindu cause, or more localized Derawal community goals. Thus, voting patterns can hardly be taken as solid evidence of ideological moorings among the Punjabi Hindus in Delhi. The support for Mehar Chand Khanna accrued primarily from his affinity with the Hindu refugee community and not from his political or ideological leanings. The party he represented through his person was less important than the possibilities of representing the community interest through him within the largest political party and the Union government. He emerged as a key political figure among the Hindu refugees in Delhi when he took over the refugee rehabilitation portfolio in the cabinet of ministers. He was expected by the refugees to redress their long-standing grievances with a lot more compassion than the previous ministers who had no personal experience with Partition migration. I was often told during the interviews that 'after all, he was our own man'.

According to the DI Khan society members, the allotment of land in Delhi for cooperative housing societies, became a much easier process, if it was organized around home-town associations like Derawal Nagar, Gujranwala Town, etc. Mehar Chand Khanna was known to be firm with his ministerial colleagues on the question of concessions to refugees. He also favoured the Hindu tenants of Muslim landlords who, after their landlords left for Pakistan, technically came to occupy the evacuee property. Under the Displaced Persons Act, 1954, this property became a part of the state property to be rented, allocated, and administered by the state. Mehar Chand proposed that those Muslim-owned properties valued under Rs 10,000 and occupied by non-displaced persons should be allotted to the current occupants.[19] Such a decision was considered partisan towards Hindus since in reality, Muslim tenants of evacuee Muslim landlords were not recipients of such favours;[20] in fact, they were often the targets of eviction campaigns launched by the rehabilitation department. This very partiality towards the Hindus earned Mehar Chand a solid constituency among the Hindus—both locals and refugees—in the city. Such anecdotes of his heavy-handed decisions, often unfavourable to Muslim tenants, were recounted to me as a proof of his commitment to the Hindu community.

A glance through the Lok Sabha as well as Legislative Assembly elections results in Delhi tends to emphasize this widespread ambivalence and frequent electoral tilts between the Congress and the BJP (and its earlier incarnation, the BJS). The BJS emerged as a major competitor to the Congress from the very first election in 1951, even though it failed to manage any major electoral victory till the 1967 general elections. The 1962 and 1967 election results throw up interesting comparisons that help show a general characteristic of Delhi politics. In 1962, the Congress swept Delhi with a 50.68 per cent vote share compared to the 32.66 per cent of the Jan Sangh. It won in all the five constituencies of Delhi including the New Delhi seat where Mehar Chand Khanna won with 57 per cent of the vote (see Table 8.1). His nearest rival was the Jan Sangh candidate Balraj Madhok, an Arya Samaj member who had joined RSS in 1938 while studying in DAV College in Lahore. Both Madhok and Khanna were Hindu Khatris, one of the prime caste groups in Punjab that had taken to the Arya Samaj since the end of the 19th century. But in the 1967 elections, the Jan Sangh nominee M.L. Sondhi, an articulate non-refugee Punjabi Hindu from Amritsar, defeated Khanna. The electoral loss suffered by Khanna was not a singular event since most Congress nominees, barring one from the Outer Delhi seat, lost to Jan Sangh candidates in Delhi in that election. Following the 1967 election, the Jan Sangh/BJP and the Congress are regularly faced with alternate electoral reverses in Delhi (see Tables 8.2 and 8.3).

Table 8.1: New Delhi constituency results (1962 and 1967)

	Winner	Nearest Rival
1962	Mehar Chand Khanna, Indian National Congress (57%)	Balraj Madhok, Jan Sangh (38%)
1967	Manohar Lal Sondhi, Jan Sangh (56%)	Mehar Chand Khanna, Indian National Congress (38%)

Source: Gupta (1997) and V.B. Singh (2000).

Table 8.2: Lok Sabha elections: percentage of valid votes polled in Delhi (1951–99)

	1951	1957	1962	1967	1971	1977	1980	1984	1989	1991	1996	1998	1999
BJS/BJP	25.92	19.72	32.66	46.72	29.57	68.15	37.89	18.85	26.19	40.21	49.62	50.73	51.75
INC	49.43	54.32	50.68	38.79	64.39	30.15	50.40	68.72	43.41	39.57	37.29	42.64	41.96

Source: Gupta (1997) and V.B. Singh (2000).

Table 8.3: Delhi legislative assembly: percentage of valid votes polled (1951–2003)

	1951	1972	1977	1983	1993	1998	2003
BJS/P	29.05	38.47	52.58	43.17	42.82	35.82	35.22
INC	52.09	52.54	39.05	47.50	34.48	47.76	48.13

Source: Gupta (1997) and V.B. Singh (2000).

The electoral upsets in Delhi need to be read along with the changes in political fortunes at an all-India level. In the years immediately after Independence, the Congress governed India under the charismatic leadership of Nehru. It was fulfilling the promise of independent nationhood through economic planning (five-year plans); a focus on agriculture (construction of big dams); and higher education, with the establishment of scientific research and training institutes like Indian Institute of Technology (IIT), to name a few areas. Nehru had also gained in terms of foreign policy through his foundational role in the Non-Aligned Movement (NAM) that positioned him as a statesman leading the third-world countries. India had managed a *Panchsheel* agreement with China that spoke of mutual trust, peace, and harmony with neighbouring countries. The occasional bickering with Pakistan over the share of state assets and boundary disputes in Kashmir was yet to become grave. The 1951, 1957, and 1962 general elections were held against this background, and not surprisingly the Congress swept to victory each time. It was only after Nehru's death in 1964 that the imperfections of the Congress leadership became a matter of public debate. The debacle of the 1962 war with China now stood as a clear failure of the Nehru government, even though it was the Chinese who were blamed for the breach of trust in the public discourse.

The adulation for Nehru almost turned into denigration after his death, more so when his daughter Indira Gandhi took over as prime minister in 1967 (see Maxwell 1974).[21] In the 1967 general elections, the Congress barely managed a victory under Indira Gandhi's leadership (see Frank 2000).[22] For the first time, the BJS won four out of five constituencies in Delhi, in keeping with the national trend of a weak performance by the Congress. In 1971, the Congress won with a huge margin following the success in the Indo–Pak war. Indira Gandhi was popularly anointed as an incarnation of the Hindu goddess Durga, the vanquisher of evil, after the humiliating surrender of the Pakistani army. She was said to be supported by the RSS in that period, more so when she was seen as the protector of the Hindu faith against the Muslim intruders. The election results in Delhi again kept up with these national level developments and the Congress won all the seats with an astoundingly high 64.39 per cent of the vote share. This level has been exceeded only by the 1984 victory of the Congress party following the assassination of Indira Gandhi, when the Congress won in Delhi with a 68.72 per cent vote share. The resounding defeat in the 1977 elections is attributed to the imposition of internal Emergency in India in 1975. In Delhi, the BJS won in 1977 with a convincing 68.15 per cent vote share to mark its best performance in Delhi ever. While Indira Gandhi made a comeback in 1980, reducing the BJS to a 37.89 per cent vote share in Delhi, the Congress reached its electoral peak in 1984, cashing in on the post-assassination nation-wide sympathy wave. Delhi was the site of worst-ever massacres since Partition, after Indira Gandhi's Sikh bodyguards assassinated her. The anti-Sikh riots were also a turning point in the distanced relationship Punjabi Hindus had come to acquire with their ethnicity. The electoral trends in Delhi, in short, seem to work well within the frame of national trends at any given moment in the last half-a-century.

The point here is not to explain the electoral losses or victories obtained in Delhi, but to bring forth the consistent reversals that have become a feature of Delhi electoral politics. More than anything, it helps show that voting patterns do not necessarily reflect the ideological leanings of the electorate, nor are they expressions of identity. They simply depict a political surface that needs to be penetrated thoroughly to understand the underlying identification processes. Two inferences can already be isolated: one, electoral ambivalence underscores the existence of a consensual Hindu identity that overrides party-level competitiveness, and two, such a consensual identity is concretized through democratic electoral practices. Christophe Jaffrelott (2000) points to the 'middle ground' that the Congress and the BJP have come to inhabit since they together represent the urban Delhi populace: the local Hindu merchants as well as the Punjabi Hindu refugees.[23] The political middle ground is also representative of the predominantly Hindu middle class and upper caste groups that define the social make-up of urban Delhi. While BJP seeks to represent the Hindu interests in the city, the Congress has never been known as an anti-Hindu party despite the allegations of Muslim appeasement during Partition. The frequently shifting electorate also suggests that Hindus in Delhi do not identify themselves entirely with right-wing Hindu politics as is commonly suggested.

LABELS AND CHOICES

Clearly, the identity label is not a permanent given: rather, it is a matter of choice and personal consideration. At the time of Partition the most prominent identity marker was religion especially when given religious identities—Hindu, Muslim, and Sikh—became the basis for internecine violence and forced migration. It is not surprising, therefore, that refugees from Punjab were initially received in Delhi as 'Hindus' who had been uprooted from their homes by the Muslims. At this moment Hindu-ness became the most important aspect of the migrant's personal and collective identity. There are several accounts narrated by the local residents about the funds that they had routinely raised for the benefit of refugees from Punjab. Often the young men in a given residential area would go around with a *chador* (cloth sheet) to collect money, clothes, food, and other useful items to be distributed in the refugee camps (ibid.).[24] The Hindus from Punjab did not risk becoming a religious minority in the new place because as Hindus they were joining another large body of Hindus in the city. It was the local Muslims who had turned into a minority after more than 300,000 among them chose to leave for Pakistan. Of the various problems that the new migrants confronted upon their arrival in Delhi, persecution and discrimination due to their professed religious faith was not one. They had now become a part of the Hindu majority in independent India.

A common Hindu identity, however, was not enough to ensure a conflict-free local–refugee association in the city. The simmering low-key rift was primarily poised on cultural differences produced by distanced ethnicities. The regional roots of the refugees in Punjab, or their Punjabi-ness, emerged as an explanation of the differences that largely remain invisible to outsiders in the city.[25] The widespread discourse on the local–refugee 'differences' centres around the contrasting figures of erudite, sophisticated and materially content local residents, who were, after 1947, unfairly pitted against the conniving, boisterous, and manipulative Punjabi refugees. There is a well-known story often recounted in Delhi to emphasize the enterprising spirit of Punjabi refugees as they strove to establish themselves in a place dominated by local Hindu traders (see Chapter 1). The story can be read in different ways: one that states the obvious sense of pride among the Punjabis for their venturesome spirit, and the other that reveals the ungrateful response of the refugees to the magnanimous openness in business practices shown by the local traders.

The local Hindu trader's inability to compete with the newcomers is seen by Punjabis as a result of the local lifestyle that encouraged incompetence and supported a laid-back attitude to business. Bir Sahni, a Punjabi trader from Lala Lajpat Rai Market in Chandni Chowk, recounted his own experience upon arrival in Delhi during Partition. He had set up a stall on the pavement in Chandni Chowk to sell handkerchiefs, combs, hairpins, and other trinkets.

I would hawk on the pavement from morning till evening in order to sell my stock. While the well-established traders in their shops could afford to hold their stock till they got a good price, I could not do the same. I had to sell the same day in order to feed my family. So, I would sell at the lowest price possible. Since the local shopkeepers had good infrastructure and proper showrooms to display their wares, they also had to incur constant expenditure to run the establishment. Small-time traders like me had no such overhead costs and thus lower expenditures. In the face of such competition, very few local traders survived. I got a shop allotted in Lajpat Rai market and now have five people in my employment. Many traders who had makeshift tent shops (*khokhas*) were allotted shops in this market complex by the government.[26]

Earning one's livelihood was clearly an imperative for the refugees that made them adopt aggressive selling strategies. This contingent approach in earning a livelihood, even when the government was supporting the refugees in a variety of ways, can be understood as a common sense response shaped by Punjabi tradition, which differentiates between *mool* (capital) and *sood* (interest earned on the capital). This is evident in a popular saying *mool nalon sood changa* (the interest earned is even better than the capital invested). It is often used to describe the desire for a male heir in the family, wherein a grandson is even better than the son, because he will carry on the line further. In everyday life this means that capital resources owned by the family are never used for routine expenditure but kept safe for the difficult times. Partition proved to be the proverbial rainy day when savings had to be employed for everyday living expenses. But the urge to keep whatever capital one had, secure from consumption, required the refugees to begin earning their livelihood again as soon as possible. Many small traders like Bir Sahni were not completely without basic resources in the form of cash, gold, and silver ornaments, but it was almost considered taboo to utilize those family resources except in the gravest of circumstances.

The everyday life in the refugee camps had slowly lost the critical edge that befitted an emergency and therefore did not merit any support from the reserve resources. Seemingly this is what differentiated the Punjabi Hindu refugees from the local Hindu traders and the difference was attributed to the differing ethnic roots.

The ethnic qualification is an accepted parameter even in the academic discourse on Punjabi refugees. V.N. Dutta, a renowned historian and himself a refugee from Punjab, explained the success of Punjabi refugee traders in terms of their 'superior initiative and enterprise' which allowed them to take over around 90 per cent of the commercial ownership in Delhi while local resident shopkeepers were reduced to a mere 10 per cent.[27]

This observation reflects the discourse on successful resettlement popular among the Punjabis and, in fact, adds a measure of pride to Punjabi ethnicity. Stephen Keller (1975: 252), in his elaborate study of Punjabi refugees, noted that refugees were often seen as the usurpers of the local trader's territory who had taken a lead due to their cunning and aggressive business strategies that were often a cause of social tension.[28] He explains this as the risk-taking behaviour typical among Punjabis, visible in the instances of frequent emigration in Punjab, the choice of tough professions like armed services, and the fact that they took recourse to long-drawn litigations in the courts. Each of these features symbolizes the inherent gambling instincts, that is, the risk-taker can never be sure of the end results since it could be total success or total failure.

Even though Keller wants to emphasize the daring–speculative character of the Punjabis, what emerges even more strongly is the cautious instinct inherent in their chosen livelihood strategies. While migration abroad, for example, to the British protectorate in East Africa in the early 19th century, was a fairly common strategy, giving up one's landholding at home was never a part of the overall migration plan. The land was reserved as a fall-back option in case the endeavour abroad did not succeed. Similarly the farmers-turned-soldiers came back to their lands after retirement to resume farming. This shows a flexible approach to shifting occupations and moving between places. The risks are never taken at the cost of losing the capital base, but capital security is used as a springboard for other enterprises.

But such a discourse around Punjabi ethnicity has become a source of the mythical Punjabi persona who is fun-loving, enterprising, skilful, large-hearted, and courageously speculative. The Punjabi myth is believed by many, and most of all by the Punjabis themselves. It extends to physical matters also, especially about outward appearance. Manchanda, a refugee from Multan described the Delhi residents in the following terms when he saw them for the first time when the refugee special train he was travelling in stopped at the newly established India–Pakistan border. The Hindu train was being exchanged at the border in return for safe passage of the Muslim train from Delhi.

This was for the first time I had seen anybody from Delhi. They were Muslim refugees from Old Delhi on their way to Pakistan. I was surprised to find that they were Muslims. Because we always thought of Muslims as tall and well-built like the Punjabi Muslims in our district. Even the Punjabi Hindus were well-built. The Delhi residents looked traumatized. But we were fine though we had faced similar circumstances. Even their women looked strange, not like our Punjabi women who are tall and fair and have well-defined features. The Hindus of Delhi were just like their Muslim counterparts, meek and spiritless.[29]

Though religious separatism had formed the basis of Partition, it did not become a common ground for those belonging to the same faith. In this account, the identity derived from the region, Punjab, becomes more important than the one derived from religion. The Hindus and Muslims shared similar characteristics visible in their tall, fair, and seemingly attractive appearance as well as their spirited approach to life. The Hindus in Delhi were comparatively unattractive and devoid of spirit just like their Muslim counterparts. The listless description of local Hindus allows for the Punjabi myth to prevail, as is evident among the members of DI Khan Service Society in North Delhi: 'I should not say this but the Delhi residents had no jest for life. They were laid-back in their attitude and had a poor lifestyle. They did not even eat good food. We have taught them how to live and enjoy life'.[30]

Thus, the two identities—Hindu and Punjabi—frequently compete with one another, yet continue to occupy a common space. But over the years, it is the third prominent identity derived from the Indian nation that has superseded ethnic identities. The idea of being an Indian, rather than just Punjabi or Hindu, finds greater favour among the former refugees and their successors in Delhi. This complicates the identification process further, as multifarious identity claims are forwarded, scrutinized, rejected, or accepted in response to historical developments. Identity claims often derive from and simultaneously contribute to popular discourses, myths, folklore, and history. They carry discursive meanings, embellish given historical myths, as a result of which the identity bearers can claim part in the ancient traditions or distant historical episodes to which otherwise they would have little connection. For instance, the claim to Aryan heritage allows an individual in Delhi to link up with an alleged 5000-year-old-history. If such identity claims give larger-than-life meanings to the otherwise ordinary individual lives, then the individual identity bearers also see themselves as precursors and guardians of the continued future of that identity.

Thus, 'identity label' assumes the qualitative sense of an adjective. This means that the bearers of an identity label—Indian, Hindu, or Punjabi—carry the ascriptive meanings of Indian-ness, Hindu-ness, or Punjabi-ness in their very persons and their way of life. The labels as such are often challenged and negotiated, but they allow the bearer to create associations and gain access into new social spaces. In a newly independent nation, identity labels also become visible symbols of sacrifice, loyalty to the nation-state and patriotism, which later enables the bearer to present a legitimate claim to the resources, opportunities, or privileges the new state-society has to offer. The Hindu refugees from Punjab already had a claim to the Indian nation by the very nature of their forced displacement. The Partition of British India had almost become a pre-requisite to gain independence from colonial rule, since the demand for Pakistan had become a firm part of the agenda in the tripartite talks between the British Indian government, Congress, and the Muslim League. The population displacement was, thus, an undeniable part of the foundations of the independent Indian nation. Even though the circumstances of forced displacement, by their very definition, cannot be termed as personal sacrifice on the part of the Punjabi refugees since they would most likely not have chosen to move if they were not forced to, in hindsight, the displacement and loss of homes did become a pre-condition for birth of the Indian nation.

Upon their arrival in Delhi, the refugees at once became a part of the Hindu religious majority and legal citizens of India according to the newly instituted Constitution. The widening Hindu–Sikh rift since the late 1960s and the militant movement in Punjab calling for a separate Sikh nation state meant that Sikhs were seen as anti-nationals and traitors, who were challenging Indian territorial integrity. Almost as a corollary to the Sikh separatism and anti-Hindu militant activities by extreme Sikh groups, the Hindus became natural allies of the Indian state, committed to territorial defence, and firmly in opposition to yet another partition of India to create a Sikh state. The 1984 anti-Sikh riots in Delhi and surrounding areas concretized the Hindu–Sikh rift. As a result, the ideas of being a Hindu and being an Indian were not separate any more, whereas the Hindus from Punjab had increasingly become distanced from their Punjabi ethnicity.

'WE ARE FIRST INDIANS...'

The title of this section is the first part of a popular slogan from the mid-1980s, when the Congress government led by Rajiv Gandhi launched an extensive national integration programme. The campaign was necessitated by a number of secessionist movements gaining currency in different parts of India that threatened its territorial nationhood.[31] The continuous separatist violence in Punjab and Kashmir along the Pakistani border was a constant source of worry for the Indian state. The focus, in such circumstances, was on the lack of national unity that would otherwise make India a strong and indivisible entity. In a bid to fill this perceived lack, the government launched campaigns around unity in diversity, communal harmony, and national integration.[32] The aim was to inculcate pride and a sense of belonging towards the Indian nation.

This campaign took an institutionalized form after the assassination of Rajiv Gandhi in 1991. The Congress government set up special tasks for the Home Ministry, aimed at promoting national integration and communal harmony through various levels of the administration. The result was a government agency called the National Foundation for Communal Harmony, established in 1992, which promoted harmony by 'mobilising constructive forces of society in the cause of national unity and solidarity and giving them leadership and articulation'.[33] An annual award worth Rs 2.5 lakh to be awarded to individuals and organizations for the 'promotion of communal harmony and/or national integration' was also instituted the same year.[34] The very fact that such concerted campaigns, generous state funding, and incentives for public recognition are offered to promote national unity shows the lack of a readymade Indian nation wherein one's personal identification with the nation is paramount. That regional affiliations in various parts of India are stronger than the national affiliation is borne out by a series of successful name-change movements in many cities. Of the four metropolitan cities in India, Bombay was renamed Mumbai, Madras as Chennai, and Calcutta as Kolkata to erase the colonial imprints and simultaneously emphasize the ethnic identification with the Marathi, Tamil, and Bengali languages respectively. The name-change of cities—from colonial to local—is symbolic of the complex processes of identification that involves individuals and groups trying to make sense of their colonial history, and the post-colonial nation-building exercise, while contesting an erosion of their local/regional identities. The change in nomenclature seemingly circumvents the 'national' identification to a large extent.

Among the four cities, Delhi is the only one where state-led campaigns for national unity have had visible success. The very first pointer is the extent to which the national identity of being Indian is chosen over the ethnic/regional identity of being Punjabi. A majority of the survey respondents identified themselves with the Indian nation rather than with a region or a religion. This brings the history of Partition displacement and communal tensions between Hindus and Sikhs in juxtaposition to the state-led campaigns for national integration. As shown earlier, the camps for the Partition refugees had become a site for experimentation in nationalism, where various state agencies attempted to produce citizens for the newly independent nation. The interaction of migrants with the state agencies was rather frequent in Delhi since it was the political capital of India, and refugee resettlement was expected to be a model for other states in India. The displacement, in a way, encouraged the migrants to attempt new social and occupational adjustments, as a result of which cooperative business enterprises and residents associations/societies became an accepted feature of the city.[35]

The Hindu–Sikh fractures meant that Punjabi ethnicity now stood in opposition to the Indian nation, as the territory of Punjab was marked for secession from India. The territory of Punjab and the Punjabi language were now linked to Sikhs, while Hindus grew closer to Hindi and the Indian nation. The religious background of Punjabi Hindus in the Arya Samaj later made it easier for them to identify with the RSS and the larger right-wing Hindu movement in their opposition to Sikh militancy. This was reflected in the choices—with respect to language, politics, and new religious symbols—that Punjabi Hindus made. First, the mother tongue, Punjabi, was rejected in favour of the national language, Hindi. This was a clear signal of detachment from Punjabi identity. Second, the popular acceptance of the cult of the eight-armed goddess brought Punjabi Hindus closer to the militant Hindu politics propagated by the RSS. The religious demarcations between Hindus and Sikhs had always been blurred in Punjab due to a strong tradition of Sufi-inspired syncretism. This blurred space to move between two religions was constricted by the new symbolism of Sheran Wali Mata, with whom the Punjabi Hindus could exclusively identify. The story of her origin, frequent movement, and armed preparedness for defence reflected her devotees' history of displacement and their battles with the Muslims. The cult therefore became a bridge between the migrants and the Indian nation, which was similarly threatened by Muslim Pakistan.

The closer identification between the labels of Hindu and Indian is also borne out by the 2003–4 campaign 'India Shining' launched by the BJP-led government. The campaign was aimed at instilling pride and belonging in the Indian nation, just like the earlier popular campaigns from the 1980s. The difference lies between the sponsors of the two campaigns: earlier it was the Congress party with its secular credentials that attempted to reiterate Indian nationalism whereas later, it was the right-wing Hindu BJP and its allies that were making similar attempts. Somewhere between these two campaigns and coupled with the occupation of the mainstream political space by the Congress and the BJP, the identity of being Hindu has written itself into being Indian. This on one hand means that Hindus have become synonymous with India, but on the other indicates that they have distanced themselves from the extreme Hindu right-wing identity in preference to the Indian national identity.[36] This is clearly visible in Delhi, where urban middle class, Hindi/English-speaking devotees of the eight-armed goddess identify themselves with the Indian nation.

Conclusions

The above discussions have shown that the notion of identity is relative, that is, the process of identification depends on historically generated moments where individuals/groups need to associate with or delink from given labels. The labels themselves are the visible products of the processes activated and steered by agencies of religious/social/political groups. Individuals choose to appropriate or reject symbols of identification contingent upon the critical response they receive from others around them. A survey of social response is important vis-à-vis acceptance or defiance of community groups by an individual. Among the Punjabi Hindu migrants in Delhi, the identification with the Indian state has been strong for several reasons: (1) both the state and the refugees began restoring and restructuring their lives simultaneously after Partition, (2) the absence of a strong regional identity in Delhi meant that Indian national identity did not compete with region-based ethnicity like in West Bengal, and, finally, (3) the Hindu–Sikh cleavages meant that Punjabi Hindus distanced themselves from their Punjabi identity partly to preserve their own religious identity and partly to prove their patriotism towards the Indian state. Thus, identification with the Indian nation-state is deeper among the displaced Punjabi Hindu population, which has been delinked from its ethnic identity following displacement.

Notes

1. Personal interview with Subhash Chaturvedi, a fourth generation resident of Delhi, December 2000.
2. A popular slogan in the 1980s to promote national integration and communal harmony supported by the Congress-led central government. The slogan could be used in various regional and religious contexts: the first line was 'We are first Indians.....', and could be followed by any given regional or communal identity. The entire initiative was called *Mera Bharat Mahaan* ('My India is Great') under which a variety of professionally produced television, radio, and print campaigns were broadcast on a daily basis.
3. Such themes are derived from individual-oriented psychological studies in the realm of social sciences, wherein conceptual bodies of large social groups replace the individual. A pointer to the arrival of the identity question in the social sciences is the fact that till the mid-1960s, the *Encyclopedia of Social Sciences* contained only one entry on identity, one that pertained to the psycho-social study of identity crises among adolescents (Hobsbawm 1996). Some of the agenda-setting work on social identities came in the form of human development theory that tried to combine psychological stages of development with the social responses each such development receives (see Erikson 1968). Though Erikson's work has been subjected to criticism for being structured-stage-oriented and for demanding a strenuous methodology of employing 'psycho-histories' of important individuals to understand larger social changes, his idea of critical social response to life situations forms a useful basis for this study. It puts the context of identity

formation in a dialogical mode, wherein individuals or social groups interact with others to construct their identities. This is particularly helpful, as we will find, in perceiving why some identities are flaunted while others are hidden from public view. Identity as a socially constructed concept in the social sciences enables us to see how people introduce themselves to others, represent their selves, and organize their surroundings to produce an explanatory device that seeks to cast ordinary lives into meaningful stories.

4. If primordialists seek to root social identities within the given social existence, larger national and ethnic identities are considered recent inventions inevitably created to meet the needs of modern nation states (see Gellner 1983; Hobsbawm 1990). The social constructivists follow Elie Kedourie (1960) who viewed the construction of national identity as a proof of collective will and ideology attained through active mobilization. The traces of this 'invention' approach are clear in the influential account of nation as an 'imagined political community—imagined as sovereign, finite and horizontal' (Anderson 1991).

5. Several political parties were mentioned in the questionnaire, but most of the respondents tended to name either the BJP or the Congress as the preferred one. There was also an option for 'any other'.

6. Paul Brass (1974), *Language, Religion and Politics in North India*, Cambridge, University of Cambridge Press, pp. 294–7.

7. A similar observation is also made in Aditi Mukherjee's (1996) comparative linguistic study on Punjabi and Bengali migrants of Partition in Delhi.

8. While Punjabis are seen to have experienced a 'language shift', the Bengalis have maintained their mother tongue Bangla (Mukherjee 1996: 173).

9. Quote taken from Tapan Basu et al. (1993: 8).

10. Personal interview.

11. *Sudarshan Chakra* is the wheel-like destructive weapon worn on the index finger by Lord Krishna in the Hindu epic, Mahabharata.

12. The mobilization of Hindu women in right-wing Hindu politics has been a much-researched theme in the last decade (see Sarkar (1996); Banerjee (1996); and also Hansen (1994)) 'Controlled Emancipation: Women and Hindu Nationalism' in *European Journal of Development Research*, vol. 6, no. 2.

13. This was one of the causes; others included the music played in temples, routes for religious processions, and carcasses of dead cows and pigs thrown in temples and mosques respectively. See Hansen (2002).

14. I must thank Dipankar Gupta for pointing this out to me.

15. During most of the personal interviews, the respondents mentioned that they had never heard such loud singing when they had just come to Delhi.

16. Christophe Jaffrelot (2000).

17. Election Commission of India, Statistical Report on General Elections 1951 to the First Lok Sabha, vol. 1, p. 82.

18. Personal interview with the members of DI Khan Seva Samiti, December 2000.

19. Letter from Mehar Chand Khanna to Gobind Ballabh Pant dated 4 October 1955 (D.O. Number 324/PSMR/Conf. Department of Rehabilitation, Ministry of Home Affairs, New Delhi).

20. In his reply to M.C. Khanna, Pant expressed his concerns about Khanna's proposal. See letter from Pant to Khanna dated 8 October 1955 (Number D-6346/55 HM, Department of Rehabilitation, Ministry of Home Affairs, New Delhi).

21. See Neville Maxwell (1974) 'Reconsiderations: Jawaharlal Nehru: Of Pride and Principle' in *Foreign Affairs* April 1974.
22. See Kathrine Frank's (2000) biography *Indira: The Life of Indira Nehru Gandhi.*
23. Christophe Jaffrelott (2000).
24. Personal interview with Subhash Chaturvedi, a fourth generation resident of the city, December 2000, New Delhi.
25. The term 'Punjabi' pertains to region-based identity, that is, those hailing from the northern state of Punjab. It includes both Hindus and Sikhs.
26. Bir Sahni (b. 1928) migrated from Rawalpindi to Delhi in 1947. Personal interview, December 2000.
27. V.N. Dutta in a personal interview conducted in December 2000. Also see V.N. Dutta (1986).
28. See Stephen Keller (1975) *Uprooting and Social Change: The Role of Refugees in Development,* p. 252.
29. Personal interview with P. Manchanda (b. 1932), December 2000.
30. Personal interview with K.K. Pahwa (b. 1928), December 2000.
31. Various secessionist movements in Punjab, Kashmir, Assam, Manipur, and movements for autonomy like Chhattisgarh, Jharkhand, and Uttarakhand confronted India from the early 1970s onwards. At the same time, there was tension in south India over the issue of the Hindi language.
32. The first extensive campaign called *Mera Bharat Mahaan* ('My India is Great') was launched by Rajiv Gandhi during the 1989 general election campaign. The mainstay of the campaign was professionally produced advertisements that appeared in daily newspapers, television, and public hoardings.
33. This is stated on the publicity leaflet for the '2002 Communal Harmony Awards' issued by the National Foundation for Communal Harmony, Lok Nayak Bhawan, New Delhi.
34. Ibid. Also see the Annual Report 1999–2000 of Ministry of Home Affairs, particularly chapter 9, entitled 'National Integration'.
35. Among numerous examples of cooperative enterprises, the well-known Central Cottage Industries Emporium (CCIE) on Janpath in Delhi best exemplifies the migrant/state partnership. In 1947, CCIE was formed to sell handlooms, handicrafts, etc., produced in the work centres for refugees managed by the CRC. Similarly, resident associations were encouraged by the government to manage the day-to-day affairs in a given colony. Resident Welfare Associations, or RWAs as they are popularly called, are now an essential part of the city's urban infrastructure.
36. The rise of religious violence associated with extreme right-wing Hindu politics has led upwardly, mobile urban Hindus to distance themselves from it. The curbs on personal freedom imposed by right wing organizations have further contributed to this detachment.

9. A Community of Narrative

In late February 2002, the MCD brought its demolition campaign in Lajpat Nagar to a halt. The demolitions had not only caused widespread protests among the residents but also unprecedented ire against the authorities in the rest of Delhi city. Two residents in the area had died of heart attacks caused by panic and unrest during the demolitions.[1] The MCD had deployed around 400 of its employees and an armoury of bulldozers, tractors, trucks, and other demolition equipment. The municipal contingent had demolished more than 800 structures out of the 3500 notified buildings and caused destruction of property worth Rs 4 crore before it closed its campaign. It was not the residents' deaths that had stopped MCD from continuing its operations, but the imminent elections to the Delhi municipality which had just been announced by the Election Commission.[2]

The Congress-led state government in Delhi along with the central government steered by the BJP[3] were in a fix as the MCD operation was bound by a legal order from the Supreme Court and could not be reversed without approaching the court. The alterations and additional structures constructed in Old Double Storey not only flouted the building bye-laws but also jeopardized the master plan for Delhi city which envisaged aesthetically pleasing architecture and a well-planned urban layout. However, the literate, politically astute, and vociferously vocal middle class electorate in Lajpat Nagar was too significant to be ignored on either legal or architectural pretexts by any political party. Moreover, the resident's protests had gained substantial sympathy from the middle classes in Delhi, who could easily identify with the residents' plight and pangs of dislocation. The various levels of state authority in Delhi, as a result, set out to find solutions that would not contravene any court order and yet satisfy the residents.

As a first measure, the Urban Development Minister at the centre, Ananth Kumar of the BJP, announced 'the constitution of an eight member committee to look into the issue of regularisation of unauthorised colonies and to study the part two of the Malhotra Committee report.'[4] The Malhotra Committee had earlier recommended that building bye-laws be changed to allow commercial structures in residential areas and the construction of additional floors in residential buildings. If the recommendations of this report were incorporated as law, then 'unauthorised' constructions in Lajpat Nagar would become legal, beyond the reproach of any court. Since the residents could not be assuaged without contravening the law in the current circumstances, the law itself was proposed to be altered through the invocation of this report. Clearly, such extreme measures were resorted to by the BJP government since its leadership represented the Lajpat Nagar area not only in the municipal council (Shakuntala Arya), but also in the state legislative assembly (Sushil Chaudhry), and Parliament (Vijay Kumar Malhotra). Following the cue from the Urban Development Ministry, the MCD promised to follow a three-step procedure that would make the demolitions seem less arbitrary. The measures agreed by the MCD were: (1) appropriate notices would be sent to the defaulters asking them to explain their position, (2) the defaulters would get 14 days period to file a reply and get an opportunity to personally present their case, and (3) the defaulter could approach the Appellate Tribunal headed by a judicial officer to contest the demolition order. The demolition would take place only when all these options had been exhausted. The three-step approach was aimed at strategically slowing down the pace of demolitions without offending the court. These measures helped halt the process of demolition, albeit on a temporary basis.

In the two years that have lapsed between the fieldwork and the completion of this study, demolitions in Lajpat Nagar have not been raked up again. The fractured buildings have long since been patched up, while everyday life in the area has returned to normal. The perceived villain in the drama— the BJP—lost heavily in the 2002 Delhi municipal elections where its candidates won only 17 out of the 134 seats.[5] Subsequently, the BJP lost the 2003 state legislative elections as well as the 2004 general elections in Delhi. The main political actors in this drama—Sushil Chaudhry, Shakuntala Arya and the architect of the Malhotra report, Vijay Kumar Malhotra— are yet to regain the lost political ground in Delhi. The eight-member committee appointed to study the building bye-laws has not made its recommendations public so far. The final order from the Supreme Court has also been delayed because of numerous review petitions. The MCD's demolition campaign, in short, has lost its sense of urgency.

Though the conflict around unauthorized construction is far from resolved, the struggle between the state and the residents has thrown up a clear winner: the residents of Lajpat Nagar, who clearly succeeded in turning the confrontation around in their favour. The efforts by the different state authorities to remove unauthorized structures in the area were thwarted by the collective resistance shown by the residents. Skilfully staged protests, strategic negotiations with the political leadership, and humble pleas to the judicial authority were variously employed by the residents to secure themselves against the demolitions. Their ability to negotiate successfully with different public authorities shows the extent of familiarity the residents have had with the state agencies. Their success emanated not only from the resistance they put up, but also from the unprecedented sympathy they evoked from 'the entire middle class of Delhi'. The response was considered unprecedented because demolitions of unauthorized colonies and structures inhabited by poor migrants from the neighbouring states are routine in Delhi, and they hardly ever evoke sympathy or response from the middle classes. In this case, however, the middle class responded sympathetically to the cause of the Lajpat Nagar residents.

How did the residents manage to mobilize this extraordinary sympathy for their cause? Such a question can be answered through the optics of everyday past which allows us to see the present-day conflicts, circumstances, and role players in their historical context. It also shows how the past is successfully evoked in everyday life to create a powerful collective entity. The residents in Lajpat Nagar are the original migrants and their descendants who were forced to migrate from West Punjab and NWFP in 1947. The Partition migrants resettled in large numbers in different parts of Delhi and account for a majority of the urban middle class population in Delhi. In fact, the urban expansion of Delhi beyond Old Delhi and British New Delhi was a result of the state-led mass housing construction in east, west, and south Delhi between the 1940s and the late 1950s. Thus, a large part of the urban middle class in Delhi is linked through the shared experience of Partition.

It was this section of Delhi society that made common cause with the Lajpat Nagar residents. The mobilizing link was the invocation of a shared past of the 1947 Partition that continues to be a personal emotive theme for most. The protests organized by the residents were covered extensively by the local media. The staple story in various newspapers and TV channels was built around an account of the actual demolitions, the technical-legal problems that necessitated demolitions and, finally, the theme of Partition uprooting and migration that brought the Lajpat Nagar residents to Delhi in the first place. Such news items were invariably accompanied by personal accounts of Partition migration, wherein individuals recounted their heart-rending experiences. Most accounts were formed around the homelessness and dislocation they had experienced in 1947 and were about to experience again. They were dislocated in 1947 because they did not belong to Muslim-majority Pakistan, but this time dislocation was happening in their 'own' country and under a government run by their fellow Hindu countrymen. The local and national representatives from Lajpat Nagar— Chaudhry, Arya, and Malhotra—were, in fact, themselves Partition migrants.

This linkage at once compressed the historical space between 1947 and 2002 in a way that injustices, betrayals, and offences committed by the state half-a-century ago became part of the current plot. The common refrain was that no one had protected the migrants from being forced out of their homes in 1947; they had come to Delhi and struggled on their own to make homes and decent living; the government had just stood there like a bystander; and this betrayal by the state was being repeated now. The entire history of state-led refugee resettlement was circumvented in this way. The identity of the residents as 'victims' of state callousness was renewed and authenticated with this evidence from the past. The invocation of Partition history is what brought the Punjabi urban middle class outside Lajpat Nagar to make common cause with them. In other words, a community feeling among the Punjabi urban middle class across the city was activated in the process. This helps us address the theme of community and its forms during forced migration and resettlement.

In earlier discussions, community has been established as a created category, which people feel they need in order to fulfil their wish to belong. It does not exist in fixed, settled forms through which people enter to become part of a community or depart when they wish to disassociate. Community, then, becomes a symbolic constitution of boundaries that are constituted by the people themselves (Cohen 1992: 13). The creation of such a community requires that people recognize and identify a common symbol around which to mobilize. The Partition migrants have had no single visible symbol of unity since they came from divergent social groups formed around religious cults, political ideologies, caste biradaris, and places of origin among other variables. Associations like the local branches of the Arya Samaj and the RSS, and the Rehgar Mahasabha and the DI Khan society are some examples of community groups based on religio-political ideology, caste, and place of origin respectively. The very experience of migration has not led to the formation of a community among the migrants. They come from socially divergent categories and have had widely varied experiences of the same event, as was evident in Chapters 2, 3, and 4. The dispersal from their homes in West Punjab and NWFP did not necessarily lead to the recreation of their former settlements in Delhi. Most migrants settled wherever the state allocated accommodation to them. The new settlements were more on the basis of class than any other consideration. Rehgar Pura resettlement, on the other hand, was based both on caste and class discrimination, which segregated poor untouchable migrants into one single location.

The basis of a Punjabi migrant community, noticeable during the Lajpat Nagar demolitions, does not lie in the visible symbols of unity. It lies rather in the master narrative of Partition uprooting, migration, and resettlement, which discursively dissolves the socially divisive categories of caste, class, and gender. What emerges is a community of narratives that comes into existence only when the master narrative is invoked. As discussed earlier, the personal narratives of Partition migration frequently depart from the common minimum narrative that seeks to relate the experiences of the millions of migrants in a compressed collective form. These personal narratives often compete with the popular version, which has by now assumed mythical characteristics. It is a matter of enquiry as to how the 'popular' version became popular in the first place. In other words, how does one account among many get repeated over and over again and gain authenticity? The answer, as we have seen, lies within the narrative and its close identification with the narrative of the independent Indian nation itself. The popular story of Partition migrants is built around proud male Hindu and Sikh characters who were thrown out of their homes through the treachery of greedy Muslims who wanted a separate homeland. They were rendered homeless and robbed of any means of survival. This turn of fate did not destroy their desire to work hard and earn their living honestly. Many of them came to Delhi and preferred starvation to beggary. The refugees began working in all available occupations and in no time began giving tough competition to the local Hindu traders. Their hard work brought them good fortune and success.

This narrative has positive 'masculine' elements—pride, hard work, bravery, honesty—that help create an ideal type among migrants from Punjab. Any departure from such an ideal figure would mean acknowledging lack of pride, honesty, and ability to work hard in one's own person. An affiliation with the ideal type seems a better option than embracing these unflattering personal qualities. The master narrative recreates the event of Partition and the personal stories therein in a practised seamless manner that glosses over any evidence to the contrary. The narrative of personal destruction followed by resurrection is a theme that resounds with the theme of national struggle for Indian independence. The hour of independence was marred by territorial partition, movement of population, and internecine communal violence. This scenario was shared by the nascent nation as well as those who were rendered homeless. The path followed by the nation and its migrants was concurrent, and its intricacies were therefore understood by both.

The pictorial depiction of Partition in the state accounts follows the common phases of complete chaos, and then order, after which both the migrants and the nation gain control of their destinies. The first phase is the portrayal of chaos, escape, danger, and defeat—visible in the photos of fleeing refugees—that helped the state to assume a role of greater authority in the given circumstances. This is followed by another set of pictures— of orderly tents, neat rows of new houses, refugees busy in their new occupations—where order is regained through state efforts. The nation and the migrants together make this journey of restoration. This commonly cherished narrative is what becomes the pivot of a structureless, episodic community (see Fraser 1999; Turner 1995) that emerges publicly only in critical moments like the demolition in Lajpat Nagar.

This discussion on community and narrative helps contextualize the three main research questions posed at the beginning of this study about state interpretation of social conflicts and its reflection in the refugee resettlement policies; differing experiences of singular events of forced migrants; and the process of transformation from refugees to locals.

STATE, SOCIETY, AND DISPLACEMENT

This study has shown that social hierarchies and conflicts permeate into the state institutions as well. The state/society debates that tend to separate the two gloss over the close interaction which goes into making and altering policies of governance. This interaction, which may be blurred in everyday life, becomes clearly visible during moments of turbulence, when both society and state are in upheaval. The instance of Partition offers such an opportunity to examine this interaction, where violent disturbances in society—communal violence, forced migration—accompanied post-colonial state formation in India. The mass production of refugees/migrants in such an event opens up such a vulnerable point in state/society interaction, since the state is required to restore social order so as to reproduce its own authority in the public sphere. Displacement also means that the subjects of governance need to be organized in governable social categories that facilitate the business of state.

During Partition resettlement, the Indian state emerges as a 'social being' rather than as a distant entity that sits atop society. This is clearly reflected in the official Indian government policies with respect to refugee resettlement. The mass of refugees was distinguished on class, caste and gender lines that largely reproduced the pre-Partition social order. The social distinctions and contemporary normative biases influenced the state resettlement, resulting in discriminatory schemes for poor people, widows, and untouchables among the migrants. The very first pointer to this is the compensation policy, which aimed at restoring what was lost during the migration. This meant that one had to 'own' something in order to be compensated for it. This was an effective way to recreate pre-Partition class divisions (notwithstanding a number of stories where individuals succeeded in circumventing the official system to make personal gains through inflated claims of loss). The class division began at the very moment of arrival from Pakistan, when the refugees were separated according to the receipt or non-receipt of state-sponsored food rations. The clusters of refugees formed at that initial moment served to make administration easier in subsequent stages when permanent housing had to be allotted. The type and form of housing accommodation one received betrayed the methodical distinction made by the state between the 'deserving' and 'non-deserving' refugees. Mass displacement clearly did not provide a social levelling ground upon which an egalitarian society could be constructed.

The second pointer is the segregation of refugees according to their caste status. The untouchable refugees were separated from the upper caste Hindus and Sikhs, first during the population movement and later during the resettlement. This happened despite the constitutional abolition of the practice of untouchability in independent India. The state agency, the Harijan Sevak Sangh, never scrutinized the allegations of discrimination against the untouchable refugees. The state housing accommodation for the untouchable refugees was located far away from the upper caste refugee camps in an already existing colony of untouchable sweepers in Delhi. This continued the familiar upper caste practice of separating the untouchables to ward off the fear of caste 'pollution'. The accommodation for untouchables constituted of mud huts covered with plastic sheets that compared poorly with the concrete planned housing colonies for the upper caste refugees. The compensation packages were extremely meagre for the untouchables when compared with the schemes for upper caste refugees. Through these state policies, the social practice of caste discrimination became part of an institutionalized social design.

The barricaded widow colony in Lajpat Nagar points to the third piece of evidence of reproduction of social biases in state policies. In keeping with the social practice of seclusion, the state built exclusive quarters for the young widows of Partition violence. The women in this colony were secluded and protected from the male gaze by the state employees who fulfilled the role of patriarchs in traditional households. The traditional role of widow is to live in a quiet, withdrawn state within a household, where, in the absence of her husband, her father-in-law or brother-in-law takes control. The family exercises control over her sexuality and reproductivity, linked to the notion of family honour and shame, by keeping her away from public activity. The Indian state similarly reproduced this notion of honour through abstinence and seclusion by fulfilling the role of the patriarch. The honour at stake was no longer that of an individual or family, but rather that of the Indian nation, to safeguard which the state had to restore 'normalcy' by reproducing familiar practices. Thus, the state attempted restoration of all that was lost during Partition, including the restoration of the social landscape.

During Partition resettlement, the Indian state, far from its rational bureaucratic incarnation, appears as a well integrated 'social being'. It is not aloof from the social expectations or the ones it imagines society to expect from its rulers. This idea of maintaining local norms hints at the continued colonial legacy of the British rulers who would not meddle in the 'local beliefs' as long as the law and order situation was not threatened. Either way, social norms became integrated with state policies. The instances of women, untouchables, and poor refugees shows that it was not necessarily the state that was intervening in the social norms, but rather the social norms—of caste-based pollution, morality, sexual abstinence in widowhood and class segregation—that entered state policies. This has shown how the private and collective beliefs about behaviour of women, sexual practices, caste distinctions, and discrimination become nationalized (and therefore public) through official directives. The public/private split, in a way, becomes obscure when it is the overlap and not the distance between the two that becomes definitive.

ABSENCES IN DISPLACEMENT

The event of mass migration, forced or voluntary, produces new categories of migrants and refugees. The pre-migration categories based on caste, class and gender collapse to produce overarching categories to describe one's state of displacement. This study has shown that use of a new discursive category does not actually remove or alter existing social arrangements and conflicts. A mass event like Partition clearly cannot be told in a single master narrative, since each individual experienced the same event based on their class, caste, and gender positions in society. However, this discriminatory aspect remains missing from the narratives of Partition. The master narrative of Punjab Partition is told by the Punjabi elite, who have retained the onus of narrating the 'true' account of Partition, though their own experiences often differ from the general experiences they narrate. This distinction can be marked in the way a given experience is narrated: personal experiences are narrated in the first person singular form while appropriated stories are narrated in the third person plural. At first, the narrators tend to relate their own experiences to the master version told from the vantage point of upper caste, middle class migrants. It is at another level, called level 'C' in this study (see Chapter 1), that narrators talk of their personal experiences which depart from the master version. This level brings out the discursive absences in the master version and therefore challenges it.

Two types of absences have been brought forth in this study: of people and institutions. The most significant absence among people is that of untouchable refugees in the popular narratives of Partition. The experiences of untouchable refugees have neither been chronicled nor been made part of the popular discourse. The discursive space has been occupied and monopolized by the upper caste migrants who have, in a sense, denied the untouchables the right to tell their story. This is because the history of Partition migration has become a mythical tale of origin: of a successful

Punjabi migrant community and the independent Indian nation. In this myth, the upper caste, middle class Punjabis emerge as heroic survivors who battled all odds to successfully reconstruct their lives. The purity of this myth cannot be polluted by opening it to the experiences of untouchables. Equally, the upper caste stories cannot be shared by the untouchables. The discursive absence of the untouchables meant that one could hardly make a connection between the untouchable resettlement in Rehgar Pura and Partition migration. The narratives of untouchables had thus been lost in Partition history. The crucial connection between Rehgar Pura and Partition could be made only through extensive archival work.

Similarly, women and poor refugee men seldom tell their own stories. This does not mean that they do not appear in the narratives, but rather that they do not author their own history. The women appear in Partition accounts chiefly as victims of violence, abductions, and forcible conversions, while the poor men appear in the vast background of the Partition drama as part of the crowd, fleeing on train tops or in foot columns. They never appear as individuals in their own right. Their individual experiences are condensed as collective experiences that are essential to the larger narration of the Partition drama. Thus, poor men and women exist only as a mass of refugees who on the one hand constitute integral ingredients of the Partition migration, and on the other, serve as a background against which individual experiences of middle class migrants are narrated.

The second type of absence is that of the Indian state in the master version of Partition migration and resettlement. There remains a large gap between the personal narratives and the evidence of state involvement in resettlement gathered from an array of documentary sources. The most significant evidence of state presence in the process of refugee resettlement is the constitution of an exclusive Ministry of Relief and Rehabilitation as early as 6 September 1947. The ministry was formed within three weeks of Partition and was entrusted with the sole responsibility of resolving the crisis of forced migration and its aftermath. The direct participation of the state in the migration process began with the creation of the Joint Evacuation Movement Plan in mid-October 1947. The two states of India and Pakistan agreed upon a formal exchange of population that would take place under armed protection. The process included formation of transit refugee camps at the place of migration, provision of military escort and vehicles for movement from rural areas, arrangement of special refugee trains between India and Pakistan, and finally, the settlement of refugees in temporary camps at their location of arrival. The temporary refugee camps became permanent residences for the refugees for some years to come. In Delhi, Kingsway was the largest camp with an estimated number of 30,000 refugees who sought shelter there. The semi-permanent status of the camp residents meant that facilities for health care, primary education, and vocational training had to be provided within the camps. For those who could not afford to pay for their basic requirements, free rations, clothes, blankets, and cash doles were provided.

Several schemes were launched by the state around this time to facilitate permanent resettlement through housing, education, and employment. The largest project undertaken by the state was the establishment of refugee housing colonies to provide accommodation outside camps to refugees. This resulted in an unprecedented urban expansion of Delhi city through development of new residential and commercial areas. The refugees were allocated one or two room accommodations, depending on the extent of their compensation claim. The creation of additional housing facilities in the city meant that refugees not only came to acquire permanent homes but also a semblance of permanence in their daily lives.

In the meantime, the state made efforts to make available basic and specialized education to refugees through a number of incentives like waiving off or lowering fees, raising the minimum age limit for admission to various institutions, interest-free loans to refugee students studying abroad, financial aid, and land grants to educational institutions which had moved from West Punjab and opening new educational institutions. It was also made mandatory for educational institutions to not refuse admission to refugee students under any circumstances. The refugee students were also offered a choice of vocational training that would enable them to gain employment later. The refugees were encouraged to seek jobs through the state organized 'employment exchanges' that maintained a database of qualified persons who were informed of suitable vacancies as and when they arose. A lenient view was taken of basic job requirements like maximum age limit and minimum educational qualification in order to enable refugees to qualify. The state became one of the biggest employers for the refugees, as it circulated directives to various ministries, state governments, and government-owned concerns to give preference to refugee candidates wherever possible.

The personal narratives told by the refugees seldom include such information. The narratives mostly circumvent the issue of state participation. The popular version is built around the myth of ethnic Punjabi essence— hard work, honesty, sharp business acumen, and self-reliance—that could be challenged when state efforts are acknowledged. The popular refrain of 'we did everything on our own' is what characterizes the personal narratives told by successful Punjabi migrants in Delhi. This self-reliant, proud position can be maintained only by keeping a distance between the state and the self. Any authentication of the state account would soil the ethnic and personal glorification.

From Refugees to Locals

This study has focused on the twin processes of transformation that turn (1) ordinary people into refugees and (2) refugees into citizens and then locals. In other words, it is about the themes of displacement, belonging and association of people and places. The event of Partition displacement at once turned ordinary Punjabi people into an exclusive category of being refugees. The state of being homeless became their most definitive characteristic, besides of course their religious identity that led to this state of homelessness. However, the term 'refugee' cannot be applied in toto to understand this process, since it has a clear legal and historical grounding in the post-World War II developments in the late 1940s. The legality of a migrant's status was hardly a question since the exchange of population meant that migrating Hindus and Sikhs were deemed citizens of India while migrating Muslims became citizens of Pakistan. There was no deprivation or denial of personal legal status during and after the movement. The refugee identity thus has more social implications than legal ones in this case. To understand this, local expressions like sharnarthi, panahgeer, and Muhajir appear more useful than the English word, refugee. The local expressions are not only detached from legal meanings but are also independent of the current discourse on refugees that views 'refugee-ness' as a special human condition.

Any new association or feeling of belonging requires that former associations be re-evaluated and concluded. Thus, association with the old home comes under scrutiny to ascertain how deeply attached the migrants were to their original homes. The condition of movement itself, from one place to another, was not unique for the Partition migrants from Punjab. The Hindus and Sikhs had earlier moved en masse in the late 19th century from East to West Punjab as part of the colonial agrarian movement. The British state had developed a vast network of irrigation canals that brought the hitherto unproductive land in West Punjab under cultivation. The opening of new agricultural land induced mass movement of farmers and soldiers who were given land holdings as reward. An influx of population led to development of new towns and villages and often to social experimentation. For example, the religio-social reform movements like the Arya Samaj took root in newly colonized areas more extensively than in East Punjab.

The Hindu and Sikh colonizers lived in West Punjab for a little more than half-a-century before they were forced to migrate back to their ancestral land in East Punjab. It is the urban population from West Punjab which migrated to Delhi city in large numbers. The Punjabi migrants in Delhi, according to their own account, became an integral part of the city in the mid-1960s. This approximate date is significant because it is around this time (1965) that the Ministry for Relief and Rehabilitation was formally closed and merged with the Ministry of Home Affairs. The migrants, symbolically, did not need a separate apparatus of administration and were now governed by similar rules as the locals in Delhi. The state programmes of rehabilitation in Delhi and Punjab were deemed concluded since a majority had gained permanent housing and means of livelihood. The process of resettlement, however, meant that the local Hindu residents in Delhi were marginalized and alienated in many ways, though the discontent and rivalry between locals and refugees in Delhi has rarely turned into open violent conflict.

The preceding chapters in this study have shown that the process of migration and resettlement was experienced by different sections of society at multiple levels, and that no single narrative can therefore claim to represent the Partition reality. The personal and collective experiences of Partition remain a contested turf where various social groups seek to narrate and define the larger history. The differences do not however interfere in the episodic formation of a narrative-based community that ordinarily remains divided on class, caste, and gender lines. It is the adverse and critical moments that catalyse past experiences to produce a powerful, tangible community.

NOTES

1. See 'Politics in a Demolition' by Naunidhi Kaur, *Frontline*, vol. 19, issue 5, 2–15 March 2002.
2. The elections were announced on 22 February 2002 and were to take place on 24 March 2002.
3. The central government was formed by the National Democratic Alliance (NDA) of which the BJP was the principal constituent.
4. 'BJP Caught Napping', *The Hindu*, 13 February 2002.
5. 'MCD Polls: BJP tried so hard it failed', *The Indian Express*, 28 March 2002.

Bibliography

PRIMARY SOURCES

All India Congress Committee Reports (II Instalment), 1947–48.

Annual Report 1947–48, Ministry of Relief and Rehabilitation, Government of India.

Imperial Gazetteer of India (Provincial Series) (1908/1991). vol. II: The Lahore, Rawalpindi, and Multan Divisions, and Native States. Delhi: Atlantic Publishers

Ministry of Relief and Rehabilitation. *Annual Report on Evacuation, Relief and Rehabilitation of Refugees, 1947–48.* New Delhi.

Constituent Assembly of India (Legislative) Debates 1947–48. New Delhi: Federal Law Depot.

Displaced Persons Compensation and Rehabilitation Act, 1954. New Delhi: Federal Law Depot. Undated.

Displaced Persons Compensation and Rehabilitation Rules 1955. New Delhi: Federal Law Depot. 1957.

The Administration of Evacuee Property Act, 1950. Delhi: Eastern Book Company.

The Delhi Evacuee Property (Supplementary) Ordinance, 1947. Delhi: Eastern Book Company.

The East Punjab Evacuees (Administration of Property) Ordinance, 1947. Delhi: Eastern Book Company.

UNHCR (1996).UN Convention Relating to the Status of Refugees, 1951, Geneva.

PRINTED COLLECTIONS OF DOCUMENTS

Husain, S.M. (1954). *The Laws and Practice Relating to Evacuee Property in India being Commentaries on the Administration of Evacuee Property Act, 1950 and Allied Acts.* Delhi: Eastern Book Co.

Singh, K. (ed.) (1991). *Select Documents on the Partition of Punjab 1947: India and Pakistan: Punjab, Haryana and Himachal Pradesh – India and Punjab – Pakistan.* Delhi: National Bookshop.

Tirmizi, S.A.I. (1998). *Paradoxes of Partition (1937–47).* vol. I. Delhi: Manak Publications.

Zaidi, Z.H. (1993). *Jinnah Papers: Prelude to Pakistan,* vols I and II. Islamabad: National Archives of Pakistan.

PRIVATE PAPERS

Diwan Chaman Lall Papers. Delhi. Nehru Memorial Museum and Library (NMML).

G.D. Khosla Papers. Delhi. NMML.

S.P. Mukherjee Papers. Delhi. NMML.

B.K. Chandiwala Papers. Delhi. NMML.

G.C. Bhargava Papers. Delhi. NMML.

PRINTED PRIMARY SOURCES

Annual Issue, *Jampuri Patrika* (1998). New Delhi. Jampur Seva Samiti.

Government of India. (Undated). *Millions on the Move: The Aftermath of Partition*. New Delhi: Publications Division, Ministry of Information and Broadcasting.

Rao, U.B. (1967). *The Story of Rehabilitation*. New Delhi: Publications Divisions, Ministry of Information and Broadcasting.

Randhawa, M. (1954). *Out of Ashes: An Account of the Rehabilitation of Refugees from West Pakistan in Rural Areas of East Punjab*. Chandigarh: Punjab Public Relations Department.

Smarika (2000). Delhi Region's Raigar Association. New Delhi.

Saxena, M.L. (1950). *Some Reflections on the Problems of Rehabilitation*. Delhi (publisher unknown).

Singh, T. (1969). *Rural Resettlement in Punjab. Towards an Integrated Society: Refelctions on Planning. Social Policy and Rural Institutions*. New Delhi: Orient Longman.

SECONDARY SOURCES

Abrams, P. (1988). 'Notes on the Difficulty of Studying State'. *Journal of Historical Sociology* 1.1. March, pp. 58–89.

Agamben, G. (1999). *Remnants of Auschwitz: The Witness and the Archive*. New York: Zone Books.

Ahmad, F. (1988). 'Ethnicity and Politics: The Rise of Muhajir Separatism', *South Asia Bulletin*, vol. 8, pp. 35–57.

Ahmad, I. (1994). 'State, Military and Modernity', *Contemporary South Asia*, 3(1), pp. 53–67.

Ahmar, M. (1996). 'Ethnicity and State Power in Pakistan: The Karachi Crisis' *Asian Survey*, 36(10), pp. 1031–48.

Aiyar, S. (1994). 'Violence and the State in the Partition of Punjab' Ph.D. thesis, unpublished, Department of History, University of Cambridge.

—— (1998). 'August Anarchy', in D.A. Low and Howard Brasted (eds), *Freedom, Trauma and Continuities: India and Independence*. Delhi: Sage Publications.

Ali, I. (1987). 'Malign Growth? Agricultural Colonisation and the Roots of Backwardness in the Punjab', *Past and Present*, no. 114, pp. 110–32.

—— (1988). *The Punjab under Imperialism 1885–1947*. Princeton, New Jersey: Princeton University Press.

—— (1999). 'Sikh Settlers in the Western Punjab during British Rule', in P. Singh and S.S. Thandi (eds), *Punjabi Identity in a Global Context*. New Delhi: Oxford University Press.

Anand, S. (2001). 'An Unforgettable August', in A. Salim (ed.), *Lahore 1947*. New Delhi: India Research Press.

Anderson, B. (1991). *Imagined Communities: Reflections on the Origin and Spread of Nationalism*. London: Verso.

Anderson, W. and S.D. Damle (1987). *The Brotherhood in Saffron: The RSS and the Hindu Revivalism*. Delhi: Vistaar.

Appadurai, A. (1981). 'The Past as a Scarce Resource', *Man*, New Series, vol. 16 (2), pp. 201–19.

—— (1988). 'Putting Hierarchy in its Place', *Cultural Anthropology*, vol. 3(1), pp. 36–49.

Asad, T. (1993). *Genealogies of Religion: Discipline and Reasons of Power in Christianity and Islam*. Baltimore: Johns Hopkins University Press.

Auge, M. (1977). *The Anthropological Circle*. Cambridge: Cambridge University Press.

Bacchetta, P. (1996). 'Hindu Nationalist Women as Ideologues: The Sangh, the Samiti and Differential Concepts of Hindu Nation', in K. Jayawardena and M. de Alwis (eds), *Embodied Violence: Communalising Women's Sexuality in South Asia.* Delhi: Kali for Women.

—— (1997). 'All Our Goddesses are Armed: Religion, Resistance and Revenge in the Life of a Militant Hindu Nationalist Woman', in K. Bhasin, R. Menon, and N.S. Khan (eds), *Against All Odds: Essays on Women, Religion and Development from India and Pakistan.* New Delhi: Kali for Women.

Balibar, E. (1996). 'Fictive Ethnicity and Ideal Nation', in A. Smith and J. Hutchinson (eds), *Ethnicity.* Oxford: Oxford University Press.

Banerjee, H. (2001). *Inventing Subjects: Studies in Hegemony, Patriarchy and Colonialism.* New Delhi: Tulika Press.

Banerjee, S. (1996). 'Hindu Nationalism and the Construction of Women: The Shiv Sena Organises Women in Bombay', in T. Sarkar and U. Butalia (eds), *Women and the Hindu Right: A Collection of Essays.* Delhi: Kali for Women.

Bardhan, P. (1998). 'The State Against Society: The Great Divide in Indian Social Science Discourse', in S. Bose and A. Jalal (eds), *Nationalism, Democracy and Development: State and Politics in India.* Delhi: Oxford University Press.

Barrier, N.G. (1967a). 'The Arya Samaj and Congress Politics in the Punjab, 1894–1908', *The Journal of Asian Studies,* vol. 26(3), pp. 363–79.

—— (1967b). 'The Punjab Disturbances of 1907: The Response of the British Government in India to Agrarian Unrest', *Modern Asian Studies,* vol. 1(4), pp. 353–83.

Bartlett, F.C. ([1932] 1995). *Remembering: A Study in Experimental and Social Psychology.* Cambridge: Cambridge University Press.

Basu, T., P. Datta, S. Sarkar, T. Sarkar, and S. Sen (1993). *Khaki Shorts, Saffron Flags: A Critique of the Hindu Right.* Delhi Orient Longman.

Bauazizi, A. and M. Weiner (1986). *The State, Religion and Ethnic Politics .* Syracuse: Syracuse University Press.

Bauman, Z. (2001). *Community: Seeking Safety in an Insecure World.* Cambridge: Polity Press.

Bateson, G. (1972). *Steps to an Ecology of Mind: A Revolutionary Approach to Man's Understanding of Himself.* New York: Ballantine Books.

Bell, C. (1992). *Ritual Theory, Ritual Practice.* New York: Oxford University Press.

Béteille, A. (1970). *Caste, Class and Power: Changing Patterns of a Tanjore Village.* Delhi: Oxford University Press.

Bhalla, A. (1994). *Stories from the Partition of India.* Delhi: Harper Collins.

Bloch, M. (1977). 'The Past and the Present in the Present', *Man,* New Series, vol. 12 (2), pp. 278–92.

Bopegamage, A. (1957). *Delhi: A Study in Urban Sociology.* Bombay: University of Bombay.

Bourdieu, P. (1999). 'Rethinking the State: Genesis and Structure of the Bureaucratic Field', in G. Steinmetz (ed.), *State/Culture: State-Formation after the Cultural Turn.* Ithaca, New York: Cornell University Press.

—— (1984). *Distinctions: A Social Critique of the Judgement of Taste.* London: Routledge.

Bourdieu, P. and L.J. Wacquant (2002). *An Invitation to Reflexive Sociology.* Cambridge: Polity Press.

Brass, P. (1974). *Language, Religion and Politics in North India.* Cambridge: Cambridge University Press.

—— (ed.). (1997). *Riots and Pogroms.* Calcutta: Seagull Books.

Brass, P. (2000). 'The Partition of India and the Forced Displacement of the Population of Punjab in 1946–7: Means, Methods and Purposes', Paper presented at the

Conference on 'War, Famine and Forced Migration: Social Engineering and Collective Violence in Today's World', Cortona, Italy, 26–27 May 2000.

Breman, J. (1974). *Patronage and Exploitation: Changing Agrarian Relations in South Gujarat.* Berkeley: University of California Press.

Briggs, G.W. ([1920] 1999). *The Chamars.* Delhi: Low Price Publications.

Burki, S.J. (1999). *Pakistan: Fifty Years of Nationhood* . Boulder, Colorado: Westview Press.

Butalia, U. (1998). *The Other Side of Silence: Voices from the Partition of India.* New Delhi: Kali for Women.

—— (2001). 'An Archive with a Difference: Partition Letters', in S. Kaul (ed.), *The Partitions of Memory: The Afterlife of the Division of India.* New Delhi: Permanent Black.

Butler, J. (1993). *Bodies that Matter: On the Discursive Limits of 'Sex'.* New York: Routledge.

Carr, E. (1987). *What is History?* London: Penguin.

Certeau, M. de (1984). *The Practice of Everyday Life.* Translated by Steven Randall. Berkeley: University of California Press.

Chakravarty, T. (2002). 'The Paradox of a Fleeting Presence: Partition and Bengali Literarture, in S. Settar and I.B. Gupta (eds), *Pangs of Partition: The Human Dimension.* Delhi: Manohar.

Chandra, B., M. Mukherjee, A. Mukherjee, K.N. Pannikar, and S. Mahajan (1989). *India's Struggle for Independence.* Delhi: Penguin.

Chatterjee, P. (1986). *Nationalist Thought and the Colonial World: A Derivative Discourse.* London: Zed Books.

—— (1994). *The Nation and its Fragments: Colonial and Postcolonial Histories.* New Delhi: Oxford University Press.

—— (2002). 'The Films of Ritwik Ghatak and the Partition', in S. Settar and I.B. Gupta (eds), *Pangs of Partition: The Human Dimension.* Delhi: Manohar.

Chatterji, J. (2001). 'Right or Charity? The Debate over Relief and Rehabilitation in West Bengal 1947–1950', in Suvir Kaul (ed.), *The Partition of Memories: The Afterlife of Division of India.* Delhi: Permanent Black.

Chopra, M.S. (1997). *1947: A Soldier's Story. From the Records of Major General Mohindar Singh Chopra.* New Delhi: The Military Studies Convention.

Clifford, J. (1997). *Routes: Travel and Translation in the Late Twentieth Century.* Cambridge, Massachusetts: Harvard University Press.

Cohen, A. (1992). *A Symbolic Construction of Community.* London and New York: Routledge.

Cohn, B. (1987). *An Anthropologist among the Historians and Other Essays.* New Delhi: Oxford University Press.

—— (1996). *Colonialism and its Forms of Knowledge.* Princeton: Princeton University Press.

Connell, R. (1996). *Masculinities.* Cambridge: Polity Press.

Connerton, P. (1989). *How Societies Remember.* Cambridge: Cambridge University Press.

Conway, M. and D. Rubin (1993). 'The Structure of Autobiographical Memory', in A.E. Collins, S.E. Gathercole, M.A. Conway, and P.E. Morris (eds), *Theories of Memories.* New Jersey: Lawrence Erlbaum Associates, Publishers.

Conway, M. (1997). 'The Inventory of Experience: Memory and Identity', in J. Pennebaker (ed.), *Collective Memory of Political Events: Social Psychological Perspectives.* New Jersey: Lawrence Erlbaum Associates, Publishers.

Corrigan, P. (1994). 'State Formation' in G. Joseph and D. Nugent (eds), *Everyday Forms of State Formation*. Durham, NC: Duke University Press.

Corrigan, P. and D. Sayer (1985). *The Great Arch: English State Formation as Cultural Revolution*. Oxford: Blackwell.

Corruccinni, R.S. and S. Kaul (1990). *Halla: Demographic Consequences of the Partition of Punjab, 1947*. New York: University of America Press.

Dar, B.A. (1971). *Religious Thoughts of Sayyid Ahmad Khan*. Lahore: Institute of Islamic Culture.

Das, V. (1989). 'Subaltern as Perspective', in R. Guha (ed.), *Subaltern Studies-VI: Writings on South Asian History and Society*. Delhi: Oxford University Press.

—— (1995). *Critical Events: An Anthropological Perspective on Contemporary India*. New Delhi: Oxford University Press.

—— (1996). *Mirrors of Violence: Communities, Riots and Survivors in South Asia*. Delhi: Oxford University Press.

Degh, L. (1995). *Narratives in Society: A Performer-Centered Study of Narration*. Helsinki: Suomalainen Tiedeakatemia.

Dirks, N. (1993). *The Hollow Crown: Ethnohistory of an Indian Kingdom*. Ann Arbor: University of Michigan Press.

Douglas, M. (2002). *Purity and Danger*. London: Routledge.

Dua, V. (1999). *The Arya Samaj in Punjab Politics*. New Delhi: Picus Books.

Dubois, A. (1981). *Hindu Manners, Customs and Ceremonies*. Delhi: Oxford University Press.

Dumont, L. (1988). *Homo Hierarchicus*. Delhi: Oxford University Press.

Dupont, V., E. Tarlo, and D. Vidal (eds) (2000). *Delhi: Urban Spaces and Human Destinies*. Delhi: Manohar.

Durkheim, E. (1995). *The Elementary Forms of Religious Life*. London: Routledge.

Dutta, V.N. (1986). 'Punjabi Refugees and the Urban Development of Greater Delhi', in R.E. Frykenberg (ed.), *Delhi Through the Ages: Essays in Urban History, Culture and Society*. Delhi: Oxford University Press.

—— (1988). *Sati: Widow Burning in India*. Delhi: Manohar.

Economic Survey of Delhi, 2001–2002. Government of Delhi: Publications Division.

Engels, F. (1942). *The Origin of Family, Private Property and the State*. New York: International Books.

Erikson, E. (1968). *Identity, Youth and Crisis*. New York: Norton.

Farquhar, J. ([1915] 1999). *Modern Religious Movements in India*. New Delhi: Low Price Publications.

Fein (1984) 'Scenarios of Genocide: Models of Genocide and Critical Responses' in Israel Charny (ed.), *Towards the Understanding and Prevention of Genocide: Proceedings of the International Conference on the Holocaust and Genocide*. Boulder, Colorado: Westview Press.

Ferguson, J. and A. Gupta (1999). 'Beyond "Culture": Space, Identity and the Politics of Difference', in A. Gupta and J. Ferguson (eds), *Culture, Power, Place: Explorations in Critical Anthropology*. Durham and London: Duke University Press.

Foucault, M. (1972). *The Archaeology of Knowledge*. New York: Pantheon Books.

—— (1980). *Power/Knowledge: Selected Interviews and Other Writings 1972–77*. Edited by P. Rabinow. London: Penguin.

Fox, R. (1984). 'Urban Class and Communal Consciousness in Colonial Punjab: The Genesis of India's Intermediate Regime', *Modern Asian Studies*, vol. 18 (3), pp. 459–89.

—— (1985). *Lions of the Punjab: Culture in the Making*. Berkeley: University of California Press.

Frank, K. (2000). *Indira: The Life of Indira Nehru Gandhi*. London: Harper Collins.

Frankel, F. (1978). *India's Political Economy 1947–1977: The Gradual Revolution*. Princeton: Princeton University Press.

Fraser, E. (1999). *The Problems of Communitarian Politics: Unity and Conflict*. Oxford: Oxford University Press.

Freud, S. (1932[1974]). 'The Anatomy of the Mental Personality'. Lecture XXXI. In *New Introductory Lectures on Psycho-Analysis*. London: Hogarth Press, Institute of Psycho-analysis.

Fuller, C.J. (1996). *Caste Today*. Delhi: Oxford University Press.

—— and V. Benei (eds) (2000). *The Everyday State and Society in Modern India*. New Delhi: Social Science Press.

Gandhi, M.K. (1947). 'To the Protagonists of Pakistan', in S.M. Rai (1965). *Partition of Punjab: A Study of its Effects on the Politics and Administration of the Punjab (I) 1947–56*, London: Asia Publishing House.

Geertz, C. (1963). 'The Integrative Revolution: Primordial Sentiments and Civil Politics in the New States', in C. Geertz, *Old Societies and New States: The Quest for Modernity in Asia and Africa*. New York: Press of Glencoe.

—— (1993). *Primoridial Loyalties and Standing Entities: Anthropological Reflections on the Politics of Identity*. Budapest: Institute for Advanced Study.

Gellner, E. (1983). *Nation and Nationalism*. Oxford: Blackwell.

Giddens, A. (1982). *Classes, Power and Conflict: Classical and Contemporary Debates*. Basingstoke: Macmillan.

Gilmartin, D. (1988). *Empire and Islam: Punjab and the Making of Pakistan*. California: University of California Press.

Grewal, R. (1988). 'Urbanisation in Punjab 1849–1947', Ph.D. thesis, unpublished, Department of History, Guru Nanak Dev University, Amritsar.

Guha, R. (ed.) (1982). *Subaltern Studies-I: Writings on South Asian History and Society*. Delhi: Oxford University Press.

Gupta, A. (1995). 'Blurred Boundaries: The Discourse of Corruption, the Culture of Politics and the Imagined State', *American Ethnologist*, vol. 22 (2), pp. 375–402.

Gupta, D. (1991). *Social Stratification*. Delhi: Oxford University Press.

—— (1997). *The Context of Ethnicity: Sikh Identity in a Comparative Perspective*. New Delhi: Oxford University Press.

—— (2001). *Interrogating Caste: Understanding Hierarchy and Difference in Indian Society*. New Delhi: Penguin.

Gupta, N. (1999). *Delhi between the Two Empires: 1803–1931*. Delhi: Oxford University Press.

Habib, I. (1963). *The Agrarian System of Mughal India*. London: Asia Publishing House.

—— (1982). *An Atlas of the Mughal Empire*. Delhi: Oxford University Press.

Halbwachs, M. ([1950] 1980). *The Collective Memory*. New York: Harper and Row.

Hansen, A.B. (2002). *Partition and Genocide: Manifestations of Violence in Punjab 1937–47*. New Delhi: India Research Press.

Hansen, T.B. (1994). 'Controlled Emancipation: Women and Hindu Nationalism', *European Journal of Development Research*, vol. 6 (2).

—— (1996). 'Recuperating Masculinity: Hindu Nationalism, Violence and Exorcism of the Muslim "Other"', *Critique of Anthroplogy*, vol. 16 (2), pp. 137–72.

—— (1998). 'BJP and the Politics of Hindutava in Maharashtra', in C. Jaffrelot and T.B. Hansen (eds), *The BJP and its Compulsions of Politics in India*. Delhi: Oxford University Press.

—— (1999). *The Saffron Wave: Hindu Nationalism and Democracy in India.* Princeton, NJ: Princeton University Press.

—— (2000). 'Governance and Myths of State in Mumbai', in C.J. Fuller and B. Veronique (eds), *The Everyday State and Society in Modern India.* Delhi: Social Science Press.

Hansen, T.B. and F. Stepputtat (2001). *States of Imagination: Ethnographic Explorations of the Postcolonial State.* Durham and London: Duke University Press.

Haq, F. (1995). 'Rise of MQM in Pakistan: Politics of Ethnic Mobilisation', *Asian Survey,* 35(11), pp. 990–1004.

Hasan, M. (ed.) (1996). *India's Partition: Process, Strategy and Mobilization.* Delhi: Oxford University Press.

Hear, N.V. (1998). *New Diasporas: The Mass Exodus, Dispersal and Regrouping of Migrant Communities.* London: Taylor and Francis.

Heeger, G. (1972). 'Discipline versus Mobilisation: Party Building and Punjab Jana Sangh', *Asian Survey,* vol. 12 (10), pp. 864–78.

Hobsbawm, E. (1990). *Nation and Nationalism since 1780: Programme, Myth and Reality.* Cambridge: Cambridge University Press.

—— (1996). 'Identity Politics and the Left', *New Left Review* no. 217, pp. 39–48.

Hough, E.M. (1966). *The Cooperative Movement in India.* Calcutta: Oxford University Press.

Hume, D. (2003). *A Treatise of Human Nature.* Oxford: Oxford University Press.

Ibbetson, D. ([1916] 1993). *Punjab Castes.* Delhi: Low Price Publications.

Illaiah, K. (1996). *Why I am Not a Hindu: A Sudra Critique of Hindutava Philosophy, Culture and Political Economy.* Hyderabad: Somya.

Inden, R. (2000). *Imagining India.* London: Hurst.

Irwin-Zarecka, I. (1994). *Frames of Remembrance: The Dynamics of Collective Memory.* New Brunswick and London: Transaction Publishers.

Islam, M. (1995). 'The Punjab Land Alienation Act and the Professional Moneylenders', *Modern Asian Studies,* vol. 29 (2), pp. 271–91.

—— (1997). *Irrigation, Agriculture and the Raj: Punjab 1887–1947.* New Delhi: Manohar.

Jaffrelot, C. (1999). *The Hindu Revivalist Movements.* Delhi: Oxford University Press.

—— (2000). 'The Hindu Nationalist Movement in Delhi: From "Locals" to Refugees and Towards Peripheral Groups?', in Dupont, Tarlo, and Vidal (eds), *Delhi: Urban Spaces and Human Spaces.* Delhi: Manohar.

Jain, L.C. (1948). 'Some Thoughts on the Problems of Rehabilitation of Displaced Persons from Pakistan', drafted on 7 February. Diwan Chaman Lall Private Paper Collection. NMML, New Delhi.

Jalal, A. (1985). *The Sole Spokesman: Jinnah, the Muslim League and the Demand for Pakistan.* Cambridge: Cambridge University Press.

Jensen, S. (2001). *Claiming Community–Negotiating Crime: State Formation, Neighbourhood and Gangs in a Capetonian Town.* Roskilde: Roskilde University Centre.

Jones, K.W. (1968). 'Communalism in the Punjab: The Arya Samaj Contribution', *Journal of Asian Studies,* vol. 28 (1), pp. 39–54.

—— (1973). 'Ham Hindu Nahin: Arya Sikh Relations, 1877–1905', *Journal of Asian Studies,* vol. 32 (3), pp. 457–75.

—— (1976). *Arya Dharma: Hindu Consciousness in 19th-Century Punjab.* Berkeley: University of California Press.

Jordens, J.T.F. (1978). *Dayanand Saraswati: His Life and Ideas*. Delhi:Oxford University Press.

Joseph, G. and D. Nugent (1994). *Everyday Forms of State Formation: Revolution and the Negotiations of Rule of Modern Mexico*. Durham, NC: Duke University Press.

Kakkar, S. (1996). *Colours of Violence: Cultural Identities and Conflict*. Delhi: Oxford University Press.

Kamtekar, I. (1989). *End of the Colonial State in India 1942–47*. Cambridge: University of Cambridge.

Kantikar, H. (1994). 'Real True Boys': Moulding the Cadets of Imperialism', in A. Cornwall and N. Lindisfarne (eds), *Dislocating Masculinity: Comparative Ethnographies*. London: Routledge.

Kaviraj, S. (1997). 'The Modern State in India', in M. Doornbos and S. Kaviraj (eds), *Dynamics of State Formation: India and Europe Compared*. Delhi: Sage Publications.

Kaul, S. (2001). *The Partition of Memories: The Afterlife of Division of India*. Delhi: Permanent Black.

Kedourie, E. (1960). *Nationalism*. London: Hutchinson.

Keller, S. (1975). *Uprooting and Social Change: The Role of Refugees in Development*. Delhi: Manohar Publishers.

Khalique, K.A. (2002). 'Genesis of Partition', in S. Settar and I.B. Gupta (eds), *Pangs of Partition: The Parting of Ways*. Delhi: Manohar.

Khosla, G. (1950). *Stern Reckoning: A Survey of Events leading up to and following the Partition of India*. Delhi: Oxford University Press.

—— (1985). *Memory's Gay Chariot: An Autobiography*. New Delhi: Allied Publishers.

Kumar, R. (1997). 'State Formation in India: Retrospect and Prospect', in M. Doornbos and S. Kaviraj (eds), *Dynamics of State Formation: India and Europe Compared*. Delhi: Sage Publications.

Kurtz, S. (1992). *All Mothers are One: Hindu India and Cultural Reshaping of Psychoanalysis*. New York: Columbia University Press.

Laclau, E. and C. Mouffe (1985). *Hegemony and Socialist Strategy: Towards a Radical Democratic Politics*. London: Verso.

Lefebvre, H. (1991). *Critique of Everyday Life*, vol. I. Translated by J. Moore. London: Verso.

—— (2002). *Critique of Everyday Life*. vol. II. Translated by J. Moore. London and New York: Verso.

Levi, P. (1988). *The Drowned and the Saved*. Summit Books: New York.

Lippert, R. (1999). 'Governing Refugees: The Relevance of Governmentality to Understanding the International Refugee Regime', *Alternatives*, 24 (3), pp. 295–328.

Madan, T.N. (1970). 'On the Nature of Caste in India: A Review Symposium on *Homo Hierarchicus*', *Contributions to Indian Sociology*. vol. 5.

Major, A. (1998). 'The Chief Sufferers: Abduction of Women During the Partition of Punjab', in D.A. Low and H. Brasted (eds), *Freedom, Trauma and Continuities: Northern India and Independence*. New Delhi: Sage Publications.

Malhotra, A. (2002). *Gender, Caste and Religious Identities: Restructuring Class in Colonial Punjab*. Delhi: Oxford University Press.

Malik, K. (2002). 'The Unsettling: Satish Gujral and his Paintings', in S. Settar and I.B. Gupta (eds), *Pangs of Partition: The Human Dimension*. New Delhi. Manohar.

Malkki, L. (1995). *Purity and Exile: Violence, Memory, and National Cosmology among Hutu Refugees in Tanzania*. Chicago: Chicago University Press.

Mamdani, M. (1996). *Citizen and Subject: Contemporary Africa and the Legacy of Late Colonialism*. Princeton, NJ: Princeton University Press.

Marriot, M. (1959). 'Interactional and Attributional Theory of Caste Ranking', *Man in India*, vol. 39, pp. 92–107.

Marriot, M. and R. Inden (1977). 'Towards a Ethnosociology of the South Asian Caste System', in K.A. David (ed.), *The New Wind: Changing Identities in South Asia*. Chicago: Aldine.

Maxwell, N. (1974) 'Reconsiderations: Jawaharlal Nehru: Of Pride and Principle', *Foreign Affairs*, April.

Mehra, A.K. (1991). *The Politics of Urban Development: A Study of Urban Development*. Delhi: Manohar.

Mellor, A. (1951). *India since Partition*. London: Turnstile Press.

Mendelsohn, O. and M. Vicziany (2000). *The Untouchables: Subordination, Poverty and the State in India*. Cambridge: Cambridge University Press.

Menon, R. and K. Bhasin (1998). *Borders and Boundaries: Women in India's Partition*. New Delhi: Kali for Women.

Metcalf, B. (1982). *Islamic Revival in British India: Deoband 1860–1900*. Princeton: Princeton University Press.

Metcalf, B. and T. Metcalf (2002). *A Concise History of India*. Cambridge: Cambridge University Press.

Mitchell, T. (1999). 'Economy and the State Effect', in G. Steinmetz (ed.), *State/Culture: State Formation after the Cultural Turn*. Ithaca, New York: Cornell University Press.

Mitra, S. and R.A. Lewis (1996). *Subnational Movements in South Asia*. Boulder, Colorado: Westview Press.

Moon, P. (1961). *Divide and Quit*. Delhi: Oxford University Press.

Moore, S.F. and B. Myerhoff (1977). *Secular Ritual*. Amsterdam: Van Gorcum.

Moore, H. (1994). *A Passion for Difference: Essays in Anthropology and Gender*. London: Polity Press.

Mukherjee, A. (1996). *Language Maintenance and Language Shift: Punjabis and Bengalis in Delhi*. Delhi: Bahri.

Nanda, B.R. (1958). *Mahatama Gandhi: A Biography*. Delhi: Oxford University Press.

—— (1998). *The Making of a Nation*. Delhi: Harper Collins.

Nanda, J. (1948.) *Punjab Uprooted: A Survey of the Punjab Riots and Rehabilitation Problems*. Bombay: Hind Kitab Ltd.

Nandy, A. (1989). 'The Political Culture of the Indian State', *Daedalus*, 118, pp. 1–26.

Nayar, B.R. (1966). *Minority Politics in Punjab*. Princeton: Princeton University Press.

Neville, P. (1998). *Lahore: A Sentimental Journey*. Delhi: Harper Collins.

—— (2001). 'I Still Remember Lahore Burning', in A. Salim (ed.), *Lahore 1947*. New Delhi. India Research Press.

Nicholson, F. and P. Twomey (1999). *Refugee Rights and Realities: Evolving International Concepts and Regimes*. Cambridge: Cambridge University Press.

Nietzsche, F. (1998). 'First Essay which traces the Historical Origins of Morality', in D. Smith (trs.), *On the Genealogy of Morals*. Oxford: Oxford University Press.

Naimark, N.M. (2001). *Fires of Hatred: Ethnic Cleansing in Twentieth-Century Europe*. Cambridge: Harvard University Press.

Narula, O.P. (2002). *I Still Remember a Small Town in Punjab*. Delhi: Srishti Publishers.

Nijhawan, D.N. (1955). *Displaced Persons (Compensation and Rehabilitation) Rules 1955*, New Delhi: Federal Law Depot.

Oberoi, H. (2001). *The Constructions of Religious Boundaries: Culture, Identity and Diversity in the Sikh Tradition.* New Delhi: Oxford University Press.

Oran, M. (1969). 'Social Organisation', *Biennial Review of Anthropology*, vol. 6, pp. 132–90.

Pandey, G. (2001). *Remembering Partition.* Cambridge: Cambridge University Press.

Park, R. (1925). 'The City: Suggestions for the Investigation of the Human Behaviour', in R. Park, E.W. Burgess, and R.D. Mckenzie (eds), *The City.* Chicago: University of Chicago Press.

Paustian, P. W. (1925). *Canal Irrigation in Punjab.* New York: Columbia University Press.

Prasad, B. (2002). *Pathways to India's Partition: The Foundations of Muslim Nationalism.* Delhi: Manohar.

Prashad, V. (2000). *Untouchable Freedom: A Social History of a Dalit Community.* Delhi: Oxford University Press.

Propp, V. (1968). *Morphology of Folktale.* Indiana: Indiana University Press.

Qureshi, I.H. (1966). *The Administration of the Mughal Empire.* Patna: NV Publications.

Rai, Satya M. (1965). *Partition of Punjab: A Study of its Effects on the Politics and Administration of the Punjab (I) 1947–56*, London: Asia Publishing House.

Rao, V. and N.B. Desai (1965). *Greater Delhi: A Study of Urbanisation 1940–57.* New Delhi: Planning Commission of India.

Redfield, R. (1947). 'The Folk Society', *American Journal of Sociology*, vol. 52 (4), pp. 293–308.

——— (1955). *The Little Community.* Chicago: University of Chicago Press.

Rehman, J. (1994). 'Self-determination, state-building and the Muhajirs', *Contemporary South Asia*, 3 (2), pp. 111–30.

Richard, John F. (1993). *The Mughal Empire*, vol. I, Part 5, of the *New Cambridge History of India.* Cambridge: Cambridge University Press.

Ricoeur, P. (1980). 'Narrative Time', *Critical Inquiry*, vol. 7 (1), pp. 165–86.

——— (2004). *Memory, History and Forgetting.* Translated by K. Blamey and D. Pellauer. Chicago: University of Chicago Press.

Rose, H.A. ([1911] 1990). *A Glossary of the Tribes and Castes of Punjab and NWFP.* Delhi: Low Price Publications.

Rowe, W. (1991). 'The New Chauhans: A Caste Mobility Movement in North India', in D. Gupta (ed.), *Social Stratification.* Delhi: Oxford University Press.

Roy, A. (1990). 'The High Politics of India's Partition: The Revisionist Perspective', *Modern Asian Studies*, vol. 24 (2), pp. 385–408.

Rudolph, L. and S. Rudolph (1978). 'To the Brink and Back: Representation and State in India', *Asian Survey*, vol. 18 (4), pp. 379–400.

Sangari, K. and S. Vaid (eds) (1989). *Recasting Women: Essays on Colonial History.* Delhi: Kali for Women.

Sangari, K. and S. Vaid (1996.) 'Institutions, Beliefs, Ideologies: Widow Immolation in Contemporary Rajasthan' in K. Jayawardena and M. de Alwis (eds), *Embodied Violence: Communalising Women's Sexuality in South Asia.* Delhi: Kali for Women.

Sarkar, T. (1996). 'Heroic Women, Mother Goddesses', in T. Sarkar and U. Butalia (eds), *Women and the Hindu Right: A Collection of Essays.* Delhi: Kali for Women.

——— (2001). *Hindu Wife, Hindu Nation: Community, Religion, and Cultural Nationalism.* Delhi: Permanent Black.

Saksena, R.N. (1975). *Social Reform: Infanticide and Sati.* Delhi: Trimurti.

Scott, J. (1998). *Seeing Like a State: How Certain Schemes to Improve the Human Condition have Failed.* New Haven: Yale University Press.

Sen, S. (2002). *Distant Sovereignty: National Imperialism and the Origins of British India*. London: Routledge.

Seteney, S. (1996) 'Transnationalism and Refugee Studies: Rethinking Forced Migration and Identity in the Middle East', *Journal of Refugees Studies*, vol. 9 (1), pp. 3–26.

Shah, G. (ed.) (2001). *Dalit Identity and Politics*. New Delhi: Sage Publications.

Sharma, K.L. (2001). *Reconceptualising Caste, Class and Tribe*. Jaipur and New Delhi: Rawat Publications.

Shils, E. (1957). 'Primordial, Personal, Sacred and Civil Ties: Some Particular Observations on the Relationship of Sociological Research and Theory', *British Journal of Sociology*, vol. 8 (2), pp. 130–45.

Simpson, J.H. (1939). *The Refugee Problem: Report of a Survey*. London: Oxford University Press.

Singh, A.I. (1987). *The Origins of the Partition of India 1936–37*. Delhi. Oxford University Press.

Singh, K. (2001). 'Lahore, Partition and Independence', in Ahmad Salim (ed.), *Lahore 1947*. New Delhi: India Research Press.

Singh, K.S. (2000). *The Scheduled Castes*. Delhi: Oxford University Press.

Singh, R. (1991). 'Military Evacuation Organisation' in K. Singh (ed.), *Select Documents on the Partition of Punjab 1947: India and Pakistan: Punjab, Haryana and Himachal Pradesh – India and Punjab – Pakistan*. Delhi: National Bookshop, pp. 548–52.

Singh, V.B. (2000). 'Political Profile of Delhi and Support Base of Parties: An Analysis', in V. Dupont, E. Tarlo, and D. Vidal (eds), *Urban Space and Human Destinies*, Delhi: Manohar.

Somerville, J. (1989). 'Maria Avatara', in S. Nicholson (ed.), *The Goddess Reawakening: The Feminine Principle Today*. London, Madras: The Theosophical Publishing House.

Spear, P. (1958). 'From Colonial to Sovereign Status: Some Problems of Transition with Special Reference to India', *The Journal of Asian Studies*, vol. 17 (4), pp. 567–77.

Spencer, J. (1996). 'Occidentalism in the East: The Uses of the West in the Politics and Anthropology of South Asia', in J. Carrier (ed.), *Occidentalism: Images of the West*. Oxford: Clarendon Press.

Spivak, G.C. (1985). 'Subaltern Studies: Deconstructing Historiography', in R. Guha (ed.), *Subaltern Studies-IV: Writings on South Asian History and Society*. Delhi. Oxford University Press.

Srinivas, M.N. (1991). 'Varna and Caste', in D. Gupta (ed.), *Social Stratification*. Delhi: Oxford University Press.

Steinmetz, G. (1999). *State/Culture: State Formation after the Cultural Turn*. Ithaca: Cornell University Press.

Stepputat, F. (1992). *Beyond Relief? Life in a Guatemalan Refugee Settlement in Mexico*. Copenhagen: University of Copenhagen.

Strauss, C.L. (1955). 'The Structural Study of Myth', *The Journal of American Folklore*, vol. 68 (270) (Myth: A Symposium), pp. 428–44.

Symonds, R. (2001). *In the Margins of Independence: A Relief Worker in India and Pakistan, 1942–49*. Karachi: Oxford University Press.

Sørensen, N.N. (1994). *Telling Migrants Apart: The Experience of Migrancy among Domonican Locals and Transnationals*. Copenhagen: University of Copenhagen.

Sørensen, N.N. and B. Folke (2002). 'Beyond Home and Exile: Making Sense of Lives on the Move', Occassional Paper Series, Roskilde University Centre.

Talbot, I. (1988). *Provincial Politics and the Pakistan Movement: The Growth of the Muslim League in North West and North East India 1937–47*. Karachi. Oxford University Press.

—— (1996). *Freedom's Cry: The Popular Dimension in the Partition Movement and Partition Experience in North West India*. Karachi: Oxford University Press.

Tan, Y.T. and G. Kudaisya (2000). *The Aftermath of Partition in South Asia*. London and New York: Routledge.

Tandon, P. (2000). *Punjabi Saga 1857–2000: The Monumental Story of Five Generations of a Remarkable Punjabi Family*. New Delhi: Rupa.

—— (2001). 'Through Smoking Towns', in A. Salim (ed.), *Lahore 1947*. Delhi: India Research Press.

Taylor, C. (1993). 'Politics of Recognition', in A. Gutman (ed.), *Multiculturalism: Examining the Politics of Recognition*. Princeton, NJ: Princeton University Press.

Temple, R.C. ([1884] 2002). *The Legends of Punjab*. Vols I and II. Delhi: Rupa.

Turner, S. (2001). *The Barriers of Innocence; Humanitarian Intervention and Political Imagination in a Refugee Camp for Burundians in Tanzania*. Roskilde: Roskilde University Centre.

Turner, V. (1995). *The Ritual Process: Structure and Antistructure*. New York: Aldine.

Tuteja, K. (2000). 'Hindu Consciousness, the Congress and Partition', in A. Singh (ed.), *The Partition in Retrospect*. Delhi: Anamika Publishers.

UNHCR (1996) UN convention Relating to the Status of Refuges 1951, Geneva.

Van der Veer, P. (1999). *Nation and Religion: Perspectives on Europe and Asia*. Princeton: Princeton University Press.

Virilio, P. (1977). *Speed and Politics: An Essay on Dromology*. New York: Semiotexte.

Washbrook, D. (1981). 'Law, State and Agrarian Society in Colonial India', *Modern Asian Studies*, vol. 15 (3), pp. 649–721.

Weber, M. (1946). 'Politics as Vocation', in H.H. Gerth and C.W. Mills (eds), *From Max Weber: Essays in Sociology*. Oxford: Oxford University Press.

—— (1958). *Religion of India: The Sociology of Hinduism and Buddhism*. Translated by H. Gerth and D. Martindale. New York: Free Press.

Weiner, M. (1957). *Party Politics in India*. Princeton: Princeton University Press.

White, H. (1984). 'The Question of Narrative in Contemporary Historical Theory', *History and Theory*, vol. 23 (1), pp. 1–33.

Wyer, R.S. Jr and T.K. Srull (1989). *Memory and Cognition in its Social Context*. Hillsdale, New Jersey, Hove and London: Lawrence Erlbaum Associates, Publishers.

Index